CRITICAL ISSUES IN SPECIAL EDUCATION

Access, Diversity, and Accountability

AUDREY McCRAY SORRELLS

The University of Texas at Austin

HERBERT J. RIETH

The University of Texas at Austin

PAUL T. SINDELAR

University of Florida

PEARSON

Boston   New York   San Francisco
Mexico City   Montreal   Toronto   London   Madrid   Munich   Paris
Hong Kong   Singapore   Tokyo   Cape Town   Sydney

Executive Editor: *Virginia Lanigan*
Editorial Assistant: *Robert Champagne*
Executive Marketing Manager: *Amy Cronin-Jordan*
Production Editor: *Michelle Limoges*
Editorial Production Service: *P. M. Gordon Associates*
Cover Coordinator: *Kristina Mose-Libon*
Electronic Composition: *Peggy Cabot*
Composition Buyer: *Linda Cox*
Manufacturing Buyer: *Andrew Turso*

For related titles and support materials, visit our online catalog at www.ablongman.com.

Between the time Web site information is gathered and published, some sites may have closed. Also, the transcription of URLs can result in typographical errors. The publisher would appreciate notification where these occur so that they may be corrected in subsequent editions.

Library of Congress Cataloging-in-Publication Data

Critical issues in special education : access, diversity, and accountability / edited by
 Audrey McCray Sorrells . . . [et al.].
    p.   cm.
 Includes bibliographical references and index.
 ISBN 0-205-34022-9
    1. Children with disabilities—Education—United States.   2. Special
 education—Social aspects—United States.   I. Sorrells, Audrey McCray.

 LC4031.C76   2004

                                                            03-057874

Printed in the United States of America

10 9 8 7 6 5 4 3 2 1   HAM   08 07 06 05 04 03

CONTENTS

PREFACE

Access to public education is universal. All children can enter schools, but not all children, including children with disabilities, are learning. Research-based interventions have been developed that are appropriate for some individuals with disabilities, but these interventions may be unavailable or may not be culturally and linguistically responsive for other students. Fewer learners with disabilities are receiving appropriate instruction to meet their unique needs from qualified teachers. The implications of general education reform efforts to "leave no child behind" have yet to be fully understood for students with disabilities in K–12 programs.

A substantial gap of achievement persists between students with disabilities and students without disabilities. The Council for Exceptional Children, in the IDEA Reauthorization Recommendation report (CEC, 2002), summarized the current status of special education service delivery this way:

> Children and families are shortchanged when more than 37,000 teachers without appropriate licenses teach students with disabilities each year. . . . They are shortchanged when research-based educational practices are not available in schools. . . . They are shortchanged when developmentally appropriate early intervention services to eligible infants, toddlers, and preschoolers with disabilities are not available. (p. 5)

Thus, it remains necessary to keep issues of personnel quality and supply, instructional interventions, and early intervention at the forefront of special education debate and evaluation. However, special education issues do not exist in a vacuum. The evaluation of special education necessarily warrants coverage of problems and concerns with educating an increasingly diverse student population in public education. Although this text covers the perpetual issues of legal requirements, placement, identification, and classification, contemporary issues facing the field are treated with the same enthusiasm. The contemporary issues discussed here include (1) standards-based reform and the use of high-stakes testing in evaluating students; (2) the changing population and the increasingly diverse demographics of the students served in the public schools; (3) the connection between curriculum-based assessment and instruction with emphasis given also to the efficacy of instructional interventions; (4) the onset of the information age and the increasingly visible role of technology in the schools and the workplace; (5) concerns about student discipline and behavioral interventions; (6) transition, including the interface between vocational rehabilitation and special education transition services; (7) the continuing shortage of qualified and certified special education teachers; and (8) trends in higher education focused on the reform of teacher education, including changing standards for knowledge and skills and changing roles of special education teachers. To this end, the authors of this book sift through the existing research and practices to identify the best practices and the conditions that may facilitate or prohibit their implementation.

This book presents the contributions of prominent researchers, teacher educators, policy makers, teachers, and parents on current and emerging issues facing the field of special education and offers their critical thinking on how to ensure that students with disabilities from an increasingly diverse student population receive free appropriate education in the least restrictive environment. The intent of this book is to offer the sound reassertion that special education is *special* and is important for students with and without disabilities. To reach their full potential, students with disabilities cannot be denied special education and related services.

HOW THIS BOOK IS ORGANIZED

Part I, Foundational Issues, examines current foundational issues. In this part, Dave Smith presents a refreshing and thought-provoking interpretation for understanding contemporary special education through his use of historical special education philosophy and practice. Next, Yell, Drasgow, Bradley, and Justesen present a comprehensive critique of legal issues in special education, followed by Yates and Ortiz's presentation of issues surrounding the classification of disability for English Language Learners. Dorn and Fuchs revisit the longstanding challenges of placement alternatives in special education programs. This section of the book ends with McCray Sorrells, Webb-Johnson, and Townsend's call for responsibility in special education research, practice, and teacher preparation within multicultural contexts and by multiple voices.

Part II, Intervention Issues, explores the practice of special education beginning with an examination of early intervention. In this first chapter, Olive and the late McEvoy stress the need to systematically identify issues related to intervention and to reexamine family involvement and diversity from the perspectives of service delivery, family, and personnel quality in early intervention. Next, Allinder, Fuchs, and Fuchs address a critical issue, namely, curriculum-based assessment and this type of student performance monitoring for classroom instruction for students with learning disabilities. Following this is a straightforward discussion by Linan-Thompson of the complex nature of providing instructional interventions to maximize learning outcomes. This author describes the need to reevaluate what is known about teaching and learning within the contexts of classrooms, curriculum, communities, and culture. Vaughn, Klingner, and Hughes, in their chapter, use the issue of sustainability and the need to create classrooms and improve teacher knowledge and skills to promote the continuous use of research-based practices for students with disabilities. In the next three chapters, readers are provided a comprehensive analysis of current trends and issues in behavioral intervention, transition issues, and trends and issues in instructional and assistive technology. Polsgrove and Ochoa offer a review of issues associated with developing and implementing behavioral interventions. Patton provides a comprehensive overview of the area of transition. Reith, Colburn, and Bryant provide an analysis of the trends and issues associated with the use of instructional and assistive technology. Also, given the importance of interagency collaboration, particularly as it relates to transition and services for individuals upon their exit from K–12 schooling, we have included Schaller, Yang, and Chang's examination of contemporary issues of rehabilitation counseling and how rehab counseling interfaces with and influences special education practice.

Part III, Personnel Preparation Issues, presents the intricacies and findings of research literature related to personnel preparation. First, Brownell, Rosenberg, Sindelar, and Smith explore teacher education and the issues of ensuring that all children with disabilities, like their nondisabled peermates, are provided instruction from qualified special education teachers. In the second chapter in this part, Smith, Pion, and Tyler grapple with and present evidence to redress the persistent shortage of leadership personnel in higher education special education.

Finally, in Part IV, Special Education Futures, Hardman and Nagle return to the issues of access and accountability, framing these discussions around public policy and special education service delivery.

ACKNOWLEDGMENTS

First, the editors thank the authors of the chapters for their insights, professionalism, and hard work during the writing of this book. As indicated earlier, the purpose of this book was to identify and analyze current and emerging issues facing the field of special education. Also, we wanted the book to focus on the challenges of educating an increasingly diverse student population and promising practices. The charge before the authors was threefold: (1) to identify and describe the major issues in their topic area and indicate the importance of each issue to the field of special education, (2) to summarize the current research-based knowledge, and (3) to recommend and defend the need for additional research regarding each issue presented.

Second, we thank Virginia Lanigan, our wonderful, persistent, and professional editor at Allyn and Bacon. Her commitment to and enthusiasm for this book inspired us to "keep at it" from its conceptualization to the development of sixteen chapters written by thirty-seven authors.

We also thank the following reviewers for their valuable comments during the writing of this book: Maria Elena Arguelles, University of Miami; Scott K. Baker, Eugene Research Institute/University of Oregon; William H. Berdine, University of Kentucky; Daniel J. Boudah, University of North Carolina at Chapel Hill; Virginia Buysse, University of North Carolina at Chapel Hill; David Chard, University of Oregon; Shernaz Garcia, University of Texas at Austin; Michael M. Gerber, University of California at Santa Barbara; Russell Gerstein, Eugene Research Institute; Sandra Hansmann, University of Texas at Austin; Margaret McLaughlin, University of Maryland; James McLesley, University of Florida; Ed Meyen, University of Kansas; MaryJane K. Rapport, UCHSC—JFK Partners; and Wilfred D. Wienke, University of Central Florida.

Finally, Audrey McCray Sorrells thanks her husband, Tony, and their children, Whittney, Gilbert Christopher, Iris Rose, Kendra, Tony, Jr., and Tonya for their support, faith, and prayers. And a special thanks to her father, James O. Davis.

Rose M. Allinder was an associate professor of special education at the University of Nebraska, where she studied teachers' use of curriculum-based measurement for instructional planning. Currently she directs educational services for AIDS orphans in Ghana.

Renee Bradley is currently a research analyst at the U.S. Office of Special Education Programs in the U.S. Department of Education, where he serves as the special assistant to the Director of Research to Practice.

Mary T. Brownell is an associate professor in the Department of Special Education at the University of Florida. Her research interests focus on teachers' careers and professional development in special and general education. Currently, she codirects the Center for Personnel Studies in Special Education funded by the U.S. Department of Special Education.

Diane Pedrotty Bryant is the Associate Dean for Teacher Education and Student Affairs at the University of Texas at Austin. Her research interests focus on the use of instructional and assistive technology to enhance academic outcomes for students with disabilities.

Sophie Chien-Huey Chang is currently an assistant professor in the Department of Special Education, National Taiwan Normal University, Taipei, Taiwan. Her research interests include orientation and mobility training and education and rehabilitation for students with visual impairments and individuals with additional disabilities.

Linda K. Colburn is Clinical Assistant Professor in the Department of Teaching and Learning at Vanderbilt University. Her research interest focuses on the integration of technology with instruction to enhance student outcomes.

Sherman Dorn is an historian of education at the University of South Florida. His research includes the history of dropping out and the history of special education in the urban South.

Erik Drasgow is an associate professor in the Department of Educational Psychology at the University of South Carolina. His interests include language intervention for students with severe disabilities, positive behavior support, and special education law.

Douglas Fuchs is a professor of special education at Peabody College of Vanderbilt University. His research includes accommodations for individuals with disabilities in the general education classroom and reforms of general education to improve academic and social outcomes for children with disabilities and other children at risk of failure in schools.

Lynn S. Fuchs is a professor in the Department of Special Education and Nicholas Hobbs Chair of Special Education and Human Development at Vanderbilt University. Her research focuses on curriculum-based measurement in the areas of reading and math as well as instructional issues in reading and mathematics disabilities.

Michael L. Hardman is Professor and Chair of the Department of Special Education and Associate Dean for Research in the College of Education at the University of Utah. He is a co-author of *Human Exceptionality: Society, School, and Family.*

Marie Tejero Hughes is an assistant professor at the University of Illinois–Chicago. She is interested in literacy development for students with disabilities and their families. She has studied the sustainablity of research-based practices and the extent to which model schools provide effective instruction for students with disabilities.

Troy Justesen is the Associate Director for Domestic Policy at the White House. At the time this chapter was written, Dr. Justesen was a policy analyst in the Office of the Director within the Office of Special Education Programs at the U.S. Department of Education.

Janette K. Klingner is an associate professor in bilingual special education at the University of Colorado at Boulder. Her research interests include outcomes for students with learning disabilities in inclusive classrooms, professional development in research-based practices, reading comprehension strategy instruction, and the disproportionate representation of culturally and linguistically diverse students in special education.

Sylvia Linan-Thompson is an assistant professor in special education at the University of Texas at Austin. She received her doctorate at the University of Texas in Multicultural Special Education. Her research interests include reading interventions for struggling readers in primary grades, literacy acquisition of English Language Learners, and Spanish literacy development.

Mary A. McEvoy's professional contributions were many, including a classroom teacher and researcher and professor at Peabody College of Vanderbilt University. She joined the special education faculty of the University of Minnesota in 1990. During her tenure at the University of Minnesota, she served as director of the early childhood special education program, directed the Center for Early Education and Development from 1993 to 1999, and chaired the Department of Educational Psychology from 1999 to 2002.

Katherine Nagle is the director of the Education Policy Reform Institute at the University of Maryland. Her research and teaching interests include special education policy and the education of students with visual impairments and severe disabilities.

Theresa Ochoa is Special Education Assistant Professor of Emotional and Behavioral Disorders at Indiana University. As a former behavior specialist, she has research interests in cognitive behavior interventions for students with emotional and behavioral needs. Her current research agenda includes the systematic evaluation of the effectiveness of problem-based learning CD-ROM technology in the preparation of teachers for students with behavior problems.

Melissa L. Olive is an assistant professor of special education at the University of Texas at Austin. She has been working in early childhood special education for fifteen years. Her background includes early language intervention, applied behavior analysis, and assessment and intervention for challenging behaviors.

Alba A. Ortiz holds the President's Chair for Education Academic Excellence at the University of Texas at Austin. She is a professor in the Department of Special Education at the College of Education, where she is also the Director of the Office of Bilingual Education. Her research and teaching interests include early intervention strategies for English Language Learners experiencing academic difficulties, the assessment of oral language skills, and special education service delivery for English Language Learners with language and learning difficulties.

James R. Patton is currently an educational consultant and an adjunct associate professor at the University of Texas at Austin. He has taught students with special needs at the elementary, secondary, and postsecondary levels. Dr. Patton's primary areas of professional activity are transition assessment and planning, life skills instruction, adults with learning disabilities, teaching science to students with learning problems, and the accommodation of students with special needs in inclusive settings.

Georgine M. Pion is a research associate professor in the Department of Psychology and Human Development at Vanderbilt University and a senior research associate in the Center for Evaluation Research and Methodology, Vanderbilt Institute for Public Policy Studies. Her work has focused on issues surrounding the education and employment of doctoral-level personnel, including those trained in research or professional fields, and the evaluation of graduate and postgraduate training programs.

Lewis Polsgrove is a professor of special education at Indiana University whose research and teaching interests focus on the understanding and treatment of children with emotional/behavioral disorders, teacher training, and developing services delivery systems. His professional positions include clinical psychologist, school psychologist, juvenile counselor, and teacher. He is a former president of Teacher Educators for Children with Behavioral Disorders and has served as treasurer and president of the Council for Children with Behavioral Disorders.

Herbert J. Rieth is Audrey Roger Myers Centennial Professor in Education and Chair of the Department of Special Education at the University of Texas at Austin. His research interests focus on the use of technology to enhance outcomes for students with disabilities and teacher education.

Michael S. Rosenberg is a professor in the Department of Special Education at Johns Hopkins University in Baltimore. Prior to his seventeen years at Hopkins (eleven as department chair), he was a teacher of adolescents with learning and behavior problems. Currently, Dr. Rosenberg is implementing a comprehensive behavior management model (PAR) for educational settings and, as part of the Center on Personnel Studies in Special Education (COPSSE), is engaged in several research efforts related to certification and personnel preparation in special education.

James Schaller is an associate professor in Rehabilitation Counselor Education at the University of Texas at Austin. His current research interests include research design and statistical methods and emotional development for people with disabilities.

Paul T. Sindelar is Professor of Special Education at the University of Florida and Director of the Center on Personnel Studies in Special Education. Dr. Sindelar's recent research has focused on the evaluation of teacher education programs, inclusion of students with disabilities in school reform and the sustainability of those reforms, and fostering of collaborative school cultures to support inclusion.

Deborah Deutsch Smith is a research professor of special education at Peabody College of Vanderbilt University and Senior Scholar of the John F. Kennedy Center for Research in Human Development in Nashville. She currently directs the Alliance Project, a federally funded technical assistance effort for HBCUs and other minority colleges and universities for the purpose of improving these schools' performance in the personnel preparation federal grant competitions held by the Office of Special Education Programs. She also directs the IRIS Project for Faculty Enhancement and was the project director of the research study about the shortage of special education faculty, which is partially reported in her chapter.

J. David Smith is provost at the University of Virginia College at Wise. His professional experience also includes work as a public school teacher, counselor, professor, and dean. He has made numerous presentations to national and international audiences and contributes regularly to the professional literature on education, human services, and public policy through journal articles. An integrating theme of his research and writing has been a concern for the rights and dignity of people with disabilities.

Audrey McCray Sorrells is an associate professor and the undergraduate advisor in the Department of Special Education at the University of Texas at Austin. Her research interests include preservice teacher education, teacher racial identity and teaching efficacy, middle school reading and literacy development, and disproportionate representation in special education programs.

Brenda L. Townsend is a professor in the Department of Special Education and director of several preservice urban teacher education initiatives at the University of South Florida. Her scholarship includes disciplinary practices, issues around ethics, power and privilege, and strategies for African American students with academic gifts and talents.

Naomi Chowdhuri Tyler is a research assistant professor at Peabody College of Vanderbilt University in Nashville. She has ten years of experience as a special education teacher, working with students from diverse racial, ethnic, and socioeconomic backgrounds. Her professional interests include the supply and demand of special education faculty, diversity in the special education workforce, and the preparation of general educators to work with students with disabilities in inclusive settings.

Sharon Vaughn is the H.E. Hartfelder/Southland Corp. Regents Chair and Director of the Texas Center for Reading and Language Arts at the University of Texas. She is the Editor-in-Chief of *Journal of Learning Disabilities*. Her research interests address reading and social outcomes for students with reading and learning disabilities.

Gwendolyn Webb-Johnson is an assistant professor of special education at the University of Texas at Austin. Her current interests include teacher education, multicultural education, behavior disorders, and culturally responsive pedagogy.

Nancy K. Yang is currently an educational, statistical, and research consultant in Austin, Texas, and was a former associate professor in National Kaohsiung Normal University, Taiwan. Her current research interests focus on social and emotional training for students with autism, computer-assisted instruction for students with disabilities, and rehabilitation issues for individuals with autism and ADHD.

James R. Yates is the John L. and Elizabeth G. Hill Centennial Professor in Education at the University of Texas at Austin. He has a joint appointment in the Departments of Educational Administration and Special Education, where his teaching focuses on the preparation of education leaders, with a particular emphasis on special education administration. His research interests include demography, the disproportionate representation of multicultural populations in special education, and techniques for forecasting and responding to changes in education.

Mitchell L. Yell is a professor in the Department of Educational Psychology at the University of South Carolina. Dr. Yell's interests include special education law, interventions for students with emotional and behavioral disorders, positive behavior support, and curriculum-based measurement.

PART I FOUNDATIONAL ISSUES

THE HISTORICAL CONTEXTS OF SPECIAL EDUCATION

Framing Our Understanding of Contemporary Issues

J. DAVID SMITH

University of Virginia College at Wise

THE HISTORIES (NOT THE HISTORY) OF SPECIAL EDUCATION

This chapter focuses on what can be learned from considering selected stories of special education. These varying histories will take us on a journey through time, location, and perspective, and they are intended to be a sampling of what can be understood about disabilities and the education of people with disabilities by looking at both the past and the future.

Yoel Dayan, the daughter of the revered Israeli patriot and statesman Moshe Dayan, wrote, "Memories are not history. They are fragments of things and feelings that were tainted and sifted through varying prisms of present time and disposition" (1985, p. 1). Historical understandings, though perhaps differing from individual memories, are also constructed through "varying prisms" of perspective. Histories may, in fact, be viewed as collective memories of a group or generation.

Special education has numerous histories. These histories are collections of memories and stories that serve as a foundation for the field. They give special education as a discipline a richness and cohesion that would not otherwise exist. In Barry Lopez's (1990) story of Native American folk characters on a quest for wisdom, a sage tells his young visitors, "The

Portions of this chapter were previously published in the author's article "Histories of Special Education: Stories from Our Past, Insights for Our Future," which appeared in *Remedial and Special Education*, vol. 19, no. 4, July/August 1998; in his book *Inclusion: Schools for All Students,* Belmont, CA: Wadsworth, 1998; and in several of his essays published in the "Perspectives" section of *Mental Retardation*.

stories people tell have a way of taking care of them. If stories come to you, care for them. And learn to give them away where they are needed. Sometimes a person needs a story more than food to stay alive. That is why we put these stories in each other's memory. This is how people care for themselves" (p. 48).

In a very important way the stories of special education and the histories of the field have nourished and sustained its development. The stories of Itard and Victor, of Samuel Gridley Howe and Edward Seguin, and of Helen Keller and Anne Sullivan, for example, have inspired generations of special education teachers and given them direction. There also have been negative stories that have proven to be assaults on the values and aims of special education teachers. The pessimistic and limiting stories of the Kallikaks and the Jukes, for example, question the feasibility and desirability of educating people with disabilities (Smith, 1985). As will be discussed later in this chapter, the story of Carrie Buck became central to the argument for institutionalizing and sterilizing thousands of people perceived to be "defective" (Smith & Nelson, 1989).

Burton Blatt (1987) observed that stories can be nurturing or destructive. He also pointed to the great responsibility that storytellers have to those for whom and to whom they speak. In *The Conquest of Mental Retardation* he said, "Every story can enhance life or destroy it. Every story can lift us or depress us. Every story can make a hero or a scapegoat. Stories sustain if not make a person's world. And thus, the storyteller holds a certain power (and responsibility), for the storyteller is usually safer than those about whom he or she spins tales" (p. 141). Historical scholarship, however, is committed to finding the "truest" story from among the positive and negative facts that have been recorded and transmitted. Scholars seek to understand history through old and new "prisms" and to tell stories they find in the most revealing and honest manner. In this sense, the search for historical accuracy is always the search for the "good" story.

CONSTRUCTING THE MEANING OF DISABILITY

The history of constructing the meaning of disabilities is long and varied. Scholars have recognized for decades, for example, that there is a basic conceptual difference between the terms *disability* and *handicap*. A disability is a physical, mental or emotional condition; a person who is blind or deaf has a disability; that person is unable to either see or hear. A handicap, however, is a limitation socially imposed on the individual because of the disability; it is the result of attitudes and suppositions rather than objective necessities. A woman who is deaf, for example, may have more difficulty living and working in a community because of the prejudices toward her disability than because of her inability to hear.

In speaking of the social construction of the meaning of the term *mental retardation*, James Trent in his book *Inventing the Feeble Mind* describes this term as "a construction whose changing meaning is shaped both by individuals who initiate and administer policies, programs, and practices, and by the social context to which these individuals are responding" (Trent, 1994, p. 2). Trent argues that constructing the meaning of disabilities is sometimes done in the name of science, sometimes in the name of caring for people with disabilities, and sometimes in the name of social or economic necessity. Each of these reasons for defining people and their differences, however, has been used to control those perceived as threats or an inconvenience to society. From this perspective, the construction of the meaning of disabilities has been motivated more by a search for mechanisms of social management than by concern for the best interests of people with disabilities.

THE MAGNIFICENT EXCEPTION: HELEN KELLER

There are, of course, exceptions to these limiting constructions of disabilities, and they typically occur when individuals with disabilities achieve prominence through extraordinary accomplishments. Helen Keller is a striking example of someone with severe disabilities and magnificent achievements who was able to eclipse prevailing attitudes about blindness and deafness. Her life and her relationship with her teacher, Anne Sullivan Macy, are inspiring and worthy of study. Her triumphs as a person with multiple disabilities also constitute a rare story. Joseph Lash observes in his biography of Keller that her disabilities may have been vehicles for her extraordinary achievements. One of her contemporaries speculated that Keller might not have accomplished all that she did if she had not been blind and deaf. He added that perhaps it was her disability that created her "high intelligence and purity of soul." Keller agreed, saying, "I have made my limitations tools of learning and true joy" (Lash, 1980, p. 766). As shall be evident later in this chapter, however, even Keller held prejudicial attitudes toward people who had disabilities different from her own, and she questioned the fundamental value of the lives of people with mental retardation.

MARTHA'S VINEYARD: DISABILITIES AND
THE ACHIEVEMENT OF COMMUNITY

There are rare examples of whole communities that have constructed the meaning of disability in ways that do not create handicaps. A fascinating example of this is contained in Nora Ellen Groce's (1985) book *Everyone Here Spoke Sign Language*. She describes a community on Martha's Vineyard, an island off Massachusetts, that from the time of its settlement by Europeans had an inordinate number of citizens who were deaf. Their deafness apparently resulted from a genetic characteristic in several of the original families, intermarriage within these families, and the relatively low level of contact with people on the mainland.

Groce characterized the social climate of Martha's Vineyard during the eighteenth and nineteenth centuries in this way: "On the Vineyard . . . the hearing people were bilingual in English and sign language. This adaptation had more than linguistic significance, for it eliminated the wall that separates most deaf people from the rest of society. How well can deaf people integrate themselves into the community if no communication barriers exist and if everyone is familiar and comfortable with deafness? The evidence from the Island indicates that they are extremely successful at this" (Groce, 1985, p. 4). Since most people on Martha's Vineyard (both those who could hear and those who could not) could communicate through sign language, deafness was not considered a disability. A few miles away on the Massachusetts mainland, deafness was considered a major handicap with serious social implications. On the island, deafness was seen as a difference that required only a sensitivity to the communication needs of others. An older hearing resident recalled that when people came together in the small villages of Martha's Vineyard, they would "sit around and wait for the mail to come in and just talk. And the deaf would be there, everyone would be there. And they would be part of the crowd, and they were accepted. They were fishermen and farmers and everything else. And they wanted to find out the news just as much as the rest of us. And oftentimes people would tell stories and make signs at the same time so everyone could follow. . . . Of course, sometimes, if there were more deaf than hearing people there, everyone would speak sign language—just to be polite, you know" (p. 60).

During the eighteenth and nineteenth centuries about 80 percent of the deaf population on Martha's Vineyard married, about the same as the overall marriage rate on the island; in the rest of the United States, however, only 45 percent of people with deafness married. On the island only 35 percent of the residents with deafness married others with deafness. This was markedly different from the national figure. During that period, 79 percent of people in the United States with deafness married other people who could not hear. The people of Martha's Vineyard with deafness were also just as likely to have children, and large families, as were their hearing neighbors.

Groce ends her book by reflecting on a comment made by an elderly islander she interviewed: "The stories these elderly Islanders shared with me, of the deaf heritage of the Vineyard, merit careful consideration. The most striking fact about these deaf men and women is that they were not handicapped, because no one perceived their deafness as handicaps. As one woman said to me, 'You know, we didn't think anything special about them. . . . They were just like anyone else. When you think about it, the Island was an awfully nice place to live.' Indeed it was" (1985, p. 110).

SCHOOLS AND THE TRADITION OF EXCLUSION

The Martha's Vineyard experience was exceptional, of course. People with disabilities in most parts of the United States, as in most parts of the world, have more often been excluded from the usual privileges and benefits of society. This has been as true of schools as of any other social institution. Although the rhetoric of public education has often emphasized equality of opportunity, educational practice well into the twentieth century belied this rhetoric.

Institutionalized inequalities in U.S. schools are most evident in the ways through which children of racial minorities have been excluded from equitable learning opportunities. This was rationalized with the argument that they could be provided "separate but equal" schools. Less known is the history of children with disabilities being excluded through similar legal and administrative practices. In 1893, for example, the Massachusetts Supreme Court (in *Watson v. City of Cambridge*, 1893) upheld the Cambridge Public Schools' expulsion of a child because the child was "weak in mind." The wording of another court ruling illustrates the extent to which school decisions leading to the exclusion of children with disabilities were based on factors other than a child's academic ability. In 1919 the Supreme Court of Wisconsin heard the case of a child with cerebral palsy who had the academic ability and physical capacity to function well in school, but who drooled, had impaired speech, and had frequent facial-muscle contractions. The court ruled that the public school could deny the child continuation in the school because he "produces a depressing and nauseating effect upon the teachers and school children" (*Beattie v. State Board of Education, City of Antigo*, 1919).

During the first half of the twentieth century, school exclusion of children with disabilities was common and legal in every state. A striking example of the justification given for segregated education for these children is a statement made by James Van Sickle, superintendent of the Baltimore Public Schools, in 1908:

> If it were not for the fact that the presence of mentally defective children in a school room interfered with the proper training of the capable children, their [separate] education would appeal less powerfully. . . . But the presence in a class of one or two mentally or morally defective children so absorbs the energies of the teacher and makes so imperative a claim upon her attention that she cannot under these circumstances properly instruct the number commonly enrolled in a class. School authorities must . . . withdraw into small classes these unfortunates who impede the regular progress of normal children. The plan of segregation is now fairly well established in large cities, and superintendents and teachers are working on the problem of classification, so that they may make the best of this imperfect material. (Van Sickle, 1908, pp. 102–103)

THE FOUNDATION FOR CHANGE: *BROWN V. BOARD OF EDUCATION*

The beginning point for the dismantling of the "separate but equal" doctrine was the Supreme Court's landmark decision in 1954 in the case known as *Brown v. Board of Education*, in which the Court found this policy and practice to be unconstitutional. As Chief Justice Earl Warren noted in the Court's decision, "In these days, it is doubtful that any child may reasonably be expected to succeed in life if he is denied the opportunity of an education. Such an opportunity, where the State has undertaken to provide it, is a right which must be made available to all on equal terms. . . . We conclude that in the field of public education the doctrine of 'separate but equal' has no place. Separate educational facilities are inherently unequal" (*Brown v. Board of Education of Topeka, Kansas,* 1954).

It is important to note that John W. Davis, the attorney for South Carolina in *Brown v. Board of Education*, opened his argument to the Supreme Court by saying, "May it please the Court, I think if the appellants' construction of the Fourteenth Amendment should prevail here, there is no doubt in my mind that it would catch the Indian within its grasp just as much as the Negro. If it should prevail, I am unable to see why a state would have any further right to segregate its pupils on the ground of sex, or on the ground of age, or on the ground of mental capacity" (cited in Friedman, 1969, p. 1). Davis was correct, of course, in his projections of the implications of *Brown v. Board of Education*. The decision did lead the way to issues of equality for other racial groups, to gender issues in education, and to the idea that all children, regardless of disability, have the right to equal education opportunities.

Brown v. Board of Education was a profound statement of the right to equality in the schooling of all children. Its impact, however, was not as immediate as some hoped nor was it as broad in application as Davis predicted it would be. Many years would pass before the principles articulated in the case would be applied to the rights of children with disabilities. Nonetheless, through recognizing that educating African American children separately, even in supposedly "equal" circumstances, was unfair and stigmatizing, the groundwork was laid for the eventual inclusion of children with disabilities in integrated schools.

The ideas that children with disabilities are entitled to an education and should be with other children followed somewhat haltingly the school integration actions that were implemented after *Brown v. Board of Education.* Although there were increasing allocations of funds for training special education teachers and supporting special education classes during the 1960s, school districts could choose whether to participate in these incentive programs. The question of whether all children with disabilities have an unqualified right to an education was not addressed for nearly two decades after the Supreme Court's decision.

LESSONS LEARNED: HISTORICAL PERSPECTIVES AND CONTEMPORARY ISSUES IN SPECIAL EDUCATION

Studying the historical events and figures in special education can shed light on how the field developed and acquired its character as a discipline. It can also foster an appreciation for the context through which contemporary issues in the field have evolved. The following vignettes from the complex history of special education will help to elucidate the questions and challenges faced in the field today.

History as a Source of Insights on Contemporary Issues

Historical research sometimes reveals previously overlooked insights. Generations of undergraduate students, for example, have read Margaret Mead's *Coming of Age in Samoa* (1928). Most "required reading" has likely focused on the main body of the book; however, in one of the appendices Mead describes people in Samoa who have disabilities. In addition to her accounts of the characteristics of particular individuals with disabilities in that culture, she notes that Samoans "possess more charity towards weakness than towards misdirected strength" (p. 182).

Mead returned to this theme many years later. In 1959 she spoke to a conference sponsored by the American Association on Mental Deficiency (AAMD). In her remarks she referred to a statement issued by a group of Catholic sisters who worked with children with mental retardation. Mead quoted the sisters as saying that they were attempting to make it possible for the children they cared for to make a "contribution in time as well as in eternity" (Mead, 1959, p. 253).

Later in her speech she again referenced the work of the Catholic Church with people with mental retardation. She gave the example of a child with Down syndrome who had been tested, diagnosed, and given every opportunity for the best skill training. When the child was in her early teens, however, she was given religious instruction, and Mead described the change that took place in the girl's life in terms of "wholeness." She said that at the same time the girl became "Catholic, she became a human being in a way that she had not been before . . . think that what happened on the secular side with this little girl was that for the first time she met a situation where people were willing to teach her the whole instead of saying 'you are defective and you can only learn a part'" (Mead, 1959, p. 260).

Mead concluded her address to the AAMD by elaborating on the concept of education for "wholeness." She distinguished between societies where everyone participates in all aspects of the culture (e.g., Samoa) and segmented, socially stratified societies that no longer attempt to teach the "whole" to all people (e.g., the United States). She emphasized that what makes for a culture of full participation is genuine opportunities for all people to learn how to fully participate. She also warned of the "risks of complicating sections of our culture so much that we define them as things most people can't learn" (1959, pp. 258–259).

Mead's insights, unfamiliar to most special education teachers and previously overlooked by many reading her work, add new meaning to what special education teachers already know. In order for people with disabilities to be genuinely included in our culture, we must strive to make the essential "wholeness" of citizenship accessible to everyone (Smith & Johnson, 1997).

History as a Source of Comprehension and Caution

Historical research also provides the opportunity for understanding characteristics of people and events previously overlooked. Personalities and social circumstances are far too complex to fit the neat categorizations we are often drawn toward. The study of history allows us to learn from contradictions. Understanding these complexities may deepen our appreciation of the truly human and sometimes contradictory characters of even those we most admire. Consider, for example, the book *The Black Stork*, which concerns the work of a physician who openly practiced euthanasia on "defective" newborns beginning in 1915. Dr. Harry Haiselden not only allowed infants with severe disabilities to die by withholding treatment but also administered drugs to hasten the deaths of several newborns; he also campaigned for the widespread adoption of these practices. Haiselden produced and starred in a movie promoting euthanasia, *The Black Stork*, which was based on his eugenic arguments; it was shown in theaters from 1916 through the 1920s (Pernick, 1996). Helen Keller was supportive of Haiselden's eugenic campaign, and in the December 18, 1915, issue of *The New Republic* Keller expressed the following opinions:

> It is the possibilities of happiness, intelligence, and power that give life its sanctity, and they are absent in the case of a poor, misshapen, paralyzed, unthinking creature. . . . The toleration of such anomalies tends to lessen the sacredness in which normal life is held.
>
> It seems to me that the simplest, wisest thing to do would be to submit cases like that of the malformed idiot baby to a jury of expert physicians. . . . A mental defective . . . is almost sure to be a potential criminal. The evidence before a jury of physicians considering the case of an idiot would be exact and scientific. Their findings would be free from the prejudice and inaccuracy of untrained observation. They would act only in case of true idiocy, where there could be no hope of mental development. (Keller, 1915, pp. 173–174)

Burton Blatt once wrote concerning the history of mental retardation that, "virtually all histories in our field are dangerously incomplete. . . . That which is preserved may be less relevant than that which is unknown; and the 'facts,' however pertinent, are to a degree divorced from the social-psychological context of the period. . . . To understand what actually occurred (and why) requires one to know what the times were like" (Blatt, 1987, p. 17).

Keller's development as an intellectual and as an advocate took place within the context of the eugenics movement. It also occurred within the environment of political progressivism. Progressive thought held that most of the problems of society, and those of individuals, could and should be reduced to scientific terms and resolved by scientific means. Keller's trust of a "jury" of physicians is very consistent with the faith in scientific progress that characterized the cultural climate of her formative years as a social activist. Her opinion that "true idiocy" lessens the sanctity of "normal life" reflects the eugenic principles to which she was most certainly exposed (Smith, 1997). Keller was known and revered as an advocate for people with disabilities. She also became a political activist and a spokesperson for victims of poverty, economic exploitation, gender discrimination, and other forms of oppression (Foner, 1967). Her voice of advocacy was bold for its time. It was focused, however, on the potential for social intercourse and productivity in the lives of ignored, misunderstood, and exploited people. In that regard, Keller moved beyond a social context that devalued many people with blindness, deafness, and other physical disabilities, and she crusaded for their right to earn a place in society. She did not believe, however, that this right extended to those people who might never "earn" their own way. Thus, in yet another way, Keller's story depends on our comprehension of the challenges facing special education teachers today.

HISTORICAL PERSPECTIVES AND THE CONCEPT OF A "FIELD" OF SPECIAL EDUCATION

A third important value of historical research is that it may help to bring a new or different focus to the contemporary sense that special education is a singular field. Knowledge of Keller's position on euthanasia provides us with a different perspective on the issue of advocacy. Questions concerning the discipline of special education can be brought into even sharper focus by insights on the life of Laura Bridgman.

Laura Bridgman was born into a prominent Massachusetts family in 1829. At two years of age she was rendered deaf and blind by scarlet fever. In 1837 she went to live at the Perkins Institution for the Blind in Boston. There she was tutored by the founder, Samuel Gridley Howe. Howe devised a teaching method that built on Bridgman's ability to feel the differences in the shapes of objects. Through drill and practice in distinguishing shapes, he led her to the understanding that these objects could be given names. At first he used labels with raised print on them to assign the names that Bridgman came to comprehend. He then taught her to form these words using movable letters. He was thus teaching her by methods similar to those used for other students at Perkins who were blind. Eventually, however, he shifted to a communication method that had been developed for students who were deaf. He began teaching her words using finger spelling. He spelled words into her hand and then associated them with objects and actions. This was the method that would later become central to Anne Sullivan's teaching of Keller. Bridgman's fame and Howe's success in teaching her were later eclipsed, in fact, by the extraordinary accomplishments of Keller and Sullivan.

It is ironic that little note has been taken of the fact that Anne Sullivan, herself a student at Perkins, learned to communicate with Bridgman and then applied what she had learned in her teaching with Keller (Smith, 1987). For several decades during the nineteenth century, however, Bridgman attracted international attention, and Howe's work with her was heralded with as much admiration as the "miracle worker" would later receive. To many intellectuals in the United States she became a symbol, "exemplifying the power of enlightened educational techniques and their capacity to transform seemingly hopeless cases" (Gallaher, 1995, p. 282). She was held up as a model of Victorian womanhood because of her courage and intelligence in the face of grave challenges. Some girls reportedly admired her so much that they "poked their dolls' eyes out and named them 'Laura' while reluctant young students were reminded to always compare their own efforts with those of the little deaf and blind girl who had accomplished so much in the face of such overwhelming obstacles" (Freeberg, 1992, p. 199).

Howe's accounts of Bridgman's education, published in the yearly reports of the Perkins Institution, attracted the attention of leading philosophers, theologians, and writers of the time. Historians who have studied Howe's reports are convinced that he recognized from the beginning of his work with Bridgman that her education would be of interest in scholarly circles. His efforts to teach her may have been motivated by the deepest and most sincere altruism, but: "Howe recognized from the start that Laura Bridgman was not just another afflicted child in need, but 'an object of particular interest.' If he could succeed in teaching her to communicate, he surely realized, this work would have far reaching religious and philosophical implications that would capture the attention of the world" (Freeberg, 1992, pp. 194–195).

For more than a century, John Locke's argument that the mind is a blank slate had dominated philosophy. The mind, according to Locke, was created by the experiential "writings" on that slate. The senses, therefore, determined the material character of the mind. If this portrait of the mind was accurate, then Howe should have found that Bridgman's mind was empty of all images, including moral or religious formulations. As Howe began to communicate with her about ideas, however, he found that her mind was not a tabula rasa. He described her internal life as a soul jailed in a body that was "active and struggling continually not only to put itself in communication with things without, but to manifest what is going on within itself" (Howe, 1893, p. 9). Howe described Bridgman's internal life, as he discovered it in its natural untouched state, as being of the highest moral character. He found that "her moral sense is remarkably acute; few children are so affectionate or so scrupulously conscientious, few are so sensible of their rights or as regardful of the rights of others" (p. 50).

To support his argument that Bridgman was innately moral, he described her behavior toward other people after she had been liberated by his teaching and learned to communicate. He reported that she was always eager to share with others and to help take care of sick people. He also said that she showed a keen sense of sympathy for people with disabilities. Howe noted, however, one exception to Laura's expressions of natural altruism. He said she showed an "unamiable" lack of respect for the children at the Perkins Institution whom she considered to be mentally inferior to herself. Interpreting this as an understandable manifestation of her Anglo-Saxon heritage, he excused the advantage she took of these children when she expected them to "wait on her" (Howe, 1893, p. 20).

One of Bridgman's most powerful and influential visitors at Perkins was Charles Dickens. His admiration for her began with his reading of Howe's accounts of her instruction. His admiration increased when he visited her in Boston. For Dickens, Bridgman was "both charming and inspirational: a merry, graceful, and intelligent young girl, she seemed also to symbolize the possibility of spiritual awakening and redemption" (Gitter, 1991, p. 163). Dickens described his visit to Bridgman at Perkins in *American Notes*. He relayed his impressions of her and he also quoted from Howe's reports. In his account he repeated Howe's observation that she had disdain for children she believed to be intellectually inferior (Dickens, 1842).

Howe is important in the history of mental retardation. In addition to his work with students with blindness and deaf-blindness, he was an early advocate for the education of students with mental retardation. He convinced the Massachusetts legislature to fund a school for the "teaching and training of idiotic children" in October of 1848 (Howe & Hall, 1904, p. 229). The school was initially housed at the Perkins Institution. According to two of his daughters, however, Howe soon discovered that his blind students resented deeply the presence of the students with mental retardation under their roof. His daughters interpreted this resentment as an expression of fear that they might come to be associated with the retardation of these "weaker brethren" (p. 231). They quoted Bridgman's journals as evidence of this feeling of resentment. Bridgman expressed the hope that the students with mental retardation would not actually come to Perkins and the fear that if they did that they would "have our rooms . . . [and] our nice sitting room in a few days" (p. 231).

Bridgman's fears regarding the perceived association between herself and her "weaker brethren" may not have been unfounded. Indeed, a literature has developed around the very notion of the transferability of social stigma—the process by which a "normal" person is seen by others as possessing the characteristics of a stigma merely by close association with a stigmatized other. Erving Goffman (1963) has written about the acquisition of a social stigma by affiliation. There is evidence to suggest that mental retardation carries the most debilitating socially constructed stigma—more than alcoholism, depression, crime, or sexual orientation. As Edgerton (1993) has pointed out, "One might speculate that no other stigma is as . . . [devastating] . . . as mental retardation in the sense that a person so labeled is thought to be so completely lacking in basic competence" (p. 184). Gibbons (1985) contends that people with mental retardation are themselves acutely aware of this stigma and tend to react with derogation toward their own peers' social competence and physical attractiveness.

Bridgman may have been acutely aware of the very real potential of being perceived as incompetent by association and of the social consequences inherent in that perception. The threat of a devalued identity provides a powerful incentive for maintaining both physical and social distance from people more seriously stigmatized. As Goffman (1963) suggested: "In general, the tendency for a stigma to spread from the stigmatized individual . . . provides a reason why such relations tend either to be avoided or to be terminated, where existing" (p. 30). Perhaps it is this attempt to avoid stigma by association that explains the attitude of Bridgman toward mental retardation. It may also explain the phenomenon of what might be called "differential advocacy" (Smith & Anton, 1997). Recognition of this differential in the attitudes of people with varying disabilities may also help special education teachers realize that they and the people who they serve as advocates must strive to work more closely together across categorical lines to achieve the ends they wish to achieve. It may also help us to understand the importance of and the challenges to a unified "field" of special education.

SPECIAL EDUCATION: LOOKING BACKWARD, LOOKING FORWARD

A Look Backward

Edward Bellamy was a journalist and novelist; he was also a strident voice for social reform during the late 1800s. His most influential work, *Looking Backward,* was a best-seller in the years following its publication in 1888 and was very influential among American intellectuals at the time. In 1935 the philosopher and educator John Dewey ranked *Looking Backward* as one of the most important books published in the preceding fifty years (Baer, 1992).

Bellamy's novel is the story of Julian West, who falls into a trance-like sleep in 1887 and is awakened in the year 2000. West awakes to a United States that has no wars, no political imparities, and no poverty. Each citizen is an equal shareholder in the social enterprise of the country and all have equitable and sufficient incomes. Bellamy emphasizes throughout the book that West finds in the year 2000 a society deeply committed to the equality of all of its citizens. West's guide in the new millennium world to which he has awakened is a physician, Dr. Leete. One of Leete's most profound revelations is that people with disabilities are considered equal members of his society. When West expresses surprise that "charity" has become so prevalent in the United States of 2000, an intriguing exchange takes place between the two men:

> "Charity!" repeated Dr. Leete. "Did you suppose that we consider the incapable class we are talking of objects of charity?"
> "Why naturally," I said, "inasmuch as they are incapable of self-support."
> But here the doctor took me up quickly.
> "Who is capable of self-support?" he demanded. "There is no such thing in a civilized society as self-support, . . . from the moment that men begin to live together, and constitute even the rudest sort of society, self-support becomes impossible. As men grow more civilized . . . a complex mutual dependence becomes the universal rule." (Bellamy, 1888, p. 178)

Dr. Leete continues his description of the fundamental equality of all people in his society regardless of individual needs or limitations in independence and productivity. In response West asks, "How can they who produce nothing claim a share of the product as a right?" Dr. Leete answers that each generation in a society inherits most of what it knows and possesses. He asks West:

> How did you come to be possessors of this knowledge and this machinery which represents nine parts to the one contributed by yourself in the value of your product? You inherited it, did you not? And were not these others, these unfortunate and crippled brothers whom you cast out, joint inheritors, co-heirs with you? . . . What I do not understand is, setting aside all considerations of justice or brotherly feeling toward the crippled and defective, how the workers of your day could have had any heart for their work, knowing that their children, or grandchildren, if unfortunate, would be deprived of the comforts and even necessities of life. (Bellamy, 1888, p. 181)

A Look Forward

Remarkable developments in molecular biology and genetic engineering are reported in the popular press almost daily. These advances in scientific knowledge and medical technology will almost certainly change the course of human history. The eradication of many of what are considered diseases, disorders, and defects may become a reality before the end of this century. A critical question that must be asked in this pursuit, however, is how diseases, disorders, and defects are defined. Are disabilities, in this context, diseases or defects, or are they simply human differences? Are they conditions to be prevented in all circumstances or are they part of the spectrum of human variation? Depending on the answer, what does this say about the status of people with disabilities in a democracy? What does it say about their fundamental equality as people?

The danger that people with disabilities will be further devalued as genetic intervention techniques increase is illustrated by recent remarks by James Watson. Winner of the Nobel Prize and co-discoverer of DNA, Watson was also the first director of the Human Genome Project. In his capacity as leader of the effort to map and sequence the genetic makeup of human beings, Watson also advocated careful consideration of the ethical, legal, and social implications of the project. And yet in an article titled "Looking Forward" Watson dismissed the value of people with severe disabilities when he spoke of the decisions faced by "prospective parents when they learn that their prospective child carries a gene that would block its opportunity for a meaningful life" (Watson, 1993, p. 314). In the same article he speaks disapprovingly of parents who do not undergo genetic testing. "So we must also face up to the ethical and practical dilemma, facing these individuals who could have undergone genetic diagnosis, but who for one reason or another declined the opportunity and later gave birth to children who must face up to lives of hopeless inequality" (p. 315). More recently Watson spoke to the German Congress of Molecular Medicine and condemned the eugenic philosophy that resulted in the atrocities of the Nazi era. Then, in a seemingly amazing contradiction, he advocated what might be termed "parental eugenics." He asserted that the "truly relevant question for most families is whether an obvious good will come from having a child with a major handicap." From this perspective, Watson said, "seeing the bright side of being handicapped is like praising the virtues of extreme poverty" (cited in Lee, 1998, p. 16).

HISTORIES AND FUTURES

In 1927 the U.S. Supreme Court, in *Buck v. Bell* (1927), upheld the constitutionality of a Virginia law allowing a state to sterilize people diagnosed as incompetent and deemed likely to genetically transmit physical, psychological, or social disabilities to their offspring. The case involved Carrie Buck, who was the first person to be eugenically sterilized under the authority of that law. In writing the majority opinion in *Buck v. Bell*, Justice Oliver Wendell Holmes used the now-famous phase, "three generations of imbeciles are enough." His reasoning and his language were consistent with the eugenic view that many disabilities are largely hereditary in origin. Inherent in this view was the idea that even complex human characteristics could be traced directly to genetic sources. This belief, with the credibility afforded it by being grounded in what was then accepted as "scientific fact," became a powerful force in shaping public opinion and social policy toward people with disabilities.

The eugenic evidence and the predictions in Buck's case have proven to be grossly inaccurate. Buck's child, Vivian, alleged to represent the "third generation of imbeciles," grew to be an honor-roll student. Buck, labeled as being the child of an "imbecile" herself, was discharged to a mountain village after being sterilized. There she married the deputy sheriff and lived a modest but productive and respectable life. Following her husband's death, she moved to a larger town, where she earned her living caring for elderly and chronically ill people. Friends and employers attested to the fact that Carrie was not mentally retarded, and, indeed, mental health professionals who observed her late in life found no evidence of retardation (Smith & Nelson, 1989).

Buck's story is a tragic saga of one injured life. It is also an important illustration of the allure and dangers of reductionistic and deterministic thought about human beings. The ideas that created the misfortunes of Buck—that human life can be reduced to biology and that social institutions can best be guided by the realities of biological determinism—have repeatedly produced tragic results. Individuals and groups of people, including people with disabilities, have been viewed by others as being inherently and unmodifiably inferior because of their biology. On that basis they have often been deprived of their dignity and rights.

In *Backdoor to Eugenics* Duster (1990) argues that eugenics is alive and well in our society but in a more subtle manifestation. Although it is still being presented as an economic and social issue, eugenics is also being portrayed as a matter of parental responsibility or irresponsibility. Although less overt, this new form of eugenics may be even more powerful in its impact on the lives of people with disabilities.

Eugenicists in the past looked to evolutionary theory and Mendelian genetics for moral truths. They believed that natural selection and Mendelian gene distributions could provide models for social ethics. The failure of this approach was evidenced in the needless institutionalization of people deemed to be "unfit" for the social "struggle," in the sterilization of people inaccurately assessed to be the carriers of defective genes, and in the moral horrors of the Holocaust. What truths will prevail in the current eugenic climate?

Linton (1998) has called for a conceptualization of humanity, inclusive of both those with disabilities and those without, as part of an integrated universe of people. A key to this social formulation is an understanding of the complementarity, interdependence, and equality of people with differences. Commenting on the work of Nobel geneticist Barbara McClintock, Linton wrote, "If something doesn't fit, there's a reason, and you find what it is. Rather than overlook difference, for instance, by naming an exception, an aberration, a contaminant, she worked to understand its place and function" (p. 120).

As the power of genetic science grows, so does the importance of ethical questions about the implication of that power for human diversity. The greatest challenge for people with disabilities in this century may be that of having their lives understood within the contexts of the civic values of liberty, justice, and equality. This challenge, and hope, is embodied in the 1892 address that Francis Bellamy, Edward Bellamy's cousin and author of the Pledge of Allegiance, delivered during the unveiling of the pledge. Perhaps borrowing a concept from his cousin Edward, he spoke of looking forward to a new age: "We look forward. We are conscious we are in a period of transition. Ideas in education, in political economy, in social science are undergoing revisions. . . . The coming century promises to be more than ever the age of the people; an age that shall develop a greater care for the rights of the weak, and make a more solid provision for the development of each individual" (Baer, 1992, p. 41).

Indeed, let us hope we are living at the beginning of a century that will be "more than ever the age of the people," including those with disabilities. Maybe our understanding of the past and the enlightenment it provides for the future will enable us to reach this goal. Perhaps when the history of the twenty-first century is surveyed someday, it will be evident that the genetic revolution was not solely a scientific and medical revolution. Perhaps history will find it to have been an ethical revolution as well, and that the true discovery of the "wholeness" of people with disabilities was part of that revolution. Perhaps it will be seen as a period when an increasing awareness of the critical and uncoerced choices that only individuals and families can make about the character and direction of their lives was achieved. If this proves to be the case, then the history of special education in the twenty-first century will be a story that enhances the value of the lives of people with disabilities.

QUESTIONS FOR FURTHER DISCUSSION

1. Several examples of both the "nurturing" and "destructive" stories of disability were presented in this chapter. Identify other literary or historical examples of these kinds of stories. Do you have stories of each type from your own experiences?

2. Have schools largely overcome the "tradition of exclusion"? If not, what do teachers and other school leaders need to understand about the place of students with special needs in their schools? What can they learn from the history of special education?

3. Is special education a civil rights movement? In addition to the relationship with the *Brown v.*

Board of Education decision, what other parallels can you think of that show the connection between the struggle for racial equality and the effort to secure the rights of people with disabilities?

4. How likely do you think it is that acceptance and respect for people with disabilities and their families will be diminished as the capacity for genetic manipulation increases? What are the implications for people with other kinds of differences? Are we moving toward expecting all people to meet a physical and mental standard of perfection?

REFERENCES

Baer, J. (1992). *The pledge of allegiance: A centennial history, 1892–1992.* Annapolis, MD: Free Press.

Beattie v. State Board of Education, City of Antigo, 169 Wisc. 231, 172 N.W. 153 (1919).

Bellamy, E. (1888). *Looking backward.* New York: Ticknor.

Blatt, B. (1987). *The conquest of mental retardation.* Austin, TX: Pro-Ed.

Brown v. Board of Education of Topeka, Kansas, 347 U.S. 483 (1954).

Buck v. Bell, 274 U.S. 200 (1927)

Dayan, Y. (1985). *My father, his daughter.* London: Weidenfield & Nicolson.

Dickens, C. (1842). *American notes.* London: Oxford University Press.

Duster, T. (1990). *Backdoor to eugenics.* New York: Routledge.

Edgerton, R. (1993). *The clock of competence* (Rev. ed.). Berkeley: University of California Press.

Foner, P. (1967). *Helen Keller: Her socialist years, writing, and speeches.* New York: International Publishers.

Freeberg, E. (1992). An object of peculiar interest: The education of Laura Bridgman. *Church History, 61,* 191–205.

Friedman, L. (1969). *Argument: The oral argument before the Supreme Court in* Brown v. Board of Education of Topeka. New York: Chelsea House.

Gallaher, D. (1995). *Voice for the mad: The life of Dorthea Dix.* New York: Free Press.

Gibbons, F. X. (1985). Stigma perception: Social comparison among mentally retarded persons. *American Journal of Mental Deficiency, 90,* 98–106.

Gitter, E. (1991). Charles Dickens. *Dickens Quarterly, 8,* 162–168.

Goffman, E. (1963). *Stigma: Notes on the management of spoiled identity.* Englewood Cliffs, NJ: Prentice Hall.

Groce, N. E. (1985). *Everyone here spoke sign language: Hereditary deafness on Martha's Vineyard.* Cambridge, MA: Harvard University Press.

Howe, M., & Hall, F. (1904). *Laura Bridgman: Dr. Howe's famous pupil and what he taught her.* London: Hodden & Stoughton.

Howe, S. (1893). *The education of Laura Bridgman.* Boston: Perkins Institution.

Keller, H. (1915, December 18). Physician's juries for defective babies. *The New Republic,* 173–174.

Lash, J. P. (1980). *Helen and teacher: The story of Helen Keller and Anne Sullivan Macy.* New York: Delacorte Press.

Lee, T. (1998, March/April). You probably won't like James Watson's ideas about us. *Ragged Edge,* 16.

Linton, S. (1988). *Claiming disability: Knowledge and identity.* New York: New York University Press.

Lopez, B. H. (1990). *Crow and weasel.* San Francisco: North Point Press.

Mead, M. (1928). *Coming of age in Samoa: A psychological study of primitive youth for western civilization.* New York: William Marrow.

Mead, M. (1959). Research cult: Or cure? *American Journal of Mental Deficiency, 64,* 253–264.

Pernick, M. (1996). *The black stork: Eugenics and the death of "defective" babies in American medicine and motion pictures since 1915.* New York: Oxford Press.

Smith, J. D. (1985). *Minds made feeble: The myth and the legacy of the Kallikaks.* Rockville, MD: Aspen.

Smith, J. D. (1987). *The other voices: Profiles of women in the history of special education.* Seattle: Special Child Publications.

Smith, J. D. (1997). Construction of mental retardation and the challenge of advocacy: The different voices of Helen Keller and Burton Blatt. *Mental Retardation, 35,* 138–140.

Smith, J. D., & Anton, M. (1997). Laura Bridgman, mental retardation, and the question of differential advocacy. *Mental Retardation, 35,* 398–401.

Smith, J. D., & Johnson, G. (1997). Margaret Mead and mental retardation: Words of understanding, concepts of inclusiveness. *Mental Retardation, 35,* 306–309.

Smith, J. D., & Nelson, K. (1989). *The sterilization of Carrie Buck.* Far Hills, NJ: New Horizon Press.

Trent, J. W. (1994). *Inventing the feeble mind: A history of mental retardation in the United States.* Berkeley: University of California Press.

Van Sickle, J. H. (1908). Provisions for exceptional children in the public schools. *Psychological Clinic, 2,* 102–111.

Watson, J. (1993). Looking forward. *Gene, 135,* 309–315.

Watson v. City of Cambridge, 157, Mass. 56, N.E. 864 (1893).

CONTEMPORARY LEGAL ISSUES
IN SPECIAL EDUCATION

MITCHELL L. YELL
ERIK DRASGOW
University of South Carolina

RENEE BRADLEY
TROY JUSTESEN
U.S. Office of Special Education Programs

President Gerald Ford signed the Education for All Handicapped Children Act (EAHCA) into law on November 29, 1975. The EAHCA was renamed the Individuals with Disabilities Education Act (IDEA) in 1990. Since the EAHCA became law almost thirty years ago, there have been numerous changes and accomplishments in the ways that students with disabilities are educated. Providing an education to children with disabilities is a complex and controversial subject in the United States, and significant debates, often highly politicized, have surrounded the topic, many of them continuing today.

This chapter provides a brief overview of the education of children who need special education and related services. It discusses the historical developments leading to the passage of federal legislation funding special education and protecting the rights of children with disabilities. It presents an analysis of the major provisions of present federal special education law. It outlines three crucial issues in special education—free appropriate public education, least restrictive environments, and disciplining of students with disabilities—and the controversies surrounding them. The chapter ends with an analysis of future directions for these three issues.

Renee Bradley and Troy Justesen participated in this article as former teachers, university instructors, and private researchers. Opinions expressed herein are those of the authors and do not necessarily reflect the position of the U.S. Office of Special Education Programs, and no such endorsement should be inferred. For additional information on the Individuals with Disabilities Education Act or official information on this legislation and subsequent regulations, visit the Office of Special Education Programs web site at www.ed.gov/offices/OSERS/OSEP.

THE HISTORY OF THE INDIVIDUALS WITH DISABILITIES EDUCATION ACT

Federal involvement in educating children with disabilities generally parallels the development of federal support for elementary and secondary education. Until the 1960s, elementary and secondary education was viewed almost entirely as state and local functions, and federal intervention was almost nonexistent. The initial comprehensive involvement of the federal government in education began in 1965 with the passage of the Elementary and Secondary Education Act (ESEA) of 1965. The ESEA set the stage for allocating federal funds for the education of children in U.S. public elementary and secondary schools. Until 1965 federal involvement in public education was staunchly prohibited because state and local authorities as well as the public believed that federal intervention in public education was a classic example of federal intrusion in local responsibilities. Nevertheless, just one year after the passage of the ESEA, it was amended to specifically provide federal support for educating children with disabilities. This amendment, Title VI, authorized the use of federal funds to assist states in the initiation, expansion, and improvement of programs to educate children with disabilities.

In the five years after the Title VI amendment, interest groups representing children with disabilities amassed major political support sufficient to expand federal funding to improve education for and afford protections to children with disabilities and their parents. Underpinning the extension of legal rights to an education for children with disabilities were the Civil Rights Movement and the Supreme Court's landmark decision in *Brown v. Board of Education* in 1954, which led to the Civil Rights Acts of 1964 and 1968 (Justesen, in press).

Litigation and legislative efforts from 1964 to 1974 produced strong legal and political support for expanding federal oversight of the education of children with disabilities; particularly significant cases were *Pennsylvania Association for Retarded Children [PARC] v. Commonwealth of Pennsylvania* and *Mills v. Board of Education of the District of Columbia*. Congress created the Bureau for the Education of the Handicapped within the U.S. Office of Education in 1966, and in 1975 Congress enacted the most expansive legislation related to educating and providing services for children with disabilities—the Education for All Handicapped Children Act (P.L. 94-142) (EAHCA).

The education of students with disabilities was seen as a privilege rather than a right prior to 1975 (Huefner, 2000). Access to educational opportunities for students with disabilities was limited in two major ways. First, many students were completely excluded from public schools. Congressional findings in 1974 indicate that more than 1.75 million students with disabilities did not receive educational services. In fact, in the early 1970s U.S. public schools educated only an estimated 20 percent of all children with disabilities (Office of Special Education Programs [OSEP], 2000). Second, over three million students with disabilities who were admitted to school did not receive an education appropriate to their needs (Katsiyannis, Yell, & Bradley, 2001). These students were often "left to fend for themselves in classrooms designed for education of their nonhandicapped peers" (*Board of Education of the Hendrick Hudson Central School District v. Rowley*, 1982, p. 191). Because public schools offered limited educational opportunities, many parents of children with disabilities were forced into expensive, private, and almost exclusively segregated education for their children, often far from their homes (Katsiyannis, Yell, & Bradley, 2001).

The increasing acceptance of federal involvement in public education coupled with the integration of children who are African American into the public schools laid the groundwork for politicians' willingness to introduce legislation requiring local and state educational agencies to provide a minimum level of educational opportunity for children with disabilities.

THE EDUCATION OF ALL HANDICAPPED CHILDREN ACT

Congress passed the EAHCA for three reasons: (1) to ensure that children with disabilities received a free appropriate public education, (2) to protect the rights of students and their parents, and (3) to assist states and localities in their efforts to provide such services. The EAHCA provided federal funding to states that chose to accept funds appropriated under the EAHCA for the provision of special education to eligible children with disabilities covered by the EAHCA. Federal EAHCA funding was contingent on a state's passage of a state law consistent with the EAHCA. Each state was also required to demonstrate to the satisfaction of the federal government that it was complying with these laws and was providing for the education of students with disabilities consistent with the minimum standards of the EAHCA. With the passage of the EAHCA, therefore, the federal government became a partner with states in educating students with disabilities (Huefner, 2000).

The EAHCA has evolved since 1975, yet it remains the most significant legislation for children with disabilities. It is federal legislation with funding appropriated by Congress, and Congress must routinely review and reauthorize it. The EAHCA was most recently reauthorized in 1990, and among other amendments discussed later in this chapter, its name was changed to the Individuals with Disabilities Education Act (IDEA). The 1990 amendments included allocating supplemental funding for individual state and local efforts to implement the requirements of the IDEA. According to the U.S. Supreme Court, however, when Congress passed the IDEA, it "did not content itself with passage of a simple funding statute. Rather the [EAHCA, now the IDEA] confers upon disabled students an enforceable substantive right to public education . . . and conditions federal financial assistance upon states' compliance with substantive and procedural goals of the Act" (*Honig v. Doe*, 1988, p. 597).

In summary, the IDEA is a comprehensive law that provides supportive funding to the states and governs how students with disabilities will be educated. Eligible students with disabilities must be provided with a free and appropriate public education that consists of special education and related services. The term *special education* means specially designed instruction, at no cost to parents, to meet the unique needs of a child with a disability, including instruction conducted in the classroom, in the home, in hospitals and institutions, and in other settings, and instruction in physical education (20 U.S.C. §1401(25)). A student is eligible for protection under the IDEA if he or she has at least one of thirteen types of disability specifically listed under the IDEA and who, by reason thereof, needs special education and related services.

The IDEA is divided into four provisions: Parts A, B, C, and D. Part A contains the general provisions of the act, including congressional justification for authorizing the IDEA and findings of fact regarding the education of students with disabilities that existed when the IDEA was passed; it also defines the terms used in the IDEA. Part B explains what states must do to qualify for federal assistance in the education of all children with disabilities, including state and local educational agency eligibility, individualized education programs and placements, procedural safeguards, and other IDEA administration procedures. The purpose of Part B (the part most familiar to teachers and administrators) is to ensure that all children with disabilities aged three through twenty-one who reside in a state that accepts funding under the IDEA have the right to a free appropriate public education (FAPE). A state's obligation to make FAPE available to each eligible child begins no later than the child's third birthday. Part C covers infants and toddlers from birth through age two; it was formerly Part H but became Part C when the IDEA was amended in 1997. Part C provides funds to eligible states for early intervention services for infants and toddlers with disabilities or who would be at risk of experiencing a substantial developmental delay if early intervention services were not provided (20 U.S.C. §1432(1)). Part D contains provisions for national activities that are vitally important to the development of special education and related services and that improve education of children with disabilities. National activities include investments in research and technology to improve services and results for children with disabilities and technical assistance and training for parents and special education personnel. The following sections examine Parts B, C, and D in detail. Table 1 summarizes each of these parts.

TABLE 1   Individuals with Disabilities Education Act (IDEA)

PARTS OF THE IDEA	TITLE	KEY PROVISIONS
Part A	General Provisions	Purposes and definitions
Part B	Assistance for Education of All Children with Disabilities	State grant formulas Requires states to provide services to children with disabilities aged 3–21 Requires states to provide services to preschool children, ages 3–5 FAPE and procedural requirements
Part C	Infants and Toddlers with Disabilities	Authorizes grants to states to provide early intervention services to infants and toddlers, aged birth to 3.
Part D	National Activities to Improve Education of Children with Disabilities	National activities to improve the education of children with disabilities through investments in areas including research, technology, training, technical assistance and information dissemination, parent training, and evaluation. The IDEA Amendments of 1997 added State Improvement Grants to Part D. State Improvement Grants are grants awarded to states to reform and improve their systems for providing educational services for students with disabilities and their nondisabled peers.

Part B of the IDEA

In addition to setting forth the funding mechanisms by which the states receive federal IDEA funds, Part B also contains the principles that states must adhere to when educating children with disabilities. Part B is permanently funded, so it does not require periodic congressional reauthorization, although Congress may reconsider any portion of the IDEA when it considers any other part of the IDEA; in other words, it may amend Part B whenever it decides that it is necessary, including amending its funding mechanisms and major principles.

Funding Mechanisms.   Part B sets forth the eligibility requirements for states to receive federal funds. To qualify for funding a state must demonstrate to the satisfaction of the U.S. secretary of education that it has policies and procedures in effect that will ensure it meets the conditions set forth in Part B. These conditions include, but are not limited to, (1) the system for identifying, locating, and evaluating children and youth with disabilities, known specifically as the "child find provisions" of the IDEA; (2) the programs that will be used to ensure that eligible students with disabilities receive special education and related services; and (3) the procedural safeguards that will ensure that appropriate programming is provided to eligible children.

Moreover, each state shall develop and implement a comprehensive system of personnel development that includes the training of paraprofessionals and primary referral sources; is designed to ensure an adequate supply of qualified special education, regular education, and related services personnel; and is updated at least every five years. Additionally, states are responsible for the continuing development of personnel already teaching in special education. A state's plan must also set up a procedure for allocating special education funds to local school districts.

States that meet the IDEA requirements receive federal funding. The state educational agency (SEA) receives the funds and distributes them to the local educational agencies (LEAs). The federal funds do not cover the entire cost of special education but rather are intended to provide financial assistance to the states. Congress originally intended to fund 40 percent of a state's costs of providing special education and related services through the IDEA. Actual funding levels, however, have usually amounted to approximately 8–10 percent of a state's total special education expenditures. Thus, the IDEA has never been fully funded in accordance with Congress's original intentions under the 1975 EAHCA.

The federal money the states receive must not be used to supplant or substitute for state funds but to supplement and increase funding of special education and related services. This requirement, often referred to as the nonsupplanting requirement of the IDEA, ensures that states will not use IDEA funds to relieve state- and local-level financial obligations but will use them instead to increase the level of state expenditures on special education and related services. Each state is ultimately responsible for ensuring the appropriate use of funds. Each state may use not more than 20 percent of the maximum amount it may retain for any fiscal year or $500,000, whichever is greater, and each outlying area may use up to 5 percent of the amount it receives for any fiscal year or $35,000, whichever is greater, with the remaining amount required to be distributed to local educational agencies (school districts).

Concepts of Part B.   Some scholars have divided Part B into six major principles for discussion purposes (e.g., Turnbull & Turnbull, 2000; Turnbull, Turnbull, Shank, Smith, & Leal, 2001). Neither the IDEA's statutory language nor the Office of Special Education Programs recognizes the division of the law into these six principles, but it provides a useful structure for our discussion, so we briefly summarize it in the following sections.

Zero Reject. According to the zero reject principle, all students with disabilities eligible for services under the IDEA are entitled to a FAPE. This principle applies regardless of the severity of the child's disability. States must ensure that all students with disabilities aged three through twenty-one who (1) reside in the state, (2) need special education and related services or are suspected of having a disability, and (3) need special education services are identified, located, and evaluated. No eligible student with a disability can be excluded (Turnbull & Turnbull, 2000).

Protection in Evaluation. Before a student can receive special education and related services for the first time, he or she must receive a full and individual evaluation administered by trained and knowledgeable personnel in accordance with any instructions provided by the producer of the tests. Tests and other evaluation materials used to assess a child must be selected and administered so as not to be discriminatory on a racial or cultural basis; and a variety of assessment tools and strategies must be used to gather relevant functional and developmental information about the child, including information provided by the parent, and information related to enabling the child to be involved in and progress in the general curriculum, among other evaluation requirements.

Upon completing the administration of tests and other evaluation materials, a group of qualified professionals and the child's parents will determine whether the child qualifies as a child with a disability.

Free Appropriate Public Education. Students who are determined eligible for special education and related services under the IDEA have the right to receive a FAPE. Under the IDEA, this means special education and related services that are provided at public expense, under public supervision and direction, and without charge to the parents; meet the standards of the SEA; include preschool, elementary school, or secondary school education in the child's state; and are provided in conformity with an individualized education program (IEP) that meets the requirements of the IDEA. The key to providing a FAPE is individualized programming.

To ensure that each student covered by the IDEA receives an individualized education, Congress required that an IEP be developed for all students with disabilities receiving special education. The IEP is both a collaborative process between the parents and the school in which each child's educational program is developed and a written document that contains the essential components of a student's educational program (Gorn, 1997). The written document, developed by a team of educators and a student's parents, describes the student's educational needs and details the special education and related services the student will receive (Bateman & Linden, 1998). The IEP also contains the student's educational goals and objectives and the means for measuring his or her progress. The IDEA mandates the process and procedures for developing an IEP.

Least Restrictive Environment. The IDEA mandates that students with disabilities be educated with their peers without disabilities to the maximum extent appropriate. The law presumes that students with disabilities will be educated in integrated settings when appropriate. In fact, students in special education can only be removed from the regular classroom to separate classes or schools when the nature or severity of the child's disability is such that the child cannot receive an appropriate education in a general education classroom with supplementary aids and services. When this happens, the student may be removed to a more specialized and restrictive setting that meets the student's needs.

To ensure that students are educated in the least restrictive environment (LRE) appropriate for their needs, school districts must ensure the availability of a complete continuum of alternative placements. This continuum ranges from settings that are less restrictive and more typical to those that are more restrictive and specialized. The most typical and, therefore, least restrictive setting for most students is the regular education classroom, or the regular classroom combined with a resource room. Alternatives that must be available include special classes, special schools, home instruction, and instruction in hospitals and institutions.

In determining the educational placement of a child with a disability, including a preschool child, public agencies must ensure that the placement decision is made by a group of people, including the parents, who are knowledgeable about the child and the meaning of the evaluation data and that the placement options are made in conformity with the LRE provisions of the IDEA. The child's placement is reviewed at least annually, must be based on the child's IEP, and is as close as possible to the child's home. Unless a child's IEP requires some other arrangement, the child must be educated in the school that he or she would attend if the child were not disabled; a child with a disability cannot be removed from an age-appropriate regular classroom solely because of needed modifications in the general curriculum. Programming, therefore, takes precedence over placement (Yell & Drasgow, 2000).

Procedural Safeguards.   Part B of the IDEA contains an extensive system of procedural safeguards to ensure that all eligible students with disabilities receive a FAPE. The safeguards also ensure that parents are equal participants in the special education process. For example, the IDEA provides that a student's parents may participate in all meetings in which their child's identification, evaluation, program, or placement is discussed. Parental involvement is crucial to successful results for students, and this requirement is one of the cornerstones of the IDEA. The IDEA requires that informed parental consent must be obtained through an initial evaluation of the child with the parents prior to an LEA's initial provision of special education and related services to a child with a disability. Importantly, under the regulations implementing the IDEA, consent for initial evaluation may not be construed as consent for initial placement.

When the school and parents disagree on any matters involving proposals to initiate or change the identification, evaluation, or educational placement of the child or the provision of a FAPE to the child, or if the school refuses to initiate or change any of these areas, parents may initiate an impartial due process hearing. School districts or the SEA may also request an impartial due process hearing under these same matters. The IDEA amendments of 1997 require states to offer parents the option of resolving their disputes through mediation prior to requesting a due process hearing. The mediation process is voluntary and must not be used to deny or delay a parent's right to a due process hearing.

Any party in a due process hearing has the right to be accompanied and advised by counsel and by individuals with special knowledge of or training in the issues related to children with disabilities. Moreover, any party may present evidence, compel the attendance of witnesses, examine and cross-examine witnesses, prohibit the introduction of evidence not introduced five days prior to the hearing, obtain a written—at the option of the parents—or electronic verbatim record of the hearing, and be provided with the written or—at the option of the parents—electronic findings of fact and decisions by the hearing officer. The public agency shall ensure that no later than forty-five days after the receipt of a request for a hearing a final decision is reached in the hearing and a copy of the decision is mailed to each of the parties. This decision is binding on both parties. Either party, however, may appeal the decision. In most states, appeals are made to the SEA. The SEA shall ensure that no later than thirty days after the receipt of a request for a review (i.e., an appeal) a final decision is reached in the review and a copy of the decision is mailed to each of the parties. The decision of the SEA can then be appealed to state or federal court as a civil action with respect to the complaint presented to the hearing officer and appealed to the state.

Parental Participation. Since the early days of special education litigation, parents of children with disabilities have played a very important role in helping schools meet the educational needs of their children. Key provisions of the IDEA that require parental participation are scattered throughout the law. Parents must be involved in initial evaluation, IEP meetings, and placement decisions. The IDEA amendments of 1997 also required that schools regularly inform parents of children with disabilities of their children's progress (through such means as periodic report cards) at least as often as the school informs the parents of nondisabled children about their progress. The goal of this principle is to have parents play a meaningful role in the education of their children and to maintain a partnership between schools and parents. Parental involvement is crucial to successful results for students, and this provision has been and continues to be one of the cornerstones of the IDEA.

Part C of the IDEA

Congress recognized the importance of early intervention for young children when it passed the Education of the Handicapped amendments in 1986. This law, which became a subchapter of the IDEA (Part H), made categorical grants to states contingent on their adhering to the provisions of law. The amendments required participating states to develop and implement statewide interagency programs of early intervention services for infants and toddlers with disabilities or at risk for developmental delays. With the consolidation of the IDEA in the amendments of 1997, Part H became Part C.

For purposes of the law, infants and toddlers are defined as children from birth through age two who need early intervention services because they are experiencing developmental delays or have a diagnosed physical or mental condition that puts the child at risk of becoming developmentally delayed. Early intervention services are defined as developmental services that are provided under public supervision and at no cost except where federal or state law provides for a system of payments by families, including a schedule of sliding fees; these services are designed to meet the developmental needs of an infant or toddler with a disability in any one or more of the following areas: physical, cognitive, communication, social or emotional, and adaptive development needs. Early intervention services may include family training, counseling, home visits, special instruction, speech-language pathology and audiology services, occupational therapy, physical therapy, psychological services, case management services, and medical services (for diagnostic or evaluation purposes only); early identification, screening, and assessment services; health services; social work services; vision services; assistive technology devices and services; and transportation and related costs. To the maximum extent appropriate, these services must be provided in natural environments (i.e., home and community settings) in which children without disabilities participate.

The infants and toddlers program does not require that the state educational agency assume overall responsibility for the early intervention programs. The agency that assumes responsibility is referred to as the lead agency. The lead agency may be the SEA, the state welfare department, the health department, or any other unit of state government. Many states provide Part C services through multiple state agencies. In these cases, an interagency coordinating council is the primary planning body that works out the agreements between the agencies regarding jurisdiction and funding.

Part D of the IDEA

Part D, perhaps the least known section of the IDEA, even among teachers and administrators, has significantly contributed to improving practices in special education. The Office of Special Education Programs (OSEP, 2000) states that Part D programs account for less than 1 percent of the national expenditure to educate students with disabilities; however, programs funded by the Part D national programs play a crucial role in identifying, implementing, evaluating, and disseminating information about effective practices in educating all children with disabilities. These programs also provide an infrastructure of practice improvement that supports the other 99 percent of our national expenditure to educate students with disabilities (OSEP, 2000). The IDEA amendments of 1997 reauthorized seven Part D programs. These programs provide federal support for (1) researching improvements to educational programs for children with disabilities, (2) developing devices and strategies to make technology accessible and usable for children with disabilities, (3) training personnel who work with children with disabilities, (4) maintaining national programs that provide technical assistance and disseminate information, (5) training parents of children with disabilities, (6) evaluating progress in educating students with disabilities, and (7) funding state improvement grants that promote statewide reforms and improvements in the education of students with disabilities.

Part D national programs are often referred to as support programs because their primary purpose is to support the implementation of the IDEA and to assist states in improving the education of students with disabilities. These programs, even though they receive a small amount of the total federal expenditure for the IDEA, help to ensure that the field of special education will continue to move forward by translating research into practice and thus improving the future of students with disabilities.

The IDEA has been exemplary in meeting its original purpose: to open the doors of public education to students with disabilities. Today, access to an education is more assured than ever before. In fact, according to the U.S. Department of Education (U.S. Department of Education, 2000a), in the 1998–1999 school year over six million students with disabilities, aged three through twenty-one, received special education services under the IDEA. Additionally, almost 50 percent of students with disabilities, aged six through twenty-one, received educational services in the regular classroom for at least 80 percent of the school day. As former secretary of education Richard Riley stated on the twenty-fifth anniversary of the IDEA, "Twenty-five years ago, IDEA opened the doors to our schoolhouses for our students with disabilities. Today, millions of students with disabilities attend our public schools. We have made steady progress toward educating students with disabilities, including them in regular classrooms, graduating them with the proper diploma, and sending them off to college" (U.S. Department of Education, 2000b, p. 1).

Despite the successes of the past three decades, the IDEA has not been without its share of controversy. Three issues have created a great deal of disagreement and acrimony in the courts and the professional literature—determining what constitutes a free appropriate public education, determining what constitutes the least restrictive environment under specific circumstances, and disciplining students with disabilities. The following sections examine these contemporary legal controversies.

FREE APPROPRIATE PUBLIC EDUCATION

The primary intent of the EAHCA was to ensure that all children and youth with disabilities would receive a FAPE individually designed to meet each student's unique educational needs. When writing the law, Congress did not provide a substantive definition of FAPE, did not indicate what components must be included in a student's IEP, and did not state specific levels of achievement that should be met. Instead, it defined FAPE more as a process by which school districts arrived at each student's IEP. Thus, Congress provided a procedural definition of FAPE but not a substantive one.

The lack of a substantive definition has led to frequent disagreements between parents and schools regarding what constitutes an appropriate education for a particular student with a disability. Many of these disputes have been settled in due process hearings and in formal litigation. In fact, disputes regarding what constitutes a FAPE for a particular student are one of the most heavily litigated areas in special education law. Typically these disputes involve questions about what degree of educational benefit a FAPE should provide. Should a FAPE confer meaningful educational benefits, and if so, what does *meaningful* mean for a specific child in question? Or is the FAPE requirement satisfied when an education confers some benefit, rather than any particular level of benefit, for a student with a disability? The following section reviews the IDEA's FAPE requirement and FAPE litigation in the federal courts. The statutory law (i.e., IDEA) and decisions (i.e., due process hearings and court cases) presented here help to clarify the meaning of FAPE under the IDEA.

Legislation and FAPE

The IDEA defines a FAPE as special education and related services that (1) have been provided at public expense, under public supervision and direction, and without charge; (2) meet the standards of the state educational agency; 3) include an appropriate preschool, elementary, or secondary school education in the state involved; and (4) are provided in conformity with the IEP (IDEA, 20 U.S.C. §1401(8)).

The IDEA mandates specific procedures schools must follow to develop special education programs for students with disabilities. These procedures safeguard a student's right to a FAPE by ensuring that parents are meaningfully involved in the development of their child's IEP and are consulted and can participate throughout the special education process. These safeguards include prior notice, informed parental consent, the opportunity to examine records, the right to an independent educational evaluation at public expense, and the right to request an impartial due process hearing (IDEA Regulations, 34 C.F.R. §300.500–515). In fact, according to the U.S. Supreme Court, "Congress placed every bit as much emphasis upon compliance with procedures giving parents and guardians a large measure of participation at every stage of the [IEP] process . . . as it did upon the measurement of the resulting IEP against a substantive standard" (*Board of Education of the Hendrick Hudson Central School District v. Rowley*, 1982). The Court also noted that adequate compliance with the procedures would in most cases ensure a FAPE would be provided. Because of the IDEA's lack of clarity in defining a FAPE, however, many disputes arose that culminated in due process hearings and court cases. These decisions have helped to refine the legal definition of a FAPE.

Litigation and FAPE

Soon after the IDEA became law, disputes regarding FAPE found their way into the courts. Early court decisions set the standard of a FAPE as more than simple access to education but less than the best possible educational programs (Osborne, 1992). In 1982, a case from the U.S. Court of Appeals for the Second Circuit became the first special education case to be heard by the U.S. Supreme Court. In *Board of Education of the Hendrick Hudson Central School District v. Rowley* (1982; hereafter *Rowley*), the Supreme Court considered the meaning of a FAPE.

In *Rowley*, the Supreme Court held that a FAPE is a right of all children receiving special education and related services and merely access to public school programs. Justice William Rehnquist, writing for the majority, stated that a FAPE consists of educational instruction designed to meet the unique needs of a student with a disability, supported by such services as needed to permit the student to *benefit* from instruction. The Court noted that the IDEA requires that these educational services must be provided at public expense, meet state standards, and comport with the student's IEP. If individualized instruction allowed the child to benefit from educational services and was provided in conformity with the other requirements of the law, the student therefore, would be receiving a FAPE.

The Supreme Court also ruled that students with disabilities do not have an enforceable right to the best possible education or an education that allows them to achieve their maximum potential. Rather, these students are entitled to an education that is reasonably calculated to confer educational benefit. Furthermore, the *Rowley* decision enabled courts to make case-by-case determinations of whether a particular educational program confers "meaningful educational benefit." Thus, meaningful educational benefit must be decided individually for each student, because there is no generic formula applied in these cases.

Post-*Rowley* Litigation.   Other court decisions immediately following the *Rowley* decision tended to apply the decision in a strict manner. For example, the courts applied the first part of the *Rowley* test by examining the student's IEP and the procedural history of the case. Second, the courts applied the second part of the *Rowley* test by examining the student's IEP to determine whether it conferred some degree of educational benefit. Osborne's (1992) analysis of these early cases indicates that if the school district met the first part of the *Rowley* test and was able to show that there was *some* educational benefit to the student, no matter how minimal, then the court would uphold the school's provision of special education and related services as constituting a FAPE.

Yell (1998) summarizes the trend of recent court decisions to interpret the FAPE mandate in a light more favorable to students with disabilities. He contends that in most recent cases the courts have begun to rule that the law's FAPE requirement means more than simple access to an education that confers minimal benefit; instead, a FAPE must confer a *meaningful* educational benefit on the student, and one that confers minimal or trivial progress is insufficient. Yell's (1998) analysis shows that when a school district was challenged, it had to show that a student's FAPE was individually designed to provide educational advancement consistent with the student's overall ability and that there was a measurable gain in that student's progress.

Yell and Drasgow (2000) examined forty-five published due process hearings and court cases in which parents of children with autism challenged the appropriateness of a school district's educational program for their children. These hearings and cases involved disagreements between parent and school district interpretations of what constituted a FAPE for young children with autism. Specifically, parents believed that schools were not providing a FAPE and requested that school districts provide, fund, or reimburse them for a specific type of treatment program—the Lovaas treatment program—for their children. Yell and Drasgow (2000) argue that the Lovaas hearings and cases advanced FAPE to a higher level by stressing that students should receive "meaningful" educational benefits. In reaching decisions, due process hearing officers and judges examined school district program data on student progress to determine if the school district (i.e., the LEA) in question was providing a meaningful education. Moreover, Yell and Drasgow contend that hearing officers and courts were being influenced by empirical research that demonstrates effective practices for assessing and evaluating students with autism. Thus, Yell and Drasgow (2000) conclude that these cases suggest that school districts are being held to a higher standard in providing special education programs. These hearings and cases suggest that the definition of FAPE has expanded from an emphasis on access to an emphasis on quality.

The next section builds on the historical implementation of federal special education law and court interpretations that lead to the IDEA Amendments of 1997 (hereafter IDEA '97) and discusses how these amendments have affected the legal definition of a FAPE.

IDEA '97 and FAPE

When Congress passed the EAHCA in 1975, the law opened the doors of public education to the nation's students with disabilities who needed special education and related services. The original law emphasized access to educational programs rather than any level of educational opportunity (Eyer, 1998; Yell & Drasgow, 2000). Although IDEA was dramatically successful in providing access for children with disabilities, Congress determined that the promise had not yet been fulfilled for too many children (Senate Report, 1997). Therefore, the underlying theme of IDEA '97 was to improve the effectiveness of special education by requiring demonstrable improvements in the educational achievements of students with disabilities. Indeed, providing a quality education for each student with a disability became the new goal under IDEA '97 (Eyer, 1998).

Congress included a number of changes in the IEP requirements to emphasize the necessity of improving educational outcomes. For example, IDEA '97 requires that each child's IEP contain *measurable* annual goals and the methods for measuring the student's progress toward achieving them. Furthermore, IEP teams must regularly inform parents of their child's progress. IDEA '97 also conveys a clear requirement that if a student fails to make progress toward the annual goals, the IEP must be revised (Clark, 1999). Last, but not least, special education services developed in the IEP planning process must allow a student to *advance appropriately* toward attaining the annual goals. As Eyer (1998) stated, "The IDEA can no longer be fairly perceived as a statute which merely affords children access to education. Today, the IDEA is designed to improve the effectiveness of special education and increase the benefits afforded to children with disabilities to the extent such benefits are necessary to achieve measurable progress" (p. 16).

IDEA '97 requires that schools further the educational achievement of students with disabilities by developing an IEP that provides a special education program that confers measurable and meaningful educational progress.

Summary of FAPE

Throughout the three decades in which the EAHCA and then IDEA have been in effect, the requirement that schools offer all eligible students with disabilities a FAPE has proven to be a very contentious issue. In fact, FAPE has been one of the most heavily litigated areas in special education (Yell, 1998). Typically, litigation occurs when school districts believe they are offering an appropriate education to a student in special education and the parents believe otherwise. The arguments have frequently centered on whether a FAPE includes more than providing access to education and the definition of a meaningful educational program.

The Supreme Court's test for determining a FAPE clarifies some of the ambiguities facing educators as they attempt to interpret this mandate of the IDEA. In the *Rowley* case the Supreme Court gave the lower courts a standard to apply when deciding cases involving questions of what constitutes an appropriate education for students with disabilities. Although the *Rowley* test does not directly address the contents of a FAPE, it does provide guidance for courts to use in deciding, case by case, whether a school has offered a FAPE to a student with disabilities. The degree of benefit provided does not need to result in a student's achieving his or her maximum potential, nor must the FAPE be the best education possible. It must, however, provide the student with an educational program that will result in meaningful and measurable advancement toward goals and objectives that are appropriate for the student given his or her ability and as set forth in the IEP.

A second major area of controversy involved the IDEA's LRE requirement. The LRE requirement has been referred to as the inclusion or mainstreaming mandate and has been the subject of much litigation and professional debate. The next section examines this issue.

LEAST RESTRICTIVE ENVIRONMENT

One of the most controversial issues in special education is inclusion. Both the terms *inclusion* and *mainstreaming* come from the IDEA's principle of the LRE. In fact, *LRE, inclusion,* and *mainstreaming* are often used interchangeably; however, they are not synonymous concepts. The somewhat dated term *mainstreaming* is used to describe the practice of placing students with disabilities in general education classrooms with their nondisabled peers for some or all of the school day (Huefner, 2000). *Inclusion* refers to the placement of a student with disabilities, regardless of the student's level of disability, into an age-appropriate general education classroom in the local community school (Crockett & Kauffman, 1999a). *LRE* refers to the IDEA's mandate that students with disabilities be educated with their nondisabled peers to the maximum extent appropriate. The LRE is determined individually for each student with a disability, and, therefore, it is not a particular setting. The LRE requirement ensures that students with disabilities are integrated to the maximum extent possible.

Inclusion (*mainstreaming* is the term the courts usually use) is the subject of many due process hearings and court cases and of much controversy in the professional literature (e.g., Crockett & Kauffman, 1999b; Fuchs and Fuchs, 1994; Kauffman & Hallahan, 1995; Lipsky & Gartner 1998; Stainback & Stainback, 1985). Proponents of inclusion argue that the general education classroom is the appropriate learning environment for all students, with and without disabilities. Many educators, however, argue that inclusion deprives students of the specialized services that they need to meet their unique educational needs (Bateman & Linden, 1998).

Legislation and LRE

The LRE mandate consists of two requirements. First, the IDEA requires that students with disabilities must be educated with students without disabilities in the general education setting to the maximum extent appropriate. This means that the law presumes students with disabilities will be educated together with children who do not have disabilities in the general education classroom. This requirement ensures that students with disabilities are educated in the LRE that is suitable for their individual needs. The second requirement is that students with disabilities cannot be removed from general education settings unless education in those settings cannot be achieved satisfactorily and only after the use of supplementary aids and services were considered to mitigate the learning environment. This requirement means that even though school districts must educate students with and without disabilities together to the greatest degree possible, the school district may move a student to a more restrictive setting when the general education setting is not appropriate for the student with disabilities but only after the IEP team has been involved in the process of changing the student's educational placement.

To ensure that school districts are able to meet the placement needs of students with disabilities, the IDEA's implementing regulations provide for a "continuum of alternative placements," and those alternative settings vary in restrictiveness. Champaign (1993) defines *restrictiveness* as "a gauge of the degree of opportunity a person has for proximity to, and communication with, the ordinary flow of persons in our society" (p. 5). In special education this means that a student with a disability has the right to be educated with students without disabilities in the general education environment. The continuum of alternative placements includes the general education classroom, self-contained classrooms, special schools, home instruction, and hospitals and institutions. The general education environment is considered the least restrictive setting along the continuum because it is the placement in which there is the greatest measure of opportunity for proximity and communication with the ordinary flow of students in schools. From this perspective, the less a placement resembles the general education environment, the more restrictive it is considered (Gorn, 1999). Hospitals and institutions are the most restrictive settings because they are the least like the general education setting.

Each student's IEP team determines the least restrictive setting that will provide an appropriate education. The IDEA and comments to the implementing regulations make it clear that the IEP team can make this decision only by assessing each child individually and then by determining his or her goals based on this assessment. The law clearly anticipates that IEP goals may sometimes be achieved only in specialized and restrictive settings.

School administrators and teachers find that determining which educational placement constitutes the LRE for a given student with a disability is difficult (Huefner, 1994; Yell & Drasgow, 1999). Not surprisingly, disagreements often arise between parents and school district personnel because of the difficulty of making appropriate placement decisions. When such disagreements cannot be settled between the involved parties, due process hearing officers or courts may ultimately be called on to resolve disputes. Courts hear the facts of a particular dispute, apply law to the specific facts of the case, and then issue an opinion. In fact, questions regarding educational placements in LREs have been a frequent source of litigation in special education. The next section discusses the impacts of the more important of these cases on the concept of LRE.

Litigation and LRE

Unlike the FAPE issue, the U.S. Supreme Court has never heard a case regarding LRE, so there is no single legal standard for determining whether a school has meet the LRE requirement of the IDEA. Nonetheless, a number of LRE cases have made their way to the U.S. Courts of Appeals. These decisions set forth *standards*, or tests, that a court will use to apply the law to the facts of the case. Courts will use these standards adopted in LRE cases to review disagreements arising regarding the LRE requirement. When a U.S. Court of Appeals adopts a judicial standard for reviewing a particular type of case, the lower federal courts (e.g., the federal district courts) in the appellate court's jurisdiction must use the appropriate judicial standard in reaching decisions in LRE cases.

These decisions are influential in clarifying the LRE requirement in their respective circuits. Although the decisions in these cases vary, they all contain consistent principles that schools are wise to consider in developing special education programs that meet the LRE requirement of the IDEA. We believe that four major principles can be extrapolated from these decisions.

First, placement decisions must be made in accordance with the individual needs of each student with a disability. An important cornerstone of special education is individualization of special education and related services. Each student with a disability must receive a full and individualized evaluation prior to developing programming and determining placement. Educational decisions must be made in accordance with this evaluation. In making such decisions, each student's IEP team must determine (1) what educational services are required and (2) where these services can be most appropriately delivered to meet the needs of the student.

Second, all students with disabilities have a presumptive right to be educated in integrated settings. The LRE mandate in the IDEA sets forth a clear preference for these settings; that is, students with disabilities have a right to be educated in their local schools with students who are not disabled. Schools must make good faith efforts to educate students with disabilities in integrated settings. Before a child's IEP team concludes that a student should be educated in a more restrictive setting, the team must consider whether supplementary aids and services would permit an appropriate education in the general education setting. Supplementary aids and services may involve educational options such as a resource room, itinerant instruction, assigning a paraprofessional, a positive behavior intervention plan, and assistive technology devices and services. Finally, when students with disabilities are educated in more restrictive settings, the school must provide as many integrated experiences for the child as possible (e.g., recess, physical education classes, and extracurricular activities).

Third, nothing in the statutory or case law indicates that LRE considerations are intended to replace considerations of appropriateness. To the contrary, in determining special education and related services for a student, the IEP team's first consideration must be to decide what constitutes a FAPE for that student. In determining a student's special education, therefore, questions of what educational services are required must precede questions of where they should be provided (Yell, 1998). In making considerations of appropriateness, each child's IEP must address both academic and nonacademic needs (e.g., modeling, social development, communication). The IDEA's clear preference for educating students with disabilities in general education classrooms indicates that when an appropriate education can be provided in an integrated setting and the placement will not disrupt the classroom setting, inclusion is generally required (Gorn, 1997).

Fourth, when the group of qualified professionals, including the parents, determines that placement in general education with supplementary aids and services will not meet the student's needs, the group must be able to choose from the entire continuum of alternative placements to determine the appropriate setting. This does not mean that school districts must have all alternative placements within its boundaries. It means that schools must be able to access the appropriate placement if required to meet the needs of a particular child with a disability. A school district (i.e., an LEA) may use alternative means, such as contracting with larger school districts for services, to obtain the alternative placement required.

IDEA '97 and LRE

Although IDEA '97 did not include any major changes regarding LRE, it did include significant changes to language. First, the law now requires that if a student with a disability will not be integrated into the general education classroom with his or her nondisabled peers, the IEP team must explain why. This is significant because prior to the passage of IDEA '97 the law expressed a preference for participation in general education programs, but in IDEA '97 this preference clearly became a presumption. Furthermore, this presumption can be overcome only by providing evidence that education in this setting will not be appropriate even after supplementary aids and services are provided. The importance of this is that it shifts the burden of proof onto the IEP team when a student is removed from the general education setting.

Second, IDEA '97 emphasizes that the general education curriculum is presumed to be the appropriate beginning point for planning each student's IEP. Only when participation in the general curriculum with supplementary support and services will not benefit the student should an alternative curriculum be considered. Therefore, it is important that the participants in the IEP process begin with the general curriculum as the preferred course of study for all students (Yell & Shriner, 1997). We emphasize that this *does not* mean that all students in special education must be educated in the general education curriculum; instead it means that the general education curriculum is the starting point when an IEP team considers a student's educational program.

Summary of LRE

The movement to educate all students, with and without disabilities, in integrated settings is certainly one of the important and widely discussed issues in education. This chapter has presented the legal basis of inclusion (i.e., the LRE principle of the IDEA). Clearly, integrated settings are the preferred placements for all students with disabilities. The IDEA sets forth the principle that such placements are the presumptive right of all students with disabilities. The most important principles, however, in educational decision making for students with disabilities are individualization and appropriateness. Special education must be individually tailored to meet each student's unique educational needs and provide meaningful educational benefit.

DISCIPLINING STUDENTS WITH DISABILITIES

The use of disciplinary procedures for students with disabilities is a controversial and confusing issue. Although the IDEA and its implementing regulations are quite detailed, there were no specific federal guidelines regarding disciplining students with disabilities until IDEA '97. This lack of statutory or regulatory requirements resulted in uncertainty among school administrators and teachers regarding appropriate disciplinary procedures and led to many due process hearings and court cases.

Although the original EAHCA did not directly address discipline, one section of the law regarding change of placement procedures proved to be important when school districts attempted to suspend or expel students with disabilities. The next section presents a brief discussion about the legislation and litigation regarding change of placement procedures and the subsequent effect on disciplining of students with disabilities.

Legislation, Litigation, and Discipline

When an IEP team wants to substantially alter a student's educational program, it must follow the procedural requirements of the IDEA. This means that the school must request that the child's IEP team convene, including giving appropriate prior notice to the parents, to consider changes proposed by school personnel. The primary purpose of prior notice is to let parents know about the school district's proposal so that parents may fully participate in the process. Minor changes in the student's educational program that do not involve a change in the general nature of the program or a change in placement do not require prior notification. Changes that substantially or significantly affect the delivery of education or the child's IEP goals and objectives, however, do constitute a change in placement and are not permissible without full consideration of the child's IEP team.

Courts have long held that long-term suspensions or expulsions are significant changes in a student's educational program and, therefore, are changes in placement (Yell, 1998; Yell, Rozalski, & Drasgow, 2001). If a student's parents object to a proposed action, including long-term suspensions or expulsions, they may request an IEP meeting to consider if the change of placement is appropriate. If the school district decides to proceed with the proposed action, a parent may request a due process hearing. In such situations, the school district is prohibited from unilaterally changing placement by the stay-put provision of the IDEA. This provision states that "during the pendency of any proceedings . . . unless the [school] and the parents . . . otherwise agree, the child shall remain in the then current placement of such child" (IDEA, 20 U.S.C. §1415(e)(3)).

The purpose of the stay-put provision is to continue students in their current placement (a student's placement before the dispute arose) until the dispute is resolved. This provision has been the focal point in many disciplinary controversies. This is because schools have suspended or expelled students receiving special education and related services and the parents, disagreeing with the school's actions, have requested a due process hearing. Under these circumstances, the student with a disability must be returned to his or her previous setting in accordance with the requirements of the stay-put provisions unless the school and the parents agree otherwise. There is no dangerous exemption to this provision. According to the Supreme Court, the purpose of this provision is to strip schools of their unilateral authority to exclude students with disabilities from school (*Honig v. Doe*, 1988).

The decision in *Honig v. Doe* (1988) and others led many school district administrators to believe that there was a dual disciplinary standard; that is, administrators and teachers faced a different set of rules and limitations when using disciplinary procedures with students with disabilities protected by the IDEA. This became such a contentious issue that Congress finally decided to address this issue in 1994.

IDEA '97 and Discipline

Although the IDEA was originally scheduled to be reauthorized in 1994, because of the controversial nature of the disciplinary issue, reauthorization was not completed until 1997. In fact, discipline became the most controversial policy issue in the law's history (Egnor, 2003). When the IDEA was finally reauthorized in 1997, Congress addressed a number of issues related to discipline. According to the Office of Special Education Programs, the underlying assumptions of the disciplinary provisions of IDEA '97 were that (1) all students, including those with disabilities, deserve safe, well-disciplined schools and orderly learning environments; (2) teachers and school administrators should have the tools they need to assist them in preventing misconduct and discipline problems and to address those problems, if they arise; (3) there must be a balanced approach to the issue of discipline of students with disabilities that reflects the need for orderly and safe schools and the need to protect the right of students with disabilities to have a FAPE; and (4) students have the right to an appropriately developed IEP with well-designed behavior intervention strategies (Senate Report, 1997).

By including the discipline provisions in the 1997 amendments, Congress sought to expand the authority of school officials to protect the safety of all children by maintaining orderly, drug-free, and disciplined school environments while ensuring that the essential rights of students with disabilities were protected (Individuals with Disabilities Education Law Report, 1999). Congress sought to help schools officials and IEP teams to (1) respond appropriately when students with disabilities exhibit serious problem behavior, and (2) appropriately address problem behavior in the IEP process. IDEA '97 added a section on discipline to the procedural safeguards section of Part B; this section reflects Congress's intention to balance school officials' obligation to ensure that schools are safe and orderly environments conducive to learning with the school's obligation to ensure that students with disabilities receive a FAPE.

IDEA '97 requires that if a student with a disability has behavior problems (regardless of the student's disability category), the IEP team shall consider strategies, including

TABLE 2 **Discipline Provisions of IDEA '97**

KEY POINTS	EXPLANATION
Disciplinary procedures	School officials may change the placement of a student to an interim alternative education setting (IAES) another setting or to suspend the student for not more than 10 days. If a student brings a weapon, possesses or uses illegal drugs, or sells or solicits the sale of a controlled substance while at school or a school function, the student may be removed to an IAES for not more than 45 days. A hearing officer may order a change of placement to an IAES when a student presents a danger to self or others if school officials can demonstrate by substantial evidence that (1) maintaining the current placement is substantially likely to result in injury, (2) the IEP and placement are appropriate, (3) the school has made reasonable efforts to minimize the risk of harm, and (4) the IAES meets the criteria set forth in IDEA '97.
Functional behavior assessment and behavior intervention plan	If a student has behavioral problems (regardless of disability category), the IEP team shall consider strategies, including positive behavioral interventions and supports, to address these problems. In such situations, a proactive behavior intervention plan, based on a functional behavioral assessment, should be included in the IEP. If a student is suspended or put in an IAES, and the school has not conducted a functional behavioral assessment and implemented a behavior intervention plan, then the IEP team must develop a behavior intervention plan within 10 days. If a behavior intervention plan is already included in the IEP, the team must meet to review and modify it if necessary.
The manifestation determination	If school officials seek a change of placement, suspension, or expulsion, a review of the relationship between the student's disability and misconduct must be conducted within 10 days. The manifestation determination must be conducted by the student's IEP team and other qualified personnel. If no relationship exists, the same disciplinary procedures as would be used with nondisabled students are available (e.g., long-term suspension, expulsion). *Educational services must continue.* If a relationship exists, school officials may seek a change of placement but cannot use long-term suspension and expulsion.
Conducting the manifestation determination	The IEP team considers all relevant information regarding the behavior in question. This includes evaluation and diagnostic results, information supplied by parents, and direct observations of the student. The IEP team can determine that the misconduct was not a manifestation of a student's disability only when (1) the student's IEP and placement were appropriate and the IEP was implemented as written, (2) the student's disability did not impair his or her ability to understand the impact and consequences of the misconduct, and (3) the student's disability did not impair his or her ability to control the behavior at issue.

TABLE 2   Continued

KEY POINTS	EXPLANATION
The interim alternative education setting	The IEP team must determine the IAES. Although the IAES is not in the school setting, the student must be able to participate in the general education curriculum and continue to receive services listed in the IEP.
The stay-put provision	If parents or guardians of a student placed in an IAES request a hearing, they are entitled to an expedited hearing; however, the stay-put placement is the IAES.
IDEA protections for students not yet eligible for special education	Students who have engaged in misconduct or rule violation may only assert IDEA procedural protections if school officials had knowledge that the student had a disability prior to the behavior that precipitated the disciplinary sanction.
Referral to law enforcement and juvenile authorities	Nothing in the IDEA prohibits a school from reporting a crime committed by a student to appropriate authorities or to prevent state law enforcement and judicial authorities from exercising their responsibilities. The SEA may require LEAs to transmit copies of school district records regarding special education records and disciplinary records to appropriate authorities.

positive behavioral interventions, and supports to address them. In such situations the student's IEP must include a proactive behavior management plan, based on a functional behavioral assessment.

IDEA '97 also addresses discipline procedures that may be used with students receiving special education. School officials may discipline a student with a disability in the same manner they discipline students without disabilities with a few notable exceptions. Table 2 lists the disciplinary requirements of IDEA '97.

Summary of Discipline

IDEA '97 attempts to balance a school's need to maintain a safe and orderly environment with the right of students with disabilities to receive a FAPE. Perhaps the most important discipline provisions of IDEA '97 are those requiring IEP teams to take a proactive, problem-solving approach to addressing problem behaviors of students with disabilities. IEP teams must become competent in conducting appropriate assessments and evaluations. Furthermore, the IEP team must design and deliver appropriate programming based on positive behavioral interventions and supports. This means that school districts will need to employ people who are competent in conducting functional behavioral assessments and developing positive behavior intervention plans to include in a student's IEP. Finally, IEP teams need to become proficient at developing data-collection systems to determine each student's progress toward his or her behavioral goals; moreover, instructional decisions should be based on the data collected. Future hearings, court rulings, and legislation will help to clarify these confusing issues.

CONCLUSION

The signing of the Education for All Handicapped Children Act on November 29, 1975, was a decisive event in the education of students with disabilities. Through the many developments over the past three decades, the law has been extraordinarily successful in achieving its major purpose of opening the doors of public education to students with disabilities. With the passage of IDEA '97, the primary goal of the law shifted from providing access to educational services to providing meaningful and measurable programs for all students with disabilities receiving special education and related services.

Along with the success of the IDEA is its controversy. The issues of what constitutes a FAPE, what constitutes an appropriate LRE, and how to correctly apply disciplinary procedures were, and in some ways remain, particularly contentious. These controversies have been the subject of numerous due process hearings and court cases. No doubt these issues will remain central to legislation and litigation regarding special education.

QUESTIONS FOR FURTHER DISCUSSION

1. The Individuals with Disabilities Education Act (IDEA) contains five major principles concerning the education of children with disabilities: zero reject; free appropriate public education (FAPE); least restrictive environment (LRE); protection in evaluation; and procedural due process. Explain these principles.

2. The Individuals with Disabilities Education Act requires that school districts offer a free appropriate public education (FAPE) for eligible students with disabilities. Since the original passage of the law in 1975, the issue of what constitutes a FAPE for students with disabilities has led to a great deal of confusion and controversy. What is a FAPE? What are the essential components of a FAPE? What is the primary vehicle by which school districts provide students with a FAPE? What guidance has litigation provided us regarding the content of a FAPE?

3. How have the courts changed how we provide special education services to students with disabilities? From your perspective as a researcher and teacher trainer, how should our field of special education react to these changes? Should this change affect the ways in which we prepare special education teachers, and if so, how?

4. One of the most contentious issues in special education involves the principle of least restrictive environment (LRE). Explain the LRE principle. What are the two major parts of the LRE principle? What is the continuum of alternative placements? How should IEP teams determine LREs for students with disabilities?

REFERENCES

Bateman, B., & Linden, M. (1998). *Better IEPs* (3rd ed.). Longmont, CO: Sopris West.

Board of Education of the Hendrick Hudson Central School District v. Rowley, 458 U.S. 176 (1982).

Brown v. Board of Education of Topeka, Kansas, 347 U.S. 483 (1954).

Champaign, J. F. (1993). Decisions in sequence: How to make placements in the least restrictive environment. *EdLaw Briefing Paper, 9 & 10,* 1–16.

Clark, S. G. (1999). Assessing IEPs for IDEA compliance. *Education Law Report, 137,* 35–42.

Crockett, J. B., & Kauffman, J. M. (1999a). Taking inclusion back to its roots. *Educational Leadership,* 56(2),74–77.

Crockett, J. B., & Kauffman, J. M. (1999b). *The least restrictive environment: Its origins and interpretations in special education.* Mahwah, NJ: Lawrence Erlbaum Associates.

Egnor, D. (2003). *IDEA reauthorization and the student discipline controversy.* Denver, CO: Love Publishing.

Elementary and Secondary Education Act, PL 80-10, 20 U.S.C. §2701 *et seq.* (1965).

Eyer, T. L. (1998). Greater expectations: How the 1997 IDEA amendments raise the basic floor of opportunity for children with disabilities. *Education Law Report, 126,* 1–19.

Fuchs, D., & Fuchs, L. (1994). Inclusive schools movement and the radicalization of special education reform. *Exceptional Children, 60,* 294–309.

Gorn, S. (1997). *What do I do when: The answer book on individualized education programs.* Horsham, PA: LRP Publications.

Gorn, S. (1999). *What do I do when: The answer book on special education law.* Horsham, PA: LRP Publications.

Honig v. Doe, 484 U.S. 305 (1988).

Huefner, D. S. (1994). The mainstreaming cases: Tensions and trends for school administrators. *Educational Administration Quarterly, 30,* 27–55.

Huefner, D. S. (2000). The risks and opportunities of the IEP requirements under IDEA '97. *Journal of Special Education, 33,* 195–203.

Individuals with Disabilities Education Act, 20 U.S.C. §1401 *et seq.* (1997).

Individuals with Disabilities Education Law Report, 30 IDELR 707 (OSEP 1999).

Justesen, T. R. (in press). Federal programs to assist people with disabilities: An historical perspective. *Encyclopedia of Education* (2nd ed.). New York: Macmillan Reference.

Katsiyannis, A., Yell, M. L., & Bradley, R. (2001). Reflections on the 25th anniversary of the Individuals with Disabilities Education Act. *Remedial and Special Education, 22,* 324–334.

Kauffman, J. M., & Hallahan, D. P. (1995). The illusion of full inclusion: A comprehensive critique of a current special education bandwagon. Austin, TX: Pro-Ed.

Lipsky, D. K., & Gartner, A. (1998). Taking inclusion into the future. *Educational Leadership, 56(2),* 78–81.

Mills v. Board of Education of the District of Columbia, 348 F. Supp. 866 (D.D.C. 1972).

Office of Special Education Programs (2000). IDEA 25th anniversary web site. Retrieved March 2002 from http://www.ed.gov/offices/OSERS/IDEA 25th.html.

Osborne, A. G. (1992). Legal standards for an appropriate education in the post-Rowley era. *Exceptional Children, 58,* 488–494.

Pennsylvania Association for Retarded Children v. Commonwealth of Pennsylvania, 334 F. Supp. 1257 (E.D. Pa. 1971); 343 F. Supp. 279 (E.D. Pa. 1972).

Senate Report of the IDEA Amendments of 1997. Retrieved July 1997 from wais.access.gpo.gov.

Stainback, S., & Stainback, W. (1985). The merger of special and regular education: Can it be done? A response to Lieberman and Mesinger. *Exceptional Children, 51,* 517–521.

Turnbull, H. R., & Turnbull, A. P. (2000). *Free appropriate public education: The law and children with disabilities* (6th ed.). Denver, CO: Love.

Turnbull, R., Turnbull, A., Shank, M., Smith, S., & Leal, D. (2001). *Exceptional lives: Special education in today's schools* (3rd ed.). Upper Saddle River, NJ: Merrill/Prentice Hall.

U.S. Department of Education (2000a). Twenty-second annual report to Congress on the implementation of the Individuals with Disabilities Education Act. Washington, DC: U.S. Department of Education.

U.S. Department of Education (2000b). Education department celebrates IDEA 25th anniversary; progress continues for students with disabilities. Retrieved March 2002 from http://www.ed.gov/PressRelease/11-2000/112900.html.

Yell, M. L. (1998). *The law and special education.* Upper Saddle River, NJ: Prentice Hall/Merrill.

Yell, M. L., & Dragsow, E. (1999). A legal analysis of inclusion. *Preventing School Failure, 42,* 118–124.

Yell, M. L., & Dragsow, E. (2000). Litigating a free appropriate public education: The Lovaas hearings and cases. *Journal of Special Education, 33,* 206–215.

Yell, M. L., Rozalski, M. E., & Dragsow, E. (2001). Disciplining students with disabilities. *Focus on Exceptional Children, 33(9),* 1–20.

Yell, M. L., & Shriner, J. G. (1997). The IDEA amendments of 1997: Implications for special and general education teachers, administrators, and teacher trainers. *Focus on Exceptional Children, 30(1),* 1–19.

CLASSIFICATION ISSUES IN SPECIAL EDUCATION FOR ENGLISH LANGUAGE LEARNERS

JAMES R. YATES
ALBA A. ORTIZ
University of Texas at Austin

This chapter provides several conceptual structures that may be useful in producing a framework for observing, evaluating, and developing appropriate procedures for classifying students for special education services. The first section identifies critical forces currently affecting the educational enterprise and interprets how these forces affect classification decisions. The second section presents a model that incorporates procedures that if put into practice would address systemically many of the classification issues affecting today's educational system. The model specifically focuses on English Language Learners (ELLs), one of the most complex groups of students for educational organizations to accurately and appropriately classify for special education. Therefore, the model illustrates how educational systems can address classification issues for a group of students who are known to be often misclassified, frequently do not experience system success, and typically receive services from professionals generally unprepared for working with such students.

How students are classified for special education is an expression of many powerful forces in our society. For example, Banks (2000) has stated that "race, mental retardation, and giftedness are socially constructed categories that have been used to reinforce the privileged positions of powerful groups, established practices, and institutions" (p. 23). There is enormous sociocultural influence on the classification of individuals as eligible for special education services. This influence derives from the current perspectives held by people involved in the classification and decision-making processes. Singham (1995) observes that "In the U.S. in the 1920's, there were detailed studies that 'showed' that Jews and Slavic groups (who happened to be recent immigrants) were of lower intelligence than the Nordic groups who were already established here. No such claims are made today about these two groups" (p. 275). Relatively few classification decisions are based on so-called laboratory test data or a known criterion level that scientific measurement defines as having been met. Obtaining "good data" for use in special education classification is particularly difficult, and the problem is growing rather than diminishing.

Because of the lack of good data, students who are culturally and linguistically out of the mainstream are disproportionately affected by poor classification decisions (National Research Council, 2002). However, those making classifications decisions, rather than being evil hearted, may simply not be aware of the powerful forces influencing the educational system in its efforts to serve students with special needs.

CURRENT CONTEXT OF SCHOOLING

A force field analysis (Haskew, 1974) of the current context of schooling in the United States would identify a number of forces that facilitate or constrain student progress in the educational system. These forces are discussed in the following sections.

Changing Demographics

The demographics in the United States are changing rapidly. For example, one person in four is African American or Hispanic (U.S. Census Bureau, 2000). The median age of these ethnic groups is younger, and therefore the effect of this rapidly changing demography is more pronounced in schools than in other aspects of society. Approximately 36 percent of school-age students in the United States are culturally or linguistically diverse, and the school systems of all the nation's major cities are majority "minority." (U.S. Census Bureau, 1996). Almost ten million students come from homes and communities where a language other than English is spoken (Waggoner, 1994). Although more than a hundred language groups are represented in the schools across the country, 75 percent of this population are Spanish speaking.

In many ways these demographics should not surprise us, nor should they be seen as undermining the educational enterprise; they are not new and have been frequently identified as important to professional educators. For example, for more than ten years the majority of public school students in Texas, the second largest state in the union, have been ethnically identified as "minority" students (Texas Education Agency, 2000). Most educational professional organizations formally or informally have projects or activities described as interested in or addressing concerns of ethnically identified minority groups (Hellregiel & Yates, 1997). However, what is abundantly clear is that students from these "minority" groups have limited academic success in the U.S. educational system. They experience high rates of retention in grade (U.S. Department of Education, 1994), high dropout rates (Montecel & Cortez, 2000; U.S. Census Bureau, 1996), and disproportionate representation in special education (Rice, 1995). These indicators of a lack of academic success have not been eliminated; in fact, as the number of "minority" students has increased in the schools, so have academic achievement problems.

Demographic changes are particularly challenging for special educators. The general education system is experiencing significant difficulty finding ways to support the achievement of culturally and linguistically diverse students. Many descriptors are used to describe underachieving students; for example, the term *at risk* refers to underachieving students. The Improving America's Schools Act (U.S. Department of Education, 1994) describes "high-risk students" as children living in poverty, Limited English Proficient students, migratory students, neglected and delinquent children, homeless children, immigrant students, teen parents, refugee children, ethnically identified students such as American Indian children, and students with disabilities. Clearly, underachieving students are more likely to be students of color (Gay, 2000). History also shows that when a student is not successful in the general education system, referring the student to special education is oftentimes considered the appropriate response (Haberman, 1995).

Referral to special education typically originates from general education teachers and multidisciplinary decision teams, under the supervision of the school's principal. The majority of professionals who determine special education eligibility are general educators (Individuals with Disabilities Education Act, 1997). Referral to special education of culturally and linguistically diverse students experiencing achievement difficulties is a frequent response of the general education system to achievement difficulties of such students. One result of this practice is the disproportionate representation of ethnically identified minorities in special education. The issue of disproportionate representation is not new. The National Science Foundation (Heller, Holtzman, & Messick, 1982) reported on the phenomenon twenty years ago. And a recent National Science Foundation study found the same thing (National Research Council, 2002).

Most general education leaders have limited training or experience in special education and issues associated with culturally and linguistically distinct students (Aspen, 1992). Therefore, leaders in special education must join with those in general education to develop appropriate, systemic reforms to address the learning needs of culturally and linguistically diverse learners. Without reform, the expectation that the learning needs of these students should be served through special education will continue or more probably increase. The special education system is typically no better prepared than the general education system to address the learning needs of this diverse group of students. That is to say, even a system such as special education has limited training and experience that focuses on culturally and linguistically diverse students and their parents.

Professionalism

Lack of professionalism affects the educational system in particularly powerful ways, and addressing it is difficult because there are few quick or short-term solutions. Educators must respond to the nation's changing demographics. However, the educational enterprise is constrained from doing so for a number of reasons. For example, with some variation across the country, 75–90 percent of the teaching force in the United States is white (Digest of Educational Statistics, 1999). Since school administrators typically emerge from the teaching corps, leadership in education reflects this "whiteness." Likewise, decision-making or policy groups, such as school boards, are typically majority white.

Although an educator need not be a member of a student's ethnic group to be supportive or to respond appropriately to the student's needs, it is unusual for white teachers to have had specific training or experience that prepares them for effective responses to all their students' needs (Grossman, 1998). For example, few teacher preparation programs require students to acquire skills in teaching English as a Second Language (ESL). Yet these skills are critical to supporting the learning needs of a large number of students in the nation's schools. As the linguistically distinct increase, the number of teachers and other educational professionals that are culturally and linguistically diverse has not increased (National Center for Educational Statistics, 2000).

As the demographics of students and their parents change, so will the demographics of those in special education. However, at this time special education professionals are no better prepared than general educators to respond to these changes. For example, bilingual special education teachers are almost nonexistent in most school districts, so there are few bilingual special education programs available. But having a disability does not eliminate a student's need for a special language program. Teacher preparation programs in special education typically do not require the development of English as a Second Language (ESL) skills. Yet given the demographics of the general education student population, special educators can expect to see increased demands to serve students who are English Language Learners.

The special educator is the professional the system often turns to for help in assessing and diagnosing students. The special educator must be able to accurately distinguish between "differences" and "disabilities." Doing so is difficult and complex, and it is impossible unless the educator has adequate training, knowledge, and skill in issues such as the processes of second language development, such as dialect differences, understanding that dialectic differences are not disabilities, and so forth.

One of the most widespread problems for schools is recruiting sufficient numbers of prepared teachers. The New York City schools, for example, must attract an estimated 40,000 teachers in the next four years (Collins, 2001). An additional 2.5 million teachers will be needed nationwide in the next decade (Gregorian, 2001). But finding teachers in sufficient numbers who are adequately prepared for today's student population is extremely problematic and has become a crisis in bilingual and special education. According to a recent report to the U.S. Congress, special education faces serious personnel shortages (U.S. Congress, 1999). Staffing issues become even more complex in special education. For example, should those teaching in specialized areas requiring high levels of staffing, such as special education, be more highly compensated than those teaching in general education? And in today's world of integrating special education students into the general education classroom, to whom, when, and how does any extra compensation get distributed? Should those in special education be required to spend more time in training than general educators, given the complex nature of providing services to students with disabilities? What are the appropriate personal and intellectual characteristics necessary for those desiring to enter and continue in special education teaching? How should special educators' performance be evaluated given the individual educational planning required for students with disabilities? Can Standards-Based Accountability adequately assess achievement progress in special education and thereby serve as the basis for judging the adequacy of special education teachers?

As educational leadership knows, the issue of adequate teacher preparation is often less important than the necessity to have at least a "warm body" in the classroom with students. The nation's largest school systems are attempting to recruit teachers from India, the West Indies, South Africa, Europe, and other nations to make up for the shortfall in qualified applicants (Gregorian, 2001). Unfortunately, teacher shortages are not perceived in the same ways by society and its decision makers as, for example, doctor or engineer shortages are. Almost no one would advocate that those holding degrees in biology could be licensed as physicians after receiving a summer of training. However, it is not uncommon for responsible people to argue for licensing anyone with a degree in English or English literature, for example, to teach students how to read, one of the most complex of pedagogical activities (Coles, 2001). Even more amazing is the willingness of educational leadership to assign such inexperienced teachers to the most challenging students in the system, the poor, the culturally diverse, the English Language Learner, and those with disabilities (Kohn, 1999).

Professionalism is complex and multivariate, and a range of issues are associated with it. One important issue is obtaining and retaining adequate numbers of trained personnel. Special education and general education share many of the same constraints in developing adequate staffing. For example, fewer than half of those trained as teachers actually take positions as teachers. And less than half of those who do are still teaching four years later. Maintaining adequate staffing levels is related to providing adequate support in the teaching context (Gersten, Keating & Harniss, 2001; Hellriegel & Yates, 1997). Yet one of the supports often cited as crucial for the success of special education teachers, having paraprofessionals available to address the learning needs of special populations, has failed to measurably increase student achievement (Gerber, Finn, Achilles, & Boyd-Zaharias, 2001).

Professionalism also involves the social perceptions and expectations of teachers and the general conditions of teaching (Fusco, 2001). It is axiomatic that the educational system calls on special education to provide services to those students most difficult to educate, that is, those that the general education system has been unsuccessful in educating adequately. Therefore, special education must set standards of professional training and service that meet the expectations of the parents and students they are called on to serve. Staffing shortages cannot become the force that dictates how services are provided to students with disabilities.

Standards, Assessment, Accountability

Standards, assessment, and accountability are another set of forces influencing the nation's schools. Of the three, accountability is the least controversial. Whether policy maker, school administrator, teacher, or parent, all agree that inquiring into the progress of the system and the students in it is both rational and appropriate. However, discussion quickly departs from consensus during efforts to define the "standards" and determine how to assess or measure them. For more than twenty years (Pipho, 1979), significant public policy debate has surrounded these issues. Much like a roller coaster, the level of concern for them has risen and fallen. This has also been the case in special education (McCarthy, 1980). What is clear is that this set of forces has significant and long-term impacts on students and their families and on those who serve them in the educational system. Students are promoted or not, graduate or do not, enter college or do not based on current processes of "accountability." Teachers and administrators receive salary increases or not, are recognized or not, depending on measures of "progress." Individual schools and school systems are recognized or not, receive more resources or not, when "accountability" measures are applied to their efforts (English & Steffy, 2001; Hartocollis, 2001).

Special education brings unique and exceedingly complex variables to the issue of standards, assessment, and accountability. For example, the following questions are common to the current debate: Are special education students to be included in or excluded from accountability tests or assessments? If some special education students are included in or excluded from assessments, which ones? Should special education students' "scores" be excluded from classroom, school, and school system accountability reporting? If special education students have not been included in the assessments, will the educational system be likely to "forget" the needs of special education students when making accountability decisions? Who is accountable for special education students whose least restrictive environments are general education classrooms? What modifications are acceptable or necessary when special education students are included in accountability assessments? Who is responsible for determining and implementing modifications for special education students during assessments? What will be the effect on norming or standardization of the assessments if modifications for special education students are permitted? How much preparation for the tests or assessments is permitted for special education students? Do special education students need parental permission to participate in assessments? Can special education students be promoted or graduate without "passing" the accountability tests? Are special education teachers held to the same standards of student progress as other teachers? If so, what types of evidence of special education student progress are sufficient? Who is responsible for special education—a school's principal or the special education director? How does the special education curriculum "align" with the content of the assessment instruments? How does an individualized education plan (IEP) relate to the national or state curriculum content and its assessment? And so forth, goes the discussion concerning special education accountability.

School Finance and Economy

School finance and economy would clearly be a part of any force field analysis. Rose and Gallup (2000) found that the general public identifies having sufficient resources for the nation's schools as one of its greatest concerns. Few responsible people disagree on the importance of having adequate school financing. Discussions of school financing are extensive in legislatures and other policy-making groups. However, these discussions, while often heated and lengthy, occur within quite different bounds or ratios when compared, for example, to defense budgets or programs supportive of certain industries. Not to diminish the importance of other areas of public policy responsibility, but it is necessary for school finance discussions to be informed by the operating values and political positions assumed by policy makers and the general public. Policy makers are willing to allow teachers to be paid one-third to one-half the amount paid to other professionals who have comparable education and experience. Inequity of resources among school districts, which results in significantly different educational experiences for students, has been tolerated and often ignored for years by national, state, and local policy makers. Areas known to significantly influence a child's educational achievement—for example, poverty and student health (Maeroff, 1998)—are given little direct attention or are relegated to other agencies or organizations loosely coupled to education. For example, President George W. Bush's proposal for religious organizations to assume responsibility for certain social programs represents the latest effort to transfer focus and support from education. Interestingly, research and discussions of school finance typically do not include special education, perhaps because its costs are "mysterious" or at least different from those of the general student population.

Although there is concern for adequately financing schools, spending questions often focus on expensive programs perceived, correctly or not, as "nonessential." Special education appears to some, perhaps in private discussions, to many, to be one of these expensive programs made available to a small number of students of questionable ability to contribute to the broader social good or economy. These private values are significant in discussions of special education finance. For example, the recent advocacy by U.S. Senator Jeffords for "full funding of special education" stirred the entire political structure and stressed the separation of the executive and legislative branches of government. When special education issues are presented to policy makers, they typically display strong public support. Yet this is often followed by less public, procedural requests to determine the "costs of special education" prior to any financial allocation decisions. Current discussions of the "dramatically" increasing costs and growth of special education are generally uninformed by real data (Parrish, 2001). A variety of agencies and organizations question the ability of the school finance system to support the "rising costs of special education," and some argue that these costs are subtracting from the support of general education. However, research shows that special education costs have not subtracted from the resources for general education (Parrish, 2001).

Technology

People typically view technology as a powerful new force in the educational environment. The excitement over and potential for new computer technologies to effect the delivery of high-quality education to increasingly larger numbers of students is a part of most discussions of educational reform. The use of artificial intelligence systems to guide the decisions of instruction, assessment, and placement is moving toward reality. The individualization of instruction, delivered on demand, holds great promise for helping the educational system to reach the ideal that "all children can learn" (Cognition and Technology Group at Vanderbilt University, 1997). However, technology presents challenges that are not only technical but also involve human values and issues of fairness. For example, what does the mapping of the human genome hold for modifying and eliminating conditions of disability? Human cloning appears feasible, but many people are conflicted about its applications. Is special education to be the experimental context for the applications of a variety of emerging technologies? Is human variability, even given personal and familial suffering, desirable? Will the emerging data banks of registered DNA abnormalities be available to insurance companies and used for determining who will be "insurable"? Who should make, or be involved in, decisions related to the application of these emerging technologies? These are significant areas of concern for special educators, and they will require extensive research and broad discussion.

In less controversial applications of technology, issues of equity and access become significant. For example, should extremely expensive technologies be made initially available to "high-risk students" to facilitate their attaining levels of achievement comparable to other students? Should technologies be withheld, given limited resources, from students who do not have specific achievement deficiencies, or should they be made available first to the gifted to enhance their ability to contribute to the larger society? Should technologies be made universally available, regardless of the wealth of a school district or the students in it? Obviously, these questions are heavily value laden and the answers to them will be driven by politics. However, these are not necessarily questions only for the future. Students who are English Language Learners, for example, are known to be less likely to have access to computer technologies than other students in special education (Noonan, 1999).

Values and Politics

A community's operating values may be the most powerful force influencing the education system, since they move horizontally through the other identified forces. For example, a school's resource allocation decisions could be motivated by local politics, and professional preparation decisions, such as not requiring teachers to be prepared to serve English Language Learners, could be motivated by racism or lack of concern for those who speak a language other than English. Disproportional placement of African American male students in programs for the seriously emotionally disturbed may stem from racial bias or a perception among white decision makers that African American youths are antisocial. The history of special education makes clear that services for persons with disabilities have been developed, provided, and expanded in a context of political action that has been both an expression and a repression of operating societal values (Gallagher, 1969). Although those in special education may articulate an openness to serving "anyone" with a disability, there is no evidence that special education professionals are distinctly different in their value orientations from other educators. The political struggles of culturally and linguistically diverse members of the Council for Exceptional Children, for example, suggest that special educators have the same biases and prejudices as others (Webb-Johnson, 2000). Therefore, the necessity of information sharing, training, advocacy, social action, and even civil disobedience are a part of the future of special education if "all persons with disabilities" are to be adequately served.

SENSITIVITY IN CLASSIFICATION: A MODEL

In efforts to effectively and accurately classify students for special education services, increasing emphasis is placed on classification models designed to structure and sequence the data-gathering and decision-making processes in ways that are culturally and linguistically sensitive. The model[1] presented here (see Figure 1) is designed specifically for English Language Learners and illustrates the complexity of classifying students for special education. Unfortunately, such models are not the norm, and they require a commitment to acquiring knowledge and skills often not a part of the training and experience of most general and special educators. By using the procedures the model prescribes, schools can address some of the problems involved in classifying students for special education. Although the model specifically addresses English Language Learners, its conceptual framework can be applied to most classification issues as well as the needs of most students under consideration for special education services. The model requires special educator linkage and commitment to working with general education professionals, and it requires that general educators recognize that each student has unique learning characteristics. These efforts with general education professionals are for the purpose of preventing difficulties from developing or to provide early intervention for struggling learners. If special education classification or assessment has already begun, the model provides a structure for adapting special education procedures and the actions of professional personnel to match the unique needs of the struggling learner.

A Framework for Serving English Language Learners with Disabilities

English Language Learners (ELLs) are defined as those who have such limited English skills that they cannot profit from general education instruction without support (Kushner and Ortiz, 2000). They are typically served in bilingual education or in English as a Second Language

---

[1]This model is adapted from a model in Ortiz and Yates (2001).

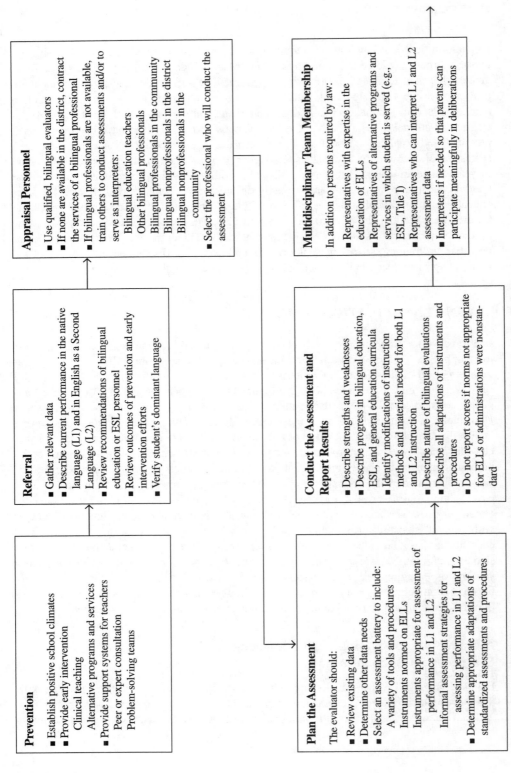

FIGURE 1 Framework for Providing Services for English Language Learners with Disabilities

Multidisciplinary Team Responsibilities

- Determine if student qualifies for and needs special education services
- Determine present level of performance and needs in L1 and L2
- Determine extent to which student will participate in bilingual education, ESL, and/or general education curricula
- Determine whether student will participate in district- or statewide assessments and the language of test-taking
- Provide assurances that problems are not primarily the result of lack of academic support, limited English proficiency, or cultural or other background characteristics
- Develop the Individualized Education Plan

Develop and Implement the Individualized Education Plan

In addition to other components required by law:

- Goals and objectives to be delivered in the native language and/or using ESL strategies
- Instructional level for all goals and objectives
- Persons responsible for L1 and L2 instruction
- Language to be used for related services
- Specialized materials, programs, technology, in L1 and L2
- Recommended instructional strategies for L1 and L2 instruction
- Modifications for bilingual education, ESL, and/or general education instruction
- Procedures to inform parents, in their native language, about their child's progress

Select Least Restrictive Environment

Instruction must address disability-related needs and provide native language and/or ESL instruction, as appropriate.

LRE options should include:

- Bilingual education with special education consultation
- General education with ESL instruction and special education consultation
- Bilingual special education resource
- Special education/ESL resource
- Self-contained bilingual special education
- Self-contained special education/ESL

Implement the IEP

Annual Review

- Evaluate progress as a result of L1 and L2 instruction
- Determine need for additional assessment
- Update language dominance and proficiency data annually
- Determine whether student continues to be eligible for special education services

If eligible, revise IEP and address any lack of expected progress and/or results of new evaluations.

If not eligible, return student to special language program.

FIGURE 1   Continued

(ESL) programs. Because education professionals are generally unprepared to serve them, ELLs experience limited academic success and are disproportionately represented in special education programs (Robertson, Kushner, Starks, & Drescher, 1994). For example, 20 percent of the fourth graders with Limited English Proficiency participating in the 1996 National Assessment of Educational Progress were identified as having disabilities (Mazzeo, Carlson, Voekl, & Lutkus, 2000).

To address the issues of academic underachievement and disproportionate representation, special education leaders must forge a close alliance with decision makers in general education. The participation of general educators in special education processes was significantly enhanced by the reauthorization of the Individuals with Disabilities Education Act (IDEA, 1997). Moreover, general education teachers, usually under the guidance of a school principal, typically initiate referrals and multidisciplinary teams, which decide whether students qualify for special education services. Yet general education administrators and teachers oftentimes have limited training in special education and the education of culturally and linguistically diverse learners. Therefore, those with leadership roles in special education must be alert to demographic changes in student populations and provide guidance in structuring a general and special education system responsive to the needs of these students.

Preventing Failure and Early Intervention for Struggling Learners

Preventing academic problems from occurring in the first place, and providing early intervention for students experiencing academic difficulties, is more cost effective than special education for students who do not have disabilities (Fashola & Slavin, 1998; Ortiz, 2000).

Prevention.   Effective schools for ELLs are characterized by strong leadership by principals, high expectations, acceptance of linguistic and cultural diversity, a challenging curriculum, instruction that supports native language and English as a Second Language (ESL) development, systematic evaluation of student progress, shared decision making, and collaborative school-community relationships (Cummins, 1989; Ortiz, 2000; Ortiz & Wilkinson, 1991). To ensure that educators understand the unique characteristics and needs of ELL students, professional development programs should focus on providing expertise in (1) native language and English as a Second Language acquisition, (2) cultural and economic influences on teaching and learning, (3) native language and English language assessment, (4) effective native language and ESL instruction, and (5) working with parents and families of ELLs.

Early Intervention.   Pre-referral intervention typically occurs too late to prevent a student from being unnecessarily referred to and placed in special education (Garcia & Ortiz, 1988). By the time teachers request assistance, the student's academic difficulties may be so serious that the teacher's interest in problem solving is half-hearted, and with good reason. If students are more than a year below grade level, even the best remedial or special education programs are unlikely to be successful (Slavin & Madden, 1989). In contrast, early intervention requires that supplementary instructional services be provided early enough, and intensely enough, to bring students quickly to a level at which they can succeed in the general education classroom (Madden, Slavin, Karweit, Dolan, & Wasik, 1991).

Clinical or diagnostic/prescriptive teaching is an excellent example of early intervention for ELLs (Garcia & Ortiz, 1988; Ortiz, 2000; Ortiz & Wilkinson, 1991). Teachers who use this approach analyze student performance as soon as they first notice a problem, identify gaps in skills and knowledge, and develop instruction to eliminate those gaps. They conduct curriculum-based assessments (e.g., using observations, inventories, and work samples) and use evaluation data to design instructional interventions (English & Steffy, 2001). Teachers maintain assessment portfolios, and if a student is ultimately referred, this portfolio accompanies the referral. If clinical teaching does not resolve the problem, general educators should have access to support systems. These might include, for example, peer and expert consultation and general education problem-solving committees such as Teacher Assistance Teams (Chalfant & Pysh, 1981). Alternative programs that offer tutorial or remedial instruction in the context of general education should also be readily available for struggling learners (Garcia & Ortiz, 1988; Ortiz, 1997; Ortiz & Wilkinson, 1991).

ADAPTING THE SPECIAL EDUCATION PROCESS FOR ELLS

When efforts to resolve achievement difficulties fail, referring the student to special education is appropriate.

Referral

Referral committees decide whether students receive a comprehensive individual assessment. This decision should be informed by data gathered through the prevention, early intervention, and referral processes (Ortiz, 1997). In addition to reviewing the student's current educational status, referral committees must solicit parents' perceptions of presenting problems. Parents will more likely consent to a comprehensive evaluation if they have concerns similar to those of school personnel or have noted the same problematic behaviors at home.

Assessments must be conducted in the student's dominant language—that is, the language in which a student demonstrates greater ability or proficiency—and disabilities must manifest themselves in this language (Ortiz & Garcia, 1990). It is important therefore that the referral committee verify the dominant language. Language data should be current, preferably no more than six months old (Ortiz et al., 1985). Bilingual education or ESL program personnel should update these assessments annually; otherwise, those conducting eligibility assessments should establish the student's dominant language.

Norm-referenced instruments, instruments developed from defined content or information appropriate for a particular age or cohort of students, yield an incomplete language profile because they typically do not assess spontaneous conversation or cognitive academic language proficiency (Cummins, 1989). Academic language proficiency refers to the more complex, abstract dimensions of language and includes literacy-related skills such as predicting or inferring. Formal assessments should be supplemented by informal measures of both conversational and academic language skills in different contexts, both at home and at school.

Qualified Assessment Personnel

Assessment personnel must have appropriate licenses or credentials and be qualified to assess ELLs. In addition to the professional development topics identified earlier, they should have expertise in (1) instruments and procedures for assessing ELLs; (2) alternative assessments and appropriate modifications of standardized tests; (3) using interpreters; (4) interpreting assessment outcomes in light of linguistic, cultural, and other background characteristics; and (4) effective instructional practices for ELLs with disabilities (Leung, 1996; Ortiz & Garcia, 1995). Moreover, they must examine their own culture, values, and beliefs and consider how these might introduce bias into the assessment or their interpretations of student performance (Leung, 1996).

School districts should contract for the services of qualified bilingual professionals if such persons are not available in the school district (Yates & Ortiz, 1995). Districts should maintain lists of bilingual evaluators in their communities, and the states' departments of education should maintain a statewide registry. If schools use interpreters, these individuals must have native-like proficiency in the target language and training related to (1) the purpose of special education and of comprehensive individual assessments, (2) maintaining confidentiality, (3) their role and that of the educational evaluator, (4) administering assessments, and (5) accurately reporting student responses. Using custodians, office assistants, or siblings as interpreters is unacceptable practice.

If it is not possible to assess a student in his or her native language, the eligibility decision will hinge on ruling out lack of English proficiency as the cause of the problem. In these instances, the assessor must establish a baseline description of the student's English proficiency. Therefore, the student must be provided ESL instruction for a period of time, with progress carefully monitored. Students without disabilities will demonstrate increased proficiency. Students with disabilities will continue to struggle in spite of effective ESL instruction. Relying on this "test-teach-test" approach to determining eligibility creates a dilemma given federal guidelines requiring timely assessments. However, if general education teachers have expertise in English as a Second Language acquisition and use diagnostic/prescription teaching approaches, they will have documented the instructional strategies they used to address students' language needs and resulting progress. This is exactly the type of information needed to rule out lack of knowledge of English as the basis of students' learning problems.

Selecting the Assessment Battery

Assessment instruments must have norms appropriate to English Language Learners and be free of racial, linguistic, and cultural biases. While it is beyond the scope of this chapter to review the availability of such instruments, the following guidelines are offered for evaluating the performance of ELLs and reporting assessment outcomes:

1. Whenever possible, use equivalent instruments in the native language and in English (e.g., the Spanish and English versions of a vocabulary test) to contrast performance across languages on comparable skills.
2. Compare results of norm-referenced instruments with those of informal assessments in the native language and in English (e.g., formal reading tests and informal reading assessments).
3. Because of the heavy emphasis on English in tests of intelligence and cognitive abilities, use nonverbal measures whenever possible.
4. Involve parents in the assessment process to help validate the assessor's observations of student performance and to affirm whether behaviors the assessor observes are typical of their child at home and in the community.

5. In reporting assessment results, give credit to students for correct responses in the native language and in English, in aggregate. For example, a student who knows ten vocabulary words in Spanish and ten different ones in English knows twenty vocabulary words. This does not mean that test scores in the native language and in English should be added but that assessments should indicate patterns of strengths and weakness and they should reflect all that a student knows or can do, regardless of the language in which the student demonstrates the skill.

Adaptations of Assessment Instruments and Procedures

Special education leaders must provide guidance on acceptable ways to adapt standardized instruments and procedures for use with ELLs. Without such guidance, there is great potential for inconsistencies in assessing ELLs and determining who qualifies for services. Adaptations of standardized procedures might include using local norms, testing limits (e.g., removing time limits), and tests normed outside the United States. However, students' scores on instruments not normed for ELLs, or obtained through adapted procedures, should not be reported since they may not truly reflect students' abilities. It would be inappropriate, for example, to calculate a discrepancy score based on the use of adapted intelligence and achievement measures. Such data can be used only for *diagnostic* purposes, not for determining eligibility.

Conducting the Assessment and Analyzing Results

The comprehensive assessment should yield information about students' academic, developmental, and behavioral characteristics and patterns of strengths and weaknesses in the native language and in English (Yates & Ortiz, 1995). Assessors should report results in writing, alerting those who will be reviewing them to the limitations of adapted procedures and thus the need for caution in interpreting assessment data obtained in nonstandard ways. They should share their clinical observations about the cultural and linguistic characteristics of the student and how these may have influenced assessment outcomes. Assessors should also offer preliminary recommendations for instruction in the native language and/or in English as a Second Language and instructional modifications that may be needed to ensure success.

MULTIDISCIPLINARY TEAMS

Team Membership

The multidisciplinary team must include representatives who understand unique considerations in educating ELLs (Yates & Ortiz, 1995, 1998). If the student is being served in alternative programs (e.g., ESL or Title I), personnel from these programs should be included on the team. An interpreter will be needed so that parents who have limited proficiency in English can participate meaningfully in deliberations and can make an informed decision about giving, or withholding, consent for services. Interpreters must be proficient in the students' dominant language and appropriately trained. Copies of team deliberations and of the IEP (or, at a minimum, accurate summaries) should be provided in the parents' native language. This information can be provided on audiotape if parents prefer.

Team Responsibilities

The multidisciplinary team considers assessment data and decides whether the student has a legally defined disability and needs special education services. Team members provide assurances that problems are not the result of linguistic or cultural differences or lack of opportunity to learn (Yates & Ortiz, 1995, 1998). The team identifies the evidence used to confirm that the disability manifests itself in the native language, not only in English. And the team indicates which data were used to show that problematic behaviors are significantly different from the behaviors of peers from the same language group and community. Documentation of previous prevention and early intervention efforts provides the data to rule out lack of opportunity to learn as the cause of achievement difficulties.

Individualized Education Plans

Providing instruction in a student's native language serves as an important scaffold for ELLs with disabilities; if this is not possible, then special education teachers must use ESL strategies (Ortiz, 2000). IEPs for ELLs should thus specify (1) the language of instruction (i.e., native language or ESL) for each goal and objective, (2) the language to be used by related services personnel (e.g., speech therapists), (3) specialized materials and recommended strategies for L1 (the first language of the student) and L2 (the second language of the student), and (4) mechanisms for sharing progress data with parents in their native language (Ortiz, 2000; Ortiz & Wilkinson, 1989).

Least Restrictive Environment

Like their nondisabled peers, ELLs with disabilities have the right to regular education services, such as bilingual education and/or ESL services. They should have access to, for example, the following placement alternatives (Yates & Ortiz, 1998).

Bilingual Education Classroom with Special Education Consultation. The student is assigned full-time to a bilingual education classroom. The special educator serves as a consultant, helping the teacher modify native language and ESL instruction to accommodate the student's disabilities.

General Education with ESL Instruction and Special Education Consultation. General education and ESL teachers use ESL strategies to ensure that the student understands the instruction. The special educator consults with both teachers to ensure that they adapt instruction to meet disability-related needs.

Bilingual Special Education Resource Teacher. This teacher provides special education instruction in the native language and/or uses ESL strategies and coordinates instruction with bilingual education teachers.

Special Education/ESL Resource Teacher. The special education teacher uses ESL strategies and works with general education and ESL specialists to ensure the adaptation of instruction to meet disability-related needs. If the student is in a bilingual education classroom, the bilingual educator addresses native language goals and the special educator provides instruction for those goals for which ESL was identified as the appropriate instructional approach. For example, the special educator can work with ELLs with disabilities who are being transitioned from native language to English reading.

Self-Contained Bilingual Special Education Teacher. The teacher delivers special education instruction in the native language and/or uses ESL strategies, as appropriate.

Self-Contained Special Education/ESL Teacher. The teacher provides special education instruction full-time using ESL techniques.

Whenever possible, special education teachers who are monolingual should be supported by bilingual paraprofessionals (Yates & Ortiz, 1998). These assistants, rather than simply interpreting what the teacher is saying, should preview lessons in the native language that will then be taught by the teacher using ESL strategies. After the lesson, the assistant reviews important content in the native language. In this way, lessons taught in English are anchored by native language support. More importantly, though, this "preview, ESL lesson, review" sequence allows teachers to retain responsibility for instruction.

Annual Review

The annual review enables multidisciplinary teams to identify students who are not making expected progress. These students' IEPs are then modified and alternative strategies recommended to improve their performance. Since the English skills of ELLs may change dramatically over brief periods of time, more frequent reviews of performance may be necessary than might be true of other special education students. Decisions about continuing special education eligibility or dismissal cannot be made without current language proficiency data. Updating language assessments annually is essential.

COMMITMENT OF SPECIAL EDUCATION LEADERSHIP

As the cultural and linguistic demographics of schools continues to change dramatically, educational systems must reform their programs, policies, procedures, and practices to respond to the needs of students. Revising classification processes for special education is but one aspect of general systemic change that must be adapted for the current and emerging population of students. Reforms needed will be neither short term nor simple. Special education administrators can begin by becoming involved in systemwide reform efforts, such as those addressing academic achievement for culturally and linguistically distinct learners and those focusing on early intervention for struggling learners. At the same time, special education processes must be adapted to address not only students' disabilities but also their cultural and language-related needs.

Classification issues and errors are not likely to disappear in the foreseeable future. However, experimentation and systemic change, and a commitment to these by both general educators and special educators, remain the most viable options for improving services to students with disabilities and their parents.

QUESTIONS FOR FURTHER DISCUSSION

1. What do you think will be the specific impact on special education services in your school of the forces identified in the first section of this chapter? Describe which one(s) you feel should be addressed first in terms of priority planning.

2. What are some ways that cultural and linguistic disproportionality in special education can be reduced?

3. Why are general education school principals so critical to delivery of appropriate special education services to culturally and linguistically distinct students?

4. Review the model found in Figure 1 of this chapter. What components of the model are in place in your school? What components need to be developed or strengthened in your school?

REFERENCES

Aspen, M. (1992, April). *Principals' attitudes toward special education: Results and implications of a comprehensive study*. A paper presented at the annual convention of the Council for Exceptional Children, Baltimore, MD.

Banks, J. A. (2000). The social construction of difference and the quest for educational equality. In R. S. Brandt (Ed.), *Education in a new ERA, ASCD Yearbook 2000* (pp. 21–45). Alexandria, VA: Association for Supervision and Curriculum Development.

Chalfant, J. C., & Pysh, M. V. D. (1981, November). Teacher assistance teams—A model for within-building problem solving. *Counterpoint*, 16–21.

Cognition and Technology Group at Vanderbilt University. (1997). *The Jasper Project: Lessons in curriculum, instruction, assessment, and professional development*. Mahwah, NJ: Erlbaum.

Coles, G. (2001, November). Reading taught to the tune of the "scientific" hickory stick. *Phi Delta Kappan, 83*(3), 204-212.

Collins, G. (2001, April 17). Those who can't test. *The New York Times*, p. A25.

Cummins, J. (1989). A theoretical framework for bilingual special education. *Exceptional Children, 56*(2), 111–119.

Digest of Educational Statistics. (1999). *Digest of Educational Statistics*. Retrieved February 19, 2002, from http://www.NCES.ed.gov.

English, F. W., & Steffy, B. E. (2001). *Deep Curriculum Alignment*. Lanham, MD: Scarecrow Press.

Esiner, E. W. (1995, June). *Standards for American schools: Help or hindrance. Phi Delta Kappan, 76*(10), 758–764.

Fashola, O. S., & Slavin, R. E. (1998). Schoolwide reform models. What works? *Phi Delta Kappan, 79*(5), 370–379.

Fusco, S. (2001, May 9). TAAS takes toll on more than students. *The Daily Texan, Classroom Commentary*, p. 2.

Gallagher, J. J. (1969, March). Organization and administration of special education: A national perspective. Proceedings of the national conference *Common and specialized learnings, competencies, and experiences for special education administrators*. Austin, TX: National Consortium of Universities Preparing Administrators of Special Education.

Garcia, S. B., & Ortiz, A. A. (1988). Preventing inappropriate referrals of language minority students to special education. *New Focus*, No. 5. Wheaton, MD: National Clearinghouse for Bilingual Education.

Garcia, S. B., Wilkinson, C. Y., & Ortiz, A. A. (1995). Enhancing achievement for language minority students: Classroom, school, and family contexts. *Education and Urban Society, 27*(4), 441–462.

Gay, G. (2000). Improving the achievement of marginalized students of color. In *Including at-risk students in standards-based reform: A report on McREL's diversity roundtable II*. Aurora, CO: Mid-Continent Research for Education and Learning.

Gerber, S. B., Finn, J. D., Achilles, C. M., & Boyd-Zaharias, J. (2001, Summer). Teacher aides and students' academic achievement. *Educational Evaluation and Policy Analysis, 23*(2), 123–143.

Gersten, R., Keating, T., & Harniss, M. K. (2001, Summer). Working in special education: Factors that enhance special educators' intent to stay. *Exceptional Children, 67*(4), 549–567.

Gregorian, V. (2001, July 6). How to train—and retain—teachers. *New York Times*, p. A19.

Grossman, H. (1998). *Ending discrimination in special education*. Springfield, IL: Charles C. Thomas.

Haberman, M. (1995, June). Selecting "star" teachers for children and youth in urban poverty. *Phi Delta Kappan, 76*(10), 777–781.

Hartocollis, A. (2001, May 26). Bonuses for principals introduces merit pay to New York public schools. *New York Times*, p. A11.

Haskew, L. D. (1974). Force analysis. In S. P. Hencley & J. R. Yates (Eds.), *Futurism in education* (pp. 55–70). Berkeley, CA: McCutchan.

Heller, K. A., Holtzman, W. H., & Messick, S. (1982). *Placing children in special education: A strategy for equity.* Washington, DC: National Academy Press.

Hellriegel, K. L., & Yates, J. R. (1997). *Issues of diversity in education professional organizations.* Reston, VA: National Clearinghouse for Special Education, Council for Exceptional Children (ERIC Document Reproduction Service).

Individuals with Disabilities Education Act of 1997. 20 U.S.C. §1400 *et seq.* (1997).

Knapp, M. S., Shields, P. M., & Turnbull, B. J. (1995, June). Academic challenge in high poverty classrooms. *Phi Delta Kappan, 79*(6), 770–776.

Kohn, A. (1999). *The schools our children deserve.* Boston: Houghton Mifflin.

Kushner, M. I., & Ortiz, A. A. (2000). The preparation of early childhood education teachers for English language learners. In *New teachers for a new century: The future of early childhood professional development* (pp. 124–154). Washington, DC: U.S. Department of Education, National Institute on Early Childhood Development and Education.

Leung, B. P. (1996). Quality assessment practices in a diverse society. *Teaching Exceptional Children, 28*(3), 42-45.

Madden, N. A., Slavin, R. E., Karweit, N. L., Dolan, L., & Wasik, B. A. (1991). Success for all. *Phi Delta Kappan, 72*(8), 593–599.

Maeroff, G. I. (1998, February). Altered destinies. *Phi Delta Kappan, 79*(6), 425–432.

Mazzeo, J., Carlson, J. E., Voekl, K. E., & Lutkus, A. D. (2000, March). *Increasing the participation rate of special needs students in NAEP: A report on 1996 NAEP research activities.* Washington, DC: U.S. Department of Education, Office of Educational Research and Improvement.

McCarthy, M. M. (1980, November). Minimum competency testing and handicapped students. *Exceptional Children, 47*(3), 166–173.

Montecel, M. R., & Cortez, A. (2000, November–December). Nine priorities for public education policy reforms in Texas. *IDRA Newsletter, 28*(10), 1–2, 9–13.

National Center for Educational Statistics. (2000). *The condition of education.* Washington, DC: U.S. Department of Education.

National Research Council. (2002). *Minority students in special education and gifted education.* Washington, DC: National Academy Press.

Noonan, C. M. (1999). *Use of assertive technology devices with limited English proficient students receiving special education services.* Unpublished master's thesis, University of Texas at Austin, Austin, TX.

Ortiz, A. A. (1997). Learning disabilities occurring concomitantly with linguistic differences. *Journal of Learning Disabilities, 30*(3), 321–332.

Ortiz, A. A. (2000). Including students with special needs in standards-based reform: Issues associated with the alignment of standards, curriculum, and instruction. In *Including special needs students in standards-based reform* (pp. 41–64). Aurora, CO: Mid-Continent Research for Education and Learning.

Ortiz, A. A., & Garcia, S. B. (1990). Using language assessment data for language and instructional planning for exceptional bilingual students. In A. Carrasquillo & R. Baecher (Eds.), *Teaching the bilingual special education student* (pp. 24–47). Norwood, NJ: Ablex.

Ortiz, A. A., & Garcia, S. B. (1995). Serving Hispanic students with learning disabilities: Recommended policies and practices. *Urban Education, 29*(4), 471–481.

Ortiz, A. A., Garcia, S. B., Holtzman, W. H., Jr., Polyzoi, E., Snell, W. E., Jr., Wilkinson, C. Y., & Willig, A. C. (1985). *Characteristics of limited English proficient Hispanic students in programs for the learning disabled: Implications for policy, practice, and research.* Austin: University of Texas, Handicapped Minority Research Institute on Language Proficiency.

Ortiz, A. A., & Wilkinson, C. Y. (1989). Adapting IEPs for limited English proficient students. *Academic Therapy, 24*(5), 555–568.

Ortiz, A. A., & Wilkinson, C. Y. (1991). Assessment and intervention model for the bilingual exceptional student (AIM for the BEST). *Teacher Education and Special Education, 14*, 35–42.

Ortiz, A. A., & Yates, J. R. (2001, November). A framework for serving English language learners with disabilities. *Journal of Special Education Leadership, 14*(2), 72–80.

Parrish, T. B. (2001, April). Who's paying the rising costs of special education? *Journal of Special Education Leadership, 14*(1), 4–12.

Pipho, C. (1979). *Update VIII: Minimum competency testing.* Washington, DC: Education Commission of the States.

Rice, L. S. (1995). *Factors related to disproportionate representation of Hispanics in programs for students with learning disabilities.* Unpublished doctoral dissertation, University of Texas at Austin, Austin, TX.

Robertson, P., Kushner, M. I., Starks, J., & Drescher, C. (1994). An update of participation rates of culturally and linguistically diverse students in special education: The need for a research and policy agenda. *Bilingual Special Education Perspective, 14,* 1, 3–9.

Rose, L. C., & Gallup, A. M. (2001, September). The 33rd annual Phi Delta Kappa/Gallup poll of the public's attitudes toward the public schools. *Phi Delta Kappan, 83*(1), 41–58.

Rose, L. C., & Gallup, A. M. (2002). The 34th annual Phi Delta Kappa/Gallup poll of the public's attitudes toward the public schools. *Phi Delta Kappan, 84*(1), 41–46.

Singham, M. (1995, December). Race and intelligence: What are the issues? *Phi Delta Kappan, 77*(4), 271–278.

Slavin, R. E., & Madden, N. A. (1989, February). What works for students at risk: A research synthesis. *Educational Leadership,* 4–13.

Texas Education Agency. (2000). *Snapshot school district profiles.* Retrieved March 3, 2002, from http://www.tea.state.tx.us/perfreport/snapshot/.

U.S. Census Bureau. (1996). *Resident population of the United States: Middle series projections, 2035–2050, by sex, race, and Hispanic origin, with median age.* 1996 census of population. Washington, DC: U.S. Government Printing Office.

U.S. Census Bureau. (2000). *Census 2000 redistricting (Public Law 94-171).* Summary file, tables PL1 and PL2. Washington, DC: U.S. Department of Commerce.

U.S. Census Bureau. (2001, March). *Overview of race and Hispanic origin: Census 2000 brief.* Washington, DC: U.S. Department of Commerce.

U.S. Congress. (1999).Twenty-second annual report to the Congress on the implementation of the Individuals with Disabilities Education Act, *To assure the free and appropriate public education of all children with disabilities.* Retrieved February 18, 2002, from http://www.ed.gov/offices/OSERS/OSEP.

U.S. Department of Education. (1994). *The improving America's schools act of 1994: Summary sheets.* Washington, DC: Author.

Waggoner, D. (1994). Language minority school-age population now totals 9.9 million. *NABA News, 18*(1), 1, 24–26.

Webb-Johnson, G. (2000, Fall). Message from the president. *DDEL News, 10*(1), 1–2.

Yates, J. R., & Ortiz, A. A. (1995). Linguistically and culturally diverse students. In R. S. Podemski, G. E. Marsh II, T. E. C. Smith, & B. J. Price (Eds.), *Comprehensive administration of special education* (2nd ed., pp. 129–155). Englewood Cliffs, NJ: Prentice-Hall.

Yates, J. R., & Ortiz, A. A. (1998). Issues of culture and diversity affecting educators with disabilities: A change in demography is reshaping America. In R. J. Anderson, C. E. Keller, & J. M. Karp (Eds.), *Enhancing diversity: Educators with disabilities in the education enterprise.* Washington, DC: Gallaudet University Press.

TRENDS IN PLACEMENT ISSUES

SHERMAN DORN

University of South Florida

DOUGLAS FUCHS

Vanderbilt University

Debates over the appropriate placement of students with disabilities, from placing them in the general education classroom to placing them in institutionalized settings, are informed by arguments about justice and individual education, and about special education in schooling more generally. Those further interested in this topic can read the many analyses written by special educators over the past fifteen years (e.g., Baker & Zigmond, 1990; Braaten, Kauffman, Braaten, Polsgrove, & Nelson, 1988; Carnine & Kameenui, 1990; Ferguson, 1995; Fuchs & Fuchs, 1991, 1994, 1995, 1998; Gartner & Lipsky, 1987; Gerber, 1988; Hallahan, Kauffman, Lloyd, & McKinney, 1988; Kauffman, 1989, 1992; Kavale & Forness, 2000; Kozleski & Jackson, 1993; Lipsky & Gartner, 1989, 1991; Reynolds, Wang, & Walberg, 1987; Roach, 1995; Roberts & Mather, 1995; Snell & Drake, 1994; Stainback & Stainback, 1992; Taylor, 1988, 1995; Wang & Walberg, 1988; Zigmond & Baker, 1994; Zigmond, Jenkins, Fuchs, Deno, Fuchs, Baker, Jenkins, & Couthino, 1995). This chapter, rather than focusing on policy arguments or analyzing the debate itself, gives a broad overview of issues. This overview includes three separate topics: legal issues, psychological research, and social science perspectives on placement in special education for students with disabilities.

LEGAL ISSUES IN PLACEMENT

Judicial Restraint and Placement

Public school systems have enormous power in determining the placement of students with disabilities, as long as they can document that they have provided appropriate educational opportunities. In a court of law, if a public school system can document that it has done everything that is professionally appropriate to include students with disabilities in an appropriate environment as close to peers as possible, the court will generally *not* side with parents in a

57

dispute. This perspective does not reflect anything having to do with justice, but rather it is a statement of realistic court expectations for public school systems. By contrast, public school systems are far more likely to lose court cases where they are unable to document that they have taken appropriate steps to attempt to include students with disabilities in an environment close to peers. In other words, as long as public school systems can document that they have been professional and have taken all appropriate steps that research suggests, they are usually protected from arguments about appropriate placement for students with disabilities, as well as from arguments about the appropriate education of individuals with disabilities (Yell, 1995; Yell & Drasgow, 1999, 2000).

This judicial restraint has its origins in the often ambiguous language in federal law and regulations that implement the Individuals with Disabilities Education Act (Education for All Handicapped Children Act, 1975; IDEA, 1997). Federal law recognizes neither the term *mainstreaming* nor the term *inclusion.* The term *least restrictive environment,* which education inherited from earlier legal language on residential institutions, is rather confusing because it refers not to absolute placement criteria but to a nebulous statement that "to the maximum extent appropriate, children with disabilities . . . are educated with children who are nondisabled" (34 CFR §300.550 (b)(1)). As occurs elsewhere in IDEA, this is a recursive definition because it assumes that one can easily identify what an appropriate education is and what the "maximum extent" of contact with nondisabled children is that is appropriate (Yell & Drasgow, 2000). The IDEA regulations, moreover, require a variety of steps in the individualized education program (IEP; see other chapters in this volume for more information). If a public school system follows these steps in a way that meets both the procedural and substantive standards of appropriate education, the public school system is relatively immune from legal challenges where placement is concerned. While federal law and regulations include substantive mandates, these rely on the procedural steps for resolution, for they describe steps for decision making rather than hard-and-fast criteria for those decisions. The one additional placement criteria that is relevant legally is whether or not a public school system has taken reasonable steps to attempt to include a student in the least restrictive environment— that is, as close to peers as is the "maximum extent appropriate."

Arguments about this interpretation are usually vivid, as is elsewhere true in special education. Those who would like to see the vast majority of students with disabilities in general education classrooms emphasize the general guidelines that children with disabilities belong in a general education environment, requiring positive justification of (and thus an implicit burden of proof for) any deviation from a general standard of full inclusion. Here, the IDEA regulations (based on 20 U.S.C. §1412(a)(5)) suggest that the burden of proof is on those who see separation as necessary, requiring "that special classes, separate schooling or other removal of children with disabilities from the regular educational environment occurs only if the nature or severity of the disability is such that education in regular classes with the use of supplementary aids and services cannot be achieved satisfactorily" (34 CFR §300.550(b)(2)). Yet those who prefer to conserve what has been called the full continuum of services, from placement in general education classrooms to institutionalized settings, point to adjacent regulations requiring that "each public agency shall ensure that a continuum of alternative placements is available to meet the needs of children with disabilities for special education and related services" (34 CFR 300.551(a)). Such "conservationists" (see Fuchs & Fuchs, 1991) generally see no need for school systems to put students with disabilities in environments in which the school systems and parents may see impending failure or in which the child has experienced failure in the past. Neither of these views, however, has been considered explicitly by courts, and what happens in a courtroom is very different from arguments about what is just or right. In practice, decisions at the main appellate level of the federal court system (circuit courts) have been quite consistent (*Daniel R. R. v. State Board of Education,* 1989; *Hartmann v. Loudoun County,* 1997; *Roncker v. Walter,* 1983; *Sacramento City Unified School District v. Rachel H.,* 1994) and demonstrate a single approach as described by Yell and Drasgow (1999).

In order to understand how courts make decisions, one must realize that the federal courts are becoming generally reluctant to interfere in the traditional operating sphere of local school systems (e.g., Orfield, Eaton, & the Harvard Project on School Desegregation, 1996). IDEA is a very powerful tool for advocates for children with disabilities, but courts place relatively high barriers that plaintiffs (those bringing suit) must meet in order to demonstrate that the school system is incompetent in dealing with students with disabilities. Where school systems violate procedural rights of children with disabilities in their families, courts and hearing officers are usually willing to intervene. However, where the issue concerns appropriate education or other substantive educational decisions, and where the procedural guidelines are moot, courts are usually reluctant to intervene. This is true in a wide variety of areas in educational law, not just in special education. Where a school system violates the normative assumption that it is both fair and professionally competent, administrating hearing officers and courts are willing to question substantive decisions. Where that condition does not hold— where there are not obvious snafus or legal evasions by a school system—school systems are much more likely to prevail in court. Courts thus maintain a great deal of judicial restraint in dealing with special education. That is, courts are reluctant to replace professional educational judgment with judicial judgment. Courts intervene in a variety of matters primarily where they conclude that the school system is demonstrably incompetent. This is true in placement issues as well as in other areas of special education law.

The "Stay-Put" Provision, Amended

When Congress wrote the Education of All Handicapped Children Act in 1975, it created a provision to encourage collaborative decision making among school officials and the families of children with disabilities. Congress decided that in a case where there was no clear agreement about what should happen with a student's IEP, the child should stay put in the existing arrangement. This "stay-put" provision was intended to encourage collaborative decision making and, in cases of disagreement, protect the due process rights of children who otherwise might be stampeded by school systems into inappropriate placements. The history of schools' arbitrarily placing a large number of children in separate classrooms before the enactment of the federal law was probably the key reason for the provision. This stay-put provision restricted one option for the discipline of children with disabilities when the Supreme Court decided that suspension of more than ten days constitutes a change of placement under the law (Hartwig & Ruesch, 2000; *Honig v. Doe,* 1988; Yell, 1989; Yell & Shriner, 1998). Suspending the child for more than two weeks without the agreement of parents or guardians constituted a decision that required an IEP conference and, therefore, fell under the stay-put provision. In other words, any action of the child related to the child's disability could not provoke more than ten days of suspension during a year without either parent/guardian agreement or a due process hearing the school system called. The enforcement of the stay-put provision provoked a bureaucratic response from school systems. Schools created, with the consent and advice of the federal Department of Education, an administrative process to determine whether or not the disciplinary incident was a manifestation of the child's disability. These manifestation hearings were a way to manage the discipline of a student and separate out, at least theoretically, that discipline that was connected to the child's disability and those discipline decisions that were not connected to the child's disability (e.g., *Letter to Boggus*, 1993).

The problem with such manifestation hearings, in practice, has been that making such distinctions is splitting legal hairs. Is a child with learning disabilities acting out because the child is undisciplined or because she or he is highly frustrated with the problems of learning a difficult skill? Parents and guardians have an incentive, with such hearings and with the recent move to "zero tolerance" school policies, to insist that virtually everything a child does is tied to the disability (or disabilities), while school officials are motivated to explain that virtually nothing is a manifestation of a disability. In this particular adversarial setting, the common obligation to solve problems is often lost. In part because of school responses that focus on manifestation hearings, what has been largely absent has been a discussion of what positive steps schools and families can take together to teach children to behave more appropriately. The suspension of a child (and the taking of other disciplinary actions that remove a child from instruction) is noneducational because the child is not receiving instruction at all. Certainly, researchers and ethical educators who work with children whose behaviors are problematic (especially those children labeled with emotional and behavior disorders) have consistently argued that the best practices for children with disabilities involve teaching better behavior. Functional behavioral assessments have long been a recommended practice, despite the legalistic focus on manifestation hearings (e.g., Hartwig & Ruesch, 2000).

Regardless of professionally recommended practices, the debate during the mid-1990s focused on what changes, if any, would an amended IDEA include that might change the stay-put provision and the disciplining of children with disabilities. Administrators wanted the freedom to remove children from existing settings based on relatively minimal evidentiary standards (the suspicion of future misconduct), a proposal that many advocates for children with disabilities fought (Alpert, 1996). The compromise provision that Congress finally enacted allows school systems, when students bring weapons to school or are engaged in drug selling in school or on school grounds, to remove those children from the existing placement approved in the students' IEPs into a more restrictive setting (as an interim placement) for forty-five days. A school may also petition a hearing officer for a forty-five-day interim placement if it can demonstrate with significant evidence (more than a preponderance) that the student is likely to injure self or others. Balancing this provision, as least theoretically, is the requirement that IEPs include behavioral components where appropriate (including positive behavior interventions) and for problem solving to include functional behavioral assessment. Codified in law is the requirement for manifestation hearings at various points. In practice, the 1997 IDEA amendments regarding discipline have been in place for too short a time to gauge their impact. What is notable, from a political perspective, is that Congress did not respond to a debate over the prior ten years regarding full inclusion or inclusion more generally, but only in the area of students who were discipline problems. Most of the battles about full inclusion were rhetorical and concerned the courts. Congress left intact legal language from the prior versions of the law. Where the education of students with disabilities appears to affect schools in general (such as in school safety or funding), legislators were more likely to focus on calls for change.

PSYCHOLOGICAL ISSUES IN THE PLACEMENT OF CHILDREN WITH DISABILITIES

In addition to understanding the legal guidelines regarding placement, educators should understand the psychological debates over appropriate placement. Much of the debate regarding the best setting for children with disabilities revolves around the priorities that one sets for schools (are they primarily for learning specific skills and knowledge or for socialization, for example). These debates also concern very concrete issues regarding the settings in which children can engage in various activities and the settings in which education can best happen. Much of the debate centers on the following four questions:

1. Where can the learning of specific or general skills (academic, behavioral, or otherwise) best happen?
2. In which settings do children feel the best about themselves?
3. In which settings can children with and without disabilities best learn how to interact, as children and as citizens of a democratic republic?
4. In which settings do the current skills of teachers best fit the needs of children with disabilities for the goals as stated in various questions above, and how are teachers' skills developed for different settings?

Those questions, of course, interact. For example, if children who need to learn behavioral skills can only be with teachers who can teach the skills effectively in a certain setting, then the placement issues for that child should concern the behavioral issues. On the other hand, if children can perform reasonably well in a general education setting with minimal interventions, or if the general education teacher has skills at least equal to the skills of special education teachers in that school, then a child is as likely to succeed in the general education environment as elsewhere—and then other concerns such as socialization trump concerns over skills. The following sections describe some of the issues central to these questions.

Where to Learn Skills

Curricular Expectations.   The choice of settings in which to learn various skills involves several factors, whether one is discussing core academic skills in the general curriculum, specific social or behavioral skills, or what Brown, Branston, Hamre-Nietupski, Pumpian, Certo, and Gruenewald (1979) have described as skills that are immediate and immediately useful. The first important consideration is the set of curricular expectations in a given environment—that is, what is possible for a child to learn in the environment, and what do teachers and fellow students expect the child to learn. (This discussion of explicit expectations is separate from issues of hidden curricula—e.g., Jackson, 1968—and what children may learn on their own.) One can rarely expect students to learn, in the general education environment, what the teacher does not explicitly set forth in academics, such as the format of writing, reading comprehension skills, math, science, or history as part of a curriculum. Behavioral expectations, as well, are important, and such expectations can (and, one would hope, should) include explicit skills for children to learn. So, too, with social skills and other skills, depending on what an IEP contains. These considerations depend on individual goals and also the capacity of an environment and school. There are many resource teachers who have not had sufficiently high expectations for their students' academic goals, many general education teachers who have had low expectations for their students or have inadequately analyzed students' performance, and also teachers (both general education teachers and special education teachers) who have not understood their students' needs for specific social skills and goals (e.g., Farlow & Snell, 1989; Fuchs & Fuchs, 1985). All of these issues of expectations should connect to an IEP, and expectations must be expressed, through concrete goals and analysis of student performance, in order for the education to be appropriate.

Support Expectations.   A second issue regarding expectations addresses the expected support available to children. Put simply, for a setting to be appropriate teachers must acknowledge the needs of children for scaffolding, modeling, reteaching, and other interventions. Work in transenvironmental programming and reintegration of children into less restrictive environments strongly suggests that explicit comparisons of expectations for students, including the expectations of support teachers, can be crucial in helping students move smoothly between environments (Anderson-Inman, 1981, 1986; Fuchs, Fuchs, & Fernstrom, 1992, 1993; Fuchs, Fuchs, Fernstrom, & Hohn, 1991; Shinn, Habedank, Rodden-Nord, & Kautsen, 1993; Shinn, Powell-Smith, & Good, 1996; Shinn, Powell-Smith, Good, & Baker, 1997). In many cases, general education teachers can provide support that they would not for most students, if explicitly expected and when assisted. In other cases, teachers may have neither the inclination nor the technical assistance to provide the best support for students, even with concerted efforts to boost general educators' capacity to accommodate students with disabilities (Baker & Zigmond, 1990; Zigmond & Baker, 1994; Zigmond, Jenkins, Fuchs, Deno, Fuchs, Baker, Jenkins, & Couthino, 1995). In yet other cases, teachers in a variety of settings rely on a limited repertoire of accommodations instead of individualizing interventions for that child. Needless to say, this aspect of what students learn is closely tied to professional development for teachers, discussed later in this chapter.

Requirements of Specific Techniques.   Some specific techniques and instructional goals may require that settings be in certain locales. For example, Brown, Schwarz, Udvari-Solner, and Kampschroer (1991; also see Brown, Nisbet, Ford, Sweet, Shiraga, York, & Loomis, 1983) pointed out that for children with developmental disabilities, where one sometimes cannot expect generalization, the school itself is an insufficient environment and an inappropriate place to learn skills such as crossing a street or interacting in a store, where proximal location is crucial to mastery. One cannot learn how to cross a street safely within a school building. Teaching in the standard academic curriculum also may require unusual levels of intervention for students with disabilities. Mastropieri, Scruggs, and Butcher (1997) presented evidence that many students with disabilities may be unable to deduce scientific principles from observation without coaching. Such coaching can often occur in general education classrooms, but some specific techniques (especially those that benefit from individualization, such as coaching individual students on their *individually best* cognitive strategies) may need teachers in one-on-one instructional settings to maximize learning. More generally, a quiet environment is a requirement for many techniques that require one-on-one instruction.

The considerations above do not either rule in or rule out any specific setting for an individual child. Many of these issues are flexible insofar as the specifics are concerned. In some schools, general education teachers have appropriate expectations, effectively use interventions with individual children, and have the approval of other staff as they devote resources and time to serving the needs of individuals with disabilities in the general education environment. We certainly wish there were more such teachers and schools! However, we and many parents know that those situations depend on local circumstances that can change with teacher and administrative turnover. The general education environment is appropriate for teaching skills where teachers have the necessary skills, resources, and assistance, and where principals support the endeavors. Such teachers do not exist everywhere.

Where to Feel Better

One set of arguments over the appropriate placement of children with disabilities centers on what children perceive about their environment and specifically what children with disabilities understand about where they are during the school day. Certainly, much writing in educational psychology has focused on children's perceptions of general policies. Shepard and Smith (1989) make the vivid point that kindergarten students who are retained understand that they are "flunking," and euphemisms (such as "retention") do not hide that fact. The work of Coles (e.g., 1967) makes clear that children have a sense of morals and ethics and understand their environment in those terms. Those working with special education and what children with disabilities perceive have used Goffman's (1963) description of social stigma or similar concepts to argue, in some cases, that the placement of children in more restrictive environments has a stigmatizing effect (e.g., Snell & Drake, 1994; Stainback & Stainback, 1992). Certainly, the feelings that children have about themselves will affect their development and can either interfere or facilitate the learning of skills and maturation. However, the exact effect of setting on children's feelings about themselves and their environment is an empirical question, and the answers are not settled. In many cases, children may certainly perceive their being separated from the general education environment as a stigma. On the other hand, children may themselves be very aware of their problems and their history of failure in school. In those cases, children may well prefer a setting in which they can succeed to one in which they perceive as having inappropriate risks for themselves (e.g., Gresham, Evans, & Elliott, 1988; Jenkins & Heinen, 1989; Vaughn, Schumm, Klingner, & Saumall, 1995). The mix of resilience and risk avoidance is an individual matter, and the effect of setting on individual perceptions will vary.

Where to Socialize

Schooling has historically included a role for the socialization of children becoming adults in a broad sense. By *socialization* we mean not only the common meaning of learning social skills but also the learning of various roles in a society, such as being a voter in a republic. Many argue that this socialization in any formal organization has had evil consequences for children—for example, Goodman (1964) and Illich (1971) argue that children should not be in formal schools to socialize them for conformity. Bowles and Gintis (1976) make a similar point about schools' being a place to socialize children into the larger economic social structure. On the other hand, some have argued that schools can serve a positive role in socializing children, in antiracist education (e.g., May, 1999), in developing human capital (Becker,

1993), and for citizenship more generally (*Brown v. Board of Education,* 1954; Gutmann, 1987; Meier, 1995). Contact with children of diverse backgrounds, including with and without disabilities, serves to promote the broader social goals, according to advocates of full inclusion (Gartner & Lipsky, 1987; Lipsky & Gartner, 1989). In addition, most special educators, we would argue, see that as a useful goal in general (e.g., Fuchs & Fuchs, 1998). We agree with this general goal of contact among children with and without disabilities.

However, proponents of full inclusion have made a provocative comparison between the separation of children with disabilities from the general environment and the historical segregation based on race (e.g., Gartner & Lipsky, 1987; Stainback & Stainback, 1987; Wang & Walberg, 1988). This argument places a greater burden on schools than they have been able to carry. The Supreme Court, in *Brown v. Board of Education,* concluded that legal segregation placed a stigma on African American schoolchildren that was an intangible inequality rooted in segregation itself rather than just the tangible inequalities that were obvious (such as unequal access to books). Many have interpreted the *Brown v. Board of Education* decision as a broad ethical mandate for a diverse student population. The argument of many proponents of full inclusion, for example, focuses on the philosophical and democratic principles that, they claim, exert an automatic and unimpeachable demand for the inclusion of all children in the general education setting. There are two ways, however, in which that argument places an inappropriate burden on schools. First, there are political limits to the use of schools for reforming society. The nation has witnessed now a fifteen-year trend away from court-supervised desegregation, for reasons that include a limited taste for schools as instruments of social policy (Orfield et al., 1996). In some ways we wish this timidity did not exist, but it does, and it affects the willingness to serve children with disabilities in various settings as well as the political will to desegregate schools.

In addition to the political limits of schools as reform instruments, the complex nature of schools as organizations constrains their capacity for implementing dramatic reform. Teachers and principals are buffeted by a variety of demands on their time and energies, from high-stakes testing to concerns about school safety and the mandated curriculum. The needs of children with disabilities, even with the best of intentions, are too often lost in the shuffle (e.g., Zigmond et al., 1995). The unintended consequence can be a message to children that is the exact opposite of democratic access and the dignity of all people. We have observed several situations in schools where the inclusion of children with developmental disabilities in the general education environment has served neither to promote the socialization of skills nor, particularly, to encourage children without disabilities to see their peers with disabilities as dignified. These examples are unfortunate object lessons of the potential for unintended consequences. Specifically, we have seen general education classrooms where children with more involved disabilities were not participating fully in activities and were the targets of teachers' efforts to provide very *different* tasks in the same classroom (such as providing a set of plastic objects to manipulate and calling this "vocational therapy"), where teachers were not given assistance to deal with difficult behavioral problems, and thus where the children with disabilities became object lessons in how those with disabilities are distinctly different from everyone else and *incapable* of having common needs, feelings, and aspirations. These children served primarily as classroom mascots and problems, not peers.

We hope that readers, regardless of their disposition toward inclusion, will share our horror at these particular situations, which serve no one's interests well. The question, of course, is whether the existence of such circumstances should undermine faith in the use of schools to inculcate democratic values in children. To what extent should we trust children to make the appropriate moral judgment when they are observing unusual behavior and teachers with insufficient skills or poor guidance? The full inclusion argument implies that we should not worry about the right balance between protecting children and providing the dignity of risk, either for individuals with disabilities or for the goal of socializing citizens of a country. Those who stand on the side of excluding children with severe disabilities from general education classrooms would also not focus on developing criteria for the right balance. As a result, we have no criteria for such a balance except the vague legal guidelines that currently exist.

We suggest a different standard for the level of contact among children necessary to promote democratic socialization, one focusing on a reasonable minimum threshold rather than the maximum desirable under the best circumstances. If we agree that complete isolation of different groups of students from each other is unwise in a democratic society, we should model the standard for contact on the *minimum* interaction adults must have to agree on common interests, to communicate, and to work together. This is consistent with Gutmann's (1987) standard for education—that it provide at least *minimally sufficient* education for citizenship. What is necessary for appropriate maintenance of neighborhood social networks is the ordinary discourse that would happen when people mingle on a frequent enough basis to recognize each other as members of a community. In some older communities (and those planned as part of the New Urbanism movement—e.g., Duane, Plater-Zyberk, & Speck, 2000; Kunstler, 1996), adults sit on their porches and converse with those walking down the street or invite others onto their porches. No one expects to live constantly with all of her or his neighbors, nor is that level of contact necessary for working together. This "acknowledged neighbor" or "welcoming porch" standard encompasses a variety of situations, from joint projects planned by teachers to reverse mainstreaming and full inclusion. We propose it here as an alternative standard rather than to illustrate every situation that might meet it. This standard is, we suspect, both more feasible and defensible in the long term than either relying on rigid standards such as full inclusion or ignoring the role that schools play as institutions in a democratic culture.

How to Improve Teachers' Skills in All Settings

Federal law (IDEA, 1997) requires that states and local school systems create systems of comprehensive professional development in order to build the skills of the school system in general and to provide appropriate education for individuals with disabilities. This legal and ethical obligation extends to general classroom teachers as well as to specialists. Building that capacity is important for several reasons, not only because three-quarters of students with disabilities spend time in general education classrooms (U.S. Department of Education, 2000) but also because special education historically has had to rely on regular classroom teachers (Dorn, 1999). For all of these reasons, we think that paying attention to the skills of general classroom teachers, in addition to the skills of specialists, is crucial to the successful education of students with disabilities. At the same time, we recognize that competing demands on school systems as organizations may impede the development of skills by general classroom teachers or, more crucially, their use under intense pressures. Weatherley (1979) described competing demands that led educators, as "street-level bureaucrats," to make decisions based on limited resources. We see time and skills as two examples of such limited resources in today's relatively high-pressured environment for classroom teachers. When all but one state has high-stakes testing every year, and when the president of the United States stated his desire to have annual testing in grades 3 through 8, we understand that one of the consequences may be a "triage effect" with many children, including children with disabilities (Dorn, 1998). Such an explicit triage is unethical and, we believe, illegal. However, there are more subtle effects of these competing demands for teacher time and skills. In many places, school systems devote extraordinary professional development resources to existing general education teachers who are concerned about high-stakes testing. Whether explicit test preparation or preparing teachers with skills in helping a classroom in general meets the needs, such efforts may often compete with developing the skills necessary to accommodate individuals with disabilities in general education classrooms. In some cases, state-level policies for professional development should encourage the focus on individual skills. For example, both New York and Florida now have rules that require professional development to focus on the needs of individual children. Florida's Department of Education, for example, will now require individual professional development plans to "be related to specific performance data for the students to whom the teacher is assigned" (School Community Professional Development Act, §231.600(4)(b)5.a; see also New York Commissioner of Education, 1999). Such a mandate should encourage professional development that focuses on the needs of students with disabilities. Whether this requirement filters down into practice at the district and school levels, however, is a matter of empirical speculation at the moment.

In addition to these concerns about the skills of general classroom teachers, one must acknowledge that teachers' skills, experience, and willingness to educate children with disabilities vary widely. We wish it were not so, but it is. The needs of individual children must be met in real schools, with the teachers already there, with all their skills and flaws as human beings. To make decisions in the placement of an individual child by ignoring those concrete specific situations, in the general hope that a placement is appropriate by fiat, may be unfair to the children involved. One must ask whether the blanket placement of children with disabilities based on general philosophical principles is different from placement based on the category of eligibility for special education services. Individualization of education includes, for practical purposes, individualization of placement.

SOCIAL SCIENCE PERSPECTIVES ON PLACEMENT ISSUES

In the last thirty years, many critics of special education practices have used social science perspectives to shed light on school practices. Since Mercer's (1973) work on the identification and placement of Southern California children with disabilities in so-called mentally retarded rooms, many have similarly focused on identifying the ways school systems work in placing students with disabilities. One can use social science perspectives to analyze all special education practices, but these perspectives are perhaps most interesting and useful for providing different questions about placement. We suggest two broad categories of social science perspectives, those focusing on internal organizational attributes and those looking at the external pressures on schools. One potential conclusion of an internal perspective is that the placement of children in various classrooms is a safety-valve function of special education. Placement thus serves as a way to lower expectations for children with disabilities (e.g., Johnson, 1969). A second "internal" perspective focuses on the organizational characteristics and public schools as a whole and sees placement decisions less as a scapegoat mechanism for avoiding correcting the failures of public schools than as *part* of the repertoire by which public schools deal with problems. Placement decisions are thus pragmatic problem-solving decisions, whose broader consequences are largely unintended (e.g., Gerber & Semmel, 1984). Both conclusions, notably, assume that what happens *inside* schools determines how we interpret placement. In contrast, we think it is important to understand the placement of children with disabilities in the broader institutional behavior that places *all* children in schools. Children outside schools do not exhibit the type of age segregation, for example, that one sees in public schools. More generally, the placement of children in any particular situation is socially constructed. This latter perspective is the one we find most persuasive. In contrast with the arbitrary placement of children in schools, arguments over where children belong within that organizational structure seem awkward and incomplete.

Internal Perspectives

The debate over appropriate placement of students with disabilities *within* schools often focuses on questions of public schools as a set of systems and organizations. For example, Taylor (1988) examined the continuum of services schools provide to students; he claims they are an organizational attribute that traps individuals with disabilities inside a pernicious logic emphasizing more restrictive placement. This type of perspective, internal to schools and school systems, has had a number of consequences for the debate over mainstreaming and inclusion. The first consequence is a focus on comparison groups within schools. The "normalization" principle, popularized in the United States by Wolfensberger (1972), focused on the provocative concept (at the time) that individuals with disabilities should have experiences similar to their peers and have contact with peers in the environment of nondisabled peers. The internal perspective on placement of individuals with disabilities within school systems applies that concept to schools in a parallel manner, suggesting that individuals with disabilities need to be with age mates in the general education classroom (e.g., Stainback & Stainback, 1992).

A second consequence of the internal perspectives is the advocacy tactic of maximizing outcomes within the organizational structure of schools. One certainly would hope that those interested in welfare and students with disabilities would try to maximize outcomes, but occasionally this leads to inconsistencies. For example, many advocates, including lawyers, who have argued for full inclusion of students with disabilities within the general education class have also represented or supported parents seeking public payment for private special education schools. This practice has become a broader public policy in one state. As of spring 2001 Florida has a statewide voucher program not only for children zoned for schools labeled failing but also for children with disabilities, and the more than one thousand children in the disability voucher program dwarfed the approximately fifty in the failing-schools voucher program during the 2000–2001 school year (Hegarty, 2001). Ironically, both public-school choice programs (such as the charter school movement) and the disabilities voucher program in Florida can promote school choice as a way of separating individuals with disabilities from the general classroom environment.

External Perspectives

In contrast to internal perspectives on placement issues, one can focus instead on the role of schools in society at large and see the placement issues in that context, looking at schools from the outside. A few consequences follow. First, the common system of age grading that exists in the schools today, a system that has been the basis for comparison between students with disabilities and their same-age peers, is an institutional quirk (if often mirrored elsewhere in society, as Chudacoff, 1989, writes). Should this quirk be the basis for all comparisons among children? Instead, perhaps we should look at age–peer comparisons as something that requires a concrete justification. A *purpose-specific comparison* may certainly be based on grading age. For example, intervention in poor reading is appropriate when comparing one eight-year-old to other eight-year-olds because learning the general curriculum in school requires relatively high literacy skills (as measured by common texts used in middle and high schools—e.g., Kinder, Bursuck, & Epstein, 1992). Thus, intervention to promote literacy also promotes the general curriculum. At other times, however, the appropriate target need not be same-age peers. Students whom we may not expect to generalize skills need those skills taught in the location and with people where students need to perform adequately. Thus, the purpose-specific comparison may be the general adult population, or the hypothetical (target) same individual *with* the skills, in the environment where using those skills is necessary and appropriate. The acculturation of children who are deaf illustrates a third way of applying the notion of a purpose-specific comparison. Those who defend deaf culture (e.g., Cohen, 1994; Lane, 1994) argue that acculturating children into that culture requires their having consistent contact with people of all ages who are deaf; thus, the purpose-specific peers are those who are deaf.

A second consequence of the external perspective is the realization that outside factors, including the ability and willingness of general educators to accommodate the needs of students with disabilities, influence schools greatly. For example, the nationalization of education debate, which has promoted the use of high-stakes tests, has created an environment that, as discussed earlier, may be in the interests of students with disabilities (which we hope) and could encourage the development of professional skills that focus on individual children (which we think would be logical). We understand, however, that little of the recent discussion about standardized tests or the latest reading statistics from the National Assessment of Educational Progress (Donahue, Finnegan, Lutkus, Allen, & Campbell, 2001) has focused on students with disabilities, and we know that focusing on special education as a policy goal is a tricky political maneuver. Reforming schools in the interests of children with disabilities will require a broad coalition capable of influencing national debates. That fact is well recognized by those with different perspectives on placement of students with disabilities in schools, but we have rarely seen such a coalition with a broad impact on public policy, though individual politicians can occasionally raise concerns about issues (such as Senator Jim Jeffords's insistence in the spring of 2001 that the federal government fulfill its promise from 1975 of providing 40 percent of special education funding) (Miller, 2001; Reagon, 1995).

Finally, an external perspective requires us to recognize that schools are now in the midst of the greatest organizational shakeup in the last 150 years, and these changes—including the promotion of privatization, the charter school movement, the shrinking of desegregation as a policy tool, and the renewed push toward making schools function more like businesses—may affect the debate over placement far more than the converse. The priority of those who would emphasize the inclusion of children in the general education environment, widely differentiated goals for children that are, ideally, achieved in the same place, may be at odds with the current movement that emphasizes universal goals in different places. During the fall 2000 term, the parent of one of our students chose to use one of these "different places" to benefit her child with a disability, even though she felt uncomfortable with privatization as public policy. During the semester, this mother withdrew her son from the public schools of west central

Florida and started negotiating a place for him in a private school that focuses on children with learning disabilities and attention-deficit disorder. She explained that she was and had always been a supporter of public schools and was uncomfortable with the use of vouchers for her own child. However, she explained, she could not sacrifice her own child's interests for her own principles. For her, the goals that she had for her individual child were primary, and placement was a tool to serve these ends.

QUESTIONS FOR FURTHER DISCUSSION

1. What is the primary argument within special education over what the term *least restrictive agreement* means? How is the professional debate over the meaning of the term different from the judicial decision-making process?

2. Do you agree with the authors' concerns about the manifestation hearing process? Why or why not?

3. How do you think the new requirements for accountability in all of K–12 education (the federal No Child Left Behind Act or your own state's accountability policies) will interact with decisions on placement of students with disabilities?

4. Do you agree with the authors' suggestion of "purpose-specific comparisons" in deciding who the nondisabled peer population is for an individual student with a disability? Why or why not?

REFERENCES

Alpert, B. (1996, May 25). Schools request right to remove discipline cases. *Cleveland Plain Dealer,* p. 2A.

Anderson-Inman, L. (1981). Transenvironmental programming: Promoting success in the regular class by maximizing the effect of resource room assistance. *Journal of Special Education Technology, 4,* 3–12.

Anderson-Inman, L. (1986). Bridging the gap: Student-centered strategies for promoting the transfer of learning. *Exceptional Children, 52,* 562–572.

Baker, J. M., & Zigmond, N. (1990). Are regular education classes equipped to accommodate students with learning disabilities? *Exceptional Children, 56,* 515–526.

Becker, G. (1993). Human capital revisited. In G. Becker, *Human capital: A theoretical and empirical analysis, with special reference to education* (3rd ed., pp. 15–25). Chicago: University of Chicago Press.

Bowles, S., & Gintis, H. (1976). *Schooling in capitalist America: Educational reform and the contradictions of economic life.* New York: Basic Books.

Braaten, S., Kauffman, J., Braaten, B., Polsgrove, L., & Nelson, M. (1988). The regular education initiative: Patent medicine for behavioral disorders. *Exceptional Children, 55,* 21–27.

Brown v. Board of Education, 347 U.S. 483 (1954).

Brown, L., Branston, M. B., Hamre-Nietupski, S., Pumpian, I., Certo, N., & Gruenewald, L. (1979). A strategy for developing chronological-age-appropriate and functional curricular content for severely handicapped adolescents and young adults. *Journal of Special Education, 13*(1), 81–90.

Brown, L., Nisbet, J., Ford, A., Sweet, M., Shiraga, B., York, J., & Loomis, R. (1983). The critical need for nonschool instruction in educational programs for severely handicapped students. *Journal of the Association for Persons with Severe Handicaps, 8*(3), 71–77.

Brown, L., Schwarz, P., Udvari-Solner, A., & Kampschroer, E. F. (1991). How much time should students with severe intellectual disabilities spend in regular education classrooms and elsewhere? *Journal of the Association for Persons with Severe Handicaps, 16*(1), 39–47.

Carlberg, C., & Kavale, K. (1980). The efficacy of special versus regular class placement for exceptional children: A meta-analysis. *Journal of Special Education, 14,* 295–305.

Carnine, D. W., & Kameenui, E. J. (1990). The general education initiative and children with special needs: A false dilemma in the face of true problems. *Journal of Learning Disabilities, 23,* 141–148.

Chudacoff, H. P. (1989). *How old are you? Age conscious-*

ness in American culture. Princeton, NJ: Princeton University Press.

Cohen, L. H. (1994). *Train go sorry: Inside a deaf world.* Boston: Houghton Mifflin.

Coles, R. (1967). *Children of crisis: A study of courage and fear.* Boston: Little, Brown.

Daniel R. R. v. State Board of Education, 874 F.2d 1036 (5th Cir. 1989).

Donahue, P. L., Finnegan, R. J., Lutkus, A. D., Allen, N. L., & Campbell, J. R. (2001). *The nation's report card: Fourth-grade reading 2000.* Washington, DC: U.S. Department of Education. Available on-line at http://nces.ed.gov/nationsreportcard/pdf/main2000/2001499.pdf.

Dorn, S. (1998). The political legacy of school accountability systems. *Education Policy Analysis Archives, 6*(1), entire issue. Available on-line at http://epaa.asu.edu/epaa/v6n1.html.

Dorn, S. (1999). *The history of special education in Nashville, Tennessee, 1940-1990.* Final report prepared for the U.S. Office of Special Education Programs.

Duane, A., Plater-Zyberk, E., & Speck, J. (2000). *Suburban nation: The rise of sprawl and the decline of the American dream.* Berkeley: North Point Press.

Education for All Handicapped Children Act of 1975, 20 U.S.C. §1400 *et seq.* (1975).

Espin, C. A., Deno, S. L., & Albayrak-Kaymak, D. (1998). Individualized education programs in resource and inclusive settings: How "individualized" are they? *Journal of Special Education, 32,* 164–174.

Farlow, L. J., & Snell, M. E. (1989). Teacher use of student performance data to make instructional decisions: Practices in programs for students with moderate to profound disabilities. *Journal of the Association for Persons with Severe Handicaps, 14,* 13–22.

Ferguson, D. L. (1995). The real challenge of inclusion: Confessions of a "rabid inclusionist." *Phi Delta Kappan, 77,* 281–287.

Fuchs, D., & Fuchs, L. (1991). Framing the REI debate: Abolitionists versus conservationists. In J. W. Lloyd, N. N. Singh, & A. C. Repp (Eds.), *The regular education initiative: Alternative perspectives on concepts, issues, and models* (pp. 241–255). Sycamore, IL: Sycamore.

Fuchs, D., & Fuchs, L. S. (1994). Inclusive schools movement and the radicalization of special education reform. *Exceptional Children, 60,* 294–309.

Fuchs, D., & Fuchs, L. S. (1995). Counterpoint: Special education—Ineffective? Immoral? *Exceptional Children, 61,* 303–305.

Fuchs, D., & Fuchs, L. S. (1998). Competing visions for educating students with disabilities: Inclusion versus full inclusion. *Childhood Education, 74,* 309–316.

Fuchs, D., Fuchs, L. S., & Fernstrom, P. (1992). Case-by-case reintegration of students with learning disabilities. *Elementary School Journal, 92,* 261–281.

Fuchs, D., Fuchs, L. S., & Fernstrom, P. (1993). A conservative approach to special education reform: Mainstreaming through transenvironmental programming and curriculum-based measurement. *American Educational Research Journal, 30,* 149–177.

Fuchs, D., Fuchs, L. S., Fernstrom, P., & Hohn, M. (1991). Toward a responsible reintegration of behaviorally disordered students. *Behavioral Disorders, 16,* 133–147.

Fuchs, L. S., & Fuchs, D. (1985). The importance of goal ambitiousness and goal mastery to student achievement. *Exceptional Children, 52,* 63–71.

Gartner, A., & Lipsky, K. (1987). Beyond special education: Toward a quality system for all students. *Harvard Education Review, 57,* 367–395.

Gerber, M. M. (1988). Weighing the regular education initiative: Recent calls for change lead to "slippery slope." *Education Week, 7*(32), 28, 36.

Gerber, M. M., & Semmel, M. I. (1984). Teacher as imperfect test: Reconceptualizing the referral process. *Educational Psychologist, 19,* 137–148.

Goffman, E. (1963). *Stigma.* Englewood Cliffs, NJ: Prentice-Hall.

Goodman, P. (1964). *Compulsory mis-education.* New York: Horizon Press.

Gresham, F., Evans, S., & Elliott, S. N. (1988). Self-efficacy differences among mildly handicapped, gifted, and nonhandicapped students. *Journal of Special Education, 22,* 231–241.

Gutmann, A. (1987). *Democratic education.* Princeton, NJ: Princeton University Press.

Hallahan, D. P., Kauffman, J. M., Lloyd, J. W., & McKinney, J. D. (1988). Introduction to the series: Questions about the regular education initiative. *Journal of Learning Disabilities, 21,* 3–5.

Hartmann v. Loudoun County, 26 IDELR 167 (4th Cir. 1997).

Hartwig, E. P., & Ruesch, G. M. (2000). Disciplining students in special education. *Journal of Special Education, 33,* 240–247.

Hegarty, S. (2001, February 26). Learning disabled latch onto vouchers. *St. Petersburg Times,* pp. 1B, 7B.

Honig v. Doe, 484 U.S. 305 (1988).

Illich, I. (1971). *Deschooling society.* New York: Harper & Row.

Individuals with Disabilities Act Amendments of 1997, 20 U.S.C. §1400 *et seq.* (1977).

Jackson, P. W. (1968). *Life in classrooms.* New York: Holt, Rinehart & Winston.

Jenkins, J. R., & Heinen, A. (1989). Students' preferences for service delivery: Pull-out, in-class, or integrated models. *Exceptional Children, 55,* 516–523.

Johnson, J. L. (1969). Special education and the inner city: A challenge for the future or another means for cooling the mark out? *Journal of Special Education, 3,* 241–251.

Kauffman, J. M. (1989). The regular education initiative as Reagan-Bush education policy: A trickle-down theory of education of the hard-to-teach. *Journal of Special Education, 23,* 256–278.

Kauffman, J. M. (1992). School reform disorder: Alternative responses to nonsense. *Journal of Behavioral Education, 2,* 157–174.

Kavale, K. A., & Forness, S. R. (2000). History, rhetoric, and reality: Analysis of the inclusion debate. *Remedial and Special Education, 21*(5), 279–296.

Kinder, D., Bursuck, B., & Epstein, M. (1992). An evaluation of history textbooks. *Journal of Special Education, 25,* 472–491.

Kozleski, E. B., & Jackson, L. (1993). Taylor's story: Full inclusion in her neighborhood elementary school. *Exceptionality, 4,* 153–175.

Kunstler, J. H. (1996, September). Home from nowhere. *Atlantic Monthly,* pp. 43–59. Retrieved April 9, 2001, from http://www.theatlantic.com/issues/96sep/kunstler/kunstler.htm.

Lane, H. (1994).The education of deaf children: Drowning in the mainstream and the sidestream. In J. M. Kauffman & D. P. Hallahan (Eds.), *The illusion of full inclusion: A comprehensive critique of a current special education bandwagon* (pp. 275–287). Austin, TX: Pro-Ed.

Letter to Boggus, 20 IDELR 625 (OSEP 1993).

Lipsky, D. K., & Gartner, A. (1989). *Beyond separate education: Quality education for all.* Baltimore, MD: Paul H. Brookes.

Lipsky, D. K., & Gartner, A. (1991). Restructuring for quality. In J. W. Lloyd, A. C. Repp, & N. N. Singh (Eds.), *The Regular Education Initiative: Alternative perspectives on concepts, issues, and models* (pp. 43–56). Sycamore, IL: Sycamore.

Mastropieri, M., Scruggs, T. E., & Butcher, K. (1997). How effective is inquiry learning for students with mild disabilities? *Journal of Special Education, 31*(2), 199–211.

May, S. (Ed.). (1999). *Critical multiculturalism: Rethinking multicultural and antiracist education.* Levittown, PA: Falmer Press.

Meier, D. (1995). *The power of their ideas: Lessons for America from a small school in Harlem.* Boston: Beacon Press.

Mercer, J. R. (1973). *Labeling the mentally retarded: Clinical and social system perspectives on mental retardation.* Berkeley: University of California Press.

Miller, G. (2001, April 6). GOP senator proves the power of one. *Los Angeles Times,* p. 21.

New York Commissioner of Education. (1999). Professional development plans. Amended regulations of the Commissioner of Education §100.2 (dd).

Orfield, G., Eaton, S. E., & the Harvard Project on School Desegregation. (1996). *Dismantling desegregation: The quiet reversal of Brown v. Board of Education.* New York: The Free Press.

Reagon, B. J. (1995). Coalition politics: Turning the century. In M. L. Andersen & P. H. Collins (Eds.), *Race, class, and gender: An anthology* (2nd ed., pp. 540–546). Belmont, CA: Wadsworth.

Reynolds, M. C., Wang, M. C., & Walberg, H. J. (1987). The necessary restructuring of special and general education. *Exceptional Children, 53,* 391–398.

Roach, V. (1995). Supporting inclusion: Beyond the rhetoric. *Phi Delta Kappan, 77,* 295–299.

Roberts, R., & Mather, N. (1995). The return of students with learning disabilities to regular classrooms: A sellout? *Learning Disabilities Research and Practice, 10,* 46–58.

Roncker v. Walter, 700 F. 2d 1058n (5th Cir. 1983).

Sacramento City Unified School District v. Rachel H., 14 Fed 1398 (9th Cir. 1994).

School Community Professional Development Act, *Florida Statutes* §231.600 *et seq.* (1995).

Shepard, L. A., & Smith, M. L. (Eds.). (1989). *Flunking grades: Research and policies on retention.* New York: Falmer Press.

Shinn, M. R., Habedank, L., Rodden-Nord, K., & Kautsen, N. (1993). Using curriculum-based measurement to identify potential candidates for reintegration into general education. *Journal of Special Education, 27,* 202–221.

Shinn, M. R., Powell-Smith, K. A., & Good, R. H. (1996). Evaluating the effects of responsible reintegration into general education for students with mild disabilities on a case-by-case basis. *School Psychology Review, 4,* 519–539.

Shinn, M. R., Powell-Smith, K. A., Good, R. H., & Baker, S. (1997). The effects of reintegration into general education reading instruction for students with mild disabilities. *Exceptional Children, 64,* 59–79.

Snell, M. E., & Drake, G. P. (1994). Replacing cascades with supported education. *Journal of Special Education, 27,* 393–409.

Stainback, S., & Stainback, W. (1987). Integration versus cooperation: A commentary on "Educating children with learning problems: A shared responsibility." *Exceptional Children, 54,* 66–68.

Stainback, S., & Stainback, W. (1992). *Curriculum considerations in inclusive classrooms: Facilitating learning for all students.* Baltimore, MD: Paul H. Brookes.

Taylor, S. J. (1988). Caught in the continuum: A critical analysis of the principle of the least restrictive environment. *Journal of the Association for Persons with Severe Handicaps, 13,* 41–53.

Taylor, S. J. (1995). On rhetoric: A response to Fuchs and Fuchs. *Exceptional Children, 61,* 301–302.

Thousand, J., & Villa, R. (1990). Strategies for educating learners with severe disabilities within their local home schools and communities. *Focus on Exceptional Children, 23,* 1–25.

U.S. Department of Education. (2000). *Twenty-second annual report to Congress on the implementation of the Individuals with Disabilities Education Act.* Washington, DC: Author.

Vaughn, S., Schumm, J. S., Klingner, J., & Saumall, L. (1995). Students' views of instructional practices: Implications for inclusion. *Learning Disability Quarterly, 18,* 236–248.

Wang, M. C., & Walberg, H. J. (1988). The four fallacies of segregationism. *Exceptional Children, 55,* 128–137.

Weatherley, R. (1979). *Reforming special education: Policy implementation from state level to street level.* Cambridge, MA: MIT Press.

Wolfensberger, W. (1972). *The principles of normalization in human services.* Toronto: National Institute on Mental Retardation.

Wood, M. (1998). Whose job is it anyway? Educational roles in inclusion. *Exceptional Children, 64,* 181–195.

Yell, M. L. (1989). *Honig v. Doe:* The suspension and expulsion of handicapped students. *Exceptional Children, 56,* 60–69.

Yell, M. L. (1995). The least restrictive environment mandate and the courts: Judicial activism or judicial restraint? *Exceptional Children, 61,* 578–581.

Yell, M. L., & Drasgow, E. (1999). A legal analysis of inclusion. *Preventing School Failure, 43,* 118–123.

Yell, M. L., & Drasgow, E. (2000). Litigating a free appropriate public education: The Lovaas hearings and cases. *Journal of Special Education, 33,* 205–214.

Yell, M. L., & Shriner, G. G. (1998). The discipline of students with disabilities: Requirements of the IDEA Amendments of 1997. *Education and Treatment of Children, 21,* 246–257.

Zigmond, N., & Baker, J. N. (1994). Is the mainstream a more appropriate educational setting for Randy? A case study of one student with learning disabilities. *Learning Disabilities Research and Practice, 9,* 108–117.

Zigmond, N., Jenkins, J., Fuchs, L. S., Deno, S., Fuchs, D., Baker, J. N., Jenkins, L., & Couthino, M. (1995). Special education in restructured schools: Findings from three multi-year studies. *Phi Delta Kappan, 76,* 531–540.

MULTICULTURAL PERSPECTIVES IN SPECIAL EDUCATION

A Call for Responsibility in Research, Practice, and Teacher Preparation

AUDREY McCRAY SORRELLS

University of Texas at Austin

GWENDOLYN WEBB-JOHNSON

University of Texas at Austin

BRENDA L. TOWNSEND

University of South Florida

SCENARIO

Ayinde strolls into his fifth-period English class. He is a 13-year-old African American male who is vervistic and deeply steeped in an oral tradition. Ms. Cautious learned these descriptors of African American learners at a multicultural workshop last week. She is very concerned, however. She clearly sees some of the patterns of behavior described in the workshop, but she worries about students like Ayinde. He was included in her class as a result of an effort to promote inclusion for students with behavioral disorders. Ayinde has been in special education settings for the past five years. The multidisciplinary team documented his high intelligence, but Ayinde's behavior is absolutely unacceptable according to Ms. Cautious. He is constantly talking and moving during class. The way he walks is so arrogant. She believes he is just trying to get the attention of his peers. She has been trying to increase the number of times she calls on Ayinde. Ms. Cautious really wants to give him a chance to demonstrate his way of "knowing," but she is so frustrated. Why should she pay closer attention to differences when she knows learners like Ayinde are capable of behaving like the majority of learners in school? He needs to follow her instructions.

The bell rings as Ayinde straddles the seat and takes out his novel. He begins to rock in the chair. Ms. Cautious quickly reminds the entire class, "Remember how we are expected to be seated in this freshman classroom. Young men and young women are expected to seat themselves appropriately. Now, let's take out our books."

Ms. Cautious: *Ayinde, why don't we begin with you? I won't talk about the way you sat down, but I do hope you have your homework today. Have you read today's assignment?*

Ayinde: *Yea, Ms. Cautious. Why you always picking on me, I just sat down.*

Ms. Cautious: *Ayinde! [in a frustrated tone]*

Ayinde: *I said, yes, I read.*

Ms. Cautious: *Good, let's begin. What did you think about the ending to* Of Mice and Men*?*

Ayinde: *It was a real trip how George took Lennie out. I mean why he have to kill him?"*

[Several students look up]. "He killed Lennie?"

Ayinde: *Yea, man. It was a trip. You know I guess he thought he was doing the right thing, but man. It was a trip. It made me think about his brain probably spattering all over the place. Did you know that even though the brain only weighs about three pounds, it's all spongy and stuff? Can you imagine? It pumps like 198 gallons of blood through it everyday. I wonder how much was pumping through when Lennie got shot. I wonder if you could see all of those billion neurons splattered all over the place.*

Ms. Cautious interrupts: *Ayinde, are you on the topic? I dare say talk about a splattered brain is clearly not appropriate.*

Ayinde: *Excuse me Ms. Cautious, I was on the topic. You always tripping and interrupting. You ask a question and then you can't wait 'til I finish.*

Ms. Cautious: *Are you getting smart young man? You really need to watch your language. Standard English is the mode for this classroom.*

Ayinde [muttering under his breath]: *I'm not getting smart, I am smart, but you know you work my nerves.*

Ms. Cautious: *What did you say young man? I believe I have had quite enough. Maybe yet another trip to the office will teach you the importance of good manners and staying on the topic at hand.*

[Ms. Cautious writes Ayinde a pass to the office. Ayinde leaves the classroom softly singing, Ya'll go' make me lose my mind, up in here, up in here] (Webb-Johnson, 2002, pp. 55–56).

This scenario includes concerns often raised in discussions about effective pedagogy for students with disabilities who come from culturally and linguistically diverse backgrounds (also referred to as "students of color"). In today's education system, there are monumental demands being made of educators, families, and students as service providers strive to provide pedagogy to serve and benefit all learners. The sociopolitical context of schooling (Nieto, 1999) highlights the importance of teachers like Ms. Cautious understanding the challenges of teaching in meaningful ways and their responsibility for doing so. Teachers must learn to teach students what is expected of them in an inclusive, multicultural, pluralistic, and demo-cratic society (Gay, 2000; Howard, 1999; Ladson-Billings, 2001, 2002; Nieto, 1999). At the same time, teachers must learn to affirm students for the dynamic cultures, strengths, and skills they bring to the classroom (Neal, McCray, Webb-Johnson, & Bridgest, 2003).

However, as depicted in the scenario, teaching well and affirming students with dis-abilities, regardless of their ethnic or cultural backgrounds, can become daunting tasks for the teacher inadequately prepared for student diversity and can yield negative and incomplete schooling for students. Although Ms. Cautious attempted to teach and interact with Ayinde by applying tenets of multiculturalism she had "acquired" during a workshop on diversity, she misunderstood Ayinde's behaviors and mishandled the situation as a result. The outcome was frustration and a sense of hopelessness and resignation for Ms. Cautious, and missed opportu-nities for quality instruction for Ayinde because he was sent to the office twice in one week. He also missed an important class discussion, and this resulted in his poor performance on an English exam at the end of the week.

As you read this classroom scene, you may have considered the appropriateness of both Ayinde's behavior and Ms. Cautious's reactions to his behavior. For example, was it necessary for Ms. Cautious to single out Ayinde because of the way he walked, talked, and sat down in his chair? Was it appropriate to interrupt his response to her question? Were Ayinde's re-sponses appropriate? Should Ayinde, as suspected by several teachers on his individualized education plan (IEP) team, be returned to a self-contained setting? You may have found it easiest to respond to such challenges in terms of "best practices," or you may have simply concluded that a student's responsibility is to appropriately respond to a teacher's question. Whether you are a novice or veteran teacher, you may have felt that Ms. Cautious should have waited to see where Ayinde was going with his story, but you may also have believed that Ayinde's attitude was unnecessary. Still, you may have wanted more information before draw-ing any meaningful conclusions. All of these are important questions for, and plausible reac-tions from, educators responsible for teaching in classrooms made up of diverse learners with disabilities.

Nonetheless, a much larger set of issues, and the focus of this chapter, underlies Ms. Cautious's reactions to Ayinde. These issues drive the need to examine existing models of instruction and teaching methods in special education and to prepare teachers to provide in-struction that is unique, individualized, and culturally responsive for all students with disabili-ties. For example, can classroom teachers, whether in general or special education, of a diverse group of students with perceived or real disabilities be held responsible for their stu-dents' academic success without knowing their cognitive, psychosocial, or behavioral charac-teristics or how to respond to their ethnic, cultural, and linguistic ethos? Can teachers realistically and effectively teach these students in the absence of research-based teaching grounded in cultural responsive pedagogy, particularly when there is convergence of race, language, culture, socioeconomic status, and disability (Bos & Fletcher, 1997; McCray & Garcia, 2002; Pugach, 2001)? How do students and teachers from incongruent backgrounds and with divergent perspectives of schooling get to a point where the goals for student high achievement and teacher high quality are met? What must teachers know about multicultural education, inclusive general education, and special education in order to be effective? And, finally, where does the responsibility rest for ensuring that teachers acquire, master, and sustain cultural awareness, responsiveness, and best practices? In this chapter, we discuss two overarching needs related to these questions: (1) the need to identify research-based culturally responsive instruction in special education service delivery, and (2) the need for multicultural teacher preparation to improve the quality of classroom teachers responsible for teaching culturally and linguistically diverse students with disabilities. We begin with an overview of demographic shifts in special education and ensuing challenges for special educators; we follow this with a discussion of multicultural teacher preparation and special education teacher training programs nationwide.

WHY MULTICULTURALISM REMAINS A PROMINENT CHALLENGE FOR SPECIAL EDUCATORS

The forecast for inclusion of multicultural perspectives in special education service delivery is dismal given the low percentage of certified teachers and university faculty who come from culturally and linguistically diverse backgrounds and the low priority of diversity and diverse groups in special education research. The public schools are becoming increasingly ethnically diverse, yet the pool of K–12 teachers is made up primarily of European Americans (U.S. Department of Education, 2002b). In contrast, over one-third of the school-age population come from ethnically and linguistically diverse backgrounds. In many large urban school districts ethnically and linguistically diverse learners already represent the majority student population. Hence, teachers' cultural and linguistic backgrounds bear little resemblance to those of the students they serve (Gay, 2000), and they often bring with them limited knowledge in cultural differences. In addition, although the call for more teachers from culturally and linguistically diverse backgrounds increases, there is no guarantee that these teachers will be any more prepared to teach diverse learners than their European American colleagues. Teacher education programs must meet this challenge by providing *all* teachers with the knowledge base, skills, and experiences to teach *all* children equitably and effectively.

Whether they are in general or special education, students of color are consistently experiencing academic failure, and the education system is failing to address this by adequately delivering educational services to them. When compared with their European American peers, students of color disproportionately experience (1) failure in academic achievement, (2) suspensions and expulsions, (3) corporal punishment in school, (4) dropout, and (5) placement in special education (Children's Defense Fund, 1999; U.S. Department of Education, 2002a).

As a result of educators' indifference to student diversity in the classroom or their inability to reach diverse learners, many culturally and linguistically diverse students continue to perform poorly on standardized tests, receive poorer grades than their European American and Asian and Asian American counterparts, and are subjected to consistently lowered expectations in both general and special education settings. Academically, they continue to perform dismally in reading and mathematics: reading achievement scores indicate that only 7 percent to 24 percent of culturally and linguistically diverse learners demonstrate proficiency; their mathematics scores indicate a 3 percent to 9 percent proficiency rate (U.S. Department of Education, 2002a). Generally, the subsequent outcome of low achievement in general education is referral to and placement in programs for students with disabilities.

Indeed, many students of color, particularly African Americans and Native Americans, are disproportionately referred to and placed in special education settings compared with their representation in the overall population (U.S. Department of Education, 2002a). Nonetheless, notwithstanding the miseducation found in many general education environments, failure often occurs when students are placed in special education programs. Furthermore, unequal delivery of quality instruction and social skills development, the exclusion of appropriate assessments, and the lack of accountability for student outcomes often precipitate lifelong hardship for culturally and linguistically diverse students with disabilities and for their families during and after school (see, e.g., Keith & McCray, 2002; McCray, Vaughn, & Neal, 2001). Of the students each year who receive special education services for emotional disturbance, for example, 50 percent drop out of school (U.S. Department of Education, 2002b).

Although the Individuals with Disabilities Education Act (IDEA, 1997) mandates the inclusion, where appropriate, of children with disabilities in the statewide assessment process, there persists a desire by some school systems to exclude identified students from these standard assessment processes, even in the area of "soft" or high-incidence disability categories (e.g., learning disabilities, mental retardation, emotional disturbance). In addition, too few culturally and linguistically diverse students are provided with research-based, culturally responsive best practices (Bos & Fletcher, 1997; Irvine, 2002); too many of them are placed in classrooms with teachers not fully qualified to deliver multicultural general or special education services. Most teachers lack the confidence and knowledge to apply the culturally responsive teaching needed to construct meaningful student outcomes (Gay, 2000; Irvine & Armento, 2001; Townsend, 2002). Needless to say, diversity in race/ethnicity, culture, language, socioeconomic status, and ability among students in special education classrooms has not resulted in sound, sustained teacher preparation or identification of research-based practices in special education classrooms consistent with the low academic performance and behavior/social needs of students of color with disabilities.

It appears that public schools may be failing masses of children and youth with disabilities from diverse cultural and linguistic backgrounds because educators are failing to connect tenets found in multicultural, general, and special education. Although educational research has addressed the impact of diversity in general education settings and the need for multicultural education to enhance diverse learners' school performance (Banks & Banks, 2002), seldom has the field systematically addressed the impact of multicultural education on the school achievement of diverse learners with perceived or real disabilities. Yet without systematic and critical examination of culturally responsive practice in special education (Kea, Cartledge, & Bowman, 2002) grounded in sociocultural paradigms (Bos & Fletcher, 1997; Gay, 2002; Pugach, 2001), many culturally and linguistically diverse students with disabilities are not likely to benefit from access to the general education curriculum or from special education instruction. Moreover, the field is not likely to witness a shift in historic and systemic trends of incomplete school success for culturally and linguistically diverse youth at risk and with disabilities without transforming "best practices" in special and general education.

Also, there needs to be a transformation in the way teachers are prepared for student diversity and disability. Researchers need to evaluate how they conduct and interpret special education research to inform and sustain best practices for diverse students with myriad learning abilities and needs. Maintaining the status quo in research and teacher training will render most teachers helpless and unable to assume their charge to teach culturally and linguistically diverse students in responsive ways; they will continue to struggle to connect with students such as Ayinde and to assist them in realizing meaningful academic and social outcomes. This is true even of a teacher like Ms. Cautious, who cares about but is unprepared to work with all students. Such teachers are destined to make instructional decisions that subsequently result in missed opportunities, and these lead to continued school failure, especially in special education.

THE ABSENCE OF MULTICULTURALISM AS A PRIORITY IN SPECIAL EDUCATION TEACHER PREPARATION PROGRAMS

Since most teacher education programs have not infused multicultural content throughout their courses and field experiences, they have not prepared teachers for the increased student diversity and disabilities in urban, rural, and suburban classrooms (Delpit, 1995, 2000). Personnel preparation and leadership programs that have not deliberately incorporated culturally responsive teaching and research strategies into the curriculum and field experiences will not contribute to developing higher teacher quality for all children or improving outcomes for all children at risk for or with disabilities.

We conducted a content analysis of teacher preparation programs at the nation's top ten graduate schools in special education in 2002, as determined by *U.S. News & World Report*. We obtained doctoral-level education program course descriptions and looked for those focusing on culture, ethnicity, race, or poverty. We considered any course that contained these terms; we did not consider any special topic courses that were not listed in the school's catalog or on-line descriptions. Our findings were not promising. Only two of the universities surveyed offered courses containing these terms—The University of Texas at Austin and the University of Virginia. The University of Texas listed six required courses and the University of Virginia listed one required course focusing on multicultural/diversity issues.

We conducted a similar content analysis on the abstracts of leadership projects funded by the Office of Special Education Programs (OSEP). We reviewed sixty-six abstracts for terms such as *diversity, urban, multicultural education, ethnicity, minority, culture,* or any other term that would suggest the project would prepare participants for working with multicultural populations. Of the sixty-six abstracts reviewed, only fifteen included at least one of those terms. Although the number of teacher preparation programs whose titles or descriptions contain these terms seems to be increasing, inadequate emphasis is being placed on this topic given the discrepancy between teaching styles and learning styles apparent in the education of children from culturally, linguistically, and socially diverse backgrounds. To reverse negative educational trends for students with disabilities who come from culturally and linguistically diverse backgrounds, personnel preparation programs must move away from "business as usual" and toward providing substantive multicultural instruction so that teachers are qualified to work with all learners with disabilities. Teacher quality and performance must be linked to what we know about effectively teaching culturally and linguistically diverse students with disabilities.

MULTICULTURAL SPECIAL EDUCATION RESEARCH: RETHINKING "BEST PRACTICES"

The research community has not yet established race, ethnicity, culture, and language as legitimate content areas in the special education knowledge base (Pugach, 2001) or in its research agendas (Artiles, Trent, & Kuan, 1997; Bos & Fletcher, 1997; McCray & Garcia, 2002). Although much attention has been given to identifying and labeling diverse students with disabilities, much less attention has been given to developing research-based interventions and instructional strategies that are culturally and linguistically appropriate. To date, special education scholars have not paid enough attention to "research within the discourse on race, class, culture, and language [or] acknowledge[d] that the context within which all disability exists is always an individual's socio-culture" (Pugach, 2001, p. 448). According to Pugach, addressing issues of diversity without considering race, class, culture, and language will lead to misconceptions of disability and further subject culturally and linguistically diverse learners to meaningless learning opportunity and powerlessness. She further concludes that both context and multiple voices must inform research in special education. To address issues that provide quality personnel and research-based culturally responsive best practices in special education, researchers must examine disability within its full sociocultural context and include all variables that affect learning. The Diversity Committee of the Council for Exceptional Children–Division of Research (CEC-DR) recently posited, "The emphasis on context when conducting research with diverse populations is essential, especially given the complexity and shifting nature of interactions among political forces, institutions, communities, families, and children" (Klingner, 2003, p. 3). The committee cited further in their position statement:

> These features require attention to the physical, social, cultural, economic, and historical environment in the research process because these contextual factors often influence results in significant ways . . . the nature of teaching and learning [is] so complex, attention to context is especially critical for understanding the extent to which theories and findings may generalize to other times, places, and populations." (Shavelson & Towne, 2002, p. 5)

Other researchers also have examined the state of multicultural special education research. In a quantitative and qualitative analysis of the existing professional literature on multicultural special education published over the past twenty-seven years (1975–2002), McCray and Garcia (2002) documented omissions in the empirical research to provide directions for further research in multicultural and bilingual special education. Specifically, they found that less than 5 percent of the studies and articles published in five major special education journals addressed the issue of cultural and linguistic diversity. Table 1 lists the categories and topic areas these articles addressed.

Of the studies they reviewed, 55 percent addressed disability and race/ethnicity as a monolithic construct, and 33 percent focused on cross-categorical issues. In all of the articles people of color were referred to as "nonwhite" and were collapsed into cross-categorical special education entities rather than single and distinct categories of disability. Fifty percent of the articles described empirical research. The studies were three times as likely to be quantitative analyses rather than qualitative analyses across the issues examined. The proportion of articles focusing on particular racial/ethnic groups or special education categories ranged

TABLE 1   Research Topics Addressed in Multicultural Special Education, 1975–2002

TOPIC	PERCENTAGE OF ARTICLES ADDRESSING TOPIC
Multiethnic groups (more than one population addressed)	55
Empirical studies	50
Cross-categorical disability areas	33
Identification and assessment	32
Speech and language	26
Theoretical/conceptual	24
Learning disabilities	21
Services and treatment	19
African American	19
Hispanic American	18
Teacher preparation and teacher education	14
Position papers	11
Native American and Asian American	<3

from less than 3 percent to 32 percent. This examination of the knowledge base in multicultural special education confirms the dearth of sociocultural research on race, ethnicity, culture, and language. For example, no inquiries focused specifically on culturally and linguistically diverse youth who do have disabilities, nor was there any information about culturally responsive services that are beneficial to the development and academic success of these students.

While McCray and Garcia's literature analysis confirms that research in multicultural special education has been limited, their analysis also highlights the need for research directions around four themes: (1) authenticity, legitimacy, and multiplicity of voices; (2) validation of culturally and linguistically responsive special education service delivery models and interventions; (3) multicultural preparation of special educators; and (4) underserved populations in special education. These themes suggest that the perspectives of "insiders" (e.g., scholars of color, women, individuals with disabilities) are important in closing the existing gaps in the special education knowledge base about student diversity and disability.

Clearly, having insider perspectives in educational research is crucial (Foley, Levinson, & Hurtig, 2001) as these analysts are pushing the boundaries of special education knowledge and thereby are challenging the field to redefine special education as a system capable of responding to all stakeholders (Artiles & Trent, 1994; Gay, 2002; Harry & Kalyanpur, 1999; Patton & Townsend, 2001). Many of these insiders' works reject historic deficit theories about academic shortcomings among students from culturally and linguistically diverse backgrounds and instead focus on strength-based paradigms, particularly how these strengths relate to communal and cultural capital and resources. In addition, a growing body of literature is emerging that demonstrates the positive impact of culturally responsive curriculum and teaching, thereby challenging traditional epistemological dialogues in research agendas (Scheurich & Young, 1997) and the field's reluctance to develop training programs for multicultural special education teacher preparation. Finally, these insider perspectives address needs of underserved culturally and linguistically diverse learners with disabilities in both general and special education settings. (For more detailed discussion of insider–outsider dichotomies in research, see, for example, Banks, 1998; Scheurich & Young, 1997.)

RESEARCH AND PROGRAM DEVELOPMENT IN MULTICULTURAL TEACHER EDUCATION IN GENERAL AND SPECIAL EDUCATION

Nearly fifty years has passed since the U.S. Supreme Court ruled, in *Brown v. Board of Education* (1954), that the legal mantra "separate but equal" had no legitimate place in public education. Recent legislation, the No Child Left Behind Act of 2001 (Bush, 2001, p. 1), supports the edict that all children can and will learn in U.S. public schools. This challenges our nation to leave no teacher behind either (Townsend, 2002) in the quest to fulfill these legislative promises. Supporting teachers will be imperative, especially in special education. Issues including disproportionality and inconsistent positive outcomes of special education services, especially among students of color and those with linguistic differences, must be addressed in the research and program development if equitable educational reform is to become a reality.

Transforming Teacher Preparation Programs

As a philosophy and a process, multicultural education seeks educational equity among historically marginalized groups—that is, African Americans, Asian Americans, Hispanic Americans, Native Americans, women, low-income groups, and people with disabilities (Banks & Banks, 2002; Gay, 1997, 2000). It is "an educational reform movement designed to restructure schools and other educational institutions so that students from all social class, racial, cultural, and gender groups will have an equal and equitable opportunity to learn" (Banks & Banks, 2002, p. 7).

Because schools are presently failing large numbers of students of color—as evidenced by (1) low academic grades, (2) high suspension and expulsion rates, (3) high dropout rates, and (4) massive placement in lower track or special education classrooms—proponents of multicultural education champion the cause of reforming schools to better meet the needs of "all" students (Artiles & Trent, 1994; Ball & Harry, 1993; Banks, 2001; Banks & Banks, 2002; Cochran-Smith, 1995; Gay, 2000; Ladson-Billings, 1994, 1995, 2001, 2002).

There is a movement to create and foster programs that encourage teachers to reexamine schooling practices for diverse learners. Cochran-Smith (1995), for example, advocates preparing teachers to be builders of knowledge and theory, facilitating environments for children who are active knowers and agents "always learning, . . . and always involved in the business of making sense of what is going on around [them]" (p. 511). Further, Ladson-Billings (1995, 2001, 2002) advocates the continued development of a culturally relevant pedagogical theoretical model to guide teacher education research. This line of research affirms the use of multiple perspectives in the improvement of educational practice. Rather than dichotomizing the notion of effective teachers, she champions a continuum of teaching behaviors that facilitate academic success, cultural competence, and critical consciousness: "A culturally relevant pedagogy is designed to problematize teaching and encourage teachers to ask about the nature of the student-teacher relationship, the curriculum, schooling, and society. . . .

We need to consider methodologies that present more robust portraits of teaching. Meaningful combinations of qualitative and quantitative inquiries must be employed to help us understand the deeply textured, multilayered enterprise of teaching" (pp. 483–484).

There is much debate about the definition of multicultural education and whether it is a process, a philosophy, or an ideology, and many educators either defend or reject its efficacy (Banks & Banks, 2002). Also controversial among educators is what teachers teach and how they are prepared to do so to a diverse population. Clearly, multiple perspectives will become the foundation in planning the equitable implementation of culturally responsive pedagogy (Ladson-Billings, 2002).

Efforts to examine this process therefore require an understanding of the foundations of culture in a context that embraces the impact of race, culture, language, social class, gender, and exceptionality (Banks & Banks, 2002; Delpit, 1988, 1995; Gay, 2000; Hilliard, 2001; Ladson-Billings, 1994, 1995, 2001, 2002; Nieto, 1999; Webb-Johnson, Artiles, Trent, Jackson, & Velox, 1998). Multicultural education is rooted in cognitive, affective, and behavioral components, which advocate for an equitable education as a unique aspect of people and an American legacy of transition. In this vein, multicultural education may be the link to integrating and transforming service delivery in general and special education. While limited research exists examining the relationships between general, special, and multicultural education, thoughtful consideration of the strengths of each area may lead to more meaningful collaboration among them in teacher development. The following sections examine research and emerging practices that may assist teacher educators in transforming teacher preparation for diversity in general, and teacher preparation for culturally and linguistically diverse students with disabilities in particular.

Multicultural Teacher Education in General Education

Banks (1994) identified a typology of multicultural education that has been used to examine and assess emerging research in multicultural teacher education. Content integration, knowledge construction, prejudice reduction, equity pedagogy, and empowering school culture are dimensions that can be used to examine efforts to reform teacher education programs. However, little research to date has focused on these aspects of multicultural education in a systematic, integrated manner. For example, many researchers use vague definitions of multicultural education, have relied on teacher reports and surveys for data, or have worked in small geographic regions of the United States (Artiles, Barreto, McClafferty, & Pena, 1998). In addition, although educators advocate for an individualized approach to teaching that values the uniqueness of a student's cultural background, they may still make broad generalizations about groups of culturally diverse people (McDiarmid, 1992). Moreover, despite the strong emphasis on individualized instruction and active learning for diverse learners, many teacher educators use traditional teaching approaches (e.g., lectures) in their courses and emphasize the acquisition of factual information.

A critical limitation of this research is the selection of outcome variables. Many studies have focused on changing teacher attitudes. It is unfortunate that teacher educators and researchers in this area have not systematically assessed the impact of multicultural teacher education experiences on teacher knowledge, beliefs, and teaching practices. Moreover, there is an urgent need to conduct longitudinal studies that will allow us to determine how teacher thought processes and practices are transformed as teachers develop professionally.

With regard to course and program development, Ladson-Billings (1995) examined forty-three studies of teacher education programs in an effort to categorize recent attempts to transform pedagogical practices and infuse them with multicultural processes. She found that twelve studies (28 percent) addressed the use of content integration, nine (20 percent) dealt with knowledge construction, four (10 percent) involved prejudice reduction, and two (10 percent) described practice that reflected equity pedagogy and an empowering school culture. Fourteen of the studies (36 percent) demonstrated no applicability to any of the dimensions; Ladson-Billings posited that this demonstrates the difficulty in merging the supportive tenets of theory and practice in multicultural teacher education. She further asserts that multicultural education be "placed squarely within the debate about teacher education in general" (p. 748).

Multicultural Teacher Education in Special Education

The majority of present-day teacher preparation programs in special education provide little exposure to multicultural perspectives that would broaden teachers' understanding of diversity and disability and teaching in multicultural environments. To illustrate, Artiles, Trent, and Kuan (1997) conducted a systematic review of the literature on empirical studies of multicultural preservice teacher education. They selected studies that (1) were data based, (2) recruited preservice teachers or personnel involved in preservice teacher education (e.g., teacher educators, cooperating teachers) to participate in the studies, and (3) focused on any topic related to preparing preservice special education teachers to teach culturally and/or linguistically diverse students with learning disabilities, behavioral disorders, and noncategorical mild disabilities. They searched the ERIC database (1982–1994) using broad descriptors (e.g., *multicultural education, teacher education*) to locate as many entries as possible. The search turned up 151 records; over a dozen concerned the special education field. But as they applied their selection criteria, the number of eligible empirical articles dwindled to seven. A similar search including three additional years (1995–1997), turned up only six more eligible articles.

Most reports did not identify the underlying conceptual model of the teacher education programs. After reading program descriptions, however, the researchers concluded that most of the studies had been conducted in programs that emphasized either an academic or developmentalist tradition. The developmentalist tradition in these programs did not necessarily focus on child development issues; rather, it was concerned with particular characteristics of culturally diverse children. In a few instances the social efficiency tradition (i.e., which emphasizes teachers' abilities to thoughtfully apply a knowledge base about teaching) guided teacher education programs. For example, Dana (1992) found by examining reflective journals that student teachers experienced culture shock at the beginning of their internships. She also found that four of the five student teachers discussed in one article experienced challenges in facilitating and maintaining effective classroom management in the midst of their shock. These teachers attributed their lack of success to the backgrounds of the youth in their classrooms who were culturally diverse. Finally, these teachers did not feel they had been adequately prepared for the student teaching experience.

In addition, most studies were concerned with linking process variables (e.g., course content, fieldwork, observations) with outcome variables (e.g., attitudes, perceptions of value). Among the most frequently assessed program elements were the characteristics of candidates and staff and the content, methods, and impact of the program. Olmeda (1997), for example, found that preservice teacher field experiences in inner-city schools greatly affected the perceptions and reflections of preservice teachers. Through journal and essay analyses, preservice teachers were challenged in their assumptions about inner-city youth. The following themes emerged from the analysis of preservice teachers' initial reflections: (1) beliefs in some students' lack of motivation, (2) pity for "victims," (3) notions of the importance of being color blind, and (4) reliance on the system as the problem. Postanalyses yielded reflections and notions that (1) children want to learn, (2) good teaching can take place, (3) there is diversity within diverse groups, and (4) being color blind is not good pedagogy. Initial perceptions and reflections were stereotypical and dominated by deficit ideologies. However, postanalyses of preservice teachers' field experiences demonstrated more specific focus highlighting higher expectations and increased knowledge about cultural differences in inner-city settings.

Dana and Floyd (1993) concluded that preservice teachers benefit from discussions of case studies describing cultural and learning differences, including special education services for children. They analyzed the written reflections of preservice teachers in cooperative groups to allow students to examine their beliefs, subjectivities, and biases. They then explored how these affected teaching and learning situations. Reflections written prior to class discussions on specific case studies were frequently quite different from postdiscussion reflections. For example, few preservice teachers questioned the placement of culturally diverse students in special education settings prior to group discussions. They assumed that a student's placement in such a setting implied the student's need for it; they were not prompted to examine whether the placement itself could be a part of the educational challenge culturally diverse learners face. These preservice teachers began to understand and confront "their own subjectivities and biases and how those subjectivities and biases affect how they perceive teaching and learning situations" (p. 9).

Few reports explicitly addressed the underlying definitions of teaching and learning that guided their efforts. Furthermore, most studies focused on multicultural education approaches that single out the distinctive characteristics of students (e.g., race, ethnicity, social class, and language). Finally, the majority of studies were quantitative, using questionnaires and surveys to gather data. For example, Reiff, McCray, and Anderson (1990), in their survey of 101 special educators of culturally diverse students in a rural setting, found that respondents overwhelmingly indicated that specialized teacher training was necessary for effective service delivery. The teachers wanted to understand better the learning styles, linguistic and communication styles, behavioral characteristics, value differences, impact of poverty, and strategies for increasing parental involvement. Ford (1992), in her survey of special education administrators, found that they, too, wanted specialized training for their teachers. However, she also found that there appeared to be a lack of available personnel with the necessary expertise to provide such training. Gormley, McDermott, Rothenberg, and Hammer (1995) concluded in their survey that teacher preparation programs need to do more to assist new teachers in becoming culturally responsive to the learning needs of children, especially given the complex interactions between culture and teaching and the surveyed teachers' uncertainties in choosing strategies to teach linguistically diverse children or providing equal access to the curriculum. Examining special education teacher preparation from the perspective of multicultural training suggests that culturally responsive pedagogy cannot adequately operationalize multicultural theory without also operationalizing its applicability to practice in general and special education settings (Gay, 2000; Ladson-Billings, 1995). If the field persists in discussing the theory and practice of multicultural teacher education without systematically assessing its impact in both special and general education, there will continue to be faulty conclusions drawn about those children who are failing in school.

Researchers at the University of South Florida have undertaken at least four research initiatives that will affect multicultural teacher preparation in special education. Townsend, Thomas, Witty, and Lee (1996), after examining the demographic data detailing the rich diversity and vast disparity in educational practice and outcomes among culturally diverse youth in Florida, conducted a study examining the plight of the African American male student. They found that these students wanted to feel respected and cared about. They also found that these students shared a tremendous desire to be treated fairly in the school context. These researchers also conducted a study examining school reform and decision making as it related to African American children and their families. They found that the voices of difference were often left out of important policy decisions. They concluded that teacher education courses should be infused with multicultural principles to better prepare teachers to meet the needs of diverse youth and their families. Their findings parallel other research in multicultural special education environments.

Today's teaching force is composed predominantly of European American females, and this is not expected to change in the future; consequently, it is crucial that teacher education be grounded in culturally relevant pedagogy based on empirical research, Yet this is often met with resistance. Teachers in preparation are confronted with notions of "white privilege" that underpin resistance to multicultural teaching and corresponding philosophies (McIntosh, 1992; Sleeter, 2001). To counter such resistance, researchers must examine changes in preservice and novice teacher perceptions as a result of multicultural course work and field experiences (Trent, Pernell, Mungai, & Chimedza, 1998).

At least two projects, one in Washington, D.C., and the other in Milwaukee, Wisconsin, have the potential of gleaning the impact of culturally responsive pedagogy in general and special education settings. The Center for Research on the Education of Students Placed at Risk (CRESPAR) at Howard University in Washington, D.C., is presently involved in a series of studies to systematically describe the cultural ecology of classrooms that include significant populations of African American youth from low-income environments (Boykin, 1994, 1997, 2000, 2001, 2002; Boykin & Bailey, 2001; Ellison, Boykin, Towns, & Stokes, 2000). Researchers at CRESPAR have documented that, compared to traditional classroom instructional delivery, teachers using dimensions of African American culture as integral aspects of classroom pedagogy have improved students' academic outcomes. Researchers have also documented a preference among African American and low-income learners for communal and vervistic academic delivery.

The African American Immersion School Project in Milwaukee, Wisconsin, found data that clearly demonstrate significant academic growth among African American students. As a result of specific teacher education development in African American–centered philosophies, concepts, and strategies, the children attending the Dr. Martin Luther King Jr. Elementary School (MLK) African American Immersion School Project have steadily demonstrated improved outcomes in reading, writing, and math. For example, in the 1990–91 school year only 57 percent of third graders scored above the desired state standard in reading, whereas in the 1995–96 school year 92 percent scored above the standard. In the district as a whole, only 71 percent of all students scored above the desired standard. While growth in math was not as fruitful, students at MLK did score above the district average (Mosely, 1997).

Both of these projects demonstrate significant promise in describing and assessing the impact of culturally relevant pedagogy in general and special education teacher training. Presently, however, neither of these programs includes significant numbers of students receiving special education services. While these inquiries represent potentially promising breakthroughs in the area of multicultural teacher education in general and special education, the field must strive to be more systematic, contextual, and case-driven in examining such programs, as well as in reporting findings, developing an empirical knowledge base, and informing policy and practice.

Collaborative Teacher Education Programs to Prepare General and Special Educators

Blatton, Griffin, Winn, and Pugach (1997) examined ten teacher education programs that have transformed their preservice curriculum and instruction to "draw upon the best models of both general and special teacher education" (p. vi). These programs place multicultural education squarely within the realm advocated by Ladson-Billings (1995) by merging their general and special education teacher preparation programs. Each of these programs has embarked on a journey to "reinvent" teacher education; they encourage collaborative efforts designed "to educate all children based on a clear understanding of culture, class, and language, and how they intersect with a disability" (p. viii). These programs incorporate diversity issues into every aspect of program design and implementation and thereby may inform the creation of multicultural perspectives in other teacher education programs throughout the country. We highlight six of the ten programs in the following sections.

Syracuse University.   Syracuse University, with an undergraduate and graduate population of 14,000, has been involved in a reform effort of its teacher education practices since 1990. An initial conversation in 1987 led to the merging of special and general education teacher preparation (Meyer, Mager, Yarger-Kane, Sarno, & Hext-Contreras, 1997). Shared values in (1) inclusion and equity, (2) teacher as decision maker, (3) multiculturalism in education, (4) innovations in education, and (5) field-based emphasis provided the core conceptual framework for merging the two programs.

University of Connecticut.   The University of Connecticut, with an undergraduate and graduate population of 24,000, began its reform efforts in 1989. The merged teacher preparation program prepares 125 teachers a year (Norlander, Case, Reagan, Campbell, & Strauch, 1997). The five-year program offers reflective practice and inquiry, addresses issues of diversity and effective teaching in urban settings, and supports collaborative efforts as integral to the program.

Providence College.   Providence College, with an undergraduate and graduate population of 3,600, grounds its dual certification program in issues of diversity, collaboration, reflective inquiry, and varied field experiences. Its transformed program has been in existence since 1986 (Ryan, Callahan, Krajewski, & Flaherty, 1997). While facilitating a relatively small teacher preparation program, advocates of the merged programs have worked diligently to foster collaborative partnerships among faculty members in general and special education.

University of Florida. The University of Florida has transformed the early childhood teacher preparation program on this campus of 38,000 students. For the past seven years, early childhood educators have been prepared within the Unified Proteach Program (Correa, Rapport, Hartle, Jones, Kemple, & Smith Bonahue, 1997). The program stresses unification, competency-based instruction, diversity, quality field experiences, inclusion, collaboration, and family issues. The program was developed in response to calls for reform by national professional organizations such as the Association of Teacher Educators, the Council for Exceptional Children Early Childhood Division, and the National Association for the Education of Young Children.

University of Alabama. The University of Alabama, with a student body of 20,000, implemented the Multiple Abilities Program (MAP) in the fall of 1994 (Gregg, Ellis, Casareno, Roundtree, Schlichter, & Mayfield, 1997). MAP participants earn certification in early childhood, elementary education, and mild learning disabilities and behavior disorders. Program foundations are steeped in issues of diversity, reflection, empowerment, parent/family involvement, and authentic assessment.

University of Wisconsin at Milwaukee. The University of Wisconsin at Milwaukee is an urban university with a student body of 25,000. Using an urban professional development school model since 1994, the university has implemented the Collaborative Teacher Education Program for Urban Communities (Hains, Maxwell, Tiezzi, Simpson, Ford, & Pugach, 1997). Preparing cohorts of 20–25 students each year, the program advocates a model of collaborative efforts emphasizing diversity, family issues, and effective teaching.

Each of these programs embraces the need to prepare teachers for the growing diversity of classrooms in general and special education. Each emphasizes that all teachers should be trained to meet the education needs of all students. The programs address issues of multiculturalism explicitly and with purposeful intent to prepare teachers to embrace and teach to the strengths and differences that students bring to classrooms. These programs provide the foundation on which researchers can assess the impact of collaborative teacher education within multicultural contexts (Griffin & Pugach, 1997).

A TRANSFORMED TRILOGY

A trilogy is a series of three dramatic or literary works that share a common theme. In this chapter we have addressed multicultural perspectives in special education by examining two needs: the need for research-based teaching practices grounded in culturally responsive pedagogy to promote achievement of all children and youth, especially those from diverse cultural and linguistic backgrounds with disabilities and the need for transformed teacher preparation to prepare high quality teachers of diversity to work with students with disabilities in practice and research.

In this chapter, we have examined the consequences of ignoring the dissonance that exists in general and special education for learners at risk for and with disabilities. It is imperative to transform both teacher preparation and service delivery in special education. This undertaking will require a dynamic knowledge base informed by research that is culturally responsive. The issues guiding efforts to transform special education are compelling, but the field cannot achieve this goal in isolation; it must collaborate with and draw on the pedagogical tenets and experiences of multicultural and general education. Furthermore, each field operating as if it were independent rather than part of a whole will only maintain the status quo: masses of children failing in U.S. public schools. Education is faced with an awesome opportunity and responsibility. By constructing meaningful change in our research perspectives, teaching practices, and teacher preparation, we will help to ensure equitable, accountable, and culturally responsive pedagogy and tools that will improve academic outcomes for *all* learners. The Ayindes in classrooms throughout the country are worthy of our best efforts and actions toward this end.

QUESTIONS FOR FURTHER DISCUSSION

1. What tenets do multicultural, general, and special education share? How are these beliefs about teaching culturally and linguistically diverse students either congruent with or incompatible with teaching diverse learners with disabilities?

2. If you were assigned the responsibility of designing a teacher preparation for diversity and disability, on what research literature would you base your model and why?

3. What kinds of experiences would be imperative for a future educator before he or she could be considered a high-quality culturally responsive teacher?

4. In a small group with your peers, identify at least five strategies for teaching a student with a reading-related learning disability. Now identify another five strategies for teaching a culturally/linguistically diverse student with a reading-related learning disability. Compare these strategies in terms of their responsiveness to the students' disability, diversity, and access to success in the general curriculum.

5. Who is ultimately responsible for ensuring that all children with disabilities receive evidence-based, culturally responsive instruction and behavior management?

REFERENCES

Artiles, A. J., Barreto, R. M., McClafferty, K., & Pena, L. (1998). Pathways to teacher learning in multicultural contexts: A longitudinal case study of two novice bilingual teachers in urban schools. *Remedial and Special Education, (19)*2, 70–90.

Artiles, J. A., & Trent, S. C. (1994). Overrepresentation of minority students in special education: A continuing debate. *Journal of Special Education, 27*(4), 410–437.

Artiles, J. A., & Trent, S. C. (1997). Learning disabilities empirical research on ethnic minority students: An analysis of 22 years of studies published in selected refereed journals. *Learning Disabilities Research & Practice, 12*(2), 82–91.

Artiles, A. J., Trent, S. C., & Kuan, L. (1997) Learning disabilities empirical research on ethnic minority students: An analysis of 22 years of studies published in selected refereed journals. *Learning Disabilities Research and Practice, 12,* 82–91.

Ball, E. W., & Harry, B. (1993). Multicultural education and special education: Parallels, divergences, and intersections. *Educational Forum, 57*(4), 430–437.

Banks, J. A. (1994). *An introduction to multicultural education.* Boston: Allyn & Bacon.

Banks, J. (1998). The lives and values of researchers: Implications for educating citizens in a multicultural society. *Educational Researcher, 27*(7), 1–17.

Banks, J. A. (2001). *Cultural diversity and education: Foun-*

dations, curriculum, and teaching (4th ed.). Boston: Allyn & Bacon.

Banks, J. A., & Banks, C. (2002). *Multicultural educational research yearbook.* San Francisco: Jossey-Bass.

Blatton, L. P., Griffin, C. G., Winn, J. A., & Pugach, M. C. (Eds.). (1997). *Teacher education in transition: Collaborative programs to prepare general and special educators.* Denver, CO: Love.

Bos, C. S., & Fletcher, T. V. (1997). Sociocultural considerations in learning disabilities inclusion research: Knowledge gaps and future directions. *Learning Disabilities, Research & Practice, 12*(2), 92–99.

Boykin, A. W. (1994). The sociocultural context of schooling for African American children: A proactive deep structural analysis. In E. Hollins (Ed.), *Formulating a knowledge base for teaching culturally diverse learners* (pp. 233–245). Philadelphia: ACSD.

Boykin, A. W. (2000). The talent development model of schooling: Placing students at promise for academic success. *Journal of Education for Students Placed at Risk, 5*(1&2), 3–25.

Boykin, A. W. (2001). Comment: The challenges of cultural socialization in the schooling of African American elementary school children: Exposing the hidden curriculum. In W. H. Watkins, J. H. Lewis, & V. Chou (Eds.), *Race and education: The roles of history and society in educating African American students* (pp. 190–199). Boston: Allyn & Bacon.

Boykin, A. W. (2002). Talent development, cultural deep structure, and school reform: Implications for African American initiatives. In S. J. Denbo & L. M. Beaulieu (Eds.), *Improving schools for African American students: A reader for educational leaders* (pp. 81–94). Springfield, IL: Charles C. Thomas.

Boykin, A. W., & Bailey, C. T. (2001). *The role of cultural factors in school relevant cognitive functioning: Synthesis of findings on cultural contexts, cultural orientations, and individual differences.* Washington, DC: Center for Research on the Education of Students Placed at Risk.

Boykin, A. W., & Ellison, C. (1993). The multiple ecologies of black youth socialization: An Afrographic analysis. In R. Taylor (Ed.), *Black youth.* Newbury Park, CA: Sage.

Brown v. Board of Education of Topeka, Kansas, 347 U.S. 483. (1954).

Bush, G. W. (2001). *Transforming the federal role in education so that no child is left behind.* Retrieved February 24, 2002, from http://www.whitehouse.gov/news/reports/no-child-left-behind.html.

Children's Defense Fund. (1999). *The state of America's children yearbook.* Washington, DC: Author.

Cochran-Smith, M. (1995). Color blindness and basket making are not the answers. *American Educational Research Journal, 32*(3): 493–522.

Correa, V. I., Rapport, J. K., Hartle, L. C., Jones, H. A., Kemple, K. M., & Smith-Bonahue, T. (1997). The unified PROTEACH early childhood program at the University of Florida. In L. P. Blatton, C. G. Griffin, J. A. Winn, & M. C. Pugach (Eds.), *Teacher education in transition: Collaborative programs to prepare general and special educators* (pp. 84–106). Denver, CO: Love.

Curtis-Pierce, E., Barbus, S., Emond, S., Sweigart, M., & Prime, K. (1997). Creating a collaborative university/school partnership: Saginaw Valley State University. In L. P. Blatton, C. G. Griffin, J. A. Winn, & M. C. Pugach (Eds.), *Teacher education in transition: Collaborative programs to prepare general and special educators* (pp. 230–248). Denver, CO: Love.

Dana, N. F. (1992). *Towards preparing the monocultural teacher for the multicultural classroom.* Paper presented at the annual meeting of the Association of Teacher Educators, Orlando, FL.

Dana, N. F. M., & Floyd, D. M. (1993). *Preparing preservice teachers for the multicultural classroom: A report on the case study approach.* Paper presented at the annual meeting of the American Educational Research Association, Chicago, IL.

Delpit, L. (1988). The silenced dialogue: Power and pedagogy in educating other people's children. *Harvard Educational Review, 58,* 280–298.

Delpit, L. (1995). *Other people's children.* New York: New Press.

Delpit, L. (2000). Skin-deep learning. In P. Rodis, A. Garrod, & M. L. Boscardin (Eds.), *Learning disabilities and life stories* (pp. 157–164). Boston: Allyn & Bacon.

Donovan, S. M., & Cross, C. T. (2002). *Minority students in special education and gifted education.* Washington, DC: National Research Council.

Dunn, L. M. (1968). Special education for the mildly retarded: Is much of it justifiable? *Exceptional Children, 35*(1), 5–22.

Ellison, C., Boykin, A. W., Towns, D. P., & Stokes, A. (2000). *Classroom cultural ecology: The dynamics of classroom life in schools serving low-income African American children.* Washington, DC: Center for Research on the Education of Students Placed-at-Risk.

Foley, D. A., Levinson, B. A., & Hurtig, J. (2001). Anthropology goes inside: The new educational ethnography of ethnicity and gender. In W. Secada (Ed.), *Review of research in education* (Vol. 25, pp. 37–98). Washington, DC: American Educational Research Association.

Ford, B. A. (1992). Multicultural education training for special educators working with African-American youth. *Exceptional Children, 59*(2), 107–114.

Gay, G. (1997). Educational equality for students of color.

In J. A. Banks & C. A. Banks (Eds.), *Multicultural education: Issues and perspectives* (3rd ed., pp. 195–228). Boston: Allyn & Bacon.

Gay, G. (2000). *Culturally responsive teaching: Theory, research, and practice.* New York: Teachers College Press.

Gay, G. (2002). Culturally responsive teaching in special education for ethnically diverse students: Setting the stage. *Qualitative Studies in Education, 15*(6), 613–630.

Gormley, K., McDermott, P., Rothenberg, J., & Hammer, J. (1995). Expert and novice teachers' beliefs about culturally responsive pedagogy. American Education Research Association Conference, April 18–22, San Francisco, CA.

Gregg, M., Ellis, E. S., Casareno, A., Roundtree, B., Schlichter, C., & Mayfield, P. (1997). The multiple abilities program at the University of Alabama: Preparing teachers to meet all students' needs. In L. P. Blatton, C. G. Griffin, J. A. Winn, & M. C. Pugach (Eds.), *Teacher education in transition: Collaborative programs to prepare general and special educators* (pp. 106–127). Denver, CO: Love.

Griffin, C. C, & Pugach, M. C. (1997). Framing the progress of collaborative teacher education. In L. P. Blatton, C. G. Griffin, J. A. Winn, & M. C. Pugach (Eds.), *Teacher education in transition: Collaborative programs to prepare general and special educators* (pp. 249–270). Denver, CO: Love.

Hains, A. H., Maxwell, C. B., Tiezzi, L., Simpson, M. J., Ford, A., & Pugach, M. C. (1997). From individual and ambiguous to collaborative and explicit: Reform in urban teacher education at the University of Wisconsin-Milwaukee. In L. P. Blatton, C. G. Griffin, J. A. Winn, & M. C. Pugach (Eds.), *Teacher education in transition: Collaborative programs to prepare general and special educators* (pp. 180–206). Denver, CO: Love.

Harry, B., & Kalyanpur, S. (1999). *Building reciprocity with families: Case studies in special education.* Baltimore, MD: Paul H. Brookes.

Hilliard, A. G., III (1992). The pitfalls and promises of special education practice. *Exceptional Children, 52*(2), 168–172.

Hilliard, A. G. (2001). Race, identity, hegemony, and education: What do we need to know now? In W. H. Watkins, J. H. Lewis, & V. Chou (Eds.), *Race and education: The roles of history and society in educating African American students* (pp. 1–36). Boston: Allyn & Bacon.

Howard, G. (1999). *We can't teach what we don't know: White teachers, multiracial schools.* New York: Teachers College Press.

Individual with Disabilities Education Act. (1997). 20 U.S.C. §1400 *et seq.* (1997).

Irvine, J. J. (Ed.). (2002). *In search of wholeness: African American teachers and their culturally specific classroom practices.* New York: Palgrave.

Irvine, J. J., & Armento, B. J. (2001). *Culturally responsive teaching: Lesson planning for elementary and middle grades.* Boston: McGraw-Hill.

Kea, C. D., Cartledge, G., & Bowman, L. J. (2002). Interventions for African American learners with behavioral problems. In B. A. Ford & F. Obiakor (Eds.), *Creating successful learning environments for African American learners with exceptionalities* (pp. 79–94). Thousand Oaks, CA: Corwin Press.

Keith, J. M., & McCray, A. D. (2002). Juvenile offenders with special needs: Critical issues and bleak outcomes. *Qualitative Studies in Education, 15*(6), 691–710.

Klingner, J. (2003). Position statement on diversity. *Newsletter of the Division for Research (CEC-DR), 16*(3), 1-4.

Ladson-Billings, G. (1994). *The dreamkeepers: Successful teachers of African American children.* San Francisco: Jossey-Bass.

Ladson-Billings, G. (1995). Toward a theory of culturally relevant pedagogy. *American Educational Research Journal, 32,* 465–491.

Ladson-Billings, G. (2001). *Crossing over to Canaan.* San Francisco: Jossey-Bass.

Ladson-Billings, G. (2002). But that's good teaching! The case for culturally relevant pedagogy. In S. J. Denbo & L. M. Beaulieu (Eds.), *Improving schools for African American students: A reader for educational leaders* (pp. 95–102). Springfield, IL: Charles C. Thomas.

McCray, A. D., & Garcia, S. B. (2002). The stories we must tell: Developing a research agenda for multicultural and bilingual special education. *Qualitative Studies in Education, 15*(6), 599–612.

McCray, A. D., Vaughn, S., & Neal, L. I. (2001). Not all students learn to read by third grade: Middle school students speak out about their reading disabilities. *Journal of Special Education, 35*(1), 17–30.

McDiarmid, G. W. (1992). What to do about differences? A study of multicultural education for teacher trainees in the Los Angeles School District. *Journal of Teacher Education, 43*(2), 83–93.

McIntosh, P. (1992). White privilege and male privilege. A personal account of coming to see correspondence through work in women's studies. Working paper No. 198 (ED335262).

Meyer, L. H., Mager, G. M., Yarger-Kane, G., Sarno, M., & Hext-Contreras, G. (1997). Syracuse University's inclusive elementary and special education program. In L. P. Blatton, C. G. Griffin, J. A. Winn, & M. C. Pugach (Eds.), *Teacher education in transition: Collaborative programs to prepare general and special educators* (pp. 18–38). Denver, CO: Love.

Mosley, J. (1997). Academic progress at the Martin Luther King, Jr. elementary immersion school. Paper presented at the American Educational Research Association Annual Meeting, Chicago, IL.

Neal, L. I., McCray, A. D., Webb-Johnson, G., & Bridgest, S. T. (2003). The effects of African American movement styles on teachers' perceptions and reactions. *Journal of Special Education, 37*(1), 49–57.

Nieto, S. (1999). *The light in their eyes.* New York: Teachers College Press.

Norlander, K. A., Case, C. W., Reagan, T. G., Campbell, P., & Strauch, J. D. (1997). The power of integrated teacher preparation: The University of Connecticut. In L. P. Blatton, C. G. Griffin, J. A. Winn, & M. C. Pugach (Eds.), *Teacher education in transition: Collaborative programs to prepare general and special educators* (pp. 39–65). Denver, CO: Love.

Office for Civil Rights. (1997). Fall 1997 elementary and secondary school civil rights survey. (Report No. CA91001001). Washington, DC: U.S. Department of Education.

Olmeda, I. (1997, April). Challenging old assumptions: Preparing teachers for inner city schools. *Teaching and Teacher Education, 13*(3), 245–258.

Patton, J. M., & Townsend, B. L. (2001). Teacher education, leadership, and disciplinary practices: Exploring ethics, power, and privilege in the education of exceptional African American learners. *Teacher Education and Special Education, 24*(1), 1–2.

Pugach, M. C. (2001). The stories we choose to tell: Fulfilling the promise of qualitative research for special education. *Exceptional Children, 67,* 439–453.

Reiff, H. B, McCray, A. D., & Anderson, P. L. (1990). *Special education training to prevent minority school dropouts in rural areas.* (ERIC Reproduction 337 305).

Ryan, L., Callahan, J., Krajewski, J., & Flaherty, T. (1997). A merged elementary special education program in a 4-year liberal arts college: Providence College. In L. P. Blatton, C. G. Griffin, J. A. Winn, & M. C. Pugach (Eds.), *Teacher education in transition: Collaborative programs to prepare general and special educators* (pp. 66–83). Denver, CO: Love.

Scheurich, J. J., & Young, M. D. (1997). Coloring episte-
mologies: Are our research epistemologies racially biased? *Educational Researcher, 26*(4), 4–16.

Schools of Education. (2002). *U.S. News & World Report, 132*(12), 58.

Serwatka, T. S., Deering, S., & Grant, P. (1995). Disproportionate representation of African Americans in emotionally handicapped classes. *Journal of Black Studies, 25*(4), 492–506.

Shavelson, R. J., & Towne, L. (Eds.). (2002). *Scientific research in education.* Washington, DC: National Academies Press.

Sleeter, C. E. (2001). Preparing teachers for culturally diverse schools: Research and the overwhelming presence of whiteness. *Journal of Teacher Education, 52*(2), 94–106

Townsend, B. L. (2000). The disproportionate discipline of African American learners: Reducing school suspensions and expulsions. *Exceptional Children, 66*(3), 381–391.

Townsend, B. L. (2002). Testing while black. *Remedial and Special Education, 33*(3), 133–145.

Townsend, B. L., Thomas, D., Witty, A., & Lee, M. (1996). Diversity and school restructuring: Creating partnerships in a world of difference. *Teacher Education and Special Education, 19*(2), 102–118.

Trent, S. C., Pernell, E., Mungai, A., & Chimedza, R. (1998). Using concept maps to measure conceptual change in preservice teachers enrolled in a multicultural education/special education course. *Remedial and Special Education, 19*(1), 16–31.

U.S. Department of Education. (2002a). *Twenty-third annual report to Congress on the implementation of Individuals with Disabilities Act.* Washington, DC: U.S. Government Printing Office.

U.S. Department of Education. (2002b). *Education statistics.* Washington, DC: Author.

Webb-Johnson, G. C. (2002). Strategies for creating multicultural and pluralistic schools and societies: A mind is something wonderful to develop. In R. A. Villa, J. S. Thousand, & A. Nevin (Eds.), *Creativity and collaborative learning: A practical guide to empowering students, teachers, and families in an inclusive, multicultural and pluralistic society.* Baltimore: Paul H. Brookes.

Webb-Johnson, G. C., Artiles, A., Trent, S., Jackson, C. W., & Velox, A. (1998). The status of research on multicultural education in teacher education and special education: Problems, pitfalls, and promises. *Remedial and Special Education, 19*(1), 7–15.

ISSUES, TRENDS, AND CHALLENGES IN EARLY INTERVENTION

MELISSA L. OLIVE

The University of Texas at Austin

MARY A. McEVOY[1]

University of Minnesota

ISSUES IN EARLY INTERVENTION

Teachers in early intervention (EI)[2] and early childhood special education (ECSE) enter the workforce facing new challenges as they attempt to provide services to young children with disabilities and their families. New legislation, more diverse families, and a variety of educational contexts are just a few of the issues. Changes to legislation, such as mandated family involvement and inclusive programming in natural or least restrictive environments, have transformed the role of the service provider from exclusively teaching in a classroom to consulting with other educators of young children, implementing various therapies while consulting with therapists, and even counseling family members (McBride & Peterson, 1997).

Leaders in the field, inspired by the goal of improving outcomes for young children and their families and challenged by the changing role of the educator of young children with

---

[1]The work presented here was completed before Mary McEvoy suddenly passed away. Publishing this work continues to honor her commitment and devotion to improving the lives of young children through teacher training and research.

[2]We use the terms *early intervention* for children ages birth to three years old and *early childhood special education* for children ages three to five years old, though this may not reflect the practice in all states. Similarly, we use the term *natural environments* for those environments where there are children ages birth to three years old with and without disabilities and *inclusive environments* for those environments where there are children ages three and up with and without disabilities.

disabilities, recently embarked on a project designed to review recent literature, identify critical intervention practices, and disseminate information to bridge the gap between research and practice (Sandall & Smith, 2000). The result of this project, the *DEC [Division of Early Childhood] Recommended Practices in Early Intervention/Early Childhood Special Education* (Sandall, McLean, & Smith, 2000), is grounded in several fundamental beliefs. First, all children and their families should be respected. Second, services provided to children and their families should be high quality, comprehensive, coordinated, and family-centered. Third, all children have the right to participate actively within their families and communities.

The changing role of the early interventionist, the recommended practices for the new millennium, and recent changes in practices resulting from litigation all affect professionals in the field of EI/ECSE as well as the educators who train them. In this chapter we identify the issues facing EI/ECSE as well as the larger field of special education. We briefly review current research within each area and discuss implications for future research.

Identifying the critical issues facing the field is no easy task. In highlighting some issues, we may have overlooked others. As teacher educators, researchers, and family members, we feel that every issue is critical for young children and their families. However, it is impossible to survey thirty years of work in one chapter; therefore, we have taken great care to identify the most pressing issues facing the field today. We reviewed the *DEC Recommended Practices* to identify themes that emerged from author discussions. We conducted a cursory review of the most recent issues of journals in EI/ECSE to identify recurring themes. From there, we identified three major issues currently facing the field.

The *DEC Recommended Practices* contains recommendations for both direct and indirect services. Direct services include assessment, child-focused intervention, family-based services, interdisciplinary models, and technology applications. Indirect services, as used by *DEC Recommended Practices,* are policies, procedures, systems change, and personnel preparation. A review of the *DEC Recommended Practices* reveals several prominent themes: (1) service delivery issues such as close family involvement and services in the natural environment affect practicing professionals as well as teacher educators; (2) personnel shortages and the effects of ECSE/EI on other professions will affect personnel preparation; and (3) recent mandates for functional behavioral assessment and child-focused intervention will pose challenges for ECSE/EI professionals. In the following sections we discuss these issues, provide a brief overview of the literature addressing them, and suggest directions for future research.

Service Delivery Issues

Family Involvement. A critical tenant of EI/ECSE is the belief that services for young children be designed and implemented with close involvement of families. Families should be decision makers for their children with disabilities. Their priorities should be used to drive early intervention services. As described in Part C of the Individuals with Disabilities Education Act (IDEA, 1997), services provided to young children must be family-centered. Trivette and Dunst (2000) recommend that families and professionals share responsibility and work collaboratively when providing services to young children with disabilities. This collaborative effort is an essential component of the assessment and identification process as well as the development of the individualized education plan (IEP) and individualized family service plan (IFSP). Clearly, families are an important aspect of service delivery within EI/ECSE.

The philosophy of working collaboratively with families has a direct impact on how professionals provide services as well as how professionals should be trained to provide services to children and their families. The structure and function of American families are changing, and this directly affects professional training and service delivery. While there are many issues related to family-centered intervention services, we have identified three that appear to be most pressing in the literature: changing family diversity, changing family function, and services in natural environments.

Family Diversity.   There is great diversity in the cultural and linguistic backgrounds of today's families (Children's Defense Fund, 1999). Consequently professionals must respect these cultural and linguistic differences when working with families (Lynch & Hansen, 1998; Willis, 1999). By the year 2030, for example, non-Hispanic white children under eighteen will be in the minority of the U.S. population, and Hispanics will be in the majority (U.S. Department of Education, 1999). However, it is likely that the majority of professionals serving young children and their families will be non-Hispanic white (DEC, 1997). It seems there are two underlying issues here: training preservice professionals to value cultural and linguistic diversity and recruiting and retaining diverse service providers.

Multiple organizations recommend cultural and linguistic diversity training for pre- and in-service professionals (Council for Exceptional Children, 1997; National Association for the Education of Young Children [NAEYC], 1994; National Council for Accreditation of Teacher Education, 2000; Sandall, McLean, & Smith, 2000). Lynch and Hanson (1993) define cross-cultural competence as "the ability to think, feel, and act in ways that acknowledge, respect, and build upon ethnic, [social] cultural, and linguistic diversity" (p. 50). Lynch (1998) describes a three-step process for developing cultural competence. She recommends that professionals first develop self-awareness, that is, get to know one's self before learning about other cultures. Once there is self-knowledge, the professional can begin to learn more about other cultures. Finally, the professional is ready to develop skills in cross-cultural communication, such as learning how to read and respond to nonverbal cues or how to listen to families.

Being culturally sensitive, however, is not enough. Recruiting and retaining diverse personnel in EI/ECSE is an additional pressing issue (e.g., Barnes, 2000; Hirsch, Koppich, & Knapp, 2000; White-Hood, 2000). While approximately 35 percent of schoolchildren are from minority-status families, only 5 percent of the professionals serving them are of minority status (Futrell, 1999). Campbell, Jefferson, and Hurwitz (2000) have identified strategies to recruit diverse groups of preservice educators. Strategies such as information boards, courteous office staff, and a welcoming department have been identified as helpful in recruiting minority preprofessional students. Retaining teachers seems to be more difficult (Campbell et al., 2000). Within the first five years of service, 25–30 percent of teachers leave the profession (Futrell, 1999). Low pay, little respect, and increasing demands are just some of the reasons teachers give for leaving the field (Futrell, 1999). While the strategies to retain minority professionals seem obvious—higher pay, more bonuses and rewards, revised tenure policies (Hirsch et al., 2000)—the outlook appears grim. Although this issue is important in general special education, its effects are felt most directly in EI/ECSE given the emphasis in the field on close family involvement and the fact that many children enter the system at a very young age.

Family Function.   Families are changing in other ways as well. Today, increasing numbers of children are spending more time in care provided by someone other than their parents (Interagency Forum on Child and Family Statistics [IFCFS], 2000). For example, in 1999, 51 percent of children ages birth through two years old and 76 percent of children ages three through six years old were in nonparental care (IFCFS, 2000). This suggests that working parents may no longer be available to take their children to appointments during the regular workday. In addition, parents of children with disabilities may not be home to implement intervention strategies.

Changing parental roles directly affects how intervention services can be provided. Professionals must respect family choices to work outside the home, to home-school their children, or to enroll their children in private programs. Given changes in family demographics, it seems likely that a major service delivery model should be one where EI/ECSE personnel consult with a variety of programs where childcare is provided. However, in 1997, 77.8 percent of services for young children with disabilities were provided in outpatient "clinic" settings or through home-visiting programs (U.S. Department of Education, 1999). This means that less than 13 percent of services in 1997 were provided in settings such as preschool programs and childcare centers where many young children spend most of their time each day. It appears the predominant model for service delivery relies heavily on bringing children to the service rather than providing the service in natural environments where children spend their time.

Natural Environments.   The most recent amendments to IDEA changed the nature of service delivery for young children with disabilities. These services must now be provided in natural environments (IDEA, 1997). Natural environments are those in which children and their families participate on a daily basis. Natural environments "include home and community settings in which children without disabilities participate" (IDEA, 1997, p. 82). A natural environment is the place or setting where the child would be if a disability were not present. Natural environments include childcare and preschool programs, as well as grocery stores, restaurants, and shopping malls.

Teachers of young children with disabilities must become familiar with the range of settings where early intervention services may be provided, and they must provide a range of services in these new "classrooms," whether they are public libraries, city buses, or neighborhood recreation centers. In addition, teacher preparation programs must design practicums that provide experiences across the continuum of placement options.

Childcare providers, particularly those that provide family or in-home childcare services, are also affected by this mandate. While only 15 percent of childcare services are provided in this manner (Children's Defense Fund, 1998), children with disabilities may have more impact on these programs than on others. First, licensing requirements for these programs are often different from other environments (Buell, Gamel-McCormick, & Hallam, 1999), as are ratio regulations and training requirements. Providers may not be familiar with or have access to technical assistance, resulting in programs that are ill equipped for serving children with disabilities. In-home childcare providers may be more appealing than other environments to parents of infants and toddlers with disabilities (Galinsky, Howes, Kontos, & Shinn, 1994) because of their home-like atmosphere, small number of children, and availability during nonstandard hours; they may actually be serving higher ratios of children with disabilities than other settings.

Because the concept of natural environments is so new, few studies have focused on the provision of services and issues related to education in natural environments. However, research in and discussion of preschool inclusion, the education of children with disabilities alongside children without disabilities, have dominated the literature over the years. Odom (2000) summarized what is currently known about preschool inclusion. Positive outcomes are identified for children with and without disabilities, and families generally express favorable attitudes toward inclusive programs. Odom reports that, on the one hand, the quality of inclusive environments appears to be comparable to the quality of those programs serving children without disabilities only. On the other hand, Bricker (2000) observes that too often inclusion is viewed as a way of removing supports for young children. Children in self-contained classrooms serving only children with disabilities may receive related services more frequently than those in integrated programs, which rely on weekly or monthly provision of itinerant services.

Guralnick (2001) describes four types of inclusive programs: (1) full inclusion, where the children with disabilities are full participants in the general education program; (2) cluster model, where the children with disabilities are included in the general education program and bring their own special education staff with them; (3) reverse inclusion, where children without disabilities are included alongside children with disabilities; and (4) social inclusion, where children are located in separate locations with separate staff and there is planned contact between the two groups. Guralnick also describes the four main goals of inclusive programming: access, feasibility, developmental and social outcomes, and social integration. Although there are many barriers to inclusive programming for infants, toddlers, and preschoolers, systems change (i.e., new ways of thinking) can help overcome them. Guralnick calls for systems change, program development, and research in early childhood inclusion.

Implications for Future Research in Service Delivery.   The field is facing service delivery challenges. The changing role of the family in the intervention process is just one aspect of this. Additional empirical information is needed to ensure that special education services for young children are effective for both the child and the family. First, how effective are teacher training programs in preparing future professionals in EI/ECSE? Can valuing cultural and linguistic diversity be taught? What are families reporting about the way service delivery professionals are treating them? What can be done to diversify the cultural awareness of professionals in the field? How can those from culturally diverse backgrounds be recruited to enter and remain in the profession?

Second, although there are multiple studies on the benefits and barriers to preschool inclusion, they do not address issues related to natural environments. Several areas need immediate attention. For example, what are the issues around education in natural environments for young children? Stakeholders should help identify issues to be addressed in research and teacher training programs. Teachers, other educators, parents, and children should be involved in helping the profession understand its problems, challenges, and barriers (Bricker, 2000). Buell et al. (1999) suggest that additional research is needed to determine the best ways to encourage providers to accept children with disabilities into their programs.

Finally, what are the desirable outcomes for young children in inclusive environments (e.g., see Bricker, 2000; Odom, 2000)? Are there effective strategies for providing services in the natural environments? What strategies are currently being used? Is there any empirical evidence to support their use?

Assessment and Intervention Issues

Child-Focused Interventions.   Recommended practices, as well as IDEA (1997), suggest that child-focused intervention efforts must be individualized and adapted based on systematic data collection and evaluation (Wolery, 2000). Child-focused interventions consist of a collection of procedures used intentionally to produce specific outcomes for young children (Wolery, 2000). Environmental arrangements, modification and individualization of practices, and systematic procedures are all strategies educators can use in purposeful ways to facilitate childhood development. New regulations also require that parents or guardians be provided with ongoing reports of their child's progress toward annual goals; this is accomplished, in part, by the child's IEP, which contains a statement of measurable annual goals (Huefner, 2000; IDEA, 1997). Intervention efforts must also be intentional and effective. "Teachers must make a good faith effort to help students achieve their annual goals" (IDEA, 1997). Parents may request a due process hearing if they believe these efforts are not being made.

A recent development in the area of intervention for young children with autism further highlights this issue. Intensive, child-focused intervention is particularly of interest given the rising number of children with autism (an increase of 243.9 percent from 1993 to 1998) (U.S. Department of Education, 2000). In a recent review of litigation related to intervention for young children with autism, Yell and Drasgow (2000) investigated the courts' expectations of data-based instruction and decision making. They reviewed forty-five cases decided between 1993 and 1998. Of those, parents prevailed in thirty-four cases (76 percent). School districts prevailed when no procedural or substantive violations occurred. Examples of substantive violations included programs that failed to provide needed services (e.g., intensity of services) or those in which the child did not make adequate progress. School districts lost three cases because programs did not use data to determine child progress and six cases because the district could not prove that the child progressed in the program.

To service providers this pressure to implement individualized intervention may seem overwhelming or even impossible at times. However, research in child-focused interventions has demonstrated repeatedly the effectiveness of such intervention efforts (Hemmeter, 2000; Wolery & Gast, 2000). For example, children have been taught to acquire new skills (e.g., McEvoy, Davis, Rogers, & Olive, 2000), decrease inappropriate behaviors (e.g., Olive, Neilsen, & McEvoy, 1997), and generalize behaviors to new conditions (e.g., McEvoy, Olive, & Neilsen, 2000). These intervention efforts have been demonstrated to be effective with young children in settings such as homes, preschools, and day care centers, with teachers, parents, assistant teachers, and siblings implementing interventions that result in positive outcomes for the child with disabilities (e.g., Hancock & Kaiser, 1996; Kaiser, Hemmeter, Ostrosky, & Fisher, 1996).

While child-focused interventions within inclusive environments produce positive outcomes for children (Odom, 2000), issues do exist. In a recent discussion of historical events in classroom research for young children with disabilities, Wolery and Gast (2000) describe some of these issues. First, researchers must be able to draw on findings from other areas of study. This may include research from animal studies or those involving basic research as opposed to applied studies. Second, researchers should embrace rigorous research methods. Many threats to internal validity exist when intervention research is conducted in classrooms for young children. Finally, researchers must persist in replicating studies with promising results. Systematic replication will assist the field in determining conditions under which strategies will be effective.

As can be seen, instruction is effective when it is intentional, individualized, and guided by *ongoing data collection* and *evaluation*. Teachers must be able to collect and analyze data on a regular basis. They must be trained to work collaboratively with parents. And they must receive a strong preservice foundation in the principles of behavior analysis.

In addition to intervention development, more research is needed on linking assessment to classroom intervention. Areas receiving considerable attention in the K–12 literature are critical skills mastery and general outcome measurement (Deno, 1997; Fuchs & Deno, 1991). Both of these intervention approaches focus on monitoring growth and development of a particular skill over time. While the focus of early childhood assessment has historically been on critical skills mastery (McConnell, 2000), researchers at the Early Childhood Research Institute (http://ici2.umn.edu/ecri) have recently been focusing on procedures that educators can use to monitor rate of development over time and assess progress toward long- and short-term goals.

Systematic data collection and evaluation have their roots in applied behavior analysis (Wolery & Gast, 2000). A cursory review of leading teacher preparation programs in special education reveals that they provide intensive training on applied behavior analysis, an indication that it has been found to be important in the classroom. However, DEC, NAEYC, and the Association of Teacher Educators (ATE) do not identify it as a critical component of licensing requirements (DEC, NAEYC, & ATE, 1995). Perhaps there is an underlying assumption by graduate admission committees that master-level trainees will have a background in special education. However, this may not be the case. Many programs admit students with backgrounds in child development, speech and language pathology, and social work, professions that most likely provide no formal training in applied behavior analysis.

In addition to demonstrating skills necessary to conduct systematic data collection and evaluation, teachers must have *time* to engage in data collection. Although teachers may be able to collect some data during ongoing activities, most graphing and data evaluation take place outside of teaching activities. An educator's day may no longer be spent entirely with children, particularly given the changing role of the EI/ECSE professional, who consults to programs, conducts home visits, and leads IEP/IFSP meetings. Administrators should be aware of these changing roles when assigning caseloads.

Addressing Challenging Behaviors.   As Polsgrove and Ochoa describe in their chapter, special education is faced with serious issues regarding disciplining students with disabilities. This area has achieved national significance in EI/ECSE (Hemmeter, McEvoy, Strain, Brault, & Timm, 1998). Many organizations have devoted entire monographs to managing challenging behavior in young children (e.g., *Behavioral Disorders, Young Exceptional Children*).Three clear issues are involved in managing challenging behavior in young children. First, early childhood may be the easiest time to include children with disabilities in the general curriculum. However, challenging behavior is one of the main reasons children with disabilities are being excluded from early childhood education (ECE) programs. Providing appropriate technical support and preservice training could alleviate some of the stress that accompanies working in such programs when children with disabilities are included (McEvoy, Davis, & Reichle, 1993).

Second, interventions for challenging behavior must be proactive and based on reinforcement. Under certain conditions, a functional behavioral assessment must be conducted.

As with data collection and evaluation, functional behavioral assessment has its roots in applied behavior analysis (Arndorfer & Miltenberger, 1993). Again, the skills necessary to conduct a functional behavioral assessment take time to master, and some believe that public policy in this area has moved beyond our knowledge base (Neilsen & McEvoy, 2001; Nelson, Mathur, and Rutherford, 1999). While the issues of having a behavioral foundation have been described above, one aspect was omitted. Graduates of early childhood programs are taught to manage and respond to behavior in ways that are distinctly different from strategies used in applied behavior analysis; early childhood educators are taught to *guide* young children's behavior.

As was pointed out in DEC's position paper on challenging behavior (DEC, 1999), guidance may not be effective for some children. Young children engage in challenging behavior for two primary reasons: to *obtain* preferred objects, activities, attention, or sensory stimulation or to *avoid* objects, activities, attention, or sensory stimulation. Therefore, with *guidance* methods, a child who engages in challenging behavior to obtain teacher attention would be getting teacher attention in the form of "use nice hands, please," for example, resulting in a greater likelihood that the child's challenging behavior would continue.

Finally, research on school-age students and adults cannot simply be applied "as is" to young children without being validated as suitable and adapted to fit their needs (Arndorfer & Miltenberger, 1993). For example, functional communication training is an intervention method demonstrated to be effective at decreasing challenging behavior across a range of ages (Olive, 1999). However, teachers in early childhood programs do not readily accept this as an intervention method (Burns & Olive, 2000). Intervention plans must fit the early childhood philosophy and must be appealing to educators of young children.

Implications for Future Research.   Although researchers in the field have been collecting data for over forty years on intervention efforts for children with disabilities, more information is needed. For example, how are data collection and evaluation skills best taught? Are EI/ECSE professionals receiving education in this important area? What systems changes can be implemented to ensure that ample resources are available for professionals to perform all components of their jobs? What is the effectiveness of implementing child-focused intervention efforts throughout the school day (DEC, 1993; Hemmeter, 2000)? Can activity-based interventions be implemented in inclusive classrooms while teachers are attempting to facilitate outcomes for all children? How does progress monitoring relate to intervention evaluation? How can progress in early childhood be monitored to ensure long-lasting outcomes even into elementary school years?

Another concept to consider for future research in child-focused interventions is the manner in which research outcomes are disseminated. Kauffman (1996) recently described the gap between research on challenging behavior and classroom practice. He discussed how research articles are *not* teacher friendly and are often *unavailable* to those who need them (e.g., teachers, parents, and policy makers). Vaughn, Klinger, and Hughes (2000) observe that "the lack of 'linkage' between research and practice and the extent to which research-based practices are sustained after researchers leave target sites have been of growing concern" (p. 164). In recent years both the *Educational Researcher* (i.e., Vol. 26, No. 5, 1997), the major journal of the American Educational Research Association, and *Exceptional Children* (i.e., Vol. 63, No. 4, 1997), the major research journal for the Council for Exceptional Children, featured a series of articles addressing the issue of enhancing the impact of educational research.

Additionally, there are many types of services and strategies available to address challenging behavior in young children (DEC, 1999). However, more research is needed. Wolery and Gast (2000) and Hemmeter (2000) discuss the plausibility of classroom intervention. However, more research is needed. Studies must be experimentally sound to determine under which conditions the interventions will be effective. Studies should be replicated and validated in multiple settings and with multiple interventionists to determine key components of effective interventions.

Additional assessment and intervention information is needed. In a recent reaction to a literature review of stereotyped and self-injurious behavior, McEvoy and Reichle (2000) highlighted the need for continued development of assessments that yield results related to identifying the function of challenging behavior. At what point, for example, is a functional behavioral assessment necessary? And who is qualified to conduct such an elaborate assessment? How consistently does an intervention need to be implemented to still maintain its effectiveness? What can be done to prevent the emergence of challenging behavior? Symons (2000) suggests that researchers should try to identify the variables that lead to the initial emergence of maladaptive behaviors. Preventing this emergence and targeting more socially appropriate, efficient, adaptive behaviors should result in fewer problem behaviors. Can using augmentative and alternative communication serve to teach new behavior before maladaptive behavior can be learned?

How can teachers be better trained to deal with challenging behavior? In a recent survey of teachers in Kentucky, Meyers, and Holland (2000) found that many teachers did not understand why children engage in challenging behavior. How can teachers intervene appropriately when they lack this understanding? What elements of training programs are crucial to ensuring that teachers have a foundation in the assessment and remediation of challenging behavior?

Personnel Issues in Early Intervention/Early Childhood Special Education

Given the focus of EI/ECSE on close family involvement and the provision of services in the natural environment, other disciplines will surely be affected. These include ECE and health-related programs (DEC, NAEYC, & ATE, 1995).

Impact on Early Childhood Education.   First, the mandate of IDEA for inclusive and natural environments suggests that many children with disabilities will be served in preschools and childcare programs. Consequently, early childhood educators should have formal training in serving young children with disabilities and their families. Second, IDEA mandates that a representative from general education be present at IEP meetings. For children ages three to five, this would be a professional who is familiar with the curriculum for children in this age range (IDEA, 1997 Regulations). To be active participants at such meetings, early childhood teachers need a foundation in disability and family issues as well as an understanding of philosophies of child-focused intervention (DEC, NAEYC, & ATE, 1995).

Typically, ECE programs focus on developmentally appropriate practice, a concept supporting the philosophy that programs should be child-directed and child-led rather than teacher-directed. The difficulties in blending developmentally appropriate practice and child-focused intervention have been reviewed previously (e.g., Carta, Atwater, Schwartz,

McConnell, 1991, 1993; Johnson & Johnson, 1992). Issues such as individualization, linking curriculum and assessment, and ongoing progress monitoring seem obvious.

Impact on Medical-Model Professions.   Early childhood educators are not the only professionals affected by changes in EI/ECSE. Professionals from other disciplines who serve young children with disabilities—pediatricians, neonatologists, nurses, speech/language pathologists, and occupational and physical therapists—will also be affected (McWilliam, 2000). These professionals are typically trained under what is known as the medical model. This training is grounded in the philosophy that medical professionals dominate the decision-making processes (Liedtka & Whitten, 1997). Under this philosophy, the professional is the expert. Preservice training in this field is provider-centered rather than patient-centered (Liedtka & Whitten, 1997). Undoubtedly, this presents issues for service delivery in EI/ECSE. Graduates in these fields should have an understanding of legal and philosophical issues in family-centered service delivery. Current program requirements, however, overrun with courses to fulfill state and national licensing requirements, often do not allow for additional course work in disability issues.

Increasing Numbers of Children and Personnel Shortages.   The latest round of national statistics reveals two other issues in the field of EI/ECSE: an increasing need for services and a lack of qualified personnel to provide them (U.S. Department of Education, 2000). When pooled, their impacts on the field seem overwhelming, and the quality of services being offered to young children with disabilities is surely being compromised as a result.

In 1994 the number of infants and toddlers with disabilities receiving early intervention services was 165,351. This number increased to 197,625 in 1997 (U.S. Department of Education, 1999). Between 1992–93 and 1998–99, the percentage of three-year-olds receiving services grew 33.2 percent, and the number of four-year-olds receiving services increased 31.8 percent. The number of five-year-olds receiving services also increased but at a slower rate of only 18.8 percent. Between 1989–90 and 1998–99, the total number of preschoolers served under IDEA increased 48.8 percent (U.S. Department of Education, 2000). Programs are being stressed by having to provide services to increasing numbers of children.

Personnel shortages have intensified this situation. During the 1995 school year, for example, 12.2 percent of the positions in services for children aged three to five were either vacant or filled by personnel not fully certified (U.S. Department of Education, 2000). In the same year, an additional 4,331 staff were needed for services to children aged birth through two years (U.S. Department of Education, 2000). It seems that EI/ECSE professionals are facing the same issues those in special education are facing: too many children to serve, too few certified personnel to serve them.

Implications for Future Research.   As more and more disciplines are affected by legislation for young children with disabilities, the research agenda will broaden. Early childhood education programs will surely be impacted by IDEA. Can ECE teachers be trained effectively to serve young children with disabilities? Kunze (2000) found that teachers with degrees in special education or a combination of special and general education perceived themselves as those most capable of working with children with disabilities, particularly in inclusive classrooms. Would ECE graduates feel more confident including children with disabilities in their classrooms if their training programs were infused with special education training? Would one course in disabilities and curricular modifications be enough? How can content in EI/ECSE be incorporated into training programs for other disciplines, particularly when the underlying philosophies do not fit with program philosophies? Is this an effective means of preservice training, or should training be delivered through in-service models? As with other issues raised previously, does training result in better services for children and families?

Increasing the number of children served would obviously increase the number of positions available for EI/ECSE personnel. This would affect teacher training programs in EI/ECSE. However, higher education is also facing shortages of appropriately trained personnel (Smith, Tyler, Sindelar, & Pion, 2000). What can be done to address the shortages of personnel at both the practitioner and the university levels? Can programs, as they exist, meet the increasing demand for educators in the field? Can they do so in a timely manner?

SUMMARY

The field of EI/ECSE is no longer in its infancy. Service providers and teacher educators are faced with many challenges, and those in EI/ECSE must possess many skills in many areas, a tall order for personnel preparation programs in special education.

Recent IDEA mandates call for family-centered care in natural environments, and this is changing the role of the service provider. The service provider must understand families and family functioning while embracing linguistic and cultural diversity. The service provider must be a teacher in multiple environments: homes, childcare centers, hospitals, and preschools. Changing family demographics and the growing number of children being served have affected how services are being provided. The natural environment may no longer be a home or clinic but rather may include a variety of environments, from childcare centers and preschools to libraries and shopping malls.

Programs are being asked to serve more children with fewer dollars. Shortages of appropriately trained personnel result in large caseloads for service providers, which in turn results in less-than-adequate service delivery. Personnel are hired on an emergency basis and then required to obtain training within a set period of time.

Service providers in EI/ECSE must have a foundation in applied behavior analysis whether the training program embraces the philosophy or not. Clearly, to fulfill mandates for functional behavioral assessments and ongoing data collection and evaluation, teacher training programs must require students to enroll in at least one such course.

Special education will face many issues in the twenty-first century. Service providers in EI/ECSE will continue to wear many hats: from service coordinator, to IEP/IFSP team leader, to parent trainer, to data collector. What will the future hold for early intervention/early childhood special education, and which hat will the field be asked to wear next?

QUESTIONS FOR FURTHER DISCUSSION

1. Discuss the impact of early childhood special education and early intervention (ECSE/EI) on related fields such as childcare programs, nurses, speech therapists, and nutritionists. Generate several ideas that may be implemented to alleviate this impact (e.g., preservice or in-service training).

2. Discuss the impact of ECSE/EI on local school districts. What can be done to lessen this impact?

3. What are some strategies for addressing personnel preparation, particularly the issue around recruitment and retention of diverse personnel?

4. Describe some of the challenges of family-centered services. What are some of the challenges of assessment and intervention? What can be done to improve the assessment and intervention process?

REFERENCES

Arndorfer, R. E., & Miltenberger, R. G. (1993). Functional assessment and treatment of challenging behavior: A review with implications for early childhood. *Topics in Early Childhood Special Education, 13,* 82–105.

Barnes, C. J. (2000). Wanted: Teachers of color. *Schools in the Middle, 9,* 10–15.

Bricker, D. (2000). Inclusion: How the scene has changed. *Topics in Early Childhood Special Education, 20,* 14–19.

Buell, M. J., Gamel-McCormick, M., & Hallam, R. A. (1999). Inclusion in a childcare context: Experiences and attitudes of family childcare providers. *Topics in Early Childhood Special Education, 19,* 217–224.

Burns, M., & Olive, M. L. (2000, December). Functional communication training: An essential intervention. Poster presented at the 16th annual conference for the Division for Early Childhood of the Council for Exceptional Children, Albuquerque, NM.

Campbell, P., Jefferson, T., & Hurwitz, B. D. (2000, Winter). Ideas and strategies for recruiting and retaining diverse groups of college students. Presentation at the annual meeting of OSEP NECTAS, Washington, DC.

Carta, J. J., Atwater, J. B., Schwartz, I. S., & McConnell, S. R. (1991). Developmentally appropriate practice: Appraising its usefulness for young children with disabilities. *Topics in Early Childhood Special Education, 11,* 1–20.

Carta, J. J., Atwater, J. B., Schwartz, I. S., & McConnell, S. R. (1993). Developmentally appropriate practices and early childhood special education: A reaction to Johnson and McChesney Johnson. *Topics in Early Childhood Special Education, 13,* 243–254.

Children's Defense Fund. (1998). *The state of America's children yearbook.* Washington, DC: Author.

Children's Defense Fund. (1999). *The state of America's children yearbook.* Washington, DC: Author.

Council for Exceptional Children. (1997). *CEC international standards for entry into professional practice.* Arlington, VA: CEC.

Deno, S. L. (1997). Whether thou goest . . . Perspectives on progress monitoring. In J. W. Lloyd, E. J. Kameenui, & D. Chard (Eds.), *Issues in educating students with disabilities* (pp. 77–99). Mahwah, NJ: Lawarence Erlbaum Associates.

Division for Early Childhood. (1993). *DEC recommended practices: Indicators of quality in programs for infants and young children with special needs and their families.* Reston, VA: Council for Exceptional Children.

Division for Early Childhood. (1997). *DEC membership report.* Reston, VA: DEC/CEC.

Division for Early Childhood. (1999). *DEC concept paper on the identification of and intervention with challenging behavior.* Denver, CO: DEC.

Division for Early Childhood, National Association for the Education of Young Children, & Association of Teacher Educators. (1995). *Personnel standards for early education and early intervention: Guidelines for licensure in early childhood special education.* Denver, CO: DEC.

Early Childhood Research Institute on Measuring Growth and Development. (1998). *Theoretical foundations of the Early Childhood Research Institute on Measuring Growth and Development: An early childhood problem-solving model.* (Tech. Report No. 6). Minneapolis: Center for Early Education and Development, University of Minnesota.

Fuchs, L. S., & Deno, S. L. (1991). Paradigmatic distinctions between instructionally relevant measurement models. *Exceptional Children, 57,* 488–500.

Futrell, M. H. (1999). Recruiting minority teachers. *Educational Leadership, 56,* 30–33.

Galinsky, E., Howes, C., Kontos, S., & Shinn, M. (1994). The study of children in family child care and relative care—Key findings and policy recommendations. *Young Children, 50,* 58–61.

Guralnick, M. J. (2001). *Early childhood inclusion: Focus on change.* Baltimore, MD: Paul H. Brookes.

Hancock, T. B., & Kaiser, A. P. (1996). Siblings' use of milieu teaching at home. *Topics in Early Childhood Special Education, 16,* 168–190.

Hemmeter, M. L. (2000). Classroom-based interventions: Evaluating the past and looking toward the future. *Topics in Early Childhood Special Education, 20,* 56–61.

Hemmeter, M. L., McEvoy, M. A., Strain, P., Brault, L., & Timm, M. (1998, December). An examination of research on challenging behaviors: Implications for future research and practice. Research roundtable at the 14th annual DEC International Early Childhood Conference on Children with Special Needs, Chicago, IL.

Hirsch, R., Koppich, J., & Knapp, M. S. (2000). Reflections on teacher quality. *Journal of Staff Development, 21,* 8–13.

Huefner, D. S. (2000). The risks and opportunities of the IEP requirements under IDEA '97. *Journal of Special Education, 33,* 195–204.

Individuals with Disabilities Education Act of 1997, 20 U.S.C. §1400 *et seq.* (1997).

Individuals with Disabilities Education Act Amendments of 1997, 20 U.S.C. §1400 *et seq.* (1997).

Interagency Forum on Child and Family Statistics. (2000). *America's children: Key national indicators of well-being, 2000.* Washington, DC: Author.

Johnson, J. E., & Johnson, K. M. (1992). Clarifying the developmental perspective in response to Carta, Schwartz, Atwater, and McConnell. *Topics in Early Childhood Special Education, 12,* 439–457.

Kaiser, A. P., Hemmeter, M. L., Ostrosky, M. M., & Fischer, R. (1996). The effects of teaching parents to use responsive interaction strategies. *Topics in Early Childhood Special Education, 16,* 375–406.

Kauffman, J. M. (1996). Research to practice issues. *Behavioral Disorders, 22,* 55–60.

Kunze, M. G. (2000). Teachers' perception of ability to teach in early childhood special and general education programs. Unpublished master's thesis, University of Texas, Austin.

Liedtka, J., & Whitten, E. (1997). Building better patient care services: A collaborative approach. *Health Care Management Review, 22,* 16–24.

Lynch, E. W. (1998). Developing cross-cultural competence. In E. W. Lynch & M. J. Hanson (Eds.), *Developing cross-cultural competence: A guide for working with young children and their families.* Baltimore, MD: Paul H. Brookes.

Lynch, E. W., & Hanson, M. J. (1993). Changing demographics: Implications for training in early intervention. *Infants and Young Children, 6,* 50–55.

Lynch, E. W., & Hanson, M. J. (1998). *Developing cross-cultural competence: A guide for working with young children and their families.* Baltimore, MD: Paul H. Brookes.

McBride, S. L., & Peterson, C. (1997). Home-based early intervention with families of children with disabilities: Who is doing what? *Topics in Early Childhood Special Education, 17,* 209–233.

McConnell, S. R. (2000). Assessment in early intervention and early childhood special education: Building on

the past to project into our future. *Topics in Early Childhood Special Education, 19,* 43–48.

McEvoy, M. A., Davis, C. A., & Reichle, J. (1993). Districtwide technical assistance teams: Designing intervention strategies for young children with challenging behaviors. *Behavioral Disorders, 19,* 27–34.

McEvoy, M. A., Davis, C. A., Rogers, E., & Olive, M. L. (2000, February). Challenging behavior in early childhood/early elementary classrooms: What the research tells us about ways to remediate or prevent it. Panel research presentation at the Pacific Coast Research Conference, La Jolla, CA.

McEvoy, M. A., Olive, M. L., & Neilsen, S. L. (2000, April). Positive behavioral support in early education. Panel research presentation at the Conference on Research Innovations in Early Interventions, San Diego, CA.

McEvoy, M.A., & Reichle, J. (2000). Further consideration of the role of the environment on stereotypic and self-injurious behavior. *Journal of Early Intervention, 23,* 22–24.

McWilliam, R. A. (2000). Recommended practices in interdisciplinary models. In S. Sandall, M. E. McLean, & B. J. Smith (Eds.), *DEC recommended practices in early intervention, early childhood special education.* Longmont, CO: Sopris West.

Meyers, C. L., & Holland, K. L. (2000). Classroom behavioral intervention: Do teachers consider the function of the behavior? *Psychology in the Schools, 37,* 271–280.

National Association for the Education of Young Children. (1994). *NAEYC guidelines for preparation of early childhood professionals.* Washington, DC: Author.

National Council for Accreditation of Teacher Education. (2000). *Professional standards for the accreditation of schools, colleges, and departments of education.* Washington, DC: Author.

Neilsen, S. L., & McEvoy, M. A. (2001). *Functional behavioral assessment: Research informing policy.* Manuscript submitted for publication.

Nelson, J. R., Mather, S. R., & Rutherford, R. B., Jr. (1999). Has public policy exceeded our knowledge base? A review of the functional behavioral assessment literature. *Behavior Disorders, 24,* 169–179.

Odom, S. L. (2000). Preschool inclusion: What we know and where we go from here. *Topics in Early Childhood Special Education, 20,* 20–27.

Olive, M. L. (1999). Functional communication training: An assessment of stimulus and response generalization. Unpublished doctoral dissertation, University of Minnesota, Minneapolis.

Olive, M. L., Neilsen, S. L., & McEvoy, M. (1997, November). Proactive interventions for young children with challenging behavior. Paper presented at the annual conference of the Division for Early Childhood of the Council for Exceptional Children, New Orleans, LA.

Sandall, S., McLean, M. E., & Smith, B. J. (Eds.). (2000). *DEC recommended practices in early intervention/ early childhood special education.* Longmont, CO: Sopris West.

Sandall, S., & Smith, B. J. (2000). Introduction to the DEC recommended practices. In S. Sandall, M. E. McLean, & B. J. Smith (Eds.), *DEC recommended practices in early intervention, early childhood special education.* Longmont, CO: Sopris West.

Smith, D. D., Tyler, N., Sindelar, P., & Pion, G. (2000, July 11–12). *Leadership supply and demand: The full story.* Paper presented at the OSEP Leadership Project Directors' Conference, Washington, DC.

Symons, F. J. (2000). Early intervention for early aberrant repetitive behavior: Possible, plausible, probable? *Journal of Early Intervention, 23,* 20–22.

Trivette, C. M., Deal, A., & Dunst, C. J. (1986). Family needs, sources of support, and professional roles: Critical elements of family systems assessment and intervention. *Diagnostique, 11,* 246–267.

Trivette, C. M., & Dunst, C. J. (2000). Recommended practices in family-based practices. In S. Sandall, M. E. McLean, & B. J. Smith (Eds.), *DEC recommended practices in early intervention, early childhood special education.* Longmont, CO: Sopris West.

U.S. Department of Education. (1999). *To assure the free appropriate public education of all children with disabilities: Twenty-first annual report to Congress on the implementation of the Individuals with Disabilities Education Act.* Washington, DC: Author.

U.S. Department of Education. (2000). *To assure the free appropriate public education of all children with disabilities: Twenty-second annual report to Congress on the implementation of the Individuals with Disabilities Education Act.* Washington, DC: Author.

U.S. Department of Education, National Center for Education Statistics. (1999). Teacher quality: A report on the preparation and qualifications of public school teachers, NCES 1999-080. Washington, DC: NCES.

Vaughn, S., Klinger, J., & Hughes, M. (2000). Sustainability of research-based practices. *Exceptional Children, 66,* 163–171.

White-Hood, M. (2000). Recruiting and maintaining diverse staff. *Schools in the Middle, 9,* 16–19.

Willis, W. O. (1999). Culturally competent nursing care during the perinatal period. *Journal of Perinatal and Neonatal Nursing, 13,* 45–59.

Wolery, M. (2000). Recommended practices in child-focused interventions. In S. Sandall, M. E. McLean, & B. J. Smith (Eds.), *DEC recommended practices in early intervention, early childhood special education.* Longmont, CO: Sopris West.

Wolery, M., & Gast, D. L. (2000). Classroom research for young children with disabilities: Assumptions that guided the conduct of research. *Topics in Early Childhood Special Education, 20,* 49–55.

Yell, M. L., & Drasgow, E. (2000). Litigating a free appropriate public education: The Lovaas hearings and cases. *Journal of Special Education, 33,* 205–214.

ISSUES IN CURRICULUM-BASED MEASUREMENT

Monitoring Instruction to Increase Student Learning

ROSE M. ALLINDER
University of Nebraska–Lincoln

LYNN S. FUCHS
DOUGLAS FUCHS
Vanderbilt University

ISSUES IN CURRICULUM-BASED MEASUREMENT

Within the field of special education in recent years, few areas have garnered as much interest and attention as assessment. This is not surprising given the indispensability of assessment in all parts of special education, beginning with the assessment procedures required for students to be placed into special education, continuing throughout the development and evaluation of the individualized education plan (IEP), and culminating in a linkage to instructional planning, delivery, and evaluation. Controversy and debate encircle the topic of assessment and range from concerns about racial and ethnic bias of assessment tools and techniques (Samuda, Kong, Cummins, Lewis, & Pascual-Leone, 1991) to appropriate methods for including students with disabilities in large-scale accountability testing (Hollenbeck, Tindal, & Almond, 1998) and development of performance and other forms of authentic assessment (Fuchs & Fuchs, 1996). Any discussion of assessment issues should also include the topic of what Messick (1980) has referred to as the social consequences of testing—specifically, the degree to which the results of assessments help guide instruction and increase student learning (Gersten, Keating, & Irvin, 1995).

Early research into the use of assessment data to enhance student learning included a meta-analysis of the effects of systematic formative evaluation on academic gains of students with disabilities (Fuchs & Fuchs, 1986). Results from the analysis of twenty-nine studies yielded an effect size of 0.70, indicating strong support for using systematic formative evaluation. Additional results from the analysis indicated that greater gains were made when two factors were present: data were displayed graphically rather than in a table, and teachers applied decision rules to their students' graphed data. Thus, formative evaluation of student academic progress appears to be one assessment procedure that meets Messick's (1988) condition for validity.

There are many formative evaluation systems. One well-developed method is curriculum-based measurement (CBM) (Deno, 1985). In this chapter we present the definition and describe the development of this assessment system. We review the research base in which CBM has been used as an intervention to improve teacher planning and student achievement, and we summarize supports for and barriers to its use.

What Is CBM?

CBM is a way of systematically measuring student progress in curriculum areas with simple, reliable, and valid measures (Deno, 1985). With CBM, students complete short tests of no more than five minutes, usually one to two times a week. Measures have been developed for reading, mathematics, written expression, and spelling (Deno & Fuchs, 1987), as well as specific content areas (Espin & Tindal, 1998) and phonological awareness skills (Good & Kaminski, 1996). Extensive research has documented the reliability and validity of these measures (e.g., Espin & Tindal, 1998; Kaminski & Good, 1996; Marston, 1989).

CBM was developed primarily at the Institute for Research on Learning Disabilities (IRLD) at the University of Minnesota in the 1970s (Deno, 1992). For six years researchers at IRLD refined curriculum-based assessment procedures through a series of studies examining the technical adequacy of the measures they developed. Design features that directed the development of the measures were (1) reliability and validity, (2) ease of administration, (3) repeated and frequent administration, and (4) time efficiency and cost effectiveness. This research resulted in measures in reading, mathematics computation, spelling, and written expression, as well as procedures for administering, graphing, and interpreting student data (Deno & Fuchs, 1987).

Four components are involved in using CBM for ongoing monitoring. First, measurement materials must be created or procured (see Deno & Fuchs, 1987; Fuchs & Fuchs, 1991, 1992). Second, probes or short tests are administered and scored, either by hand or using computer programs (Fuchs, Fuchs, & Hamlett, 1992; Shinn, 1989). Next, student scores are graphed, and the initial scores are used to establish an end-of-year goal. Finally, teachers compare the student's actual rate of progress to the expected rate of progress or end-of-year goal (Fuchs, 1989). The resulting graphed data provide a means for teachers to evaluate student progress in order to determine the effectiveness of their instructional plans. To accomplish this teachers (1) set an end-of-year goal for individual students, (2) visually represent this on the student's graph by drawing a goal line connecting the initial scores and the end-of-year goal, and (3) continually evaluate the rate of student progress with the expected progress represented by the goal line on the student's graph. Teachers are encouraged to use a simple but explicit set of decision rules (e.g., raise student goal, modify instruction, continue collecting data) to evaluate the rate of student progress. Figure 1 illustrates these components on a student's graph.

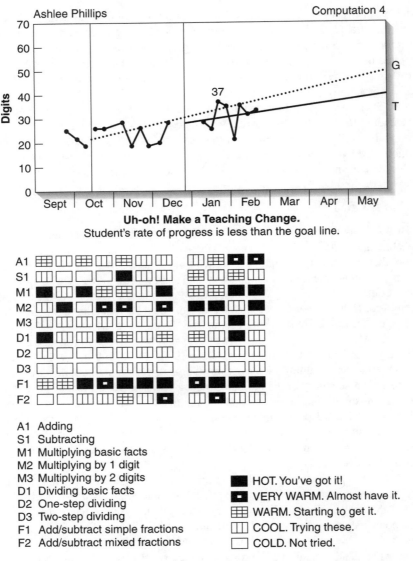

FIGURE 1   **Student Graph and Skills Analysis in Mathematics Computation**

Research on Effects of CBM on Student Achievement

Numerous studies show that the use of CBM positively affects the academic achievement of students with high-incidence disabilities. Research shows that various CBM components contribute to the increased outcomes, including teachers' use of student data to evaluate the effectiveness of instruction, teachers' goal setting, and visual presentation of data via graphs (Fuchs, Deno, & Mirkin, 1984; Fuchs & Fuchs, 1986, 1991; Fuchs, Fuchs, & Hamlett, 1989a, 1989b).

Use of Student Data

A key component of CBM is the response of teachers to students' data, not merely the act of measuring student progress. Several studies on reading instruction have underscored the importance of this. Fuchs, Deno, and Mirkin (1984) taught eighteen special education teachers to use primary components of data-based instruction, including a decision-rule procedure that required teachers to make instructional changes when a student's progress toward an individualized reading goal appeared to be insufficient over seven to ten data points. Results indicated that students whose teachers used the measurement system significantly outperformed similar students whose teachers did not use the measurement system on a passage reading test as well as the decoding and comprehension subtests of a norm-referenced standardized reading test. Jones and Krouse (1988) found similar results when they examined the use of a data-based approach to evaluating instructional effectiveness with student teachers. In this study significant improvement in oral reading and in the reading comprehension subtest of a norm-referenced standardized reading test was found for students whose teachers had used a systematic measurement system. Finally, Fuchs, Fuchs, and Hamlett (1989a) compared academic gains of students with high-incidence disabilities in reading. In this study teachers were divided into three groups: control (no use of CBM at all), CBM-M (teachers only measured student progress but did not respond to student progress data), and CBM-E (teachers evaluated student graphs and made instructional changes if sufficient student progress was not evidenced). Results indicated that students in the CBM-E group made significantly greater gains than students in the other two groups; importantly, students in the CBM-M group made gains comparable to students whose teachers did not use CBM at all.

Similar results are found in other academic areas. Fuchs, Butterworth, and Fuchs (1989) investigated the effects of applying decision rules to student-graphed CBM data in spelling with twenty special education teachers, nine of whom completed CBM with the assistance of a computer software program that graphed and applied decision rules to student data. Ten teachers completed all CBM tasks by hand, and the remaining teachers comprised the control group. Results indicated that students whose teachers used CBM had significantly greater growth in spelling compared with the control group; no differences were detected with regard to computer-assisted CBM.

In math Allinder (1996) reported that teachers who implemented CBM with greater fidelity effected greater gains among their students with high-incidence disabilities. In this study, ten teachers were assigned randomly to a control group and did not use CBM; the remaining twenty teachers used CBM for fifteen weeks. Following the completion of the study, teachers' degree of implementation of key CBM components (frequency of measurement, compliance with decision rules, and ambitiousness of goals) was examined. Teachers who were found to have implemented CBM with high quality evidenced greater gains in mathematics computation when compared with teachers who implemented CBM with lesser quality. These poorly implementing teachers produced growth only comparable to that of the control group.

Teachers and Goals

Because data are graphed, CBM lends itself naturally to using goals and goal setting as complementary components of the measurement system. How teachers use goals has been found to influence student achievement. Fuchs, Fuchs, and Hamlett (1989b) found that when teachers were prompted to raise goals for students when their rate of progress was greater than expected, students had statistically significant growth compared to students whose teachers did not use CBM. This difference in growth was associated with an effect size of 0.52. In contrast, students whose teachers conducted CBM but who did not systematically raise goals did not perform significantly better than control students. The researchers concluded that teachers routinely underestimated student progress; however, when teachers were responsive to prompts to raise student goals, greater student achievement was noted.

Students and Goals

Because CBM graphically presents data of student progress, some analysts have posited that having students examine their graphs may motivate them and thus contribute to increased academic gains. Research results to date corroborate this possibility, but support is limited.

Bean and Lane (1990) investigated the use of CBM in reading acquisition with adults in a basic education program and queried participants regarding their perceptions of CBM. These adult learners responded that seeing the goal line on the graphs of their reading data was motivating for them. The authors concluded that using CBM with adults in basic literacy programs helped maintain their interest in their learning, enhanced their knowledge about their own learning, and in general had a positive effect on student learning.

Fuchs, Butterworth, and Fuchs (1989) reported that students whose teachers employed CBM were more articulate and specific when asked about their goals in an academic area than were students whose teachers did not use CBM. In this study, teachers created graphs by hand or through a computer-assisted program; students were not systematically informed of their graphs and goals, nor did they systematically interact with them. Students in this study had significantly greater gains than did control students. The researchers hypothesized that increased awareness of goals may have contributed to student outcomes, but this did not fully explain the significant difference between the two groups of students.

Because students did not view their graphs in the Fuchs, Butterworth, and Fuchs (1989) study, it is not possible to conclude that the graphs do not have motivational properties. Subsequent research has explored this question. In two studies (Fuchs, Fuchs, Hamlett, & Whinnery, 1991; Whinnery & Fuchs, 1993) students were shown CBM graphs, and one-half of the students were shown a goal for that day's probes based on the intersection of the goal line and date; the remaining students who completed CBM also saw their graphs but without a goal or goal line specified. In neither study did students who interacted with their goal make significantly greater gains at the end of the treatment. However, in the Fuchs, Fuchs, Hamlett, and Whinnery (1991) study, students who received feedback regarding their performance via their graph and goal line had significantly less variability across time. Although this study did not support the premise that CBM graphs motivate students and thus increase their academic performance, decreased variability in student graphs is advantageous in two ways. First, it suggests that students are constantly applying more effort to their performance on biweekly tests, and, second, it produces graphs that are easier for teachers to interpret. The lack of intervention effects of student performance may be attributed to the instructional variables that teachers of all students manipulated (Whinnery & Fuchs, 1993).

In a similar examination of the effects of graphs, Glor-Scheib and Zigmond (1993) examined the effects of CBM on students' motivation. In this study, twenty-two sixth-grade students with learning disabilities were shown their CBM graphs before they read orally for one minute. In addition to examining their graphs, students set a goal for that day's reading. Following the treatment, students rated themselves significantly higher with regard to their perceived competence in reading; no differences were found on the other measures that included self-perception of general intellectual ability and global self-worth. The investigators hypothesized that this enhanced self-perception of competence in reading was the possible result of the measurement system itself (e.g., the increased opportunity to read while completing the CBM tasks) or the interaction with their graphed data and goal setting (e.g., setting a short-term goal helped them feel more capable and positive).

Tying CBM to Instructional Changes

Despite studies showing that CBM can inform teachers of the effectiveness of instruction for individual students, ample research indicates that it has not been widely implemented (Swain & Allinder, 1997), and the primary reason cited for this has been the time needed to implement CBM (Hasbrouck, Woldbeck, Ihnot, & Parker, 1999; Wesson, King, & Deno, 1984; Yell, Deno, & Marston, 1992). In response to this, computerized programs were created that administer, score, graph, and apply decision rules; this technology decreases the amount of time teachers spend on these tasks (Fuchs, Hamlett, Fuchs, Stecker, & Ferguson, 1988). This positive step had a definite downside: When computers administered, scored, and graphed student CBM data, teachers were distant from the student data and found making instructional modifications more difficult (Fuchs, Fuchs, Hamlett, & Stecker, 1990). To compensate for this loss of teacher interaction with student data, computerized applications of CBM incorporated skills analysis and expert systems to assist teachers in formulating instructional modifications.

Skills analyses have been developed for math (Fuchs, Fuchs, Hamlett, & Stecker, 1990) and spelling (Fuchs, Fuchs, Hamlett, & Allinder, 1991a). Skills analyses summarize student responses to problem types in math (e.g., addition with regrouping, multiplication of fractions, and word problems) and to phonetic patterns in spelling (e.g., short vowels and final *e* rule). Figure 2 illustrates skills analyses in mathematics computation and applications. These summaries are coupled with the graphs displaying student progress over time to provide teachers feedback regarding student progress overall within the identified curriculum area as well as information regarding student performance on specific subskills within the curriculum. Research regarding the reliability and validity has established the technical adequacy in each domain (Fuchs, Fuchs, Hamlett, & Allinder, 1989).

Research in math and spelling indicates that adding the skills analysis is beneficial. In an investigation of the effects of skills analysis in math, Fuchs, Fuchs, Hamlett, and Stecker (1990) found that teachers who used the skills analysis differed from teachers who did not—those who did identified more specific skills to be taught. Moreover, students of teachers who used CBM with skills analysis made significantly greater gains in math compared to students whose teachers did not have the skills analysis added to CBM graphs or to students whose teachers did not use CBM at all. A similar result was found in spelling (Fuchs, Fuchs, Hamlett, & Allinder, 1991a).

While skills analyses provided additional information that informed teachers' instructional decision making, teachers still found it difficult to enhance instructional programs. Thus, expert systems were developed to augment CBM computerized data collection and graphing (Fuchs, Fuchs, & Hamlett, 1994). Expert systems were developed to provide advice to teachers about instructional changes based on the input of acknowledged experts in the areas of reading, math, and spelling. The expert systems' recommendations were formulated on the basis of responses to queries regarding (1) patterns of student performance in that aca-

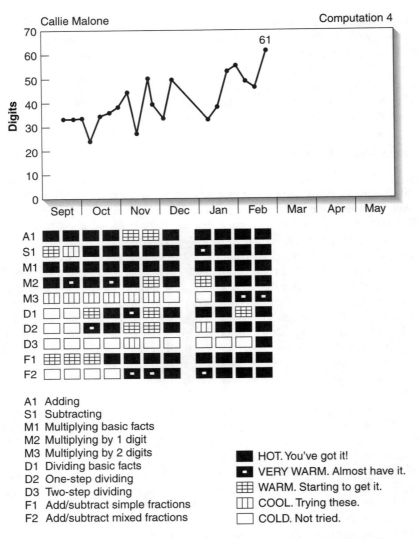

A1 Adding
S1 Subtracting
M1 Multiplying basic facts
M2 Multiplying by 1 digit
M3 Multiplying by 2 digits
D1 Dividing basic facts
D2 One-step dividing
D3 Two-step dividing
F1 Add/subtract simple fractions
F2 Add/subtract mixed fractions

■ HOT. You've got it!
▣ VERY WARM. Almost have it.
▦ WARM. Starting to get it.
▥ COOL. Trying these.
☐ COLD. Not tried.

FIGURE 2   Skills Analyses in Mathematics Computation and Applications

demic area (taken from the skills analyses in math and spelling), (2) curricular options and preferences of the teacher, (3) additional materials and supports, and (4) student factors such as motivation and interest.

Outcomes in the three main academic areas were generally strong and positive, with the results in math being clearest. In math, teachers who used the expert system made instructional changes that were much more varied than their counterparts who did not use the expert system; furthermore, students of teachers in the expert system group made significantly greater growth in math (Fuchs, Fuchs, Hamlett, & Stecker, 1991). In reading, students whose teachers used the expert systems outperformed their counterparts whose teachers used only CBM on only one outcome measure; both groups of students whose teachers used CBM out-

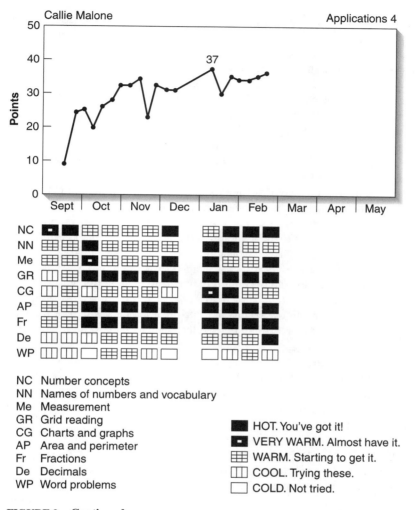

NC Number concepts
NN Names of numbers and vocabulary
Me Measurement
GR Grid reading
CG Charts and graphs
AP Area and perimeter
Fr Fractions
De Decimals
WP Word problems

HOT. You've got it!
VERY WARM. Almost have it.
WARM. Starting to get it.
COOL. Trying these.
COLD. Not tried.

FIGURE 2   Continued

performed students in the control group (Fuchs, Fuchs, Hamlett, & Ferguson, 1992). In contrast to these positive outcomes in favor of using expert systems to guide teacher instructional decision making, the addition of the expert system in the area of spelling did not result in greater gains; however, both groups of students whose teachers used CBM had significantly greater growth in spelling than did students in the control group (Fuchs, Fuchs, Hamlett, & Allinder, 1991b).

Classwide Applications of CBM

The instructional augmentations of skills analyses and expert systems were originally created to be used by special education teachers with individual students with high-incidence disabilities. In later applications teachers have also used these skills analyses for students with and without disabilities who receive their instruction from a general education teacher. Knowing that general education teachers rarely individualize instruction for unique students (Baker & Zigmond, 1990; Fuchs, Fuchs, & Bishop, 1992a), CBM use has been explored with entire classrooms in which students with high-incidence disabilities are included.

Fuchs, Fuchs, Hamlett, Phillips, and Bentz (1994) examined the use of CBM with forty general educators, each of whom had at least one student with a learning disability included for instruction in mathematics. In this study, one-half of the teachers did not conduct CBM. The remaining teachers conducted CBM with their entire classes and received feedback that included (1) copies of each student's graph and skills profile (detailing degree of mastery of each problem type), (2) a class graph depicting student progress across time for number of digits correct on CBM measures at the twenty-fifth percentile, fiftieth percentile, and seventy-fifth percentile, (3) a listing of students whose performance was below the twenty-fifth percentile, (4) the skills on which students had improved or stayed the same in the previous month, and (5) a graphic representation of all students' proficiency on problem types for the current two-week period. Figures 3 through 9 illustrate these components of a classwide report. While all twenty teachers conducting CBM received this information, ten of them also received recommendations regarding which skills to teach during whole-class instruction, which skills to teach to small groups, computer-assisted instruction, and classwide peer-tutoring assignments. The remaining ten CBM teachers did not receive these additional instructional recommendations. Results indicated that teachers who received the instructional recommendations had more variety in what they taught and how they taught it. Achievement gains were significantly greater for students with learning disabilities when teachers received instructional recommendations; no significant differences were noted between students with learning disabilities in classes in which CBM was used without instructional recommendations and those in contrast classes. The investigators concluded that general educators required instructional recommendations based on assessment data to enhance the achievement of their students.

This finding was corroborated by a second study that again examined the use of classwide CBM (Fuchs, Fuchs, Hamlett, Phillips, & Karns, 1995). As in the previous study, twenty general educators conducted CBM with their entire math class (which included at least one student with a learning disability) and received a class report that included statistics on the class as a whole and on individual students as well as graphic displays of student progress. In this study, one-half of the teachers also received suggestions for how to modify the peer-mediated portions of their math instruction for individual students. Results were similar to those of the Fuchs, Fuchs, Hamlett, Phillips, and Bentz (1994) study in that it appeared that teachers needed this type of explicit assistance to use the assessment information to inform their instructional planning and revising. Unlike in the previous study, in this case students with learning disabilities in general education classrooms in which teachers were given suggestions for specialized instructional modifications did not outperform their counterparts in the no-suggestions CBM classrooms.

Both these studies illustrate the melding of CBM assessment data with a specific instructional strategy, classwide peer tutoring, in a directive approach to help general educators accommodate increased diversity in their classrooms. In addition to the investigations of the combination of CBM and peer tutoring, which have been conducted in the area of math and which include instructional recommendations based on classwide skills profiles (Fuchs, Fuchs, Hamlett, Phillips, & Karns, 1995; Fuchs, Fuchs, Hamlett, Phillips, & Bentz, 1994), work has also been conducted in the area of reading. The CBM reading measure consists of

CLASS SUMMARY
   Teacher: Mrs. Robertson
   Report through 2/23

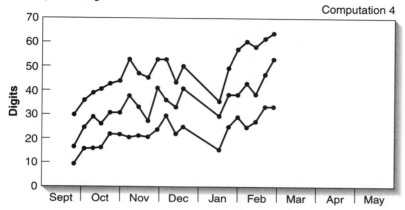

Students to Watch
   Michele Hauser
   Brandon Smith
   Anthony Williams
   Tommy Payne
   John Brendall

Areas of Improvement:
Computation
   D3 Two-step dividing
   D2 One-step dividing
   S1 Subtracting
   M1 Multiplying basic facts

Whole-Class Instruction:
Computation
   D3 Two-step dividing
   48% of your students are either
   COLD or COOL on this skill.

Small-Group Instruction:
Computation
   D2 One-step dividing

   Anthony Williams
   Ashlee Phillips
   Brandon Smith
   Jamal Walker
   Michele Hauser
   Tyrone Randall

(continued)

**FIGURE 3   Classwide Graphs in Mathematics Computation
and Applications**

grade-appropriate maze tasks that students complete using computer software (Fuchs, Hamlett, & Fuchs, 1997). Teacher feedback resembles the math feedback except that student performance on subskills or problem types is omitted (Fuchs & Fuchs, 1994).

Barriers and Supports

Despite the body of work overwhelmingly supporting the contention that teachers' use of CBM to evaluate their instructional plans increases their students' achievement, CBM is not implemented on a wide scale (Swain & Allinder, 1997; Wesson, King, & Deno, 1984), nor is it always implemented with rigor. This is a concern because research documents that the quality with which teachers implement CBM is linked to the amount of academic growth of their students (Allinder, 1996; Wesson, Skiba, Sevcik, King, & Deno, 1984). Factors that may im-

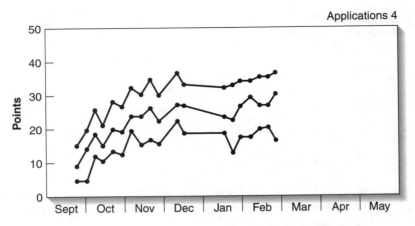

Most Improved
  LaSheika Morris
  Bryce Canyon
  Michele Hauser
  Greg Schneider
  Anthony Williams

Areas of Improvement:
Applications
  Me Measurement
  De Decimals

Whole-Class Instruction:
Applications
  De Decimals

  70% of your students are either
  COLD or COOL on this skill.

Small-Group Instruction:
Applications
  NC Number concepts

  Anthony Williams
  Jamal Walker
  Michele Hauser

FIGURE 3   Continued

pact the degree to which teachers implement CBM include those at the personal, professional, and school level.

Personal Factors.   Two personal factors that may affect the degree to which teachers implement CBM are efficacy and acceptability. Efficacy may be thought of as both personal efficacy, the extent to which teachers believe they can influence student outcomes, and teaching efficacy, the degree to which teachers believe that students benefit from school (Gibson & Dembo, 1984). In a study of thirty special education teachers who were implementing CBM, those who rated themselves higher in personal efficacy differed from their colleagues in (1) how they implemented CBM (they raised their students' goals more often) and (2) the results they obtained (their students had greater gains in math) (Allinder, 1995). In this same study there was a difference in the way teachers rated themselves in teaching efficacy. Special education teachers with higher teaching efficacy had greater goal ambitiousness and more goal changes for their students than their counterparts; no differences were noted for student achievement. Thus it seems that a readiness to set and strive for higher goals, which the high-personal efficacy teachers demonstrated, may have reflected their belief in their ability to teach students.
    Research into the acceptability of CBM has revealed variation in how well teachers (1) like CBM, (2) would continue using it, and (3) would recommend it to other teachers,

CLASS SKILLS PROFILE – Computation
Teacher: Mrs. Robertson
Report through 2/23

Name	A1	S1	M1	M2	M3	D1	D2	D3	F1	F2
Amanda Brown	■	■	■	☐	■	■	▥	▥	■	■
Analie Carter	■	■	■	■	■	▦	■	■	■	■
Anthony Williams	▣	▦	■	☐	☐	▥	☐	☐	■	☐
Ashlee Phillips	▣	▥	■	▦	▥	▦	▥	▥	■	▥
Brandon Smith	▦	☐	■	▥	▦	▦	▥	▥	■	▥
Bryan White	▣	■	■	■	■	▥	■	▦	■	▥
Bryce Canyon	■	■	■	■	■	■	■	▥	▥	▦
Callie Malone	■	■	■	■	▣	■	■	▣	■	■
Chris Allen	▦	■	■	▣	■	■	■	■	■	■
Conrad Jones	▣	▦	■	■	▦	■	■	▦	■	■
DeShawn Parrish	■	■	■	■	■	▦	■	■	■	■
Greg Schneider	■	▦	▣	■	■	▦	■	▦	▣	▦
Jamal Walker	▦	▣	■	▣	■	▣	▥	▥	■	■
Janice Baker	■	▣	■	▣	▣	▥	■	▥	■	■
Jennifer Kantner	■	■	■	▥	▦	■	■	■	■	▥
John Brendall	▥	▣	▥	▣	☐	■	▥	▣	▣	▣
LaSheika Morris	■	▦	■	▣	▦	▦	■	■	■	■
Leonard Long	■	■	■	■	■	■	▦	■	▦	▦
Lizabeth Howard	■	▦	■	■	■	■	■	■	■	■
Michele Hauser	▦	▦	■	▥	▥	▦	■	▥	▦	☐
Susannah Crockett	▦	▣	■	■	▥	▦	▦	▥	■	▣
Tommy Payne	▥	☐	▥	☐	▥	☐	☐	☐	☐	☐
Tyrone Randall	■	■	▦	☐	▦	■	▥	▥	■	▣
■ HOT. You've got it!	12	10	19	10	10	8	13	6	18	10
▣ VERY WARM. Almost have it.	4	4	1	5	2	2	0	2	2	3
▦ WARM. Starting to get it.	5	6	1	1	5	9	1	4	1	3
▥ COOL. Trying these.	2	1	2	3	4	3	7	9	1	4
☐ COLD. Not tried.	0	2	0	4	2	1	2	2	1	3

FIGURE 4   Classwide Skills Profile in Mathematics Computation

even among teachers who volunteer to participate in research projects involving CBM. In a study of twenty-one special education teachers who used CBM with at least two students with high-incidence disabilities, Allinder and Oats (1997) found that teachers who rated CBM as more acceptable differed significantly from their colleagues who also used CBM with regard to the number of probes they had students complete and how ambitious they were in setting their students' goals; the difference between the two groups of teachers in the number of times they raised their students' goals approached significance. Also important in this study was the finding that teachers who rated CBM more highly acceptable effected greater growth in their students' math progress. Thus, it appears that the degree to which teachers found CBM acceptable affected the way they used the measurement system.

CLASS SKILLS PROFILE – Applications
Teacher: Mrs. Robertson
Report through 2/23

Name	NC	NN	Me	GR	CG	AP	Fr	De	WP
Amanda Brown									
Analie Carter									
Anthony Williams									
Ashlee Phillips									
Brandon Smith									
Bryan White									
Bryce Canyon									
Callie Malone									
Chris Allen									
Conrad Jones									
DeShawn Parrish									
Greg Schneider									
Jamal Walker									
Janice Baker									
Jennifer Kantner									
John Brendall									
LaSheika Morris									
Leonard Long									
Lizabeth Howard									
Michele Hauser									
Susannah Crockett									
Tommy Payne									
Tyrone Randall									

		NC	NN	Me	GR	CG	AP	Fr	De	WP
■	HOT. You've got it!	4	11	3	17	0	7	18	3	0
▪	VERY WARM. Almost have it.	0	1	3	2	3	3	2	0	0
▦	WARM. Starting to get it.	12	8	13	2	10	8	2	4	2
▯	COOL. Trying these.	6	3	4	1	7	5	1	15	16
□	COLD. Not tried.	1	0	0	1	3	0	0	1	5

FIGURE 5   **Classwide Skills Profile in Mathematics Applications**

Professional Factors.   Professional factors that may affect the degree to which teachers implement CBM include time, training, and support. The issue of time motivated the creation of software programs to administer, score, graph, and analyze student responses (Fuchs, Hamlett, Fuchs, Stecker, & Ferguson, 1988). Training is critical if teachers are to accurately and efficiently implement CBM; in fact, Yell et al. (1992) reported that the primary barrier to CBM implementation identified by school administrators was that teachers mechanically collected and graphed CBM data but did not use this information to inform instructional planning. The administrators attributed this to lack of training for teachers.

Fuchs and Fuchs (1993) found that teachers who completed CBM activities without the assistance of technology implemented CBM as well as teachers who used software did; all

FIGURE 6   Classwide Ranking of Students by Scores in Mathematics Computation

RANKED SCORES—COMPUTATION   TEACHER: MRS. ROBERTSON   REPORT THROUGH 2/23

NAME	SCORE	GROWTH
Analie Carter	63	+1.42
DeShawn Parrish	61	+1.12
Leonard Long	60	+0.72
Lizabeth Howard	58	+1.13
Callie Malone	53	+0.99
LaSheika Morris	50	+0.42
Jennifer Kantner	50	+1.23
Bryce Canyon	49	+0.36
Chris Allen	48	+1.00
Janice Baker	46	+0.62
Conrad Jones	45	+1.04
Tyrone Randall	44	+1.04
Bryan White	43	+0.26
Amanda Brown	42	+1.10
Greg Schneider	39	+0.23
Susannah Crockett	37	+0.26
Jamal Walker	36	+1.04
Michele Hauser	34	+0.61
Ashlee Phillips	32	+0.52
Brandon Smith	27	....
Anthony Williams	18	+0.24
Tommy Payne	7	....
John Brendall	....	....

teachers performed the structure and measurement components with greater accuracy than they did the data utilization component. The investigators concluded that observation and feedback on CBM implementation were beneficial. This finding is underscored by other research that found that the way teachers initially conducted CBM is difficult to change and that unguided practice does not automatically result in accurate and efficient CBM implementation (Wesson, Deno, Mirkin, Maruyama, Skiba, King, & Sevcik, 1988).

The benefits of consultation have been illustrated in other CBM research. Much of that research relied on expert university-based consultants who supported teachers while they acquired skills in conducting and using CBM (Fuchs, Fuchs, & Hamlett, 1989c). Not all consultation has relied on this model. Wesson (1991) contrasted individual consultation with a university-based consultant and group consultation with other teachers. In this study with fifty-five teachers of students with high-incidence disabilities, teachers who implemented CBM and participated in group follow-up consultation produced greater growth in their students than did teachers who used CBM and received individual follow-up consultation or teachers who did not use CBM at all.

Given that not all teachers have access to individual university-based consultation, Allinder and BeckBest (1995) explored the benefits of teachers' self-monitoring their implementation of CBM. In this study with nineteen special education teachers in rural schools,

FIGURE 7   Classwide Ranking of Students by Scores in Mathematics Applications

RANKED SCORES—APPLICATIONS	TEACHER: MRS. ROBERTSON	REPORT THROUGH 2/23
NAME	**SCORE**	**GROWTH**
Lizabeth Howard	35	+0.69
LaSheika Morris	35	+0.84
Callie Malone	35	+0.70
Analie Carter	34	+0.84
Jennifer Kantner	33	+0.87
DeShawn Parrish	33	+0.61
Leonard Long	32	+0.47
Tyrone Randall	27	+0.89
Chris Allen	27	+0.48
Susannah Crockett	26	+0.53
Conrad Jones	25	+0.72
Janice Baker	24	+0.34
Greg Schneider	23	+0.67
Bryce Canyon	23	+0.43
Bryan White	23	+0.61
Ashlee Phillips	23	+0.60
Amanda Brown	22	+0.24
Jamal Walker	19	+0.47
Michele Hauser	18	+0.60
Anthony Williams	14	+0.10
Brandon Smith	12	....
Tommy Payne	8	....
John Brendall	....	....

nine teachers received bimonthly visits from a university-based consultant. The remaining teachers self-monitored their completion of CBM components and were prompted to request assistance or clarification on a bimonthly basis from the consultant. Results indicated no differences between the groups of teachers with regard to CBM implementation nor to student achievement. These findings suggest that self-monitoring implementation is as effective as expert university-based consultation. In a similar study Allinder, Bolling, Oats, and Gagnon (2000) explored the use of self-monitoring of an additional facet of CBM, specifically teachers' use of math skills analyses data in formulating instructional modifications. In this study with thirty-one special educators, teachers who self-monitored their understanding and use of skills analyses differed in two aspects from teachers who used CBM without self-monitoring and teachers who did not use CBM at all: Their instruction relied more on changing what and how they taught math, and their students had significantly greater growth in mathematics.

School Level Factors.   Several school-level factors have been identified as contributing to or hindering teachers' implementation of CBM. One factor is the match between the measurement system and the school or local curriculum, especially when using software to assist CBM implementation. Phillips, Fuchs, and Fuchs (1994) report that general education teach-

PEER-TUTORING ASSIGNMENTS
Teacher: Mrs. Robertson
Report through 2/23

Floater: Analie Carter

F2 Add/subtract mixed fractions	First coach	Second coach
	■ Lizabeth Howard	☐ Tommy Payne
	⊞ Leonard Long	⊡ Bryan White
	⊞ Greg Schneider	⊡ Jennifer Kantner
	⊞ Bryce Canyon	⊡ Ashlee Phillips
	▣ Tyrone Randall	☐ Michele Hauser
	■ Janice Baker	⊡ Brandon Smith
	■ Conrad Jones	☐ Anthony Williams

NC Number concepts	First coach	Second coach
	⊞ DeShawn Parrish	⊞ John Brendall
	■ Callie Malone	⊡ Amanda Brown
	⊞ LaSheika Morris	⊞ Susannah Crockett
	■ Chris Allen	⊡ Jamal Walker

FIGURE 8   Classwide Peer-Tutoring Assignments

ers who used CBM with their entire classrooms, including students with learning disabilities, felt tension between content coverage, which the district math curriculum emphasized, and content mastery, which the CBM measurement system emphasized. As a result of this information, the CBM system was broadened to include math application skills, and participating

FIGURE 9   Class Statistics for Mathematics Computation and Applications

CLASS STATISTICS: COMPUTATION + APPLICATIONS
TEACHER: MRS. ROBERTSON   REPORT THROUGH 2/23

Score

Average score	67.7
Standard deviation	21.7
Discrepancy criterion	46.0

Slope

Average slope	+1.34
Standard deviation	0.54
Discrepancy criterion	+0.80

Students Identified with Dual-Discrepancy Criterion

	Score	Slope
Anthony Williams	33.0	+0.35
Greg Schneider	46.0	+0.51

teachers were granted exemptions by their school district from meeting some aspects of the district curriculum.

Certain other schoolwide factors have been demonstrated to affect how teachers implement CBM. Using the School Organization Contexts Profile (Fuchs, Fuchs, & Bishop, 1992b), Allinder (1996) examined the way teachers who implemented CBM with high quality differed from their counterparts who implemented CBM with less quality with regard to their perceptions of schoolwide emphasis on goals and instructional leadership, friendly and tolerant atmosphere, participative decision making, perceived adequacy of materials, perceived adequacy of planning time, consultation, and uninterrupted instruction. Results revealed that teachers who differed in the quality with which they implemented CBM differed to a significant degree on only one of these factors, perceiving adequacy of planning time. Teachers in schools in which they believe they have adequate time for planning may have an advantage when it comes to learning and incorporating CBM components.

SUMMARY

This chapter examined CBM, one of the most well-developed and extensively researched assessment tools currently available. The chapter focused first on a review of the research in which CBM has been used as an intervention. In doing this, we provided ample evidence of the academic benefits that accrue when teachers use CBM with their students, particularly students with high-incidence disabilities. Having established the effectiveness of CBM, we reviewed research on how to increase teachers' use of this promising practice.

QUESTIONS FOR FURTHER DISCUSSION

1. How might we use CBM to track students' "yearly annual progress"?

2. How might CBM be best configured to encourage students to work hard and purposively?

3. How might CBM be extended to other academic areas? What would CBM look like in other domains?

REFERENCES

Allinder, R. M. (1995). An examination of the relationship between teacher efficacy and curriculum-based measurement and student achievement. *Remedial and Special Education, 16,* 247–254.

Allinder, R. M. (1996). When some is not better than none: Effects of differential implementation of curriculum-based measurement. *Exceptional Children, 62,* 525–535.

Allinder, R. M., & BeckBest, M. A. (1995). Differential effects of two approaches to supporting teachers' use of curriculum-based measurement. *School Psychology Review, 24,* 287–298.

Allinder, R. M., Bolling, R. M., Oats, R. G., & Gagnon, W. A. (2000). Effects of teacher self-monitoring on implementation of curriculum-based measurement and mathematics computation achievement of students with disability. *Remedial and Special Education, 21,* 219–226.

Allinder, R. M., & Oats, R. G. (1997). Effects of acceptability of teachers' implementation of curriculum-based measurement and student achievement in mathematics computation. *Remedial and Special Education, 18,* 113–120.

Baker, J. M., & Zigmond, N. (1990). Are regular education

classes equipped to accommodate students with learning disabilities? *Exceptional Children, 56,* 515–526.

Bean, R. M., & Lane, S. (1990). Implementing curriculum-based measurement of reading in an adult literacy program. *Remedial and Special Education, 11,* 39–46.

Deno, S. L. (1985). Curriculum-based measurement: The emerging alternative. *Exceptional Children, 52,* 219–232.

Deno, S. (1992). The nature and development of curriculum-based measurement. *Preventing School Failure, 36,* 5–10.

Deno, S. L., & Fuchs, L. S. (1987). Developing curriculum-based measurement systems for data-based special education problem-solving. *Focus on Exceptional Children, 19,* 1–16.

Espin, C. A., & Tindal, G. (1998). Curriculum-based measurement for secondary students. In M. R. Shinn (Ed.), *Advanced applications of curriculum-based measurement* (pp. 214–253). New York: Guilford Press.

Fuchs, L. S. (1989). Evaluating solutions: Monitoring progress and revising intervention plans. In M. R. Shinn (Ed.), *Curriculum-based measurement: Assessing special children* (pp. 152–181). New York: Guilford Press.

Fuchs, L. S., Butterworth, J. R., & Fuchs, D. (1989). Effects of ongoing curriculum-based measurement on student awareness of goals and progress. *Education and Treatment of Children, 12,* 63–72.

Fuchs, L. S., Deno, S. L., & Mirkin, P. K. (1984). The effects of frequent curriculum-based measurement and evaluation on pedagogy, student achievement, and student awareness of learning. *American Educational Research Journal, 21,* 449–460.

Fuchs, L. S., & Fuchs, D. (1986). Effects of systematic formative evaluation: A meta-analysis. *Exceptional Children, 53,* 199–208.

Fuchs, L. S., & Fuchs, D. (1989). Enhancing curriculum-based measurement through computer applications: Review of research and practice. *School Psychology Review, 18,* 317–327.

Fuchs, L. S., & Fuchs, D. (1991). Identifying a measure for monitoring student reading progress. *School Psychology Review, 21,* 45–58.

Fuchs, L. S., & Fuchs, D. (1992). Curriculum-based measurement: Current applications and future directions. *Preventing School Failure, 35,* 6–11.

Fuchs, L. S., & Fuchs, D. (1993). Effects of systematic observation and feedback on teachers' implementation of curriculum-based measurement. *Teacher Education and Special Education, 16,* 171–187.

Fuchs, L. S., & Fuchs, D. (1994). Strengthening the connection between assessment and instructional planning with expert systems. *Exceptional Children, 61,* 138–146.

Fuchs, L. S., & Fuchs, D. (1996). Combining performance assessment and curriculum-based measurement to strengthen instructional planning. *Learning Disabilities Research & Practice, 11,* 183–192.

Fuchs, L. S., Fuchs, D., & Bishop, N. (1992a). Instructional adaptation for students at risk. *Journal of Educational Research, 86,* 70–84.

Fuchs, L. S., Fuchs, D., & Bishop, N. (1992b). *School organization contexts profile.* Annual continuation application for "Planning and Ongoing Assessment among Classroom Teachers." Grant No. 0023E90020, U.S. Department of Education, Office of Special Education Programs.

Fuchs, L. S., Fuchs, D., & Hamlett, C. L. (1989a). Effects of instrumental use of curriculum-based measurement to enhance instructional programs. *Remedial and Special Education, 10,* 43–52.

Fuchs, L. S., Fuchs, D., & Hamlett, C. L. (1989b). Effects of alternative goal structures within curriculum-based measurement. *Exceptional Children, 55,* 429–438.

Fuchs, L. S., Fuchs, D., & Hamlett, C. L. (1989c). Computers and curriculum-based measurement: Effects of teacher feedback systems. *School Psychology Review, 18,* 112–125.

Fuchs, L. S., Fuchs, D., & Hamlett, C. L. (1992). Computer applications to facilitate curriculum-based measurement. *Teaching Exceptional Children, 24,* 58–60.

Fuchs, L. S., Fuchs, D., & Hamlett, C. L. (1994). Strengthening the connection between assessment and instructional planning with expert systems. *Exceptional Children, 61,* 138–146.

Fuchs, L. S., Fuchs, D., Hamlett, C. L., & Allinder, R. M. (1989). The reliability and validity of skills analysis within curriculum-based measurement. *Diagnostique, 14,* 203–221.

Fuchs, L. S., Fuchs, D., Hamlett, C. L., & Allinder, R. M. (1991a). The contribution of skills analysis to curriculum-based measurement in spelling. *Exceptional Children, 57,* 443–452.

Fuchs, L. S., Fuchs, D., Hamlett, C. L., & Allinder, R. M. (1991b). Effects of expert system advice within curriculum-based measurement on teacher planning and student achievement in spelling. *School Psychology Review, 20,* 49–66.

Fuchs, L. S., Fuchs, D., Hamlett, C. L., & Ferguson, C. (1992). Effects of expert system consultation within curriculum-based measurement, using a reading maze task. *Exceptional Children, 58,* 436–450.

Fuchs, L. S., Fuchs, D., Hamlett, C. L., Phillips, N. B., & Bentz, J. (1994). Classwide curriculum-based measurement: Helping general educators meet the challenge of student diversity. *Exceptional Children, 60,* 518–537.

Fuchs, L. S., Fuchs, D., Hamlett, C. L., Phillips, N. B., & Karns, K. (1995). General educators' specialized adaptations for students with learning disabilities. *Exceptional Children, 61,* 440–459.

Fuchs, L. S., Fuchs, D., Hamlett, C. L., & Stecker, P. M. (1990). The role of skills analysis in curriculum-based measurement in math. *School Psychology Review, 19,* 6–22.

Fuchs, L. S., Fuchs, D., Hamlett, C. L., & Stecker, P. M. (1991). Effects of curriculum-based measurement and consultation on teacher planning and student achievement in mathematics operations. *American Educational Research Journal, 28,* 617–641.

Fuchs, L. S., Fuchs, D., Hamlett, C. L., & Whinnery, K. (1991). Effects of goal line feedback on level, slope, and stability of performance within curriculum-based measurement. *Learning Disabilities Research & Practice, 6,* 66–74.

Fuchs, L. S., Hamlett, C. L., & Fuchs, D. (1997). *Monitoring basic skills progress* (2nd ed.) [computer programs]. Austin, TX: PRO-ED.

Fuchs, L. S., Hamlett, C. L., Fuchs, D., Stecker, P. M., & Ferguson, C. (1988). Conducting curriculum-based measurement with computerized data collection: Effects on efficiency and teacher satisfaction. *Journal of Special Education Technology, 9,* 73–86.

Gersten, R., Keating, T., & Irvin, L. K. (1995). The burden of proof: Validity as improvement of instructional practice. *Exceptional Children, 61,* 510–519.

Gibson, S., & Dembo, M. H. (1984). Teacher efficacy: A construct validation. *Journal of Educational Psychology, 76,* 569–582.

Glor-Scheib, S., & Zigmond, N. (1993). Exploring the potential motivational properties of curriculum-based measurement in reading among middle school students with learning disabilities. *Learning Disabilities, 4,* 35–43.

Good, R. H., & Kaminski, R. A. (1996). Assessment for instructional decisions: Toward a proactive/prevention model of decision-making for early literacy skills. *School Psychology Quarterly, 11,* 326–336.

Hasbrouck, J. E., Woldbeck, T., Ihnot, C., & Parker, R. I. (1999). One teacher's use of curriculum-based measurement: A changed opinion. *Learning Disabilities Research & Practice, 14,* 118–126.

Hollenbeck, K., Tindal, G., & Almond, P. (1998). Teachers' knowledge of accommodations as a validity issue in high-stakes testing. *Journal of Special Education, 22,* 175–183.

Jones, E. D., & Krouse, J. P. (1988). The effectiveness of data-based instruction by student teachers in classrooms for pupils with mild learning handicaps. *Teacher Education and Special Education, 11,* 9–19.

Kaminski, R. A., & Good, R. H. (1996). Toward a technology for assessing basic early literacy skills. *School Psychology Review, 25,* 215–227.

Marston, D. B. (1989). A curriculum-based measurement approach to assessing academic performance: What it is and why do it. In M. R. Shinn (Ed.), *Curriculum-based measurement: Assessing special children* (pp. 18–78). New York: Guilford Press.

Messick, S. (1980). Test validity and the ethics of assessment. *American Psychologist, 35,* 1012–1027.

Messick, S. (1988). The once and future issues of validity: Assessing the meaning and consequences of measurement. In H. Wainer & H. I. Braun (Eds.), *Test validity* (pp. 33–46). Hillsdale, NJ: Lawrence Erlbaum.

Phillips, N. B., Fuchs, L. S., & Fuchs, D. (1994). Effects of classwide curriculum-based measurement and peer tutoring: A collaborative researcher-practitioner interview study. *Journal of Learning Disabilities, 27,* 420–434.

Samuda, R. J., Kong, S. L., Cummins, J., Lewis, J., & Pascual-Leone, J. (1991). *Assessment and placement of minority students.* Lewiston, NY: Hogrefe and ISSP.

Shinn, M. R. (1989). *Curriculum-based measurement: Assessing special children.* New York: Guilford Press.

Swain, K. D., & Allinder, R. M. (1997). An exploration of the use of curriculum-based measurement by elementary special educators. *Diagnostique, 22,* 87–104.

Wesson, C. L. (1991). Curriculum-based measurement and two models of follow-up consultation. *Exceptional Children, 57,* 246–256.

Wesson, C., Deno, S., Mirkin, P., Maruyama, G., Skiba, R., King, R., & Sevcik, B. (1988). A causal analysis of the relationships among ongoing curriculum-based measurement and evaluation, the structure of instruction, and student achievement. *Journal of Special Education, 22,* 330–343.

Wesson, C. L., King, R., & Deno, S. L. (1984). Direct and frequent measurement: If it's so good for us, why don't we use it? *Learning Disability Quarterly, 7,* 45–48.

Wesson, C. L., Skiba, R., Sevcik, B., King, R. P., & Deno, S. (1984). The effects of technically adequate instructional data on achievement. *Remedial and Special Education, 5,* 17–22.

Whinnery, K. W., & Fuchs, L. S. (1993). Effects of goal and test-taking strategies on the computation performance of students with learning disabilities. *Learning Disabilities Research & Practice, 8,* 204–214.

Yell, M. L., Deno, S. L., & Marston, D. B. (1992). Barriers to implementing curriculum-based measurement. *Diagnostique, 18,* 99–112.

INSTRUCTIONAL INTERVENTIONS FOR STUDENTS WITH LEARNING DISABILITIES

SYLVIA LINAN-THOMPSON

The University of Texas at Austin

The goal of instructional interventions, approaches designed to increase student engagement in learning and to ameliorate learning difficulties, is to maximize learning outcomes for students with disabilities. In the thirty years since learning disabilities were first identified, researchers and leaders in the field have been developing, researching, and refining interventions that enhance learning opportunities for students with learning disabilities. Recently, two meta-analyses (Swanson, 1999; Swanson & Hoskyn, 1998) and a synthesis (Vaughn, Gersten, & Chard, 2000) have provided summaries of intervention research and identified effective instructional practices. Among the practices found to be effective are explicit instruction in skill building and the development of strategies in students' areas of academic need, reading, mathematics, and/or writing, provided in small groups. This approach to instruction provides the intensity and explicitness needed by students with learning disabilities (Swanson, 1999; Swanson & Hoskyn, 1998; Vaughn, Gersten, & Chard, 2000).

If all we had to contend with were developing, researching, and implementing effective practices, then our job would be easy. But the classrooms, schools, and communities in which instruction is provided to students at risk for and identified with disabilities are much more complex. Changes in the last few years include changes in the law, an increased awareness that not all students are benefiting from instruction, and an increase in the number of students from culturally and linguistically diverse backgrounds in schools. To ensure that practices are appropriate and effective for all students regardless of setting, we must reevaluate what we know about teaching and learning and continually strive to improve practice. One area in particular, the recent mandate to ensure that students with disabilities have access to and make progress in the general education curriculum (Individuals with Disabilities Education Act, 1997), has led to discussions and research of effective instructional practices provided to students with learning disabilities in the general education classroom. In addition, due to the importance of identifying difficulties early, prevention has become a critical part of instruction. In this chapter I discuss the use of prevention and intervention practices in the general education classroom and then look at two groups of students about whom we need to learn more, students who make minimal gains even when provided supplemental instruction and students from diverse backgrounds. In particular I consider the following questions: How do we ensure that students with disabilities have access to the general education curriculum? What type of instructional intervention do students who fail to respond to treatment need? Are current interventions responsive to the needs of students with disabilities who are from culturally and linguistically diverse backgrounds?

ENSURING ACCESS AND MEASURING PROGRESS

How do we ensure that students with disabilities have access to and make progress in the general education curriculum? The Individuals with Disabilities Education Act of 1997 mandated that students with disabilities be given access to the general education curriculum and that accommodations and adjustments that enable the students to be involved in and progress in the general education curriculum be part of students' individualized education plans. It gave students with disabilities the opportunity to receive the same curricular content as their peers without disabilities.

To improve learning for students with mild to moderate disabilities and students at risk for school failure in the general education classroom, King-Sears (2001) suggests the following three steps. First, analyze the general education curriculum to identify accessible resources and universal design features in the curriculum. Second, enhance areas of the general education curriculum as needed. Third, identify and implement minor to major modifications needed so students with disabilities can access the curriculum. In the following sections I discuss the accessibility of texts, means for enhancing general education, and a way to implement minor to major modifications in the general education classroom.

General Education Resources

Among the roadblocks to students' participation in the general education curriculum is the inaccessibility of the materials used in the general education classroom. These materials often lack the instructional design features that support the learning of students with disabilities. Although limited, reviews of basal programs and textbooks indicate that texts are generally not accessible to students with disabilities. This is particularly troubling in the content areas because textbooks often define the curriculum. At the secondary level, the match between student ability and readability of and accessibility to textbooks is critical. Reviews of history (Harniss, Dickson, Kinder, & Hollenbeck, 2001) and geography (Jitendra, Nolet, Xin, Gomez, Renouf, Iskod, & DaCosta, 2001) textbooks found that texts were limited in several ways. The text structure was often unorganized and lacked coherence (Harniss et al., 2001). The readability levels were often higher than that of the students for whom the text was intended (Harniss et al., 2001; Jitendra et al., 2001). Finally, they relied on factual information rather than on presenting the concepts and principles necessary for deeper understanding of the material (Harniss et al., 2001; Jitendra et al., 2001).

At the elementary level, Jitendra, Salmento, and Haydt (1999) reviewed seven basal mathematics programs for the inclusion of nine variables: clarity of objective, additional concepts and skills taught, explicit teaching explanations, teaching prerequisite skills, efficient use of instructional time, sufficient and appropriate teaching samples, adequate practice, appropriate review, and effective feedback. None of the programs evaluated met all nine criteria, and only two met seven or eight. Likewise, Smith et al. (2001) analyzed the phonological awareness component of four kindergarten reading programs and found that the programs lacked instructional design principles that would make them accessible to students with disabilities, such as systematically sequencing tasks, increasing opportunities to produce sounds at the phoneme level, and providing suggestions for teacher scaffolding of tasks and materials. An examination of writing process instruction in two basal programs by Gleason and Isaacson (2001) revealed that the programs did not provide information on explicit instruction of procedural strategies, reviews of concepts and skills learned, more than one opportunity to practice the genre, or suggestions for teacher modeling and scaffolding of tasks.

Inconsiderate and inaccessible texts require that teachers "fill in" the missing material and support needed by students with disabilities. Recommendations for teachers across the reviews include adding modeling and explicit instruction (Gleason & Isaacson, 2001; Smith et al., 2001), providing scaffolds (Gleason & Isaacson, 2001; Harniss et al., 2001; Smith et al., 2001), developing background knowledge (Harniss et al., 2001), and developing concepts (Harniss et al., 2001; Jitendra et al., 2001).

Enhancing the General Education Curriculum

If we view prevention and intervention as a continuum, rather than as discreet instructional categories as Keogh (1994) suggested, then the instruction provided early to students experiencing difficulties and that provided later to students with disabilities are two sides of the same coin. The basic concepts and foundational skills taught in each academic area are the same whether used as a prevention measure or an intervention; the difference is the level of intensity with which instruction is provided (Foorman & Torgesen, 2001). While this knowledge base is most developed for reading (Stanovich, 1999), we have an emerging knowledge base in mathematics and writing that permits the development of effective interventions. Kame´enui and Carnine (1998) describe the fundamental concepts and principles needed for the most efficient and broadest acquisition of knowledge within an academic area as "big ideas." Big ideas in reading are phonemic awareness, alphabetic principle and phonics, fluency, vocabulary, and the construction of meaning (Coyne, Kame´enui, & Simmons, 2001; Snow, Burns, & Griffin, 1998). The big ideas in mathematics may include number sense and estimation, spatial sense and geometric thinking, computational proficiency, patterns and relationships, and problem solving (Cawley, Parmar, Foley, Salmon, & Roy, 2001; Thorton, Langrall, & Jones, 1997). Big ideas in writing might include steps in the writing process, knowledge of the conventions of a writing genre, mechanics, functions of writing, spelling, and handwriting (Graham, Harris, & Larsen, 2001).

Furthermore, since instructional practices associated with effective outcomes for students with disabilities enhance learning outcomes for many students (Vaughn et al., 2000), practices used by special educators are finding new life in general education classrooms as prevention and intervention measures. Research on effective instructional interventions for students with learning disabilities has had an impact on both general and special education.

Prevention

The knowledge that intervening early with students who are experiencing difficulty in reading (Dickson & Bursuck, 1999; Juel, 1988; O'Connor, 2000), mathematics (Fuchs & Fuchs,

2001), and written expression (Graham et al., 2001) increases students' chances for academic success has provided the impetus to develop interventions that prevent or ameliorate learning difficulties. Instruction intended as a prevention measure is usually provided to the whole class as part of the curriculum and may only require enhancing the existing curriculum slightly. The goal is to provide students opportunities to practice and master foundational skills and concepts in the context of general education as early as possible. Fuchs and Fuchs (2001) identified three criteria for identifying appropriate prevention practices. They include those that (1) have demonstrated effectiveness, (2) are research-based, and (3) contain universal design features. In this case *universal design* refers to features or elements of instruction that support the acquisition of skills for students with disabilities and are suitable for students without disabilities (Fuchs & Fuchs, 2001; King-Sears, 2001).

Research in early intervention is promising. O'Connor (2000) found that providing whole-class, teacher-led instruction in phonological awareness to kindergarten students was effective in moving 25 percent of the students identified for possible difficulty out of the risk category. In a similar study Dickson and Bursuck (1999) found that when teachers enhanced phonological awareness and phonics instruction, the number of students who remained at risk was reduced. Graham, Harris, and Larsen (2001) reported on four studies that examined the efficacy of early intervention in writing and found that early intervention in handwriting and spelling have a positive effect on composition fluency and quality of writing. While instruction in these studies was supplemental, the aim was to accelerate the progress of struggling writers.

Fuchs and Fuchs (2001) took another approach to preventing mathematics difficulties. In their model, in addition to teacher-led instruction, all students participated in follow-up instructional activities. Peer-assisted learning strategies (PALS) were used to integrate principles of mathematics prevention into the general education classroom. These principles involve providing instruction that is based on achievement standards, is quick-paced and varied, and includes cognitive strategy instruction and physical and visual representations. Classroom teachers incorporated two thirty-five-minute sessions into their regular mathematics instruction. During each session, students working in pairs each had the opportunity to be both a tutor and a tutee on a particular skill. In addition the model includes mediated verbal rehearsal, step-by-step feedback, explanation and modeling of strategic behavior, frequent verbal and written interactions, and opportunities for tutees to apply explanations to subsequent problems (Fuchs & Fuchs, 2001), thus incorporating features of effective instruction into the model.

Prevention as it is described here goes a step beyond prereferral interventions. Rather than a teacher's waiting for a student to experience difficulty and then providing one-on-one support in response, prevention models are proactive. They enhance the learning environment for all learners by incorporating effective instructional practices that meet the definition of universal design in an effort to prevent the development of learning difficulties for some students.

Intervention

Identifying foundational skills and concepts students need has provided the knowledge base for identifying students at risk for learning difficulties early. However, prevention measures are not enough for many students (O'Connor, 2000; Torgesen, 2000; Vellutino, Scanlon, & Lyon,

2000). While the overall concepts and skills that are taught do not change, the content of lessons will be based on the specific needs of the students (Fuchs & Fuchs, 2001; Graham et al., 2001), and instruction will be more intensive and explicit. Two ways to intensify instruction are to increase instructional time and to reduce the group size in which instruction is provided (Foorman & Torgesen, 2001). Intensifying instruction gives students opportunities for higher rates of active participation, more individualized scaffolding, and corrective feedback. Explicit instruction makes visible for students with disabilities the processes effective learners use. To teach these processes or strategies, identify and model the use of skills students need to use as well as the strategies themselves, give students multiple opportunities to demonstrate the use of the skills in isolation and as part of the strategy, ask them to explain how and why they use the strategy, and provide feedback (Fuchs & Fuchs, 2001; Gersten, 1998).

Other design principles associated with effective instruction are aligning task difficulty and student level (Vaughn et al., 2000), using follow-up instruction to ensure mastery of targeted skills (Coyne et al., 2001; Fuchs & Fuchs, 2001; Graham et al., 2001), providing access to the lower-level skills students need to use higher-level skills (Vaughn et al., 2000), and ensuring opportunities for students to self-regulate learning (Fuchs & Fuchs, 2001; Graham et al., 2001). These principles are necessary to providing the support students with disabilities need to acquire complex knowledge and skills in mathematics (Fuchs & Fuchs, 2001; Parmar, Cawley, & Frazita, 1996), reading (Coyne et al., 2001; Vadasy, Jenkins, & Pool, 2000), and writing (de la Paz & Graham, 1997). Appropriate instruction supports students' development of basic skills as well as complex thinking, learning, and achievement (Gersten, 1998).

One of the goals of prevention and intervention is to ensure that students with learning disabilities have access to the general curriculum. We can ensure the meaningful participation of students with disabilities by increasing the capacity of general education (Zigmond et al., 1995) to accommodate student diversity; we can do this using prevention and intervention practices that incorporate features of effective instruction, such as giving corrective feedback, grouping students for instruction, and providing multiple opportunities for students to respond. Instruction that includes these features provides students with disabilities opportunities to acquire basic skills and gives them access to the complex concepts, skills, and problem-solving strategies that most students need (Gersten, 1998).

Implementation of Change in the General Education Classroom

One way to implement change in the general education classroom is to provide instruction that can be modified and adapted at each level. Using curriculum-based measures to monitor student progress in acquiring the necessary skills and concepts gives teachers a way to identify students requiring more intensive instruction and to monitor their progress; it also enables teachers to provide additional support to students with disabilities.

Several models of layered instruction have been developed and implemented; teachers have used these to provide additional instruction to students in primary grades struggling with reading (Dickson & Bursuck, 1999; O'Connor, 2000) and mathematics (Fuchs & Fuchs, 2001). The first layer consists of effective practices, such as delivering systematic and explicit instruction, using flexible grouping, and providing multiple practice opportunities. The teacher increases support for students who are lagging behind (Dickson & Bursuck, 1999; Fuchs & Fuchs, 2001; O'Connor, 2000). The degree of intensity, explicitness, and teacher support varies according to the students' skills and diverse learning needs (Dickson & Bursuck, 1999). By providing different levels of instruction, teachers can give students who are experiencing difficulty multiple opportunities to learn and practice new skills and concepts.

O'Connor used layered or leveled instruction to reduce early reading failure by providing instruction across four levels that varied in length (number of minutes per session), intensity (number of times per week and group size), and duration (number of weeks). Level 1, prevention, consisted of ninety whole-class, teacher-led sessions of phonological awareness activities. In level 2, students received one-on-one instruction that reinforced the activities in level 1. Students in level 2 received twelve-minute sessions, three times a week for ten weeks. Level 3 targeted first-grade students and began in November. Students in this level received thirty-minute sessions four times a week for fourteen weeks in groups of three or four. Students in the project moved in and out of supplemental instruction for two years (kindergarten through first grade) on the basis of their scores on progress monitoring measures. At the end of first grade, reading failure among the at-risk students had declined. However, the proportion of students referred for special education services did not decrease. Dickson and Bursuck (1999) implemented a three-tiered system that varied along the same dimensions studied by O'Connor. Students at risk for reading failure benefited the most when they were placed in small-group intensive intervention. Both O'Connor (2000) and Dickson and Bursuck (1999) attributed the failure to decrease referrals to special education to teachers' lack of time and resources and their resulting inability to provide the intensity of instruction struggling readers needed.

Fuchs and Fuchs (2001) designed three levels for math instruction. The first level, prevention, focused on principles that met the criteria for universal design, was research based, and was proven to be effective. Instruction was integrated into the general education curriculum through PALS along with the regular mathematics curriculum. For the second level, prereferral, the general education curriculum was modified in ways that were feasible for the teacher, minimally invasive for the target student, and unobtrusive for other students. Goal setting, self-monitoring of task completion and work quality, computer-assisted instruction, and concrete representations of numbers and number concepts were incorporated into the first level of instruction. Finally, the third level of instruction, intervention, was provided to students who did not respond adequately to the first two levels. In the third level, instruction focused on the individual student and included intensive instructional delivery and explicit contextualization of skills-based instruction.

Coyne, Kame´enui, and Simmons (2001) developed and implemented a schoolwide model of prevention and intervention in beginning reading instruction. Staff at participating schools coordinated with the researchers to establish reading benchmarks, devise a method for identifying and monitoring students struggling with reading, and develop differentiated instruction for students with a wide range of reading abilities and skills. Instruction was based on six instructional design principles: big ideas, mediated scaffolding, conspicuous strategies, strategic integration, primed background knowledge, and judicious review. While there were no predetermined levels of instruction beyond the standard curriculum, collaborative teams within each school made decisions about the allocation of instructional time, the use of supplemental materials, and instructional focus to meet the needs of individual students.

These three studies have several factors in common. First, they all track student progress through progress monitoring. Second, the first level consists of the regular curriculum enhanced with instructional practices that fit the universal design criteria. Third, the successive levels of instruction vary in intensity and explicitness from the first level. Using levels of instruction is a way to prevent learning difficulties and ensure that students with disabilities benefit from instruction in the general education classroom. However, researchers need to continue to explore ways to reach students who make minimal gains within the scope of existing resources in the schools (O'Connor, 2000; Torgesen, 2000; Vellutino et al., 2000). This is not an easy task given the personnel constraints placed on schools by budgets.

For students with disabilities to have meaningful access to the general education curriculum and to ensure their progress in it, we must continue to advocate for it as well as refine instructional practices and identify models and frameworks for implementing these. These changes will require careful attention to professional development for both preservice and inservice teachers; they will need to know how to employ progress monitoring and research-based models of instruction for all students (Vaughn & Linan-Thompson, in press).

RESPONDING TO STUDENTS WHO RESIST TREATMENT

What type of instructional intervention do students who fail to respond to treatment need? We have made great strides in identifying effective interventions for students with learning disabilities; however, some students make minimal gains despite our best efforts. Often labeled *treatment resisters*, these students do not respond to well-designed and implemented interventions. After reviewing four studies that provided reading interventions for students struggling with reading, Torgesen (2000) determined that between 2 and 4 percent of students in schools today will fail to make substantial gains in reading even after being provided intensive instruction. Other researchers (O'Connor, 2000; Vadasy et al., 2000; Vaughn et al., in press) have documented the existence of this group of children. In all four studies students at risk for or identified as having learning disabilities were provided intensive reading instruction in small groups or one on one. Although the majority of the students who participated in these studies made adequate gains, some students in each study did not.

To date we have no way of identifying which students will fail to respond to treatment prior to intervention and we have yet to determine the best way to meet the needs of this group of children. Identifying interventions that are effective with students who make minimal gains is imperative if we are to ensure that all students have access to the general curriculum. As Torgesen (2000) stated, "to know what kind of instruction is most effective is not the same thing as knowing how much of that instruction, delivered under what conditions" (p. 63) is enough. This question remains to be answered.

RESPONDING TO CULTURALLY AND LINGUISTICALLY DIVERSE STUDENTS

Are current interventions responsive to the needs of students with disabilities from culturally and linguistically diverse backgrounds? Students from diverse backgrounds are represented in general education and special education in increasing numbers. The *Twenty-third annual report to Congress on the implementation of the Individuals with Disabilities Education Act* (U.S. Department of Education, 2002) reports that 15.8 percent of students with learning disabilities are Hispanic, 18.3 percent are African American, 1.4 percent are Asian American, and 1.4 percent are American Indian. Seventy-three percent of the 174,530 students who have limited proficiency in English speak Spanish as their first language. In addition, 27.8 percent of students with one disability live in households with incomes below the poverty level. Although we have extensive research on the efficacy of instructional interventions, many of these studies do not include students from culturally, linguistically, or economically diverse backgrounds. If they do, results are not disaggregated from majority students (Swanson, Hoskyn, & Lee, 1999). Given the increasing number of students from diverse backgrounds, it is imperative that we support research that not only includes students with disabilities from culturally and linguistically diverse backgrounds but also documents the extent to which these interventions are appropriate for students from diverse backgrounds.

Figueroa, Fradd, and Correa (1989) noted the dearth of research documenting interventions that improve the academic abilities of English Language Learners. Gersten and Baker (2000) located only nine studies that examined interventions and included control groups that contributed to that knowledge base. The knowledge base for students from other culturally and linguistically diverse backgrounds is just as sparse. We are just beginning to explore the effectiveness of using interventions developed for monolingual English speakers with English Language Learners. There is a small but growing body of research that has documented the efficacy of instructional interventions in reading (Gunn, Biglan, Smolkowski, & Ary, 2000; Linan-Thompson, Vaughn, Hickman-Davis, & Kouzekanani, 2003; Quiroga, Lemos-Britton, Mostafapour, & Berninger, 2002) with English Language Learners. In all three studies English Language Learners not only benefited from the instructional intervention but benefited regardless of their English language proficiency.

In mathematics Rodriguez, Parmar, and Signer (2001) examined the understanding of number line concepts of culturally and linguistically diverse fourth graders with disabilities. They found that students' difficulty in solving number-line-based word problems extended beyond lack of language proficiency and included a limited range of strategies and failure to apply the number line to solve problems. These difficulties are similar to the difficulties experienced by monolingual English students with disabilities. While preliminary, these findings seem to indicate that while language considerations are important, interventions that have proven effective for students with disabilities who are monolingual English speakers can improve outcomes for English Language Learners.

The call for research that focuses on instructional interventions with students from culturally and linguistically diverse backgrounds continues. Areas that require further study include distinguishing between language growth and academic growth (Gersten & Baker, 2000) and the efficacy of instructional interventions in all academic areas involving students from culturally and linguistically diverse backgrounds. However, if we are to make a significant impact on the education of students from diverse backgrounds, research in this area must increase at a more rapid rate.

CONCLUSION

As we enter the twenty-first century, we are still facing enormous challenges. Even though we get converging evidence on effective practices for teaching students with learning disabilities, factors that affect instruction—such as increasing student diversity, the failure of some students to make adequate gains, and changing expectations for students with disabilities—continue to change. Mandates for students with disabilities to have increased access to the general education curriculum and to participate in accountability testing require that we continue to develop and refine instructional interventions. Providing different levels of instruction in the general education classroom is one way of enhancing instruction for all students prior to referral; it will ensure that all students will have meaningful access to and can progress in the curriculum.

QUESTIONS FOR FURTHER DISCUSSION

1. How does the focus on prevention affect the current approaches for identifying students with disabilities?

2. How much extra instruction and individualized attention is feasible in a general education classroom?

3. What factors might affect schools' ability to institute a prevention model?

4. Is it feasible to expect that all students will have access to and make progress in the general curriculum?

5. What are the implications of this approach for students from cultural and linguistically diverse backgrounds?

REFERENCES

Carnine, D., Jones, E. D., & Dixon, R. (1994). Mathematics: Educational tools for diverse learners. *School Psychology Review, 23*(3), 406–428.

Cawley, J., Parmar, R., Foley, T. E., Salmon, S., & Roy, S. (2001). Arithmetic performance of students: Implications for standards and programming. *Exceptional Children, 67*(3), 311–328.

Coyne, M. D., Kame´enui, E. J., & Simmons, D. (2001). Prevention and intervention in beginning reading: Two complex systems. *Learning Disabilities Research and Practice, 16*(2), 62–73.

de la Paz, S., & Graham, S. (1997). Strategy instruction in planning: Effects on the writing performance and behavior of students with learning difficulties. *Exceptional Children, 63*(2), 167–181.

Dickson, S. V., & Bursuck, W. D. (1999). Implementing a model for preventing reading failure: A report form the field. *Learning Disabilities Research and Practice, 14*(4), 191–202.

Figueroa, R. A., Fradd, S. H., & Correa, V. I. (1989). Bilingual special education and this special issue. *Exceptional Children, 56*(2), 174–178.

Foorman, B. R., & Torgesen, J. (2001). Critical elements of classroom and small-group instruction to promote reading success in all children. *Learning Disabilities Research and Practice, 16*(4), 203–212.

Fuchs, L. S., & Fuchs, D. (2001). Principles for the prevention and intervention of mathematics difficulties. *Learning Disabilities Research and Practice, 16*(2), 85–95.

Gersten, R. (1998). Recent advances in instructional research for students with learning disabilities: An overview. *Learning Disabilities Research and Practice, 13*(3), 162–170.

Gersten, R., & Baker, S. (2000). What we know about effective instructional practices for English-language learners. *Exceptional Children, 66*(4), 454–470.

Gleason, M. M., & Isaacson, S. (2001). Using the new basals to teach the writing process: Modifications for students with learning problems. *Reading and Writing Quarterly, 17,* 75–92.

Graham, S., Harris, K. R., & Larsen, L. (2001). Prevention and intervention of writing difficulties for students with learning disabilities. *Learning Disabilities Research and Practice, 16*(2), 74–84.

Gunn, B., Biglan, A., Smolkowski, K., & Ary, D. (2000). The efficacy of supplemental instruction in decoding skills for Hispanic and non-Hispanic students in early elementary school. *Journal of Special Education, 34*(2), 90–103.

Harniss, M. K., Dickson, S. V., Kinder, D., & Hollenbeck, K. L. (2001). Textual problems and instructional solutions: Strategies for enhancing learning from published history textbooks. *Reading and Writing Quarterly, 17,* 127–150.

Individuals with Disabilities Education Act, 42 U.S.C. §12101 *et seq.* (1997).

Jitendra, A. K., Nolet, V., Xin, Y. P., Gomez, O., Iskold, L., Renouf, L. I., & DaCosta, J. (2001). An analysis of middle school geography textbooks: Implications for students with learning problems. *Reading and Writing Quarterly, 17,* 151–173.

Jitendra, A. K., Salmento, M. M., & Haydt, L. A. (1999). A case analysis of fourth-grade subtraction instruction in basal mathematics programs: Adherence to important instructional design criteria. *Learning Disabilities Research and Practice, 14*(2), 69–79.

Juel, C. (1988) Learning to read and write: A longitudinal study of 54 children from first through fourth grades. *Journal of Educational Psychology, 80*(4), 437–447.

Kame´enui, E. J., & Carnine, D. W. (1998). *Effective teaching strategies that accommodate diverse learners.* Upper Saddle River, NJ: Merrill.

Keogh, B. K. (1994). What special education research agenda should look like in the year 2000. *Learning Disabilities Research and Practice 9*(2), 61–69.

King-Sears, M. E. (2001). Three steps for gaining access to the general education curriculum for learners with disabilities. *Intervention in School and Clinic, 37*(2), 67–76.

Linan-Thompson, S., Vaughn, S, Hickman-Davis, P., & Kouzekanani, K. (2003). Effective reading instruction for English language learners with reading difficulties. *Elementary School Journal 103*(3), 221–238.

O'Connor, R. E. (2000). Increasing the intensity of intervention in kindergarten and first grade. *Learning Disabilities Research and Practice, 15*(1), 43–54.

Parmar, R. S., Cawley, J. F., & Frazita, R. R. (1996). Word problem-solving by students with and without mild disabilities. *Exceptional Children, 62*(5), 415–429.

Quiroga, T., Lemos-Britton, Z., Mostafapour, E., & Berninger, V. (2002). Phonological awareness and beginning reading in Spanish, ESL first graders: Research practice. *Journal of School Psychology, 40,* 85–111.

Rodriguez, D., Parmar, R. S., & Signer, B. R. (2001). Fourth-grade culturally and linguistically diverse exceptional students' concepts of number line. *Exceptional Children, 67*(2), 199–210.

Sexton, M., Harris, K. R., & Graham, S. (2001). Self-regulated strategy development and the writing process: Effects on essay writing and attributions. *Exceptional Children, 64*(3), 295–311.

Smith, S. B., Simmons, D. C., Gleason, M. M., Kame´enui, E. J., Baker, S., Sprick, M., Gunn, B., Thomas, C. L., Chard, D. J., Plasencia-Peinado, J., & Peinado, R. (2001). An analysis of phonological awareness instruction in four kindergarten basal reading programs. *Reading and Writing Quarterly, 17,* 25–51.

Snow, C. E., Burns, M. S., & Griffin, P. (Eds.). (1998). *Preventing reading failure in young children.* Washington, DC: National Academy Press.

Stanovich, K. (1999). The sociopsychometrics of learning disabilities. *Journal of Learning Disabilities, 32*(4), 350–361.

Swanson, H. L. (1999). *Interventions for students with learning disabilities: A meta-analysis of treatment outcomes.* New York: Guilford.

Swanson, H. L., & Hoskyn, M. (1998). Experimental intervention research on students with learning disabilities: A meta-analysis of treatment outcomes. *Review of Educational Research, 68,* 277–321.

Swanson, H. L., Hoskyn, M., & Lee, C. (1999). *Interventions for students with learning disabilities.* New York: Guilford.

Thorton, C. A., Langrall, C. W., & Jones, G. A. (1997). Mathematics instruction for elementary students with learning disabilities. *Journal of Learning Disabilities, 30*(2), 145–150.

Torgesen, J. (2000). Individual differences in response to early interventions in reading: The lingering problem of treatment resisters. *Learning Disabilities Research and Practice, 15*(1), 55–64.

U.S. Department of Education. (2002). *Twenty-third annual report to Congress on the implementation of the Individuals with Disabilities Education Act.* Washington, DC: U.S. Government Printing Office.

Vadasy, P. F., Jenkins, J. R., & Pool, K. (2000). Effects of tutoring in phonological and early reading skills on students at risk for reading disorders. *Journal of Learning Disabilities, 33*(6), 579–590.

Vaughn, S., Gersten, R., & Chard, D. (2000). The underlying message in LD intervention research: Findings from research syntheses. *Exceptional Children 67*(1), 99–114.

Vaughn, S., & Linan-Thompson, S. (in press). What's special about special education for students with learning disabilities? *Journal of Special Education.*

Vaughn, S., Linan-Thompson, S., Khouzekanani, K., Bryant, D. P., Blozis, S. A., & Dickson, S. (in press). Grouping for reading instruction: Students with reading difficulties who are Monolingual English or English Language Learners. *Remedial and Special Education.*

Vellutino, F. R., Scanlon, D. M., & Lyon, G. R. (2000). Differentiating between difficult-to-remediate and readily remediated poor readers: More evidence against the IQ-achievement discrepancy definition of reading disability. *Journal of Learning Disabilities, 33*(3), 223–238.

Zigmond, N., Jenkins, J., Fuchs, L. S., Deno, S., Fuchs, D., Baker, J. N., Jenkins, L., & Couthino, M. (1995). Special education in restructured schools. *Phi Delta Kappan, 76*(7), 531–541.

SUSTAINABILITY OF RESEARCH-BASED PRACTICES
Implications for Students with Disabilities

SHARON VAUGHN

University of Texas at Austin

JANETTE K. KLINGNER

University of Colorado at Boulder

MARIE TEJERO HUGHES

University of Illinois-Chicago

Research is increasingly being promoted as a decision-making tool in special education (Carnine, 1997; Gersten, Vaughn, Deshler, & Schiller, 1997; Kauffman, 1993). Furthermore, local school districts and state departments of education are supporting the use of research-based instructional practices. This push to consider what we know and to use this knowledge to influence what we do in education is part of a new wave of accountability.

This renewed interest in research and its influence on education is grounded in the concern that too little of what is done in education is based on the findings of rigorous inquiry (Cooper, 1996; Walberg, 1998). This is not because we do not know the answers to highly important questions in education. According to Chall (2000), a base of rigorous scientifically determined research exists on the most important issues in education, including (1) best practices in teaching, (2) effective instruction, and (3) standards of practice for improving outcomes in reading and math. The problem is that what we know empirically is not implemented systematically and continuously as part of educational practice.

As Vaughn and Dammann (2001) note, not only does lack of implementation of effective practices deprive students of the best education possible, it is particularly heinous in that it is *regressive*. It deprives the very students who need it the most from the most effective instruction. This is particularly concerning for students with special needs who can not make up for lost time and do not learn well on their own. The provision of the most effective instruction available is essential to provide them with the opportunities needed for success.

Identifying and implementing research-based practices in education are essential first steps in improving education for all students, particularly students with special needs. However, initial implementation without sustained follow-through is little improvement over not making the best decision in the first place. This chapter will discuss what sustainability is and what we know about sustaining research-based practices.

WHAT IS SUSTAINABILITY?

Sustainability refers to the extent to which an instructional practice is adopted and used over time, such as one academic year. Often sustainability is considered by researchers who are engaged in school or classroom change and have worked extensively at the school or classroom level to assist teachers in implementing effective practices in a particular target area, such as behavioral supports or reading. Researchers are interested in the extent to which these target practices are maintained after the committed period or after the support provided by the research team has gone.

Gersten, Chard, and Baker (2000) note that when considering sustainability, it is important to distinguish between whether the innovation to be sustained is part of a "structural" or "core-of-teaching" innovation:

> "Structural" innovations we define as those innovations that target non-instructional changes that may only tangentially affect what teachers teach in their classroom. These include co-teaching, institutionalization of native language instruction for English-language learners, the use of special education teachers to provide post-secondary transition services, and moving from period to block scheduling in middle and high schools. All of these innovations require changes outside of teachers' instructional practices. "Core-of-teaching" innovations target instructional practices used in teaching the core disciplines: reading, writing, mathematics, and science. (Gersten, Chard, & Baker, 2000, p. 447)

In this chapter we discuss sustainability from the perspective of "core-of-teaching" practices that are sustained by districts, schools, and teachers. These practices include curriculum modifications as well as the instructional practices or tools that are designed to enhance their instruction. Such practices would include, for example, the use of computer-assisted instruction, peer-assisted learning, phonemic awareness instruction, verbal math problem-solving strategies, and strategies for enhancing essay writing.

Variations of Sustainability

We believe that there are at least four ways to sustain an instructional practice. These vary depending on the teacher's level of enthusiasm for the practice, implementation fidelity, and understanding of the practice. These variations of sustainability can be envisioned along a continuum, with *proactive sustainability* on one end and *partial sustainability* on the other. We have found numerous examples of these different types of sustainability in our own and others' research.

Proactive sustainability is characterized by high levels of enthusiasm, implementation, and understanding. This first type of sustainability refers to when a practice is highly valued by the teacher—so much so that the teacher wants others to use it. These teachers not only maintain use but also are associated with use by others; that is, they persuade and teach others to use the same practice and promote its ongoing sustainability. These teachers also regularly implement the practice, much like it was taught to them. They also clearly understand the theory behind the practice, as demonstrated by their ability to tailor implementation procedures to meet the needs of their students and the demands of their instructional setting (e.g., creating new, more efficient record-keeping forms). For example, Heidi is a special education teacher who has motivated other teachers in her school to learn research-based practices she learned in a yearlong professional development program (Klingner, Arguelles, Hughes, & Vaughn, 2001). During observations in Heidi's inclusion classrooms (three years after she first learned the practices), it was clear that her students were experts in the procedures involved in each practice. All students were on task, engaged, and discussing the material at hand (including the students with learning disabilities and the student with autism). In both of Heidi's classrooms there are many references to all practices (e.g., posters, charts). She has adapted each of the practices slightly, making them more "gamelike" to match her teaching style (Klingner, Vaughn, Hughes, & Arguelles, 1999).

Routine sustainability is characterized by teachers for whom the practice has become routinized as part of their instructional repertoire. In these cases the teachers may take occasional "vacations" from the practice, discontinuing its use and then resuming implementation later. These teachers continue to use the practice much as they learned it and do not feel compelled to share it or teach it to others, though they might make a few modifications. When asked, they are able to explain the key components of the practice and understand what makes it effective. For example, Leigh, a third-grade teacher, currently uses partner reading with her class twice a week as one of the centers students rotate through during language arts. She has implemented partner reading consistently over the years since she learned the practice but modified the approach slightly to save time. At times she temporarily discontinues use of the practice, such as when she is preparing students for high-stakes testing (Klingner et al., 1999).

In *modified sustainability* teachers continue using several elements of the practice but other elements are either eliminated or significantly modified. In these cases teachers may modify the practice in ways that improve the effects of the practice for the students or the teacher; however, their modifications may also compromise its effectiveness. All modifications are not improvements. Teachers modify practices for a variety of reasons, including time constraints, students' wishes, their own philosophy, forgetting, and boredom (discussed more fully later in this chapter). In some cases teachers modify a practice because they do not fully understand the theory that supports the practice or its essential components. Occasionally, teachers modify a practice so significantly that the essence of the practice is lost, and consequently, so is its effectiveness. Teachers with modified sustainability believe that they are still implementing the practice but "have just made a few changes." For example, Kelly, a third-grade teacher, has made so many changes to partner reading that it is not clear whether she is actually doing partner reading or has adapted it so much that it has become a different instructional practice. Students often read content area textbooks instead of trade books, sometimes omit partner reading and rereading, and are placed in groups of three rather than two (Klingner et al., 1999).

In *partial sustainability* teachers adopt and use at least some of the ideas or elements of a practice. However, they do not implement the instructional practice as they learned it. These teachers, when asked, do not claim that they are implementing the practice and may or may not even be aware that they have incorporated a portion of the practice into their instructional routine. For example, three years after Leigh first learned collaborative strategic reading (CSR), she no longer implements it. She insists that she likes the approach, however, and that she did not consciously stop using it. Instead, she has been providing whole-class reading comprehension instruction. Although Leigh no longer uses CSR, she has students who use the CSR "clunking" strategy while reading the *Weekly Reader* as part of a whole-class activity.

Our longitudinal research on the sustained use of instructional practices reveals that teachers who learn practices and have implemented them several times in their classroom can often be categorized into one of the above-discussed broad descriptions. However, we did not examine sustained use by teachers who were involved in learning the practice in a cursory manner, such as through short-term professional development courses.

HOW DO RESEARCHERS STUDY SUSTAINABILITY?

Researchers have often lamented the lack of follow-up after an intervention has been implemented to ensure that the outcomes for students have been maintained over time. Of even more concern is the lack of research investigating the extent to which teachers who have implemented practices continue to use them over time. In part, it is because this type of research is exceedingly difficult to do. Locating the teachers, ensuring their participation, and conducting ongoing observations are challenging and time-consuming pursuits. Even more troublesome is the lack of measures available to determine sustainability of a practice. One of the few exceptions is the measure described next that has been used to determine and categorize levels of sustained use of instructional practices.

The "Levels-of-Use Questionnaire" (Hall, Loucks, Rutherford, & Newlove, 1975) provides a means of categorizing the sustained use of practices by assessing the ways teachers use the practices.

LEVELS-OF-USE CODING SYSTEM

The purpose of the Levels-of-Use Coding System is to document the individual variation in levels of use of an innovation or instructional practice. In essence, the levels were designed to document teacher change as it relates to the application of an innovative or instructional practice. The ratings of Levels of Use from this measure were designed to be applied from the results of an extensive and carefully conducted interview of the teacher to determine the teacher's knowledge and use of the instructional practice. Thus, the measure relies on self-report.

The measure does not attempt to define causality but to describe and better understand what the user is doing. The information gathered from the interview about the use of the innovative practice is categorized as the user "progresses from familiarization with to increased sophistication in using an innovation" (Hall et al., 1975, p. 6). Table 1 provides an overview of the Levels of Use and the corresponding categories: knowledge, acquiring information, sharing, assessing, planning, status reporting, and performing. The names of the levels are informative and signal the progression of a practice, from nonuse to orientation, preparation for use, mechanical use, and ultimately routine use of the practice, and on to the more advanced levels, such as refining the practice, integrating it, and renewing it.

WHY IS SUSTAINABILITY IMPORTANT?

Sustainability is an important issue because it is linked to such critical factors as stability, effectiveness of use, and educational reform. Sustainability is often used as the marker of whether a link has been made between research and practice. Kauffman (1996) states that sustainability is relevant because the instructional practices targeted to be sustained are ones that are associated with improved outcomes for schools and/or students. Also, special attention needs to be directed to issues of sustaining research-based practices once they have become part of the school and classroom protocol.

Furthermore, sustainability of effective practices in special education is important since students with disabilities are unlikely to make adequate gains unless teachers implement the most effective practices. Unlike many students in general education who can compensate for less than adequate instruction, life outcomes for individuals with disabilities are related to the extent to which they are provided effective practices that are sustained long enough to yield positive outcomes.

Why are effective instructional practices not sustained? While bridging the gap between research and practice in education is not a new concern, it has received renewed discussion in special education and reading instruction in recent years (Carnine, 2000; Kauffman, 1996; Lloyd, Weintraub, & Safer, 1997; Malouf & Schiller, 1995; Stanovich, 2000). In addition, the push to require research-based practices as part of educational decision making has even made it into federal guidelines (see, for example, No Child Left Behind Act, 2001).

Vaughn, Klingner, and Hughes (2000) proposed explanations for low rates of sustainability in research-based practices:

> Many teachers think that the instructional practices they are currently using are at least moderately effective; unless they are disturbed by the progress of a student or group of students, they are unlikely to seek alternative instructional interventions.

> Unless teachers are conducting on going progress monitoring, the immediate effects of implementation of an effective practice may not be visible to them. If an instructional practice requires additional work or effort on their part and the gains for students are not obvious, the practice may not be sustained.

> Teachers know that there are many effective ways to teach students, and unless the practice they are using is not working they may not be motivated to make a change.

> Sustaining the use of an instructional practice requires some change on the part of the teacher. Change is always difficult, particularly when the person who may have the most to gain from the change (the student) may not be the one who has to make the change.

TABLE 1   LoU Chart

LEVELS OF USE	CATEGORIES		
Scale Point Definitions of the Levels of Use of the Innovation	*Knowledge*	*Acquiring Information*	*Sharing*
Levels of Use are distinct states that represent observably different types of behavior and patterns of innovation use as exhibited by individuals and groups. These levels characterize a user's development in acquiring new skills and varying use of the innovation. Each level encompasses a range of behaviors but is limited by a set of identifiable *decision points*. For descriptive purposes, each level is defined by seven categories.	That which the user knows about characteristics of the innovation, how to use it, and consequences of its use. This is cognitive knowledge related to using the innovation, not feelings or attitudes.	Solicits information about the innovation in a variety of ways, including questioning resource persons, corresponding with resource agencies, reviewing printed materials, and making visits.	Discusses the innovation with others. Shares plans, ideas, resources, outcomes, and problems related to use of the innovation.
Level 0			
NON-USE: State in which the user has little or no knowledge of the innovation, has no involvement with the innovation, and is doing nothing toward becoming involved.	Knows nothing about this or similar innovations or has only very limited general knowledge of efforts to develop innovations in the area.	Takes little or no action to solicit information about this or similar innovations when it happens to come to personal attention.	Is not communicating with others about the innovation beyond possibly acknowledging that the innovation exists.
DECISION POINT A	*Takes action to learn more detailed information about the innovation.*		
Level I			
ORIENTATION: State in which the user has acquired or is acquiring information about the information and/or has explored or is exploring its value orientation and its demands on user and user system.	Knows general information about the innovation such as origin, characteristics, and implementation requirements.	Seeks descriptive material about the innovation. Seeks opinions and knowledge of others through discussions, visits, or workshops.	Discusses the innovation in general terms and/or exchanges descriptive information, materials, or ideas about the innovation and possible implications of its use.
DECISION POINT B	*Makes a decision to use the innovation by establishing a time to begin.*		

CATEGORIES

Assessing	Planning	Status Reporting	Performing
Examines the potential or actual use of the innovation or some aspect of it. This can be a mental assessment or can involve actual collection and analysis of data.	Designs and outlines short- and/or long-range steps to be taken during process of innovation adoption, i.e., aligns resources, schedules activities, meets with others to organize and/or coordinate use of the innovation.	Describes personal stand at the present time in relation to use of the innovation.	Carries out the actions and activities entailed in operationalizing the innovation.
Takes no action to analyze the innovation, its characteristics, possible use, or consequences of use.	Schedules no time and specifies no steps for the study or use of the innovation.	Reports little or no personal involvement with the innovation.	Takes no discernable action toward learning about or using the innovation. The innovation and/or its accouterments are not present or in use.
Analyzes and compares materials, content, requirements for use, evaluation reports, potential outcomes, strengths, and weaknesses for purpose of making a decision about use of the innovation.	Plans to gather necessary information and resources as needed to make a decision for or against use of the innovation.	Reports presently orienting self to what the innovation is and is not.	Explores the innovation and requirements for its use by talking to others about it, reviewing descriptive information and sample materials, attending orientation sessions, and observing others using it.

(continued)

TABLE 1   Continued

LEVELS OF USE	CATEGORIES		
Scale Point Definitions of the Levels of Use of the Innovation	*Knowledge*	*Acquiring Information*	*Sharing*
Level II			
PREPARATION: State in which the user is preparing for first use of the innovation.	Knows logistical requirements, necessary resources, and timing for initial use of the innovation and details of initial experiences for clients.	Seeks information and resources specifically related to preparation for use of the innovation in own setting.	Discusses resources needed for initial use of the innovation. Joins others in pre-use training and in planning for resources, logistics, schedules, etc., in preparation for first use.
DECISION POINT C	*Begins first use of the innovation.*		
Level III			
MECHANICAL USE: State in which the user focuses most effort on the short-term, day-to-day use of the innovation with little time for reflection. Changes in use are made more to meet user needs than client needs. The user is primarily engaged in a stepwise attempt to master the tasks required to use the innovation, often resulting in disjointed and superficial use.	Knows on a day-to-day basis the requirements for using the innovation. Is more knowledgeable on short-term activities and effects than long-range activities and effects of use of the innovation.	Solicits management information about such things as logistics, scheduling techniques, and ideas for reducing amount of time and work required of user.	Discusses management and logistical issues related to use of the innovation. Resources and materials are shared for purposes of reducing management, flow, and logistical problems related to use of the innovation.
DECISION POINT D-1	*A routine pattern of use is established.*		
Level IV A			
ROUTINE: Use of the innovation is stabilized. Few if any changes are being made in ongoing use. Little preparation or thought is being given to improving innovation use or its consequences.	Knows both short- and long-term requirements for use and how to use the innovation with minimum effort or stress.	Makes no special efforts to seek information as a part of ongoing use of the innovation.	Describes current use of the innovation with little or no reference to ways of changing use.
DECISION POINT D-2	*Changes use of the innovation based on formal or informal evaluation in order to increase client outcomes.*		

	CATEGORIES		
Assessing	*Planning*	*Status Reporting*	*Performing*
Analyzes detailed requirements and available resources for initial use of the innovation.	Identifies steps and procedures entailed in obtaining resources and organizing activities and events for initial use of the innovation.	Reports preparing self for initial use of the innovation.	Studies reference materials in depth, organizes resources and logistics, schedules and receives skill training in preparation for initial use.
Examines own use of the innovation with respect to problems of logistics, management, time, schedules, resources, and general reactions of clients.	Plans for organizing and managing resources, activities, and events related primarily to immediate ongoing use of the innovation. Planned-for changes address managerial or logistical issues with a short-term perspective.	Reports that logistics, time, management, resource organization, etc., are the focus of most personal efforts to use the innovation.	Manages innovation with varying degrees of efficiency. Often lacks anticipation of immediate consequences. The flow of action in the user and clients is often disjointed, uneven, and uncertain. When changes are made, they are primarily in response to logistical and organizational problems.
Limits evaluation activities to those administratively required, with little attention paid to findings for the purpose of changing use.	Plans intermediate and long-range action with little projected variation in how the innovation will be used. Planning focuses on routine use of resources, personnel, etc.	Reports that personal use of the innovation is going along satisfactorily with few if any problems.	Uses the innovation smoothly with minimal management problems; over time, there is little variation in pattern of use.

(continued)

TABLE 1 Continued

LEVELS OF USE	CATEGORIES		
Scale Point Definitions of the Levels of Use of the Innovation	*Knowledge*	*Acquiring Information*	*Sharing*
Level IV B			
REFINEMENT: State in which the user varies the use of the innovation to increase the impact on clients within immediate sphere of influence. Variations are based on knowledge of both short- and long-term consequences for clients.	Knows cognitive and affective effects of the innovation on clients and ways for increasing impact on clients.	Solicits information and materials that focus specifically on changing use of the innovation to affect client outcomes.	Discusses own methods of modifying use of the innovation to change client outcomes.
DECISION POINT E	*Initiates changes in use of innovation based on input of and in coordination with what colleagues are doing.*		
Level V			
INTEGRATION: State in which the user is combining own efforts to use the innovation with related activities of colleagues to achieve a collective impact on clients within their common sphere of influence.	Knows how to coordinate use of the innovation with colleagues to provide a collective impact on clients.	Solicits information and opinions for the purpose of collaborating with others in use of the innovation.	Discusses efforts to increase client impact through collaboration with others on personal use of the innovation.
DECISION POINT F	*Begins exploring alternatives to or major modifications of the innovation presently in use.*		
Level VI			
RENEWAL: State in which the user reevaluates the quality of use of the innovation, seeks major modifications of or alternatives to present innovation to achieve increased impact on clients, examines new developments in the field, and explores new goals for self and the system.	Knows of alternatives that could be used to change or replace the present innovation that would improve the quality of outcomes of its use.	Seeks information and materials about other innovations as alternatives to the present innovation or for making major adaptations in the innovation.	Focuses discussions on identification of major alternatives or replacements for the current innovation.

Source: Procedures for adopting educational innovations project, research and development, Center for Teacher Education, University of Texas at Austin, 1975, N.I.E. Contract No. NIE-C-74-0087.

	CATEGORIES		
Assessing	*Planning*	*Status Reporting*	*Performing*
Assesses use of the innovation for the purpose of changing current practices to improve client outcomes.	Develops intermediate and long-range plans that anticipate possible and needed steps, resources, and events designed to enhance client outcomes.	Reports varying use of the innovation in order to change client outcomes.	Explores and experiments with alternative combinations of the innovation with existing practices to maximize client involvement and to optimize client outcomes.
Appraises collaborative use of the innovation in terms of client outcomes and strengths and weaknesses of the integrated effort.	Plans specific actions to coordinate own use of the innovation with others to achieve increased impact on clients.	Reports spending time and energy collaborating with others about integrating own use of the innovation.	Collaborates with others in use of the innovation as a means for expanding the innovation's impact on clients. Changes in use are made in coordination with others.
Analyzes advantages and disadvantages of major modifications or alternatives to the present innovation.	Plans activities that involve pursuit of alternatives to enhance or replace the innovation.	Reports considering major modifications of or alternatives to present use of the innovation.	Explores other innovations that could be used in combination with or in place of the present innovation in an attempt to develop more effective means of achieving client outcomes.

Teachers are bombarded with new instructional practices and requests for curriculum changes. Even when an instructional practice has evidence to support its use, it is difficult to sustain it when requests for new and/or different approaches come from the district, principal, or another professional.

Teachers are continually required to make decisions about what they will teach and how they will teach it. Sustaining an instructional innovation is affected by all of the factors that influence these decisions about what and how they will teach (discussed in the next section).

The complexities involved in and the dynamics of one adult providing instruction for numerous students cannot be overstated. The extent to which a practice is implemented and then sustained is in no small part a function of whether the teacher can determine how to do so: "Even when we are confronted with what appear to be examples of teachers' resistance to change and misunderstanding of the usefulness of new ideas . . . we must try to understand teachers' actions and reactions from their perspective in the classroom, because what may look like foolishness to an observer in the back of the room may look like the only route to survival from behind the teacher's desk" (Stanovich & Stanovich, 1997, p. 479).

WHAT FACTORS FACILITATE OR IMPEDE SUSTAINED IMPLEMENTATION?

Perhaps the factor most frequently associated with sustained use of practice is "leadership." Research on school change, school restructuring, and school reform supports the importance of the building-level principal in sustaining the change process (Berman & McLaughlin, 1976). In fact, when we initiated our study investigating the most important factors associated with sustained use of instructional practices by teachers, we were repeatedly told that the answer was already known: the school principal. If a principal strongly supports the sustained use of an instructional practice, then it bodes very favorably for the continued use of this practice by the teachers in the school. If a school principal does not support a practice, the practice will flounder. While our and others' research certainly confirms the critical role of district and school leadership in sustaining a practice, we were able to identify other factors that contribute to the sustained use of instructional practices.

Klingner et al. (1999) examined the sustained use of three instructional practices by seven teachers who had participated in a yearlong professional development program. These teachers were then individually interviewed, engaged in conversations, and observed during the three years following the program. Six teachers sustained one or more of the three practices at a high rate. Teachers reported on factors that enhanced or interfered with their sustained use of practices. The following are factors the teachers reported as enhancing their sustained use of the practices:

Support network. Having a support network that included other teachers, paraprofessionals, and individuals from the university helped teachers to maintain the practices. Teachers found that listening to ideas from other teachers who were using the same practice was helpful and made them feel like they were part of a team rather than on their own. One teacher stated, "One of the reasons that this program has been so successful is because we are all doing it."

Administrative support. Teachers identified administrative support as a critical factor in their decisions to use the practices. Teachers knew that their principals valued the practices and expected to see teachers using them in the classroom. This support provided the nudge some teachers needed to use the practices, which they might not otherwise have done. Teachers reported that principals discussed the value of the practices in faculty meetings.

Student benefits. Teachers identified student benefits as strongly influencing their sustained use of the practices. Teachers were impressed by the ways students used the practices and how they influenced students' thinking, reading, and writing. When students made gains, teachers reported that they did not want to discontinue use of the practices.

Student acceptance. Teachers reported that student acceptance influenced their sustained use of practices. If students liked the practices, teachers were much more likely to continue using them than if students did not like the practices.

Flexibility. If teachers could modify a practice to suit their instructional style or their students' needs rather than having to implement the practice rigidly, teachers were more inclined to sustain use of that practice.

Materials readily available. Teachers reported that they simply did not have time to hunt around for materials, locate books, or make the materials necessary to sustain a practice. If the materials were readily accessible, teachers were much more likely to sustain the use of the practice.

In contrast to the above stated factors that were associated with sustained use of practices, teachers also identified those factors that *impeded* their sustained use of practices:

High-stakes testing. Teachers view high-stakes testing as interfering with their use of instructional practices. Teachers indicated that they felt intense pressure to prepare their students for the state level assessments and that to do this they needed to use the test preparation materials; thus, they did not use the instructional practices for several months a year. They also recognized that if an instructional practice appeared to be associated with improved outcomes on the high-stakes test, they were more likely to sustain use of that practice than if this were not the case.

Content coverage. Teachers identified content coverage as a possible barrier to the sustained use of a practice if, for example, the practice in any way slowed down how quickly they were able to cover the content. Teachers recognized that covering the content was not the same as students' "knowing" the content, but they were still concerned that subsequent teachers would be disappointed if all of the appropriate content from the previous year had not been taught.

Time constraints. Teachers identified time constraints as a compelling reason for not sustaining the use of practices. When the school or district mandated that teachers do other things, teachers needed to adjust what and how they taught in order to meet the demands. Teachers reported that this meant they might discontinue using a particular instructional practice even though they perceived it as valuable.

Mismatches. A mismatch between a teacher's style or personality and the instructional practice may keep a teacher from using a practice. For example, one of the instructional practices that we taught involved use of cooperative groups. One of our teachers said, "Cooperative groups just don't click with my personality."

Forgetting. Many teachers offered their forgetting to use the practice as the reason the practice was not sustained over time. Teachers both forgot to use it and forgot how to use it. One teacher had changed grade levels and no longer had the support of a co-teacher who was using the practice. She commented, "With so much change, you forget."

The teachers participating in this study provided very informative insights into why and how instructional practices were sustained over time as well as the reasons that practices may be lost or infrequently used. As stated in a previous analysis of sustainability (Vaughn, Klingner, & Hughes, 2000), we were more impressed with the number of teachers who sustained the practices in a quality manner than we had anticipated. This is much more than giddy optimism or romantic ideas about teachers and their work. It is a genuine appreciation for the challenges that we all have in making change and sustaining the use of that change over time.

WHY IS SUSTAINING A RESEARCH-BASED INNOVATION SO HARD?

When we are inclined to change a routine or practice in our life, we choose to do so most often for our own sake. That is to say, if we are changing our eating habits, sleeping habits, exercise routines, or driving patterns, we do so because there is evidence that we will benefit. However, when we ask teachers to make changes, their doing so often requires that they do additional work, devote more time, or give special consideration to the benefits someone else will reap—hopefully, their students. Thus, we view the fact that many teachers change their instructional practice and sustain this change as quite positive—even though there are teachers who do not.

Change is always difficult, and compliance with requests to change routines is always low. There are many sources of data to support this point, but certainly the medical literature is rampant with evidence about the difficulty in getting patients to comply with practices, even when there are life-threatening consequences to their lack of compliance. Even when changes requested are simple, such as taking a pill, compliance is quite low (Vaughn et al., 2000).

Despite the fact that change is difficult and sustaining an innovative practice may be challenging to many teachers, there are steps that school and district leaders can make to improve the sustained use of practices (Gersten et al., 2000; Klingner et al., 2001; Vaughn et al., 2000); for example, principals who are highly engaged in making sure the practices are used consistently by teachers are much more likely to have sustained use of targeted practices.

Identify the instructional practices that the school and district want to sustain, and clearly specify these to teachers.

Develop effective and ongoing professional development to ensure that teachers acquire the targeted practices to a minimum level of competency so that teachers can use them independently and automatically.

Devise a plan to ensure that sustaining the practices is reasonable for teachers.

Do not provide extensive requests for teachers to learn or implement other practices while they are learning the targeted instructional practices.

Communicate effectively with teachers the importance of the targeted instructional practices and why it is valuable for them to be sustained.

Identify teachers who are implementing the practices effectively and allow other teachers opportunities to observe.

Develop resources and materials so teachers can readily observe via videotape, for example, or benefit from the materials other teachers devise.

Provide time for teachers to implement the practices, talk with other teachers about issues related to the practice, develop and share materials related to the practices, and reflect on their practice and communicate with others who know and use the practices.

Give systematic and ongoing feedback to teachers about their students' progress as it relates to their implementing the target practice.

Give teachers opportunities to adjust and fine-tune the instructional practices to work in their settings with their students.

One of the significant obstacles to successful implementation of research findings in education is a prevailing pessimism among teachers and even researchers about the importance and use of research (Stanovich & Stanovich, 1997). For many educators, it is difficult to sort out the credible from the phony claims about research in education. The actual consumption and interpretation of the research base on any given issue in education is complex even for researchers whose full-time work it is to synthesize and contribute to research in education. Understanding the range of educational topics needed by most classroom teachers requires precise, accurate, and corroborated information. In many ways, the research community has failed to support practicing professionals by not making this information accessible and readily available to them.

We have been interested in the barriers and facilitators identified by teachers as contributing to sustaining target instructional practices. We are also interested in the extent to which teachers might sustain a practice if the barriers identified were removed. For example, for teachers who indicated that they had insufficient planning time to implement the practice, would they indeed implement and sustain use of the practice if additional planning time were provided? We suspect that for some teachers removing barriers would be sufficient to influence their use of the practice, and for others there simply is little or nothing that could be done to enhance use.

COMMUNITIES THAT SUSTAIN CHANGE

There is a growing consensus that some habits and cultures foster reflective thinking about instructional practices and promote sustained use of innovative practices (Darling-Hammond & McLaughlin, 1995; Elmore, 1996). Among these are learning communities that extend beyond the often solo work of teaching. As we have learned, sustaining change—whether through dieting, exercising, or investing for retirement—seems to be easier when the effort is shared with someone else or a group. We suppose this in part explains the proliferation of support groups around every topic imaginable.

Researchers from Juniper Gardens (Abbott, Walton, Tapia, & Greenwood, 1999) present a blueprint for closing the gap between research and practice in local schools. They argue that the traditional professional development model has not led to direct change in classroom practice. Furthermore, the top-down research model also has not produced interventions that affect practice. Both of these problems exist largely because research has failed to obtain input from the critical stakeholders—teachers—and thus the gap between research and practice persists. They, like others, suggest that the gap can be bridged with ongoing interchange between researchers and practitioners (Fuchs & Fuchs, 1998; Stone, 1998).

According to Englert and Tarrant (1995), researchers can foster a collaborative culture by viewing teachers as coparticipants in the research process. They contrast this with more traditional models in which researchers view teachers as recipients of knowledge. Collaborating with teachers creates relationships that can lead to deeper, more long-lasting changes than would be possible in traditional staff development or teacher education programs. Furthermore, individuals' interacting can address both real-world and theoretical problems (Oakes, Hare, & Sirotnik, 1986). Perhaps most noteworthy about the research on collaborative learning groups for teachers is the finding that through them teachers have altered their self-views in ways that make the continued implementation of practices more enduring (Hendricks-Lee, Soled, & Yinger, 1995).

Berman and McLaughlin (1976) describe the importance of the school community's participation in selecting an innovative practice in response to an identified need in the school or district. They found that schools were more likely to maintain the practice for extended periods of time when they had identified it as addressing their specific needs. Furthermore, practices were more likely to be sustained if they replaced an existing practice rather than added to what teachers were already doing. Other factors that influenced continued use were professional development that addressed practical classroom issues and the use of experts and available materials. McLaughlin (1990) observes that factors that contribute to teacher change are less likely to be policy structure issues than those in teachers' proximal environment, such as their colleagues, school association, and professional networks.

Senge (1990) states that "people learn what they need to learn, not what someone else thinks they need to learn" (p. 345). Senge's comment surely relates to issues about teachers' sustaining innovative practices. Whether or not teachers do so will in part be influenced by the extent to which they view the requested change as necessary. This is particularly important in the United States, where teachers have a lot of autonomy about what and how they teach; without teachers' support of practices, desired outcomes are difficult to achieve (Cuban,

1990)—unless, of course, there are significant changes in the incentive system for teachers (Elmore, 1996).

IMPLICATIONS FOR RESEARCH AND PRACTICE

There are many opportunities for research to inform our understanding of the sustained use of innovative practices by districts, schools, and teachers. Much can be gained by further investigating teachers' proclivities about using research-based practices. We have some initial evidence to suggest that what teachers think of research findings and the appropriateness of these findings for their setting and students may influence the extent to which they use and sustain the use of targeted innovative practices (Arguelles, Vaughn, Gould, Hughes, & Klingner, in press). For example, in focus groups conducted with teachers of students with emotional/behavioral disorders, investigators found that teachers believed that the so-called research-based practices the district was promoting had not been tested with their students in mind and would not meet the needs of their classrooms. They were further skeptical that anyone at the school or district level had even considered the types of students they taught and the appropriateness of the implementation. As one teacher stated, "This research doesn't mean anything to me because it doesn't speak to my students."

Teachers may also believe that research does not apply universally but is applicable only to the particular group under investigation. Furthermore, some teachers may have difficulty understanding that a particular principle (e.g., code-based instruction for beginning reading) has been supported by universal converging findings and is likely to be applicable to their setting. One teacher told us, "Teachers don't use research; they use what works for them in their particular situation."

We are also interested in research that addresses the extent to which different levels of professional development result in implementation and sustained use of a practice. While there has been considerable criticism of traditional professional development in which teachers are provided with information about an innovative practice and then expected to implement it (Richardson, 1994), few studies have systematically investigated the effectiveness of more or less intensive professional development opportunities and their influence on sustained use. Additionally, we think it would be valuable to determine the extent to which teacher teams might be able to inform each other of innovative practices and work cooperatively to sustain implementation.

We also think that it would be beneficial to understand ways to develop a cadre of teachers who are experts about the scientific knowledge base in education and are able to serve as mentors and guides for their fellow teachers (Vaughn & Dammann, 2001). A beneficial outcome of scientific inquiry is the establishment of a community of experts who access the scientific knowledge and contribute to it through their own research. For classroom teachers this scientific inquiry would be through their own classroom implementation in which they document progress. This evidence-based approach to instruction makes scientific knowledge part of teachers' repertoires and provides them with the muscle they need to challenge the system when poorly constructed or ill-advised ideas are promoted. Professional preparation in education has failed to make teachers consumers of and participants in the scientific process in education. We believe that it would be highly valuable to devise a model for engaging educational professionals in this process.

In summary, sustainability of research-based practices is an essential issue in education. Schools, districts, or teachers may select effective practices to implement with their students, but if the implementation of the selected practices is not sustained, the effectiveness of these practices is significantly compromised. In this chapter we discussed two approaches to categorizing the sustained use of instructional practices by teachers. Through our research we identify teachers who sustain interventions proactively, routinely, through modifications, and partially. We presented factors that contribute or inhibit sustained use of practices and recommended areas for future research on sustainability.

QUESTIONS FOR FURTHER DISCUSSION

1. How would you define a sustainable practice? Can you provide an example?

2. If educational practices are sustained but changed substantially in implementation, can we still call them the same practice?

3. What are the barriers and facilitators to sustaining effective practices from a teacher's perspective? What suggestions do you have to promote facilitators and reduce barriers?

4. Why is sustainability important, and what can educators do to promote sustainable practices?

REFERENCES

Abbott, M., Walton, C., Tapia, Y., & Greenwood, C. R. (1999). Research to practice: A "blueprint" for closing the gap in local schools. *Exceptional Children, 65*(3), 339–352.

Arguelles, M. E., Vaughn, S., Gould, A., Hughes, M., & Klingner, J. K. (in press). Special education teachers' views on research-based practices. *Journal of Special Education.*

Berman, P., & McLaughlin, M. (1976). Implementation of educational innovations. *Educational Forum, 40*(3), 345–370.

Carnine, D. (1997). Bridging the research-to-practice gap. *Exceptional Children, 63,* 513–521.

Carnine, D. (2000, April). Why education experts resist effective practices. Washington, DC: The Thomas B. Fordham Foundation. Retrieved from http://www.edexcellence.net/library/carnine.html.

Chall, J. S. (2000). *The academic achievement challenge.* New York: Guilford.

Cohen, D. K., & Ball, D. L. (1990). Relations between policy and practice: A commentary. *Educational Evaluation and Policy Analysis, 12*(3), 249–256.

Cooper, H. (1996). Speaking power to truth: Reflections of an educational researcher after 4 years of school board service. *Educational Researcher, 25*(1), 29–34.

Cuban, L. (1990). Reforming again, again, and again. *Educational Researcher, 19*(1), 3–13.

Darling-Hammond, L., & McLaughlin, M. W. (1995). Policies that support professional development in an era of reform. *Phi Delta Kappan, 76*(8), 597–604.

Elmore, R. (1996). Getting to scale with good educational practice. *Harvard Educational Review, 66*(1), 1–26.

Englert, C. S., & Tarrant, K. L. (1995). Creating collaborative cultures for educational change. *Remedial and Special Education, 16,* 325–336, 353.

Fuchs, D., & Fuchs, L. S. (1998). Researchers and teachers working together to adapt instruction for diverse learners. *Learning Disabilities Research and Practice, 13*(3), 126–137.

Gersten, R., Chard, D., & Baker, S. (2000). Factors enhancing sustained use of research-based instructional practices. *Journal of Learning Disabilities, 33*(5), 445–457.

Gersten, R., Vaughn, S., Deshler, D., & Schiller, E. (1997). What we know about using research findings: Implications for improving special education practice. *Journal of Learning Disabilities, 30*(5), 466–476

Hall, G. E., Loucks, S. F., Rutherford, W. L., & Newlove, B. W. (1975). Levels of use of the innovation: A framework for analyzing innovation adoption. *Journal of Teacher Education, 26*(1), 5–9.

Hendricks-Lee, M. S., Soled, S. W., & Yinger, R. J. (1995). Sustaining reform through teacher learning. *Language Arts, 72,* 288–292.

Kauffman, J. M. (1993). How we might achieve the radical reform of special education. *Exceptional Children, 60*(1), 6–16.

Kauffman, J. M. (1996). Research to practice issues. *Behavioral Disorders, 22*(1) 55–60.

Klingner, J. K., Arguelles, M. E., Hughes, M. T., & Vaughn, S. (2001). Examining the schoolwide "spread" of research-based practices. *Learning Disability Quarterly, 24,* 221–234.

Klingner, J. K., Vaughn, S., Hughes, M. T., and Arguelles, M. E. (1999). Sustaining research-based practices in reading: A 3-year follow-up. *Rase: Remedial & Special Education, 20*(5), 263–274, 287.

Lloyd, J. W., Weintraub, F. J., & Safer, N. D. (1997). A bridge between research and practice: Building consensus. *Exceptional Children, 63*(4), 535–538.

Loucks, S. F., Newlove, B. W., & Hall, G. E. (1975). *Measuring levels of use of the innovation: A manual for trainers, interviewers, and raters.* Austin, TX: Research and Development Center for Teacher Education, University of Texas.

Malouf, D. B., & Schiller, E. P. (1995). Practice and research in special education. *Exceptional Children, 61*(5), 414–424.

McLaughlin, M. W. (1990). The Rand change agent study revisited: Macro perspectives and micro realities. *Educational Research, 19*(9), 11–16.

No Child Left Behind Act. (2001, August 2). Retrieved from http://www.nochildleftbehind.gov/.

Oakes, J., Hare, S. E., & Sirotnik, K. A. (1986). Collaborative inquiry: A congenial paradigm in a cantankerous world. *Teachers College Record, 87*(4), 545–561.

Richardson, V. (1994). Conducting research on practice. *Educational Researcher, 23*(5), 5–10.

Senge, P. (1990). The fifth discipline: The art and practice of the learning organization. New York: Doubleday Currency.

Stanovich, K. E. (2000). *Progress in understanding reading.* New York: Guilford Press.

Stanovich, P. J., & Stanovich, K. E. (1997). Research into practice in special education. *Journal of Learning Disabilities, 30*(5), 477–478.

Stone, C. A. (1998). Moving validated instructional practices into the classroom: Learning from examples about the rough road to success. *Learning Disabilities Research & Practice, 13*(3), 121–125.

Vaughn, S., & Dammann, J. E. (2001). Science and sanity in special education. *Behavior Disorder, 27*(1), 21–29.

Vaughn, S., Klingner, J. K., & Hughes, M. (2000). Sustainability of research-based practices. *Exceptional Children, 66*(2), 163–171.

Walberg, H. J. (1998). Foreword. In K. Topping & S. Ehly, *Peer-Assisted Learning* (pp. ix–xii). Mahwah, NJ: Erlbaum.

TRENDS AND ISSUES IN BEHAVIORAL INTERVENTIONS

LEWIS POLSGROVE
THERESA OCHOA
Indiana University, Bloomington

PROBLEM BEHAVIORS OF CHILDREN

Many children with disabilities display a variety of "problem" behaviors that pose challenges to those who are responsible for fostering their academic and social development. It is generally recognized that these behavior patterns are the product of a complex interaction of such variables as temperament, cognitive endowment, environmental privation, and learning history. Although considerable overlap in problem behaviors has been identified among various types of children's disabilities, the topography and severity of these generally vary with the particular disability. Children with developmental disabilities such as autism or severe mental retardation, for example, are prone to stereotypic motor patterns, eating disorders, disruptive outbursts, self-injurious behavior, and other forms of aggression (Pyles & Bailey, 1990). Children with information processing and cognitive disorders, such as learning disabilities, mild mental retardation, and attention deficit hyperactivity disorders, typically pose instructional and motivational difficulties but may show episodic disruptiveness, noncompliance, and outbursts of anger (Barkley, 1998). Children identified as having emotional/behavioral disorders (EBD) present the most difficulties, however, because of the variety, frequency, and severity of their problem behaviors.

Occasional displays of troublesome behavior are natural occurrences in childhood and adolescent development. In fact, most children are considered problematic by at least one of their teachers during their school years (Rubin & Balow, 1978), and the line between normal and abnormal behavior often is a matter of degree and situational circumstances. Critics of the field of special education have used such facts to argue that perceived differences among children are minimal, that labels such as EBD are merely "social constructs" rather than markers describing a particular group of children. They view labeling children as stigmatizing (Dunn, 1968), distortional (Lilly, 1979), and a major factor influencing teachers' differential treatment of children (Reynolds & Birch, 1982). Some doubt the existence of children's disabilities altogether (Danforth & Rhodes, 1997). Such positions dismiss centuries of recognition of mental illnesses by virtually all human culture (Carson, Butcher, & Mineka, 1996) and ignore a half-century of research on the abnormal behavior of children and youth (Kauffman, 2001).

Considerable empirical evidence indicates that even without a formal label, children with EBD are identifiable by dint of their socially unacceptable behaviors. In their observational analyses of the social interactions of hundreds of families of children with behavioral disorders, for example, Patterson, Reid, Jones, and Conger (1975) showed that these children are 4.5 times more likely than nonaggressive peers to perform negative physical acts and 4.7 times more likely to show destructive behavior. They also were two to four times more likely than nonaggressive children to display other oppositional and antisocial behaviors: high rates of noncompliance, high teasing, humiliation, whining, crying, and negativism. Coie and Kupersmidt (1983) demonstrated that within minutes of placing highly aggressive boys in play groups, their nonaggressive peers showed clear signs of rejecting them. Curci and Gottlieb's (1990) observations disclosed that even when classroom teachers were unaware of their student's disability label, they showed lower rates of instructional interaction and feedback, and greater signs of rejection, for children identified as EBD.

Studies have consistently shown that a significant number of children, estimated at between 3 and 10 percent of the school-age population (Department of Health and Human Services, 2002; Kauffman, 2001) show frequent and/or severe problem behaviors such that they require ongoing services. Their difficulties appear to arise from a complex interaction of genetic predisposition, temperament, and social learning interactions, with environmental variables playing the most influential role (Bandura, 1969, 1977; Chess & Thomas, 1977; Patterson, Reid, and Dishion, 1992; Plomin, 1989). These children's maladaptive behavioral patterns can result in the direst outcomes to themselves, their families, and society. Left unchecked these patterns can result in a lifetime of difficulties, including school failure, social rejection, low self-esteem, depression, antisocial behavior, delinquency, substance abuse, adult adjustment problems, unemployment, and institutionalization (Kauffman, 2001). Recent evidence indicates that some of these patterns become so thoroughly ingrained at an early age they are largely unmodifiable and are considered chronic medical conditions similar to cerebral palsy or diabetes that require long-term services (Walker, Colvin, & Ramsey, 1995; Wolf, Braukmann, & Ramp, 1987).

These and other findings provide clear and formidable evidence that children's emotional and behavioral disorders—conditions such as antisocial behavior, bipolar disorders, anorexia, social anxiety, phobias, autism, personality disorders, and various psychoses—are real and chronic. They require early and intensive interventions that may not be available in traditional general education classrooms and schools (Braaten, Kauffman, Braaten, Polsgrove, & Nelson, 1988; Kauffman, 1999; MacMillan, Gresham, & Forness, 1996; Walker et al., 1995). Unfortunately, as many as 90 percent of children who might qualify as EBD go unidentified, and most of those who do qualify often receive inadequate school-based services (Department of Health & Human Services, 2002; Kauffman, 2001; Knitzer, Steinberg, & Fleisch, 1990).

Over the past four decades considerable advances have been made concerning the nature of children's EBD and their assessment and treatment. However, these have gone largely ignored by practitioners in the public schools, and programs for these children have changed little in the past thirty years. In this chapter we provide a brief history of the development of behavioral interventions, identify those that have empirical evidence supporting their effectiveness, and identify major barriers to developing more advanced systems of services for children with EBD.

We face a daunting task in attempting to untangle the complex issues related to the term *behavioral interventions.* A logical starting point, therefore, would involve reducing the ambiguity of this term, for if left undefined, it could refer to strategies of any source, tested and untested, for changing any type of behavior. In this chapter the term *behavioral interventions* refers to empirically based strategies used to reduce problem behavior and enhance the acquisition of developmentally appropriate and socially acceptable behavior. As schools are the most important influence on cognitive and social development for most children, most of the interventions we present involve educational settings as a primary site. Although some of the interventions we review fall within a strict behavioral framework, others involve a combination of approaches. However, each includes some component based on behavioral psychology, and all have received substantial external validation of their effectiveness.

PERSPECTIVE ON BEHAVIORAL INTERVENTIONS

Historical Backdrop

It would be an understatement to say that much of our current knowledge about how to manage children's problem behavior is based on behavioral psychology. However, the tenets of this discipline are poorly understood among educators, and its viability and appropriateness for use in instruction and social development continues to be debated in the educational literature (Brigham & Polsgrove, 1998; Meyer & Evans, 1993; Nelson, Scott, & Polsgrove, 1999). The epistemology of behavioral psychology rests on a radical "positivist" philosophy that rejects metaphysical, unobservable explanations of phenomena. For positivists, physical phenomena and human behavior can be adequately explained only by collecting and comparing information based upon observable data. Thus, the behavioral "model" seeks to identify scientific "truths" by collecting facts under controlled conditions and verifying these through evaluation by a community of scholars.

A major activity of a positivist approach to knowledge building involves first formulating hypotheses regarding the effects of one or more environmental variables on others. Researchers conduct a series of experiments in which they manipulate controllable ("independent") variables and then observe and measure the effects of doing so on others ("dependent variables"). The main goals of positivist science are to establish a reliable body of information and to use this information to predict and control outcomes (Leahey, 1980). In the case of children's behavior problems we are concerned with identifying what variables increase or decrease the probability of one or more behaviors in various contexts or settings. This knowledge allows assessment of the most effective and ethically appropriate intervention.

In the early history of the field primarily two schools dominated psychology: structuralism and functionalism. Structuralism attempted to locate and describe sensations in the "mind" and map its "structure," and functionalism focused on the functions that perceptions and thoughts served in guiding behavior. Both disciplines relied on introspection whereby investigators subjectively interpreted their perceptions and derived "scientific" conclusions based on their perceptions. For over two hundred years these "subjectivist" approaches limited the advancement of the field of psychology to philosophical introspection and speculation (Hernshaw, 1987).

Behaviorism emerged early in the twentieth century as a radical reaction to the constraints imposed by subjectivism and to establish a science of human behavior (Leahey, 1980). This required eliminating reliance on introspective methods and limiting investigations to behavioral reactions (behaviors) of various "organisms" to verifiable public stimuli. A primary objective of this new behavioral science was the prediction and control of behavior. Ultimately, through controlled and independently replicated experiments based on observational data, behaviorists hoped to identify universal principles that would apply across species (Skinner, 1974). Although it often goes unrecognized in the education literature, behavioral psychology was considerably influenced by the psychologists and pragmatist philosophers Charles Sanders Peirce and John Dewey, especially in their efforts to make scientific information useful in improving the human condition (Leahey, 1980). Thus, an undercurrent of behavioral psychology has always been the application of empirically derived scientific principles for solving societal problems and improving human conduct and learning (Skinner, 1953, 1956). This literature has exerted a significant influence on educational and clinical practices with children.

Beginning in the early 1960s, the development of effective behavioral interventions for treating children's EBD was propelled by a series of conceptual and empirical breakthroughs. First, professionals became increasingly dissatisfied with the dominant "medical" model and psychoanalysis as a theoretical and treatment paradigm. Psychoanalytic theory did not provide empirically testable hypotheses or verifiable treatment outcomes (Kazdin, 1978). Szasz (1960) and others argued that psychological and behavioral problems were the results of a social learning process and "problems of living" rather than biogenic causes or subconscious conflicts. Second, critiques of psychiatric and psychotherapeutic treatment approaches presented damaging evidence regarding their effects with adults (e.g., Eysenck, 1965) and children (Levitt, 1963). Third, studies based on behavioral principles were producing effective results. Skinner (1953) had described how principles affecting animal behavior could explain and be used to change complex human behavior. Soon, a number of reports began appearing in the literature of successful applications of behavioral principles for changing adult and child behavior in natural settings (Kazdin, 1978; Ulman & Krasner, 1966).

The growing success of behavioral applications in natural settings fostered a highly influential movement in the field aptly termed "applied behavior analysis," or ABA. This approach has a primary assumption that psychological disorders are primarily learned behavior and the goal of interventions is to teach more functional or effective behavior. Thus, ABA focuses on development of a systematic methodology that can be used in natural settings to produce significant and verifiable changes in socially significant observable behaviors. After three decades, the literature on ABA principles and procedures boasts hundreds of studies documenting the effectiveness of ABA in explaining and treating children's EBD. This methodology has produced an array of strategies such as functional behavior analysis, differential reinforcement, shaping, chaining, token economies, extinction, DRO, timeout, and response cost (Kazdin, 1994). Moreover, hundreds of studies have demonstrated that these strategies can be used effectively in natural environments by caregivers and service providers, including teachers and parents.

While Skinner's operant model formed the basis of ABA applications, Bandura (1969, 1977) expanded this paradigm into a social learning/cognitive behavioral theory that explained how complex behavioral repertoires could be acquired and modified through observation and imitation of social models. Kanfer and Karoly's (1972) model of behavioral self-regulation added yet another breakthrough and led to the development of a number of useful strategies for teaching children to control their behavior (Meichenbaum & Asarnow, 1979). These advances have produced a large behavior change literature termed *cognitive behavior modification* (CBM), which bridged the chasm between behavioral and constructivist theory.

The CBM literature, which focuses on teaching individuals behavioral self-control, provides a credible response to philosophical critiques raised about the "data-driven," "value-free" approach to interventions associated with radical behaviorism (Donnellan & LaVigna, 1990; Meyer & Evans, 1993). Teaching children cognitive behavior modification techniques such as goal-setting, self-monitoring, self-evaluation, self-reinforcement, self-instruction, and interpersonal problem-solving focuses on moving the "locus of control" to the child and decreasing his or her reliance on external or environmental controls (Meichenbaum & Asarnow, 1979; Mischel, 1968). Studies have clearly demonstrated that CBM provides a powerful complement to "external" behavior management strategies (Reid, 1999; Polsgrove, 1979). Some of the more notable of these include rational emotive therapy (Ellis, 1970), self-instructional and metacognitive training procedures (Meichenbaum & Asarnow, 1979), problem solving (D'Zurilla & Goldfried, 1971; Spivack, Platt, & Shure, 1976), self-control (Thoresen & Mahoney, 1974), and social skills training (e.g., Goldstein, Sprafkin, Gershaw, & Klein, 1979).

These advances, taken together, have provided the conceptual foundation for a number of current practices in classrooms, clinics, and treatment programs for children with EBD. A considerable number of studies conducted in natural settings have used behavioral interventions to address problem behaviors of children. Overwhelming evidence from meta-analyses of individual studies has demonstrated empirically based behavioral and cognitive/behavioral interventions to be highly effective in improving both academic and behavioral functioning of children exhibiting problem behavior (Skiba and Casey, 1985). Highly significant results also have been reported with applications of cognitive behavior modification with children's hyperactivity-impulsivity and aggression (Robinson, Smith, Miller, & Brownell, 1999). Considerable evidence suggests that behavior modification and other related "positivist" interventions produce reliable and highly significant outcomes. Forness, Kavale, Blum, & Lloyd (1997), in a meta-analysis of special education interventions, reported some of the most highly significant effect sizes (< .65) for behavior modification, cognitive behavior modification, early intervention, and formative assessment.

Current Status

Over the past four decades hundreds of studies in applied settings (home, school, community) have provided a body of factual and independently confirmed evidence that empirically based strategies can produce significant positive changes in both academic achievement and behaviors of children and youth (Greenwood & Abbott, 2001; Peacock Hill Working Group, 1991; Walker, Zeller, Close, Webber, & Gresham, 1999). These have provided the foundation for the current genre of studies that have emerged recently in the behavior-management literature involving multicomponent intervention "packages." Multicomponent interventions are not focused on simply targeting problem behavior as many earlier studies did but involve identification and modification of "context" variables, such as setting events, expectations, and behavior of significant others (e.g., Lewis & Sugai, 1999). Some of these interventions involve intensive services with the child and significant others across various ecological settings (e.g., Conduct Problems Prevention Research Group, 1999; Borduin, Mann, Cone, Henggeler, Fucci, Blaske, & Williams, 1995; Henggeler, 1997). These programs have been highly successful and each is composed of principles of behavioral change based on empirical studies. We will highlight a few of these as illustrations of the second generation of behavioral interventions. Note that each of the studies goes well beyond simply demonstrating the effectiveness of a single behavioral technique with one or two children. All involve groups of children, rely on teachers and, in some cases, parents as primary "interventionists," and were conducted in natural settings. Finally, each has an empirically validated positive outcome in children's problem behaviors.

In an early investigation Walker and Hops's (1993) RECESS program demonstrated that a combination of behavior modification strategies (praise, token-reinforcement, and response cost) and an intensive academic basic skills training program could produce significant improvements in the positive social interactions and reduction of negative interactions of children (Walker et al., 1995). The Prepare Curriculum provides training in problem solving, situational perception, anger replacement, stress management, empathy, recruitment of social models, cooperation, and group dynamics, and it has been shown to be effective in several evaluation studies (Goldstein, 1988). Second Step (Frey, Hirschstein, & Guzzo, 2000), a violence prevention and reduction program for teaching students empathy, social problem solving, and anger management, has produced significant results in a control group comparison.

A major criticism of behavioral intervention studies is they tend to be restricted to small, short-term studies. However, we are witnessing the emergence of highly effective group applications of behavioral intervention, and some are showing significant long-term effects. Metzler, Biglan, Rusby, and Sprague (2001), for example, recently reported data in a three-year evaluation of a positive behavioral approach to schoolwide discipline. Results indicated that the school climate became more positive, disciplinary referrals and social aggression declined, and a greater number of students reported feeling safe in various school settings.

Strain and Timm (2001) recently reported positive long-term results on forty cases involved in a "regional intervention program." The program enlists parents in a home-school partnership and trains them in behavioral and social skills training and family planning designed to reduce aggression and antisocial behavior. Analysis of three- and nine-year follow-up data from home and school observations, behavioral-rating scales, and interviews revealed high rates (97 percent) of positive parent-child interactions, high behavioral ratings, high employment and academic achievement, low rates of school discipline referral, and no aggressive or antisocial behavior.

Another behavioral intervention project, FAST Track (Conduct Problems Prevention Research Group, 1999) evaluated the long-term effects of training parents in behavioral techniques, children in social and academic skills, and parent-teacher consultation. Results across nearly nine hundred children located in four states indicated that receiving the FAST Track intervention produced significant positive effects on peer ratings of aggression and hyperactive-disruptive behaviors and increases in observer ratings of classroom atmosphere. Moderate positive effects were noted on children's social, emotional, and academic skills; peer interactions and social status; and conduct problems. Reliance on special education services decreased. Parents also reported using less physical discipline, more appropriate and consistent discipline, experiencing greater satisfaction and ease in parenting, feeling more positive toward their child, and increasing their involvement with the school.

Multisystemic therapy (MST) represents another empirically based behavioral intervention package that has been demonstrated to be highly effective in reducing the course of delinquency among repeat offenders (Borduin et al., 1995). MST uses an ecological approach to service delivery that focuses on multiple determinants of violent and antisocial behavior involving the youngster's family, peers, school performance, and neighborhood. MST therapists conduct interventions using a combination of insight, affective, relationship-building, and behavioral techniques in a family therapy setting offered twenty-four hours a day, seven days a week.

Several well-controlled long-term multisite studies have demonstrated MST to be effective in improving parent–youth relationships and reducing re-arrest rates, recidivism for sexual offenses, and substance abuse among participants. Most impressive is a four-year longitudinal study in which 176 participants were randomly assigned to either an MST or a traditional individual therapy group. In addition to improved peer and family relations, the recidivism rate for those who completed MST was 22 percent versus 71 percent for those who completed individual therapy. The recidivism rate for MST dropouts was 47 percent versus 71 percent for individual therapy dropouts. Both those who completed MST and those who dropped out were involved in significantly fewer serious crimes compared with the group who participated in individual therapy (Henggeler, 1997).

The studies presented above represent only the highlights of a large and persuasive body of evidence supporting the conclusion that practitioners currently have at their disposal very powerful behavioral interventions. These have been empirically validated in "field-based" studies in producing positive and significant changes in behavior and adjustment of children and youth in individual, group, and systemwide applications. Developing such a solidly researched base has been an incredible accomplishment and a powerful advantage in the treatment of children's EBD. However, the key to affecting services hinges on convincing services providers to draw on research-based information in planning and implementing interventions. Under these circumstances one would logically conclude that such effective approaches would be widely adopted and highly used by practitioners. Unfortunately, this is decidedly not the case; there exists a large and persistent discrepancy—a "gap"—between research and practice that has been documented by a number of researchers (e.g., Kauffman, 1999; Meyer & Evans, 1993; Peacock Hill Working Group, 1991; Walker et al., 1999).

Over a decade ago Knitzer and her colleagues (1990), in an extensive national study of school programs for children with EBD, found that these programs characteristically overemphasized and misused token economies, rarely used academic teaching strategies, offered few opportunities to learn adaptive social skills, provided limited access to counseling and therapy services, and paid little attention to helping students with developmental or programmatic transitions. However, little has changed since Knitzer's study. In the next section, we identify barriers to fuller implementation of effective evidence-based practices in the field and offer recommendations for the adoption and sustained use of research-validated practices.

ISSUES IN BEHAVIORAL INTERVENTIONS

Futurologist Alvin Toffler (1980) anticipated the global chaos we are currently witnessing, interpreting it as a clash of "waves" of three concomitant social-cultural-technological revolutions. The first and second waves, the agricultural and industrial revolutions, are still operating in some developing parts of the world. The third wave, currently in motion, involves deconstruction of the industrial model with its emphasis on standardization, specialization, and centralization and its replacement with a new, stable global culture and economy based on information technology; this wave embraces individuality and racial, ethnic, and religious diversity and portends a more equal distribution of power among various groups.

The social sciences are not immune to general forces shaping the cultural and political landscapes. The field of special education appears to be grappling with influences similar to those Toffler identified. Thus, over the past two decades we have witnessed in the special education literature considerable and often acrimonious debate concerning what constitutes appropriate assumptions and practices regarding children with disabilities. Some have identified these debates as a revolution, a "shift in paradigms," the reconceptualization of the field of special education from an outmoded, indifferent, valueless scientific approach to a new, postmodern, value-based, democratic model (Skrtic, Sailor, & Gee, 1996).

The field of emotional and behavioral disorders has unavoidably been drawn into this conflict, and over the last decade considerable attention has focused on defending the appropriateness of reliance on evidence-based research to guide practices and related service delivery models (Braaten, Kauffman, Braaten, Polsgrove, & Nelson, 1998; Kauffman, 1999; MacMillan, Gresham, & Forness, 1996). These developments have divided the leadership and the rank and file of special education, tarnished our public image, and clouded the future of the field (Walker et al., 1999). Most importantly, they have generated considerable confusion regarding what constitutes appropriate and effective practices for children who are struggling with academic and emotional/behavioral difficulties. We consider the most important issue related to behavioral interventions with children with EBD to be a failure to capitalize on our current knowledge for developing effective comprehensive services for them. In the next section we identify the main barriers to establishing appropriate practices and services and suggest that these stem from ideological disputes, the willingness of practitioners to employ untested interventions, and a severe shortage of adequately trained personnel.

IDEOLOGICAL DISPUTES

One of the most politically significant barriers to establishing an effective services system for children with EBD involves a deep ideological rift that exists in the special education leadership concerning the viability of basic assumptions and practices related to providing services for children with disabilities. This considerably complex dispute is primarily embodied in the "postmodern critique" of the empirical/scientific, evidenced-based, or "modernist" model that provides a compass for practices in the field. In truth, the postmodern position is not a "critique" intended to reform current practices and policies in the field of special education. Rather, it has become a political movement to dismantle the empirically based services delivery framework and replace it with a new "paradigm" based on postmodern philosophical ideals and approved practices (Lipsky & Gartner, 1997; Skrtic, 1995; Skrtic & Sailor, 1996). Toward this end, some special educators have assumed the mantle of critical philosophers and launched multifaceted campaigns through a flurry of publications and public presentations.

A major distinction between the empirical (modern) and postmodern positions involves the concept of "truth." For empiricists, objective information can be established by collecting verifiable facts through observation and controlled experiments. The results of experiments are cross-validated through the replication of studies by independent observers. A body of information gains acceptance as accurate through collegial review in public forums and publications that are continually reevaluated and revised. The process of continually evaluating and refining empirical information is, by design, methodical and time consuming. In the case of interventions with children and youth, potentially effective strategies are developed through careful research and refined through subsequent replication in applied settings. These strategies are then disseminated to practitioners, who essentially function as responsible users of interventions.

Although differences can be drawn between their various positions (Skrtic et al., 1996) postmodern special educators staunchly reject the philosophical tenets of the empirical position and related practices. A basic point of departure between these views involves the status of "objectively" derived information. If observer subjectivity is always inherent in collecting and interpreting information, postmodernists argue, then objective "truth," per se, cannot be established. Thus, postmodernists argue that every idea, no matter what its source or basis, is equal to another. No external source or method can be employed to test the validity of one idea over another. It follows, then, that there can be no established authority, no "experts," no "facts." Postmodernists also reject the idea of "progress" as a function of empirical activities. Instead, they view empirical knowledge building as nothing more than a socially constructed and directionless narrative having no more validity than any other "voice" (Danforth, 1997; Skrtic, Sailor, & Gee, 1996).

To some postmodernists, empirical "narratives" are simply political mechanisms. For example, postmodern special educators have argued that the concept of human deficits and associated labels such as mental retardation and EBD are not "real" phenomena but fabrications by the social services industry that perpetuate the myth of human abnormality and limitation (Brantlinger, 1997; Danforth, 1997). Rhodes (1995) cast empiricism as a form of imperialism that, through the labeling and provision of special services process, creates and maintains social castes: the privileged (children without disabilities) and the underprivileged (children with disabilities). Danforth (1997) has painted empiricism as a male-dominated activity serving the needs of a select professional class. Further, postmodern special educators argue that practices based on empirical research have failed and reliance on the evidence-based practices cannot be justified (Brantlinger, 1997).

The ultimate objective of postmodern special educators is the "deconstruction" of the current system of identifying appropriate or best practices and the "social construction" of a new services delivery "model" based on consumer-determined values and a "new social logic" involving, according to Skrtic, Sailor, & Gee (1996), "voice, collaboration, and—above all—inclusion" (p. 143). Skrtic (1995) suggests replacing traditional special educational services with "adhocracies." These he describes as "ambiguous and uncertain" collaborative organizations created to invent "new practices" based on a socially just and participatory "dialogue" among all stakeholders to determine appropriate practices. For postmodernists, any approach to intervention, however untested, is considered viable. Throughout their many publications, Skrtic and his colleagues seem unconcerned with the outcomes their proposed educational experiments might produce in the lives of children with disabilities.

Unfortunately, the ideological rift in special education is not just a debate among academics. It is significantly affecting the course of educational programs for children with all types of disabilities. The repeated arguments in the literature that disabilities are mere "social constructions," that empirical practices are ineffectual, and that current special education services should be dismantled has generated considerable confusion among practitioners, administrators, and policy makers and is contributing to the endorsement and adoption of questionable practices and services. This atmosphere of uncertainty has fostered the general impression in the field that any intervention is acceptable without need for documentation of its effectiveness.

UNEVALUATED INTERVENTIONS

Full Inclusion. The most obvious example of the adoption of an intervention without research support involves the movement toward "full inclusion" of children in the educational mainstream. Using value-laden slogans such as "children are more alike than they are different" and "it's the right thing to do" (Kauffman, 2002), full inclusionists have persuaded many stakeholders that all children should be educated in the regular classroom regardless of whether these settings can adapt to meet their needs or they can educationally benefit from such a placement. Thus, rather than basing services on assessed educational needs of children with disabilities, schools have increasingly adopted this "one size fits all" approach. Nearly 90 percent of students with mild disabilities currently are served in regular education classes (Katsiyannis, Conderman, & Franks, 1995; McLeskey, Henry, & Hodges, 1999).

The concept of a "value-based" practice such as inclusion is appealing in theory. It is safe to say that for most special educators, postmodernists and empiricists alike, the ultimate goal for children with disabilities involves their successful maintenance in natural environments. However, given the complexities of the service needs of children with EBD, some observers have questioned the feasibility of inclusion of children with EBD. The key to successful inclusion involves the provision of adequate supportive services to children with disabilities who are placed in regular education classes. For children with EBD this requires a school ecology that provides positive alternatives plus ancillary support such as school-based or wraparound services (Lewis & Sugai, 1999; Metzler et al., 2001; Skiba, Polsgrove, & Nasstrom, 1996). However, evidence indicates inclusion is far from an educational panacea and may be detrimental if appropriate educational services cannot be provided in the educational mainstream (Baker & Zigmond, 1995; Braaten et al., 1988; Fuchs & Fuchs, 1994; Kauffman, 1999; MacMillan, Gresham, & Forness, 1996). Studies further indicate that inclusion actually may not be an acceptable alternative to parents of children with either mild or severe disabilities (Garrick-Duhaney & Salend, 2000; Palmer, Fuller, Arora, & Nelson, 2001).

The placement of increasing numbers of children in regular education classrooms—inclusion—has occurred largely without evidence supporting the effects of this practice or considering the "voices" of parents, teachers, or students. Few controlled studies have shown inclusion to be an effective alternative to properly implemented special education interventions, nor has federal funding been available for full-scale longitudinal studies of its effects. In the medical profession this would be equivalent to vaccinating large numbers of children with a serum that had not been approved by the FDA. Logic would dictate that a system relying on empirical research to inform parents and teachers regarding "best practices" would be much safer and more ethically responsible than one guided by a "value-based" philosophy rife with contradictions.

"Alternative" Practices. Historically, the literature in special education has been punctuated by reports of interventions having little theoretical validity or research support. Instructional and behavior-management techniques are continually emerging from field practices and ideas generated by armchair theorists. These sources may provide new ideas for interventions. However, their adoption and use poses potential risks to children until they have been evaluated. Potential negative outcomes of using untested interventions include loss of valuable instruction time, squandering of finances, exacerbation of learning and/or behavior problems, production of harmful psychological effects, and creation of false hope for service providers and parents. The empirical validation process has, over the years, provided a valuable service in identifying effective interventions and winnowing out ineffective interventions in special education. Empirical analysis has demonstrated, for example, that strategies such as "patterning," ability training, modality training, learning styles, colored lenses, auditory integration training, gentle teaching, and facilitated communication appear to have little effect in ameliorating children's disabilities. On the other hand this research has demonstrated positive effects of structured learning environments, multi-modal instruction, direct instruction, behavior management, mnemonic training, and planned instruction.

Ironically, despite a large body of research on effective and ineffective practices, parents and practitioners, in their desire to exhaust all possible options to help their children with disabilities, appear prone to adopting interventions based on anecdotes, testimonials, and "guru" hyperbole (Palfreman, 1993). Several factors can account for this phenomenon. First, the originators of the technique continue to promote it. Second, teachers and other practitioners often are not trained to discriminate between interventions based on sound research and those based on unverified information. Third, parents and teachers often are not in the information loop and are uninformed about research related to a particular intervention. Fourth, they also may be naïve about the importance of research or distrust the research process. Fifth, desiring to exhaust every method for helping their children, they are susceptible to adopting strategies that provide quick or miraculous "cures." Finally, the "demand characteristics" and positive expectancies practitioners hold about a particular strategy ensure that virtually any intervention will be successful with some children, and, consequently, these are interpreted as appropriate for all children.

The practice of facilitated communication (FC) provides a vivid example of how an untested intervention can gain widespread acceptance and use throughout the educational community. Introduced to this country by Douglas Biklen in the early 1990s, FC was heralded as a breakthrough in the treatment of autism because it enabled children with autism to communicate with the "outside world" (Biklen & Schubert, 1991). In FC a "facilitator" (e.g., a parent or a teacher) guides a child's hand or finger to type out messages on a keyboard or other communication device. Presumably, the message originates with the child and represents the child's inner speech. Taught to express themselves through FC, children with autism and other disabilities and who were mute or incommunicative, and who in some cases manifested severe management problems, appeared suddenly to become able not only to communicate their physical needs but to demonstrate high-level intellectual skills such as writing poetry, essays, and advanced mathematics.

To advance FC, Biklen established the Facilitated Communication Institute at Syracuse University and launched a series of training workshops for parents and teachers around the country. Through a stream of books and journal articles, he and other academics (e.g., Biklen, 1993; Crossley & Remington-Gurley, 1992; Donnellan, Sabin, & Majure, 1992) lent authoritative credibility to the procedure. Some have even claimed the FC process "works" because individuals with autism possessed a magical "sixth sense" (Haskew & Donnellan, 1993). The technique gained the endorsement of the Association of Persons with Severe Handicaps

(TASH), and articles and programs in the media touting FC as a "breakthrough" in the treatment of disabilities caught public attention (Mostert, 2001). Given such hyperbole, parents and practitioners fervently embraced FC and began pressuring training programs, agencies, and school districts to incorporate FC into the curriculum and hire facilitators.

The advent of FC caused considerable stir in the academic community. Its presence and origin challenged the empirical approach to determining best practices and aroused considerable advocacy and public policy concerns. Decades of research had concluded that children with autism have severe cognitive and language deficits that profoundly limit their ability to communicate. Thus, demonstrating the efficacy of FC at once would establish that children with autism and other forms of disabilities possessed normal cognitive functions, undermine the legitimacy of empirical research, and question the field's reliance on evidence-based practices. Further, it would establish that a subjective or "interpretist" approach to research was as viable as an experimental one. The potential policy and economic implications of adopting FC were enormous. It would require training for practitioners and using public monies to support facilitators for children with severe disabilities in schools, programs, and even university settings across the nation.

Although controlled studies raised doubt about the validity of FC, this information may never have become public were it not for a number of court cases in which parents, through FC, were accused of sexually abusing their children and arrested. Their lives and reputations shattered, they filed a class-action lawsuit against the facilitators and school districts involved in using the practice and the Facilitated Communication Institute (FCI). The efficacy of FC was "tried" in court, and expert testimony revealed that in almost all cases the facilitator—not the child—authored the messages (Palfreman, 1993). In addition, studies have consistently failed to find evidence that children actually communicate through FC. Howlin (1997), for example, reviewed 45 controlled studies on FC involving over 350 students and concluded that only 6 percent of their responses could be traced to independent communication while 90 percent were attributable to their facilitators. Mostert's (2001) more recent review concluded that controlled studies find FC to be largely ineffective while anecdotal studies are universally favorable.

Facilitated Communication has been openly rejected by professional organizations such as the American Medical Association, the American Academy of Pediatrics, the American Psychological Association, and others. However the Association of Persons with Severe Handicaps (TASH) continues to endorse FC. Curiously, despite all the negative publicity and research indicating its ineffectiveness and potential for harm, the FCI continues to disseminate information and provide training in FC, FC support networks continue to be active, and parents and service providers apparently continue to seek out FC as an "alternative" treatment option.

As function of the "alternative" (to evidence-based) movement, practitioners are being widely encouraged in the special education literature to adopt vaguely defined "alternative" interventions that have little or no research bases. Despite the absence of controlled research on their effectiveness, Poplin (1988, 1996) has repeatedly urged teachers to use what she terms the new "liberatory pedagogies" (1996, p. 4): critical education, sociocultural constructivism, holism, whole language instruction (despite its abysmal instructional effectiveness), and feminist analyses. The effectiveness of these strategies, she indicates, will be based on "classroom tales" told by teachers (Poplin, 1996, p. 6). Along similar lines Skrtic and Sailor (1996) assert that practices should be based on "correct choices." "Because there are not objective criteria for making these decisions, values provide the grounds for judging the merit of our choices" (p. 276); however, Skrtic and Sailor fail to reveal what criteria will be used to determine the best values and who will ultimately decide which values take precedent over others.

Perhaps the most absurd alternative intervention for children with EBD was Rhodes's (1987) recommendation to use "quantum logic . . . to mediate the child's cognitive capacities for expanding . . . her projection into her environment" (p. 59). Such recommendations have been made in a sea of articles and books, generating an "anything goes" atmosphere regarding appropriate practice. This invisible "deconstruction" of the field is being translated into local classroom practices with an unexamined effect on children.

What kind of outcomes are such unfounded recommendations producing? In our work with public school teachers, we frequently witness and are told about incidents in which children's lives are being negatively affected through the application of philosophy-driven or "value-based" interventions. Some local school districts have created inclusion classrooms that include children with severe to mild disabilities who rarely have access to special education teachers. We have visited classrooms in which teachers shirk the practice of using small group instruction or using materials at grade level for children with disabilities because doing so would call attention to these children's limitations. One of our graduate students in school psychology recently reported that a teacher with whom she was working had suspended repeatedly three boys in her class because they refused to work and frequently terrorized the other students. She refused to use suggested behavior modification strategies because these were at odds with her "teaching philosophy." She had defined herself as a "constructivist" whose function, she said, was guiding the children to develop their own reasons for behaving properly.

As we have discussed, a major barrier to the application of evidence-based knowledge for guiding and improving services for children with EBD concerns the considerable "noise" generated by people in positions of influence who have constructed a largely fallacious case against empirical methodology and interventions. Simultaneously, they advocate the use of practices that, in some cases, have little empirical support for their effectiveness. It is to their credit that some advocates of "new" approaches to interventions recognize this shortcoming (e.g., Anderson & Barrera, 1995; Richardson, 1996). Some researchers have observed that an integration of approaches might prove fruitful (Harris & Graham, 1994).

However, a number of articles appearing in the recent special education literature have promoted the conclusion that "value-based," "holistic," "constructivist," "alternative," and "interpretist" interventions are the coming wave of acceptable practices and that the "research" on which these are based is irrelevant. This conflicted social and political landscape creates considerable confusion among parents and service providers and deters them from selecting the most productive developmental goals and effective interventions for their children and students. For children with EBD, the effect of the current services zeitgeist may indeed lead to dire outcomes.

Personnel Training

Recent events suggest that the federal government is becoming increasingly concerned about the largely ignored mental health needs of children and youth with EBD. A recent conference of educators, mental health professionals, justice system representatives, and policy makers addressed this issue, and results were summarized in a report from the U.S. Surgeon General's office, which established a national agenda for children's mental health (Department of Health and Human Services, 2002). A main recommendation of this report was the need to rely more heavily on evidence-based information to improve diagnosis of and interventions for children with EBD. However, as Kauffman (1999) observed, the broad resistance to the use of research-based interventions and even insistence on adhering to concepts and practices actually work to "prevent the prevention" of children's emotional and behavior disorders. We would add to Kauffman's list several personnel training issues that chronically inhibit both the prevention and provision of adequate services for children with EBD.

Personnel Shortages.   Students with EBD continue to be grossly underserved in schools. Although as many as 10 percent of school-age children in the United States could qualify as EBD, only about 1 percent are actually identified and are receiving school-based services (Maag & Katsiyannis, 1999; Kauffman, 2001). Many of these children reportedly suffer various forms of abuse and neglect (Oseroff, Oseroff, Westling, & Gessner, 1999), and they display well-documented academic limitations and severe disruptive behavior that require much more attention from teachers and more supportive services than other children (Katsiyannis, Landrum, Bullock, & Vinton, 1997; Maag & Katsiyannis, 1999; Whelan & Simpson, 1996).

Providing effective school-based services for these children and youth requires the cooperative effort of regular and special education teachers, administrators, and other support professionals (e.g., psychologists, counselors, social workers). In recognition of the right for children with disabilities to appropriate services, the 1997 Individuals with Disabilities Education Act (IDEA) includes specific provisions and funding for training qualified teachers and support personnel (Katsiyannis et al., 1997). Unfortunately, there exists a long-standing extreme shortage of skilled service providers for children and youths with EBD. Fifty-three percent of special education program directors in Grosenick, George, and George's (1987) survey indicated that all of their teachers were fully certified in this area and about 30 percent were working under an "emergency" license. In addition, the population of children with EBD continues to grow, and the movement to "inclusive schools" has increased the number of service venues in which these children require services. While regular educators represent a potential source of help, most have little training in this area; many are reluctant to assume responsibility for these students (Schumm & Vaughn, 1992). Thus, not only are more educational specialists needed to staff special classes; they also need additional skills to provide consultative/cooperative services to aid transition to regular education classrooms (Bullock, Ellis, & Wilson, 1994).

To compound these problems, a high attrition rate has long existed among special educators. Lawrenson and McKinnon (1982) estimated that as many as 48 percent left their positions for various reasons within three to four years. Some may move to other positions, and some may return (George, George, Gersten, & Grosenick, 1995; Singer, 1992); nevertheless, Singer (1992) and Brownell, Smith, McNellis, and Miller (1997) reported attrition rates among teachers of children with EBD about double that of teachers in other areas. Other studies have reported the attrition rate at 140 percent above that of regular educators (Huntze & Grosenick, 1980). Studies have identified several explanations for this trend: insufficient training, significant discipline problems, lack of administrative support, and poor school climate (Brownell et al., 1997; Miller, Brownell, & Smith, 1999). Another explanation may involve the sheer demands placed on special educators in the workplace. Teachers of children with EBD have reported spending an average of fifty-six hours a week performing their duties, most of it (60 percent) in noninstructional activities (Gable, Hendrickson, Young, & Shokoohi-Yekta, 1992). Thus, the shortage, preparation, and retention of knowledgeable and skillful personnel to provide effective behavioral interventions represent major issues facing the field (Whelan & Simpson, 1996).

Quality Standards.   Both common sense and research underscore the necessity for those assigned to teach and supervise children with EBD to have a thorough knowledge of their unique needs, be capable of planning and executing effective interventions strategies, and orchestrate appropriate transition and support services. For these reasons it is essential to identify the knowledge and skills required by professionals to deliver services to these students (Bullock, Ellis, & Wilson, 1994). As Whelan and Simpson (1996) observed, "The depth and breadth of professional skills needed for success with students with EBD require significant development above and beyond those of general educators" (p. 49).

Unfortunately, this ideal is far from the reality in actual practice. Due to burgeoning demand for teachers of children with disabilities, school districts across the nation are having to appoint general educators on "emergency licenses." Some states allow teachers certified in any area to teach children and youth with EBD. There is a growing movement in some states toward quickly certifying, with a few basic courses, holders of college degrees in critically needed areas. Although appointing uncertified or minimally prepared teachers solves the immediate problem of staff shortages, these practices have considerable risks.

First, insufficient training has been linked to high rates of teacher attrition (Miller et al., 1999). Thus, assigning a novice teacher to provide services to children who challenge the skills of even veteran professionals may provide only a temporary solution. Second, and most importantly, we have witnessed devastating consequences that have resulted from misguided interventions used by poorly trained personnel. Assigning unqualified individuals to work with children and youth with EBD may endanger their own safety as well as that of other students and staff. Although the outcomes may not be immediately detectable, inadequately trained teachers and other service providers may employ strategies that exacerbate behavior problems, accelerate school failure, and hasten the downward spiral in which many children with EBD are entrapped (Kauffman, 2001; Walker et al., 1995). A major concern in training teachers in the area of EBD, therefore, involves ensuring that they have the appropriate knowledge and skills to effectively fulfill the demands of their professional roles.

The enterprise of preparing teachers of children with EBD could benefit from more information on the knowledge and skills practitioners need. Some progress has been made in this area. A succession of surveys over the last four decades has provided information on the competencies teachers of children with EBD require (e.g., Bullock, Dykes, & Kelly, 1974; Gable et al., 1992; Mackie, Kvaraceus, & Williams, 1957; Polsgrove & Rieth, 1979). These and other studies have contributed to the development of a loose agreement among practitioners and teacher educators on the knowledge and skills teachers need.

This consensus is reflected in a section identifying standards for teachers of these students in *International Standards for the Preparation and Certification of Special Education Teachers,* published and distributed by the Council for Exceptional Children (1995). In addition to core requirements for all beginning special education teachers, the section on EBD includes twenty-seven knowledge and twenty-five related-skills standards in the following areas:

Philosophical, historical, and legal foundations

Characteristics of children with EBD

Assessment methods

Planning instructional and behavioral interventions

Delivering appropriate instruction

Behavior management

Consultation and collaboration

Professionalism and ethical practices

The Council for Exceptional Children (CEC)-EBD standards, which were approved by the National Council for Accreditation of Teacher Education (NCATE), offer a guide for state educational agencies (SEAs) and university program developers for determining training requirements for preservice teachers. However, the extent to which these standards have been incorporated into certification and program requirements varies. Available information suggests that the field has largely ignored the standards and that there is little uniformity among requirements in various state teacher certification and university training programs.

Two studies specifically addressed this issue. Katsiyannis et al. (1997) compared SEA requirements in EBD with CEC standards. Reports from twenty-seven states that required certification in EBD indicated an emphasis on only the most "essential features of teaching": assessment, instruction, and behavior management. Maag and Katsiyannis (1999) described similar results in comparing requirements of sixty-seven university training programs in EBD reporting in their study. Although most programs (90+ percent) provided training in instructional content, assessment, behavior management, and characteristics of EBD, training was underemphasized in important areas such as planning and managing (77 percent), philosophical, historical, and legal foundations (58 percent), collaboration (58 percent), and counseling (17 percent).

Variation in state and university requirements for teacher preparation programs is a major issue in the provision of quality services for children with EBD. Although absolute congruence in teaching standards across all states and university training programs would be virtually impossible, it seems reasonable and professionally appropriate to expect these entities to at least adopt the minimal standards established by professional organizations such as those offered by CEC/NCATE (Bullock et al., 1994; Katsiyannis et al., 1997; Maag & Katsiyannis, 1999). Unfortunately, no mechanism requires that SEAs and institutes of higher education (IHEs) adopt these standards to receive program accreditation. In many cases complex professional and political barriers (e.g., theoretical and philosophical disagreement, proprietorship, turf, ignorance, and individual diffidence and stubbornness) hamper realization of this goal. Without personnel with advanced training, however, it is improbable that more comprehensive school-based services for children with EBD will develop in the near future.

Generic Certification.   Perhaps the most prominent issue in the area of personnel training concerns a migration from specialized or categorical to generic or noncategorical training. Guided by inclusive school policies, postmodern philosophy, and anti-special education rhetoric, as well as cost-savings advantages, school districts across the nation have moved increasingly to integrated and multicategorical classrooms and away from self-contained classrooms. Some school administrators have discontinued classrooms for children with EBD and moved them to general education classes in an effort to minimize problems created by these children (J. Easterday, personal communication, February 3, 2002). Unfortunately, few regular education teachers have the specialized training required to meet the needs of these children, and such assignments may result in increased stress and negative outcomes for the children (Brownell et al., 1997).

Whether following or leading this trend, SEAs appear to be moving toward "generalist" special education certification for teachers of children with mild to moderate disabilities and away from specialized certification in areas such as EBD. Katsiyannis, Landrum, Bullock, and Vinton (1997), for example, reported that only 60 percent of forty-seven states responding to their survey required EBD certification; nineteen states required generic special education training. In Maag and Katsiyannis's (1999) survey only 51 percent of 101 universities responding from thirty-two states offered training programs in EBD. If the trend toward generic certification continues, we expect institutions will phase out training programs in EBD in order to compete for students.

A decade ago Bullock, Ellis, and Wilson (1994) forecast a continuing need for teachers with specialized preparation to work with students with EBD, who typically require interventions that are more intensive. Ironically, SEAs and IHEs seem to be moving to generalist training programs. Although it is technically possible to certify "generalists" who are minimally prepared to provide services to children and youths with mild academic and behavior problems, it seems highly unlikely they will be prepared to meet the needs of children with more severe difficulties. Given a long history of neglect of children with EBD, we foresee a further watering down of the scant services currently available. It remains highly doubtful whether children with severe EBD can be provided effective services in general education settings (MacMillan, Gresham, & Forness, 1995). Further, without highly trained specialists, the goal of developing an effective comprehensive system of services is remote.

There are additional drawbacks to moving to generic training patterns. Teachers trained in EBD often provide technical know-how and leadership to colleagues who have not received this training. In their roles as functional assessors, developers of individual behavioral plans, behavioral consultants, and leaders of teacher assistance teams, these teachers provide important services in countless schools across the country. Thus, eliminating training in EBD could, as trained personnel retire, result in the dismantling of frontline services, often the only services available to many children with EBD. Those who cannot "fit" in inclusion classrooms face placement in multicategorical classrooms, reassignment to "home-bound" instruction, or institutional referral. The possibility of developing effective school-based, ecological, or wraparound services will become more remote.

Training to Practice Gap.   Even the most effective teacher preparation program cannot guarantee that graduates will actually practice the knowledge and skills they were taught. One issue concerns whether students perceive this information as relevant to job responsibilities. Studies on beginning teachers' perceptions of professional preparedness have produced mixed and sometimes conflicting results. Teachers of EBD in a study by George et al. (1995) reported that their college training poorly prepared them to deal with professional demands. Teachers also may become jaded after a few years on the job. Gable et al. (1992) found that newer teachers of EBD perceived the quality of their teacher preparation as good to very good, whereas veteran teachers viewed their university training as significantly unimportant.

These results may also indicate a gap between theory and practice. Gunter and Denny (1996), for example, found two-thirds of teachers reported that their college course work was poor preparation for their teaching environments and indicated that they learned their classroom management strategies from other teachers rather than from their course work. Furthermore, the strategies with empirical validation may not be those used by teachers (Gunter & Denny, 1996). Research is needed that evaluates which classroom management strategies are used, how they are used, and how often teachers of students with EBD use them.

The "user friendliness" of a strategy also may affect the probability a teacher will employ it. In particular, behavioral interventions often are seen as manipulative and barriers to the development of intrinsic motivation in children and youth with behavior disorders. Some may be reluctant to use punishment strategies due to the negative publicity associated with these interventions (Polsgrove, 1991). A growing educational literature indicates that positive behavioral support plans may be more favorably viewed by teachers and can play an important and positive role in the treatment of students with challenging behaviors (Lewis & Sugai, 1999; Metzler et al., 2001; Walker et al., 1995). These plans provide scripts for use of more proactive practice and positive alternatives to inappropriate and challenging student behavior. However, there is little information on whether teachers will actually use this approach consistently.

Several other factors may explain teacher resistance to using evidence-based interventions. First, teachers may lack training in discriminating between effective and ineffective interventions and are likely to accept a practice based on anecdotal evidence (Kauffman, 1999). Second, they may be naturally drawn to interventions that promise a quick remedy and require less time. For example, teachers' continued use of interventions such as FC, despite the lack of research evidence supporting it, perhaps can be explained in terms of the reinforcement teachers receive from "seeing" students instantly overcome their disabilities. One sees what one believes to be true; parents and teachers, and even investigators, are thus susceptible to being duped into drawing erroneous conclusions without the guidance of independent and objective evaluation. In addition, other issues such as time to plan and implement an intervention also may affect whether a teacher will use a particular strategy (Gunter & Denny, 1996).

Earlier, we observed that ensuring adequate teacher preparation is a major issue in the delivery of effective interventions and developing comprehensive systems of services for children and youths with EBD. The perennial shortage of teachers appears to be increasing, and the population continues to grow. As a partial response, increasing numbers of children with disabilities, including those with EBD, are being integrated into regular education classes. Yet general education teachers are not trained to provide special education services, nor are they particularly inclined to assume this responsibility (Baker & Zigmond, 1995). Although children with EBD are notoriously underidentified and thus underserved, no recent studies have investigated the extent or quality of services these children are receiving, and we have little information of the impact of inclusion on this population.

Logic would dictate that well-prepared teachers are those who receive intensive training in effective and useful academic and behavioral interventions for addressing the needs of children with EBD and that SEAs and IHEs would follow standards established and recommended by professional organizations. However, there appears to be a considerable gap between certification and university program requirements and standards widely perceived as critical to delivery of effective services. Thus, despite the availability of more effective interventions, we do not appear to have come much closer to overcoming the miasmic conditions

Knitzer, Steinberg, and Fleisch (1990) observed over a decade ago in classrooms for children with EBD. In fact, available evidence suggests that the extent and quality of services may be becoming more limited. As demands increase to teach more widely diverse populations of children in larger classes, and as qualified teachers of EBD are pressured to assume more responsibilities, attrition and transfers can be expected to increase. Struggling to meet the intense demands for services, school districts are routinely hiring unqualified personnel.

The trend toward SEAs eliminating certification requirements specific to EBD and special education preparation programs transitioning to generalist training portend a further reduction in the availability of qualified personnel and quality services. We think that it is unlikely that administrators, policy makers, and university personnel will recognize the errors and consequences inherent in this movement, and, like many "school reform" bandwagons in education, it will have to run a dialectical course. Unfortunately, the main victims in this social experiment are children and their parents.

PERSPECTIVE AND RECOMMENDATIONS

In this chapter we discussed the remarkable advances in educational and treatment services for children with emotional and behavioral disorders that have been made through empirical research over the last four decades. These we traced to the abandonment of a subjective-philosophical method of studying human behavior that dominated the field of psychology and education for two centuries and the emergence of a scientific-experimental approach. We showcased an impressive array of behavioral interventions, documented in hundreds of studies, that parents and service providers can draw on to produce long-term and significant outcomes. Why, we asked, have these innovations not gained greater acceptance or been incorporated into schools and treatment programs on a larger scale? We identified three major barriers that appear to affect the realization of this goal: confusion generated by ideological disputes, competition from nonempirical or "alternative" interventions, and issues related to personnel training.

Currently the field of special education is in the throes of a continuing debate between those persuaded by an empirical approach to interventions and those adhering to a philosophical values-driven position. This dispute can be traced to the ancient and unresolved behaviorist-humanist debate. Radical behaviorists view human action as determined by the same laws as animal behavior and thus largely influenced by immediate environmental variables. Radical humanists reject such deterministic notions and view human behavior as guided solely by conscious planning, problem solving, free choice in decision making, and free will (Kazdin, 1978). Perhaps "truth," if one believes in such a concept, lies somewhere between these positions.

It seems most feasible that both environmental stimuli and cognitive processes influence human behavior. That is, while individuals are strongly influenced by environmental consequences, they also have the ability to consciously direct their behavior and influence the environment to produce desirable outcomes, a view widely held by many current behaviorists (e.g., Bandura, 1969, 1977). A subtle evolution has occurred within the field of children's EBD over the last four decades in which interventions based exclusively on radical behavioral tenets have been blended into more cognitive, ecologically based, contextualized, and consumer-driven approaches. During this period, empirical interventions have become less reliant on radical behavioral determinism and have incorporated more "cognitive" approaches such as self-monitoring, self-evaluation, social problem solving, modeling, environmental planning, behavioral rehearsal, self-instruction, mnemonic training, and cognitive strategy training. These strategies have not only provided much greater flexibility in teaching children and youth but also offer much greater opportunity for developing behavioral self-control and self-determinism. There is an abundant literature in this area; though not intentionally, it addresses many of the philosophical complaints about the evils of behaviorism and empiricism related to interventions and the structure of services for children and youths with disabilities and EBD (e.g., Kanfer & Goldstein, 1986; Hughes, 1988; Meichenbaum & Asarnow, 1979; Masters, Burish, Hollon, & Rimm, 1987; Thoresen, 1973; Thoresen & Mahoney, 1974).

Unfortunately, critics have failed to register these advances and continue to adhere to an outdated monolithic perspective about behavioral and other empirical approaches to practices and services delivery. Postmodern special educators strongly view themselves as protectorates of individuals with disabilities from the influences of "modernist empiricism," and they have embarked on a mission of "deconstruction" of the existing "empirically driven paradigm" of services and practices and "reconstruction" of a new and more "humane" approach based on "socially just" ideals (Skrtic, 1995). Critical inspection easily leads to the conclusion that the postmodernist position is itself a constructed reality. It is essentially an epistemological foundation, and it has no logical tenets, no theoretical anchor, no knowledge base, and no reliable way of determining best practices or services models. It is particularly ironic that postmodern special educators who so adamantly oppose a scientific approach to determining appropriate practices are willing to experiment with the futures of children and youth with disabilities based on the intuitive appropriateness of vaguely defined "values-driven" and "alternative" interventions.

The lack of consensus by empiricists and postmodernists on fundamental questions, such as whether "truth" can be established, whether an objective or a subjective approach to research is acceptable, and how values should be determined, represents a fundamental and irreconcilable ideological difference. This ongoing battle among the leadership in the field of special education has led to considerable confusion among service providers and policy makers about what constitutes best practices. It presents a major barrier to the development and adoption of effective behavioral interventions and development of a comprehensive system of services for children with EBD. In the midst of this turmoil profound changes are taking place in our approach to training personnel and certifying teachers.

Perhaps our best solution for coping with such conflict is to recognize this era as an evolutionary phase in the field. The field of special education, ill defined as it is, is really only in its infancy. We are experiencing the first philosophical crisis since pioneers in the field nobly set out to provide equitable treatment to children with disabilities. We do not yet have a clear "theory" of special education explaining EBD and other disabilities. We have borrowed many of our guiding principles and approaches to practice from other fields. However, we have, through research, developed a set of research-based interventions that improve our capability to predict and change children's responses to academic and social stimuli and thereby produce reliable positive outcomes. Such knowledge bases have been essential to the advancement of all human endeavors since the beginning of recorded history (Bronowski, 1974) and play critical roles in science, public health, business, technology, physical education, and the arts.

Unlike their counterparts in the natural sciences, many special education philosophers, on the one hand, seem to poorly understand scientific methodology and clearly are unaware of advances in evidence-based practices. They seem not to understand that successful "revolutions" in science involve replacing one body of facts with one more comprehensive and explanatory than its predecessor (Brigham & Polsgrove, 1998). They are not skilled in detecting weaknesses in empirical rationale and providing constructive critical analyses. On the other hand, empiricists in special education are not accustomed to criticism of their values and methodology. They have responded with vehement rejection of the postmodernist critique and ignored, in some cases, suggestions for reform of traditional practices that may have little empirical or practical validity.

The ideological disputes that have raged in the field of special education for nearly two decades appear to have resulted in what Sasso (2001) termed a retreat from knowledge; they have created a fertile environment for a weakening of the credibility of empirical approaches to interventions and the resulting proliferation of unproven and even bogus approaches. The hyperbole associated with the large assortment of untested interventions that are continuously marketed to parents and teachers provides another source of confusion among these "consumers" of intervention approaches. Many of them are untrained to discriminate between effective and ineffective interventions and fall prey to approaches offering false hope and quick cures.

No social reconstruction of reality can alter the fact that problems presented by children with EBD are real and that we need the best and most advanced practices available to address their needs. Our deepest concern is that the new postmodern "paradigm" has preempted the implementation of extremely promising practices such as early identification, functional assessment, individualized instruction, behavioral intervention plans, positive behavioral supports, and the establishment of a sorely needed comprehensive, school-based system of services for children and youth with EBD.

One solution to these confusing times is to continue with studies that yield reliable and effective practices and to devote more time than in the past to publicly disseminating the results. This would involve researchers' actively promoting practices that have been consistently and clearly demonstrated to be effective rather than relying exclusively on publication in scholarly journals. Another solution would be to devote more time and research to addressing the issues raised by critics of the empirical process, such as looking more closely at what parents and teachers think about inclusion and monitoring its long-term effects on children with EBD. Organizations within the field of special education also might consider publishing position papers presenting the views of the membership and its leaders on critical issues. These organizations might also develop and disseminate public bulletins reporting evidence that supports or questions the use of a particular practice. We see a great need for organizations within the field of special education, such as the Council for Children with Behavioral Disorders (CCBD), to become more political, to develop closer ties to other organizations, such as the National Institute for Mental Health, National Association for School Psychologists, and Federation of Families for Children's Mental Health, and to strengthen and coordinate advocacy and congressional lobbying activities. Furthermore, professional organizations should become more active in educating the general public and professional service providers about the importance of relying on evidence-based practices.

Indeed, the ultimate solution to closing the gap between research and practice and increasing parents' sophistication may lie in providing the best training possible to future generations of professionals, who will ultimately bear responsibility for determining what practices will be implemented. There is an intense need for research on the impact on the current services zeitgeist on teacher training patterns and how these are affecting the extent and quality of services for children with and in the area of EBD. Toward this end Whelan and

Simpson (1996) identified four critical research questions: First, what competencies do experts consider essential for teachers to successfully work in the area of EBD? Second, what are the most effective strategies for training preservice teachers to acquire skills in and employ evidence-based best practices? Third, what evidence indicates that preservice teachers are actually taught these skills in their university training programs? Fourth, to what extent can teachers demonstrate these skills in their classrooms?

To Whelan and Simpson's list we would add a fifth question: Can teachers produce positive outcomes with children with EBD after receiving appropriate and intensive instruction on selected CEC/CCBD standards? Finally, a more pressing issue that needs research attention in light of the growing trend toward generalist, or generic, training: How do teachers appropriately trained in EBD compare with teachers receiving generic training? Specifically, are there differences in their feelings of preparedness and confidence, skill in delivering instruction, effectiveness in managing problem behaviors, and ability to produce positive outcomes for children with EBD? There is a great need for research that establishes clear connections between training program curricula and graduates' skill at delivering services that consistently produce educationally and clinically significant outcomes.

QUESTIONS FOR FURTHER DISCUSSION

1. What factors have contributed to the rather large gap between special education research and practice?

2. How could the research-to-practice gap be closed?

3. Why is the empirical method so misunderstood and maligned these days?

4. Why are critics of special education research and practices, i.e., postmodernists, constructivists, deconstructivists, critical theorists, and holists, not required to present an accurate account of these and research in support of their position?

5. What criteria should be used to determine the validity of a recommended intervention for children with disabilities?

REFERENCES

Anderson, G. L., & Barrera, I. (1995). Critical constructivist research and special education. *Remedial and Special Education, 3, 142–149.*

Baker, J. M., & Zigmond, N. (1995). The meaning and practice of inclusion for students with learning disabilities: Themes and implications of the five cases. *Journal of Special Education, 29, 163–180.*

Bandura, A. (1969). *Principles of behavior modification.* New York. Holt Reinhart.

Bandura, A. (1977). *Social learning theory.* Englewood Cliffs, NJ: Prentice Hall.

Barkley, R. A. (1998). *Attention-deficit hyperactivity disorder: A handbook for diagnosis and treatment* (2nd ed.). New York: Guilford.

Biklen, D. (1993). *Communication unbound: How facilitated communication is challenging traditional views of autism and ability/disability.* New York: Teachers College Press.

Biklen, D., & Schubert, A. (1991). New words: The communication of students with autism. *Remedial and Special Education, 12, 46–57.*

Borduin, C. M., Mann, B. J., Cone, L. T., Henggeler, S. W., Fucci, B. R., Blaske, D. M., & Williams, R. A. (1995). Multisystemic treatment of serious juvenile offenders: Long-term prevention of criminality and violence. *Journal of Consulting and Clinical Psychology, 63,* 569–578.

Braaten, S. R., Kauffman, J. M., Braaten, B., Polsgrove, L., & Nelson, C. M. (1988). The regular education initiative: Patent medicine for behavioral disorders. *Exceptional Children, 55,* 21–28.

Brantlinger, E. (1997). Using ideology: Cases of nonrecognition of the politics of research and practice in special education. *Review of Educational Research, 4,* 425–460.

Brigham, F. J., & Polsgrove, L. (1998). A rumor of a paradigm shift in the field of children's behavior disorders. *Behavioral Disorders, 23,* 166–170.

Bronowski, J. (1974). *The ascent of man.* Boston: Little, Brown.

Brownell, M. T., Smith, S. W., & McNellis, J. R., & Miller, M. D. (1997). Reflections on attrition in special education: Why teachers leave the classroom and where they go. *Exceptionality, 7,* 143–155.

Bullock, L. M., Dykes, K., & Kelly, T. (1974). Competency-based teacher preparation in behavioral disorders. *Exceptional Children, 41,* 192–194.

Bullock, L. M., Ellis, L. L., & Wilson, M. J. (1994). Knowledge/skills needed by teachers who work with students with severe emotional/behavioral disorders: A revisitation. *Behavioral Disorders, 19*(2), 108–125.

Carson, R. C., Butcher, J. N., & Mineka, S. (1996). *Abnormal psychology and modern life.* New York: Harper Collins.

Chess, S., & Thomas, A. (1977). Temperamental individuality from childhood to adolescence. *Journal of the American Academy of Child Psychiatry, 16,* 218–226.

Coe, D. A., & Matson, J. L. (1990). On the empirical basis for using aversive and non-aversive therapy. In A. C. Repp & N. N. Singh (Eds.), *Perspectives on the use of non-aversive and aversive interventions for persons with developmental disabilities* (pp. 465–475). Sycamore, IL: Second way.

Coie, J., & Kupersmidt, J. (1983). A behavioral analysis of emerging social status in boys' groups. *Child Development, 54,* 1400–1416.

Conduct Problems Prevention Research Group. (1999). Initial impact of the fast track prevention trial for conduct problems: Vol. II. Classroom Effects. *Journal of Consulting and Clinical Psychology, 67,* 648–657.

Council for Exceptional Children (1995). *What every special educator must know: The international standards for the preparation and certification of special education teachers.* Reston, VA: Council for Exceptional Children.

Crossley, R., & Remington-Gurley, J. (1992). Getting the words out: Facilitated communication training. *Topics in Language Disorders, 12,* 29–45.

Curci, R. A., & Gottlieb, J. (1990). Teachers' instruction of non-categorically grouped handicapped children. *Exceptionality, 1,* 239–248.

Danforth, S. (1997). On what basis hope? Modern progress and postmodern possibilities. *Mental Retardation, 2,* 93–106.

Danforth, S., & Rhodes, W. C. (1997). Deconstructing disability. *Remedial and Special Education 18,* 357–366.

Department of Health and Human Services. (2002). Report of the Surgeon General's Conference on Children's Mental Health: A national action agenda. Washington, DC. Retrieved January 3, 2001, from www.surgeongeneral.gov/topics/cmh/.

Donnellan, A. M., & LaVigna, G. W. (1990). Myths about punishment. In A. C. Repp & N. N. Singh (Eds.), *Perspectives on the use of non-aversive and aversive interventions for persons with developmental disabilities* (pp. 33–58). Sycamore, IL: Sycamore.

Donnellan, A. M., Sabin, L. A., & Majure, L. A. (1992). Facilitated communication: Beyond the quandary to the questions. *Topics in Language Disorders, 12,* 69–82.

Dunn, L. M. (1968). Special education for the mildly retarded—Is much of it justifiable? *Exceptional Children, 35,* 5–22.

D'Zurilla, T. J., & Goldfried, M. R. (1971). Problem solving and behavior modification. *Journal of Abnormal Psychology, 78,* 107–126.

Ellis, A. (1970). *The essence of rational psychotherapy. A comprehensive approach to treatment.* New York: Institute for Rational Living.

Eysenck, H. J. (1965). The effects of psychotherapy. *International Journal of Psychiatry, 1,* 99–244.

Forness, S. R., Kavale, K. A., Blum, L., & Lloyd, J. W. (1997). What works in special education and related services: Using meta-analyses to guide practice. *Teaching Exceptional Children, 29,* 4–9.

Frey, K. S., Hirschstein, M. K., & Guzzo, B. A., (2000). Second step: Preventing aggression by promoting social competence. *Journal of Emotional and Behavioral Disorders, 8,* 102–112

Fuchs, D., & Fuchs, L. (1994). Inclusive education and the radicalization of educational reform. *Exceptional Children, 60,* 294–309.

Gable, R. A., Hendrickson, J. M., Young, C. C., & Shokoohi-Yekta, M. (1992). Preservice preparation and classroom practices of teachers of students with emotional/behavioral disorders. *Behavioral Disorders, 17*(2), 126–134.

Garrick-Duhaney, L., & Salend, S. (2000). Parental perceptions of inclusive educational placements. *Remedial and Special Education, 21,* 121–128.

George, L., George, M. P., Gersten, R., & Grosenick, J. K. (1995). To leave or to stay? An exploratory study of teaches of students with emotional and behavioral disorders. *Remedial and Special Education, 16,* 227–236.

Goldstein, A. P. (1988). *The prepare curriculum: Teaching prosocial competencies* (4th ed.). Champaign, IL: Research Press.

Goldstein, A. P., Sprafkin, R. P., Gershaw, J., & Klein, P. (1979). *Skillstreaming the adolescent. A structured learning approach to teaching prosocial skills.* Champaign, IL: Research Press.

Greenwood, C. R., & Abbott, M. (2001). The research to practice gap in special education. *Teacher Education and Special Education, 24,* 276–289.

Grosenick, J. K., George, M. P., & George, N. L. (1987). A profile of public school programs for the behaviorally disordered: Twenty years after Morse, Cutler, and Fink. *Behavioral Disorders, 12,* 159–168.

Gunter, P. L., & Denny, R. K. (1996). Research issues and needs regarding teacher use of classroom management strategies. *Behavioral Disorders, 22*(1), 15–20.

Harris, K. R., & Graham, S. (1994). Implications of constructivism for students with disabilities and students at risk: Issues and directions. *Journal of Special Education, 28,* 233–247.

Haskew, P., & Donnellan, A. M. (1993). *Emotional maturity and well-being: Psychological lessons of facilitated communication.* Madison, WI: DRI Press.

Henggeler, S. W. (1997). *Treating serious antisocial behavior in youth: The MST approach.* Juvenile Justice Bulletin. Washington, DC: U.S. Department of Justice, Office of Juvenile Justice and Delinquency Prevention.

Hernshaw, L. S. (1987). *The shaping of modern psychology.* New York: Routledge & Kegan Paul.

Howlin, P. (1997). Prognosis in autism: Do specialist treatments affect long-term outcome? *European Child & Adolescent Psychiatry, 6,* 55–72.

Hughes, J. N. (1988). *Cognitive behavior therapy with children in schools.* New York: Pergamon Press.

Huntze, S. L., & Grosenick, J. K. (1980). *National needs analysis in behavior disorders: Human resource issues in behavior disorders.* Columbia, MO: University of Missouri–Columbia, Department of Special Education.

Kanfer, F. H., & Goldstein, A. P. (Eds.). (1986). *Helping people change.* New York: Pergamon Press.

Kanfer, F. H., & Karoly, P. (1972). Self-control: A behavioristic excursion into the lion's den. *Behavior Therapy, 3,* 398–416.

Katsiyannis, A., Conderman, G., & Franks, D. (1995). State practices on inclusion: A national review. *Remedial and Special Education, 16,* 279–287.

Katsiyannis, A., Landrum, T. J., Bullock, L., & Vinton, L. (1997). Certification requirements for teachers of

students with emotional or behavioral disorders: A national survey. *Behavioral Disorders, 22,* 131–140.

Kauffman, J. M. (1996). Research to practice issues. *Behavioral Disorders, 22*(1), 55–60.

Kauffman, J. M. (1999). How we prevent the prevention of emotional and behavioral disorders. *Exceptional Children, 65,* 448–468.

Kauffman, J. M. (2001). *Characteristics of emotional and behavioral disorders of children* (7th. ed.). Columbus, OH: Merrill/Prentice Hall.

Kauffman, J. M. (2002). *Education deform: Bright people sometimes say stupid things about education.* Lanham, MD: Scarecrow.

Kazdin, A. E. (1978). *History of behavior modification.* Baltimore: University Park.

Kazdin, A. E. (1994). *Behavior modification in applied settings.* Pacific Grove, CA: Brooks/Cole.

Knitzer, J., Steinberg, Z., & Fleisch, B. (1990). *At the school house door: An examination of programs and policies for children with behavioral and emotional problems.* New York: Bank Street College of Education.

Lawrenson, G., & McKinnon, A. J. (1982). A survey of classroom teachers of the emotionally disturbed—Attrition and burnout factors. *Behavioral Disorders, 8,* 41–49.

Leahey, T. H. (1980). *A history of psychology.* Englewood Cliffs, NJ: Prentice Hall.

Levitt, E. E. (1963). Psychotherapy with children: A further evaluation. *Behaviour Research and Therapy, 1,* 45–51.

Lewis, T. J., & Sugai, G. (1999). Effective behavior support: A systems approach to proactive schoolwide management. *Focus on Exceptional Children, 21*(6), 1–24.

Lilly, M. S. (1979). *Children with exceptional needs: A survey of special education.* New York: Holt, Rinehart & Winston.

Lipsky, D. K., & Gartner, A. (1997). *Inclusion and school reform: Transforming America's classrooms.* Baltimore: Paul Brookes.

Maag, J. W., & Katsiyannis, A. (1999). Teacher preparation in E/BD: A national survey. *Behavioral Disorders, 24*(3), 189–196.

Mackie, R. Kvaraceus, W., & Williams, H. (1957). *Teachers of children who are socially and emotionally handicapped.* Washington, DC: U. S. Government Printing Office.

MacMillan, D. R., Gresham, F. M., & Forness, S. R. (1996). Full inclusion: An empirical perspective. *Behavioral Disorders, 21,* 145–159.

Masters, J. C., Burish, T. G., Hollon, S. D., & Rimm, D. C. (1987). *Behavior therapy.* New York: Harcourt Brace.

McLeskey, J., Henry, D., & Hodges, D. (1999). Inclusion:

What progress is being made across disability categories? *Teaching Exceptional Children, 31,* 60–64.

Meichenbaum, D., & Asarnow, J. (1979). Cognitive-behavior modification and metacognitive development: Implications for the classroom. In P. C. Kendall & S. D. Hollon (Eds.), *Cognitive-behavioral interventions* (pp. 11–35). New York: Academic Press.

Metzler, C. W., Biglan, A., Rusby, J. C., & Sprague, J. R. (2001). Evaluation of a comprehensive behavior management program to improve school-wide positive behavior support. *Education and Treatment of Children, 24,* 448–479.

Meyer, L. H., & Evans, I. M. (1993). Science and practice in behavioral interventions: Meaningful outcomes, research validity, and usable knowledge. *Journal of the Association of Persons with Severe Handicaps, 18,* 224–234.

Miller, M. D., Brownell, M. T., Smith, S. W. (1999). Factors that predict teachers staying in, leaving, or transferring from the special education classroom. *Exceptional Children, 65,* 201–218.

Mischel, W. (1968). *Personality and assessment.* New York: Wiley.

Mostert, M. P. (2001). Facilitated communication since 1995: A review of published studies. *Journal of Autism and Developmental Disabilities, 31,* 287–313.

Nelson, C. M., Scott, T. M., & Polsgrove, L. (1999). A revisitation of the behavioral perspective on emotional/behavioral disorders: Assumptions and their implications for education and treatment. CEC Monograph Series. Reston, VA: Council for Exceptional Children.

Oseroff, A., Oseroff, C. E., Westling, D., & Gessner, L. J. (1999). Teachers' beliefs about maltreatment of students with emotional/behavioral disorders. *Behavioral Disorders, 24,* 197–209.

Palmer, D. S., Fuller, K., Arora, T., & Nelson, M. (2001). Taking sides: Parent views on inclusion for their children with severe disabilities. *Exceptional Children, 67,* 467–484.

Patterson, G. R., Reid, J. B., & Dishion, T. J. (1992). *A social interaction approach: Antisocial boys.* Eugene, OR: Castalia.

Patterson, G. R., Reid, J. B., Jones, R. R., & Conger, R. E. (1975). *A social learning approach to family intervention.* Vol. 1: *Families with aggressive children.* Eugene, OR: Castalia.

Palfreman, J. (Producer). (1993, October). *Frontline: Prisoners of silence* [Videotape]. Boston, MA: WGBH Public Television.

Peacock Hill Working Group. (1991). Problems and promises in special education and related services for children and youth with emotional or behavioral disorders. *Behavioral Disorders, 16,* 299–313.

Plomin, R. (1989). Environment and genes: Determinants of behavior. *American Psychologist, 44,* 105–111.

Polsgrove, L. (1979). Self-control: Methods for child training. *Behavioral Disorders, 4,* 116–130.

Polsgrove, L. (1991). *Reducing undesirable behaviors. Working with behavioral disorders.* CEC Mini-Library Series. Reston, VA: Council for Exceptional Children.

Polsgrove, L., & Rieth, H. (1979). A new look at competencies required by teachers of emotionally disturbed/behaviorally disordered children and youth. In F. H. Wood (Ed.), *Teachers of secondary school students with serious emotional disturbance* (pp. 25–46). Minneapolis, MN: University of Minnesota, Department of Special Education.

Poplin, M. S. (1988). Holistic/constructivist principles of the teaching/learning process: Implications for the field of learning disabilities. *Journal of Learning Disabilities, 21,* 401–416.

Poplin, M. S. (1996). Looking through other lenses and listening to other voices: Issues for the 21st century. In M. S. Poplin & P. T. Cousin (Eds.), *Alternative views of learning disabilities,* (pp. 1–13). Austin, TX: Pro-Ed.

Pyles, D. A. M., & Bailey, J. S. (1990). Diagnosing severe behavior problems. In A. C. Repp & N. N. Singh (Eds.), *Perspectives on the use of non-aversive and aversive interventions for persons with developmental disabilities* (pp. 181–401). Sycamore, IL: Sycamore.

Reid, R. (1999). Attention deficit hyperactivity disorder: Effective methods for the classroom. *Focus on Exceptional Children, 32*(4), 1–20.

Repp, A. C., & Singh, N. N. (1990). *Perspectives on the use of non-aversive and aversive interventions for persons with developmental disabilities.* Sycamore, IL: Sycamore.

Reynolds, M. C., & Birch, J. (1982). *Teaching exceptional children in all America's schools.* Reston, VA: Council for Exceptional Children.

Rhodes, W. C. (1987). Ecology and the new physics. *Behavioral Disorders, 13,* 58–61.

Rhodes, W. C. (1995). Liberatory pedagogy and special education. *Journal of Learning Disabilities, 28,* 458–462.

Richardson, V. (1996). From behaviorism to constructivism in teacher education. *Teacher Education and Special Education, 19,* 263–271.

Robinson, T. R., Smith, W. S., Miller, M. D., & Brownell, M. T. (1999). Cognitive behavior modification of hyperactivity-impulsivity and aggression: A meta-analysis of school-based studies. *Journal of Educational Psychology, 91,* 195–203.

Rubin, R. A., & Balow, B. (1978). Prevalence of teacher

identified behavior problems: A longitudinal study. *Exceptional Children, 45,* 102–111.

Sasso, G. M. (2001). The retreat from inquiry and knowledge in special education. *Journal of Special Education, 34,* 178–193.

Schumm, J. S., & Vaughn, S. (1992). Planning for mainstreamed special education students: Perceptions of general classroom teachers. *Exceptionality, 3,* 81–98.

Simpson, R. L. (1999). Children and youth with emotional and behavioral disorders: A concerned look at the present and a hopeful eye for the future. *Behavioral Disorders, 24*(4), 284–292.

Singer, J. D. (1992). Are special educators' career paths special? Results from a 12-year longitudinal study. *Exceptional Children, 59,* 262–279.

Skiba, R., & Casey, A. (1985). Interventions for behaviorally disordered students: A quantitative review and methodological critique. *Behavioral Disorders, 10,* 239–252.

Skiba, R., Polsgrove, L., & Nasstrom, K. (1996). *Developing a system of care: Interagency collaboration for students with emotional/behavioral disorders.* Reston, VA: Council for Exceptional Children.

Skinner, B. F. (1953). *Science and human behavior.* New York: Free Press.

Skinner, B. F. (1956). *What is psychotic behavior? Theory and treatment of the psychoses.* Seattle: University of Washington Press.

Skinner, B. F. (1974). *About behaviorism.* New York: Knopf.

Skrtic, T. M. (1995). Special education and student disability as organizational pathologies: Toward a metatheory of school organization and change. In T. M. Skrtic (Ed.), *Disability & democracy: Reconstructing (special) education for postmodernity* (pp. 190–232). New York: Teachers College Press.

Skrtic, T. M., & Sailor, W. (1996). School-linked services integration. Crisis and opportunity in the transition to postmodern society. *Remedial and Special Education, 17,* 271–283.

Skrtic, T. M., Sailor, W., & Gee, K. (1996). Voice collaboration and inclusion: Democratic themes in educational and social reform initiatives. *Remedial and Special Education, 17,* 142–157.

Spivack, G., Platt, J. J., & Shure, M. B. (1976). *The problem-solving approach to adjustment.* San Francisco: Jossey-Bass.

Strain, P. S., & Timm, M. (2001). Remediation and prevention of aggression: An evaluation of the regional intervention program over a quarter century. *Behavioral Disorders, 26,* 297–313.

Swan, W. W., & Sirvis, B. (1992). The CEC common core of knowledge and skills essential for all beginning special education teachers. *Teaching Exceptional Children, 25,* 15–20.

Szasz, T. S. (1960). The myth of mental illness. *American Psychologist, 15,* 113–118.

Toffler, A. (1980). *The third wave.* New York: Bantam Books.

Thoresen, C. E. (1973). Behavioral humanism. In C. E. Thoresen (Ed.), *Behavior modification in education.* Chicago: National Society for the Study of Education, University of Chicago Press.

Thoresen, C. E., & Mahoney, M. J. (1974). *Behavioral self-control.* New York: Holt, Rinehart & Winston.

Ullman, L. P., & Krasner, L. (Eds.). (1965). *Case studies in behavior modification.* New York: Holt, Rinehart & Winston.

Walker, H. M., Colvin, G., & Ramsey, E. (1995). *Antisocial behavior in school: Strategies and best practices.* Pacific Grove, CA: Brooks/Cole.

Walker, H. M., & Hops, H. (1993). *The RECESS program for aggressive children.* Seattle, WA: Educational Achievement Systems.

Walker, H., Hops, H., & Greenwood, C. R. (1981). RECESS: Research and development of a behavior management package for remediating social aggression in the school setting. In P. Strain (Ed.), *The utilization of classroom peers as behavior change agents* (pp. 261–303). New York: Plenum.

Walker, H. M., Sprague, J. R., Close, D. W., & Starlin, C. M. (1999–2000). What is right with behavior disorders: Seminal achievements and contributions of the behavior disorder field. *Exceptionality, 8*(1), 13–28.

Walker, H. M., Zeller, R. W., Close, D. W., Webber, J., & Gresham, F. (1999). The present unwrapped: Change and challenge in the field of behavioral disorders. *Behavioral Disorders, 24,* 293–304.

Whelan, R. J., & Simpson, R. L. (1996). Preparation of personnel for students with emotional and behavioral disorders: Perspectives on a research foundation for future practice. *Behavioral Disorders, 22*(1), 49–54.

Wolf, M. M., Braukmann, C. J., & Ramp, K. A. (1987). Serious delinquent behavior as part of a significantly handicapping condition: Cures and supportive environments. *Journal of Applied Behavior Analysis, 20,* 347–359.

TRANSITION ISSUES
Process, Practices, and Perspectives

JAMES R. PATTON

University of Texas at Austin

In the field of special education the subspecialty area of *transition,* preparing adolescents for adult roles, is relatively new as a formal area of study. One must be cautious in regard to identifying a clear starting point for transition activities. Many professionals in the field of special education, particularly those who worked in work-study programs of the 1950s and 1960s, were apt to be performing duties that are similar in nature to what we now call transition services. Therefore, care is called for when proclaiming the new achievements in the area of transition in the last fifteen years.

For all practical purposes, the incipient stages of transition efforts as we know them today began in the early 1980s. The U.S. Department of Education's publication of Madeline Will's (1984) *OSERS Programming for the Transition of Youth with Disabilities: Bridges from School to Working Life,* what has become known as the "bridges" document, marks the beginning of the movement. Her work introduced us not only to one of the first metaphors of transition but also to a model and framework from which the subspecialty of transition services has evolved.

From the late 1980s until today, transition has received increasing levels of attention. It would be wonderful to propose that professional interest in this topic was spurred by the realization that implementing a school-initiated mechanism to assist students with disabilities in moving more smoothly from high school to adult life is a good idea. However, in reality early efforts in transition during the 1980s were precipitated in part by the availability of federal support. In the early 1990s another major factor arose that encouraged school systems to become more interested in the issue of transition. With the reauthorization of the Education of All Handicapped Children Act in 1990, all students with disabilities who were sixteen years old were to have a statement of transition services in their individualized education plans (IEPs). Not addressing the issue of transition planning was to be out of compliance with federal law. However, as will be discussed later in this chapter, federal mandate does not necessarily ensure compliant behavior.

Even though there are some forceful reasons for "interest" in transition which have nothing to do with best or recommended practices, professional efforts to identify a valid knowledge base have increased. Over time, a growing number of professionals have chosen transition as a field of study and primary professional activity. Expanding professional interest in and consolidation of the field is evidenced by the growth of the Division on Career Development and Transition (DCDT) of the Council for Exceptional Children (CEC). This particular division of CEC has enjoyed increased membership and well-attended conferences since its formation.

School-based professionals, mostly by necessity and sometimes by career choice, need to increase their level of knowledge and develop their skills in the area of transition. Accordingly, many school districts across the country have provided a wealth of in-service activities to their staff. Almost all special education teachers who completed their preparation programs prior to the mid-1990s would not have had any exposure to basic information about transition. So the need for useful information at the in-service level has been extensive.

During the mid-1990s, some teacher preparation programs in special education in the United States began to offer entire courses on transition. Most of these courses were designed as general courses on transition for those who would become special educators. They were not intended to prepare transition specialists/coordinators (i.e., individuals who are key staff members at the secondary level with primary responsibility for transition-related activities within their schools). The reality, however, was that many of these preservice teachers would be given transition-related responsibilities on graduation. A broader perspective, endorsed in some programs, was that all special education personnel, regardless of level of schooling, play some role in the transition process.

Perhaps the most telling sign that transition has come of age is the number of textbooks specifically addressing transition (e.g., Flexer, Simmons, Luft, & Baer, 2001; Rusch & Chadsey, 1998; Sitlington, Clark, & Kolstoe, 2000; Wehman, 2001). Another signal of the increasing importance of this topic is coverage given to it in introductory and methods/materials textbooks in special education. This coverage is important because it may be the only exposure many students have to the topic. Table 1 briefly outlines the extent, though not the quality, of coverage in some of the leading introductory and methods/materials textbooks in the field today.

A BRIEF HISTORICAL PERSPECTIVE

To understand the major issues in the field of transition, a brief overview of the evolution of the transition movement is necessary. Table 2 presents the key historical themes and events in the field of transition. Table 2 focuses on events that immediately preceded and for the most part postdate the passage of the Education of All Handicapped Children Act of 1975. Other sources (e.g., Neubert, 1997) provide a more expansive discussion of the history of preparing adolescents for adult roles. Without question, certain events prior to 1970 affected current transition practices more than others (e.g., the increasing importance of occupational knowledge and intent of work-study programs).

As Table 2 shows, the federal government has played a crucial role over the years in the transition movement. Moreover, by looking at the different themes that have arisen over the years, one recognizes that an embedded theme of empowerment has emerged. Because of space limitations, the table intentionally omits many important professionals who have made significant contributions to the field of transition.

TABLE 1   Textbook Coverage of Transition

SOURCE	INDEX LISTING	DEDICATED CHAPTER	COVERAGE (# OF PAGES)
Methods/Materials Books			
Bos, C. S., & Vaughn, S. (2002). *Strategies for teaching students with learning and behavior problems* (5th ed.). Boston: Allyn & Bacon.	Y	Y	27
Cegelka, P. T., & Berdine, W. H. (1995). *Effective instruction of students with learning difficulties.* Boston: Allyn & Bacon.	Y	Y	24
Hammill, D. D., & Bartel, N. R. (1995). *Teaching students with learning and behavior problems* (6th ed.). Austin, TX: PRO-ED.	Y	Y	36
Mastropieri, M. A., & Scruggs, T. E. (2002). *Effective instruction for special education* (3rd ed.). Austin, TX: PRO-ED.	Y	Y	17
Mercer, C. D., & Mercer, A. P. (2001). *Teaching students with learning problems* (6th ed.). Upper Saddle River, NJ: Merrill/Prentice Hall.	Y	Y	22
Polloway, E. A., Patton, J. R., & Serna, L. (2001). *Strategies for teaching learners with special needs* (7th ed.). Upper Saddle River, NJ: Merrill/Prentice Hall.	Y	Y	35
Introductory Books			
Gargiulo, R. M. (2003). *Special education in contemporary society: An introduction to exceptionality.* Belmont, CA: Wadsworth/Thomson Learning.	Y	N	~15
Hallahan, D. P., & Kauffman, J. M. (2003). *Exceptional learners: Introduction to special education* (9th ed.). Boston: Allyn & Bacon.	Y	N	~32
Hardman, M. L., Drew, C. J., & Egan, M. W. (2002). *Human exceptionality: Society, school, and family* (7th ed.). Boston: Allyn & Bacon.	Y	Y	*
Heward, W. L. (2003). *Exceptional children: An introduction to special education* (7th ed.). Upper Saddle River, NJ: Merrill/Prentice Hall.	Y	N	~14
Hunt, N., & Marshall, K. (1999). *Exceptional children and youth* (2nd ed.). New York: Houghton Mifflin.	Y	Y	37
Smith, D. D. (2004). *Introduction to special education: Teaching in an age of opportunity* (5th ed.). Boston: Allyn & Bacon.	Y	N	~29
Turnbull, H. R., Turnbull, A. P., Shank, M., Smith, S., & Leal, D. (2002). *Exceptional lives: special education in today's schools* (3rd ed.). Upper Saddle River, NJ: Merrill/Prentice Hall.	Y	N	~25
Wood, J. W., & Lazzari, A. M. (1997). *Exceeding the boundaries: Understanding exceptional lives.* Belmont, CA: Wadsworth/Thomson Learning.	Y	Y	29

Whether transition activities, which are currently part of students' programs, would be implemented without legislative mandate is debatable. Given the importance of federal law and regulations in ensuring that students with disabilities are provided transition planning, it is instructive to take a close look at the changes that have occurred in the Individuals with Disabilities Education Act (IDEA). In addition, an examination of the transition requirements of IDEA points out various critical elements that are part of transition planning. Table 3 shows the progression of the transition initiative within IDEA, as tracked by Stodden (1998). The first time schools were required to include transition information in a student's IEP was in 1990; however, the original law and the reauthorization in 1983 contained elements that are clear precursors to the features that emerged in the reauthorizations of the act in 1990 and 1997.

MAJOR ISSUES IN TRANSITION

In this section I examine the key issues in the field of transition, including broad topics (e.g., the concept of transition), practice-related topics (e.g., assessment), and policy-related topics

TABLE 2 Historical Overview

TIMEFRAME	KEY THEMES/CONCEPTS	SIGNIFICANT EVENTS	KEY LEGISLATION	FEDERAL INITIATIVES	DCDT POSITION PAPERS
1970s	■ "Criterion of ultimate functioning" (Brown et al., 1976). ■ Career education. ■ Prevocational/vocational education.	■ Division on Career Development established. ■ Life Centered Career Education (LCCE).	■ Education for All Handicapped Children Act (EHCA) (P.L. 94-142).		■ Career/vocational assessment. ■ Gifted.
1980s	■ Transition movement begins. ■ Supported employment. ■ Community-based instruction.	■ "Bridges" model (Will, 1984). ■ Expanded transition model (Halpern, 1985).	■ Job Training Partnership Act. ■ EHA reauthorization (P.L. 98-199). ■ Carl D. Perkins Vocational and Technical Act (P.L. 88-210).	■ Funds to support demonstration projects. ■ Support for the National Longitudinal Transition Study (NLTS).	
1990s	■ Inclusion. ■ Self-determination/self-advocacy. ■ Standards-based movement. ■ Access to the general education curriculum. ■ Community-based programs. ■ Community transition teams. ■ Quality of life focus. ■ Student-focused conferences and planning.	■ Secretary's Commission of Achieving Necessary Skills (SCANS) report. ■ Best practices research (Kohler, 1993). ■ NLTS results published.	■ IDEA reauthorization (P.L. 101-476). ■ Americans with Disabilities Act (P.L. 101-336). ■ Carl D. Perkins Vocational and Applied Technology Education Act (P.L. 1091-392). ■ Rehabilitation Act amendments (P.L. 102-569). ■ School-to-Work Opportunities Act (P.L. 103-239). ■ IDEA reauthorization (P.L. 105-17).	■ Funds to support 5-year systems-change programs.	■ Career development elementary levels. ■ Life skills. ■ Definition of transition. ■ Transition assessment. ■ Self-determination.

TABLE 3 Progress of the Transition Initiative within IDEA

1975 IDEA (P.L. 94-142)	1983 IDEA (P.L. 98-199) REAUTHORIZATION	1990 IDEA (P.L. 101-476) REAUTHORIZATION	1997 IDEA (P.L. 105-17) REAUTHORIZATION
■ Ensured FAPE for children with disabilities. ■ Outlined due-process procedures. ■ Established an Individualized Education Plan (IEP) process for each child with a disability.	■ Federal funds were provided to demonstrate transition models. ■ OSERS transition model was developed. ■ Transition outcomes were specified in legislative language.	■ Transition services are defined in legislation. ■ Legislation included a statement of needed transition services in the IEP for each student aged 16 or younger. ■ Promoted educational planning focused on postschool goals.	■ Focused on self-determination for students and families in trasition planning. ■ Focused on short- and long-range goals rather than objectives within the IEP. ■ Focused on student planning and participation in the general educational curriculum. ■ Focused on integrating transition planning within the process of educational planning starting at age 14 years. ■ Based educational planning and programming on postschool results.

Source: From Stodden, R. A. (1998). School-to-work transition: Overview of disability legislation. In F. R. Rusch & J. G. Chadsey (Eds.), *Beyond high school: Transition from school to work* (p. 67). Belmont, CA: Wadsworth Publishing.

(e.g., preservice/in-service training). This list is by no means exhaustive; it is simply representative of the kinds of issues special educators face in the field today.

Researchers have been identifying critical issues in transition and related concepts since the mid-1970s. Early studies focused primarily on career education, vocational preparation, and life-skills instruction. The more recent studies have focused primarily on transition-related practices. Table 4 provides examples of changing research agendas over time.

The first column of Table 4 represents the results of a conference sponsored by the Research Branch of the Bureau of Education for the Handicapped (BEH) (1975) and highlights five critical research needs in the field. The second column outlines the findings of a study on emerging themes in the field conducted by the Division on Career Development (Wimmer & Sitlington, 1981). The third column highlights the results of a study Kohler (1993) conducted to identify best practices in transition. The last column outlines the findings of a study sponsored by the DCDT (Bassett, Patton, White, Blalock, & Smith, 1997) to identify which research issues were most important to practitioners and other professionals in the field of transition. A number of observations can be made after reviewing Table 4:

■ Some themes continue to be identified as areas of focus, for example, interagency agreements.

TABLE 4   Examples of Research Agendas over Time

BEH[a] (1975) "CRITICAL RESEARCH AREAS"	DCD[b] (1981) "RESEARCH AGENDA" (WIMMER & SITLINGTON, 1981)	KOHLER (1993) "BEST PRACTICES"	DCDT[c] (1997) "TOP 10 CRITICAL RESEARCH ISSUES" (BASSETT ET AL., 1997)
■ Attitudes that impede choices for career level and employment. ■ Critical variables in keeping/losing/advancing in jobs. ■ Development of decision-making, problem-solving, and coping skills. ■ Development of interagency agreements improves articulation between all agencies delivering career education services to persons with disabilities. ■ Identification of developmental sequences associated with concepts, facts, and behaviors fundamental to career education competencies.	■ Instructional methodologies and settings for skill training. ■ Delineation of essential competencies for vocational and community adjustment. ■ Attitudes that prevent entry into the world of work. ■ Efficacy of various vocational skill training programs for students with disabilities. ■ Essential competencies for successful vocational adjustment. ■ Effects of instruction in various settings (mainstreamed vocational education, special class, infusion with regular class, etc.). ■ Effects of various teaching methods in training persons with disabilities in personal, social, human relationship skills. ■ Essential competencies for successful community adjustment. ■ Effects of various teaching methodologies in training work skills among persons with disabilities. ■ Opinions/attitudes that interfere with the entrance of individuals with disabilities into the world of work.	■ Vocational training. ■ Parent involvement. ■ Interagency collaboration and service delivery. ■ Social skills training. ■ Paid work experience. ■ Individualized transition planning.	■ Teacher training for transition. ■ Inclusion of student with special needs into vocational education. ■ Family involvement in transition. ■ Transition plans, goals and objectives, linkage activities. ■ Interagency collaboration. ■ Facilitation of student self-determination and self-esteem. ■ Functional transition assessment to support transitional planning. ■ Models of K–12 career development and transition planning. ■ Social skills curriculum, assessment, and training. ■ Collaboration with general education.

[a]Bureau of Education for the Handicapped.
[b]Division on Career Development.
[c]Division on Career Development and Transition.
Source: Adapted from Bassett et al. (1997).

■ Many key issues, such as essential competencies for successful community adjustment, are as vital today as they were when the field was in its infancy.

■ An evolving emphasis on issues related to transition practices and student/family involvement is evident.

The following sections will discuss issues highlighted in Table 4 as well as related issues and provide professional commentary on these issues from the literature.

THE CONCEPT OF TRANSITION

Outside the field of special education, mention of the term *transition* is often met with blank stares and remarks indicating a lack of understanding. Pure and simple, it is an "insider" term. Yet while this term has meaning to special educators, does everyone in the field agree on its definition?

The original notion of transition, "an outcome-oriented process" (Will, 1984), has endured over time and remains a major theme in IDEA. To more precisely define it, it is necessary to examine what is meant by the services that accompany transition efforts.

Transition services are defined in IDEA (§1401(30)) as a coordinated set of activities for a student with a disability that

■ is designed within an outcome-oriented process, which promotes movement from school to postschool activities, including postsecondary education, vocational training, and integrated employment (including supported employment), continuing and adult education, adult services, independent living or community participation;

■ is based on the individual student's needs, taking into account the student's preferences and interests; and

■ includes instruction, related services, community experiences, the development of employment and other postschool adult living objectives, and, when appropriate, acquisition of daily living skills and functional vocational evaluation.

What we learn from this definition is that some "set of activities" should occur that prepares the student for and helps with moving to various postschool options. The definition is, at times, confusing and not clearly presented. Although other explanations of transition services can be found in the literature (e.g., Everson & Guillory, 1998), few definitions provide the clarity and exactness necessary to facilitate the enormous task of preparing students for and moving them into any number of new postschool settings. As a result, state and local educational agencies must decide on their own how to accomplish these tasks, often with deleterious consequences for students.

There is no doubt that transition is a complex process. It is not simple procedure that can be implemented quickly and marginally. Successful transition services involve the efforts of school-based personnel (assessing needs, developing plans, providing appropriate instruction, and establishing necessary linkages to postschool entities) and coordination, cooperation, and communication from a variety of agencies (Patton & Dunn, 1998). In a recent study on policy compliance and best practices, McMahan and Baer (2001) found that the most influential way to obtain compliance and the implementation of best practices is through the existence of a school-based interagency transition team. Establishing a transition process that involves different parties is not easy and, too often, does not occur.

The focus of transition services must be comprehensive; that is, transition activities must consider all key areas of adult functioning, including but not limited to employment and further education, as is the case in many school settings. Other areas transition services must address include activities of everyday living, physical and emotional health, leisure, community participation, transportation, self-determination, and interpersonal relationships. The concept of "criterion of ultimate functioning," which was introduced almost thirty years ago by Brown, Nietupski, & Hamre-Nietupski (1976), still functions as a great way to understand that the outcome of transition services is to produce young adults who are competent in many areas across a range of settings (Ward & Kohler, 1996b). It refers to the ever changing, expanding, localized, and personalized cluster of factors that each person must possess in order to function as productively and independently as possible in socially, vocationally, and domestically integrated adult community environments (Brown et al., 1976).

Professional Commentary

■ "The concept of transition is not fully accepted, developed, or integrated into schools. Until a common understanding of transition is developed, it will be difficult to identify strategies for including students." (Lehmann, Bassett, & Sands, 1999, p. 167)

■ "Too many schools interpret the transition mandate as primarily an arrangement of services from other agencies and fail to recognize its functional skills/career development curriculum requirements." (Brolin, 1995, p. 443)

■ "Transition services, which we once thought consisted of a relatively simple individualized planning process culminating in a written statement of transition services, are finally being recognized as much more complex." (Everson & Guillory, 1998, p. 299)

■ "Transition planning is complex because it must encompass both educational and postsecondary community services and includes not only academic skills but also vocational, residential, social, leisure, and community living skills." (Repetto, White, & Snauwaert, 1990, p. 111)

■ "Early models of transition planning have been expanded from a focus only on employment goals to a more comprehensive view of postschool outcomes." (Morningstar, Kleinhammer-Tramill, & Lattin, 1999, p. 14)

■ "I firmly believe that there is much more to the quality of life than employment. Friends, experiencing joy, feelings of self-esteem, adventure and excitement, freedom of choice, reasonable living situations—the range of events, feelings, and experience we all value—make up quality." (Edgar, 1988, p. 5)

KEY ELEMENTS OF THE TRANSITION PROCESS

A certain degree of confusion exists about what constitutes transition services. Federal law provides general guidelines, but it stops short of clearly articulating the essential elements of the transition planning and services process. Patton and Dunn (1998) described a very general model for understanding the implications of the transition process (see Figure 1). The core features of the transition reflected in this model include:

■ School-based personnel, the student, his/her family, and adult services must work collaboratively to ready the individual for dealing successfully with the demands of adulthood.

■ Essentially, the student needs to acquire certain knowledge (facts, concepts, ideas) and skills (performance) to be successful—this task is addressed through instruction and manifested as IEP goals.

■ The student also needs to be linked with various supports and services that are either required or useful to be successful—this task is addressed through various linkage activities and manifested as transition goals.

■ This process must start early in a student's school career. Certain efforts should begin at the elementary level (Clark, Field, Patton, Brolin, & Sitlington, 1994), and more systematic activity must be in evidence at the middle school level. Pursuant to the requirements of IDEA, a "statement of transition service needs" must be in the IEP by age 14 and a "statement of needed transition services" must be in the IEP by age 16.

■ This process involves the development of comprehensive plans (i.e., a two-step process of assessment and individual planning based on the assessment results) and earnest action on the plan that is generated.

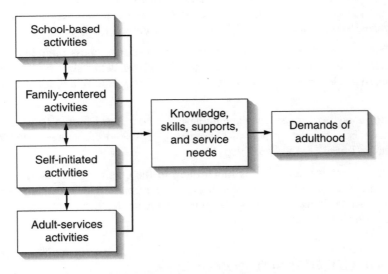

FIGURE 1   Key Elements of the Transition Process

Source: Patton, J. R., & Dunn, C. (1998). *Transition from school to young adulthood: Basic concepts and recommended practices.* Austin, TX: PRO-ED. Reprinted by permission.

■ Transition planning meetings, as required by IDEA, become the major venue for discussing and resolving many transition-related issues. These meetings demand adequate preparation, regular communication between school and home, involvement of key adult service personnel, and the active participation of the student. Far too frequently these features are absent (Gallivan-Fenlon, 1994; Lehmann et al., 1999; Shearin, Roessler, & Schriner, 1999).

■ The active involvement of all players, especially the student, is crucial.

■ Sensitivity to cultural issues must pervade the entire transition planning process.

A very important point that is too often overlooked in understanding the key aspects of transition services is that the planning stage typically should generate two different, but related, types of goals. *Instructional goals* are of an academic, social, and/or behavioral nature. *Linkage goals* are principally oriented toward making connections with various services in which the student will be involved or will need in his/her postschool life. For instance, a student with learning disabilities who is headed to college and who has some serious problems in note taking could benefit from both types of goals. A goal should be developed in the student's IEP whereby the student receives instruction in how to take better notes. In addition, a linkage goal should be generated that specifies that the student determine what services the college the student will be attending offers to its students to enhance their study skills.

Kohler (1998) describes the educational process of transition in the following way: (1) postschool goals are identified based on student abilities, needs, interests, and preferences; (2) instructional activities and educational experiences are developed to prepare students for their postschool goals; and (3) a variety of individuals, including the student, work together to identify and develop the goals and activities (p. 181).

Professional Commentary

■ "The paucity of critical transition-related resources/opportunities, general confusion about how to encourage student involvement in activities, and underutilization of the transition planning meetings suggests that the current delivery of transition services is stagnant." (Lehmann et al., 1999, p. 168)

■ "The concept of *transition planning* means different things to different people. Many in the field of special education view transition planning from a narrow perspective that focuses specifically on a student's movement from school to immediate postschool activities." (Kohler, 1998, p. 180)

BEST PRACTICES IN TRANSITION

A field of study becomes legitimate when evidence-based practices exist. Unfortunately, this is not the case in the area of transition. Many professionals (Browning, 1997; Greene & Albright, 1995; Johnson & Rusch, 1993; Neubert, 1997) have remarked that a solid research base on transition practices is lacking. Few would argue that many practices that are espoused in the transition literature are sound on face value; however, few practices have received the research attention that is essential to validate their effectiveness and ultimately their continued use. Table 5 is a summary of transition practices that have been identified in the literature as having some face validity in terms of effectiveness. The table, developed by Morningstar and colleagues (1999), is based on their analysis of opinion-based and research studies.

Most professionals in the area of transition would support the implementation of the practices listed in Table 4. However, empirical evidence supporting the use of most of the practices has not been found as yet. Interestingly, Kohler (1993, 1996) found that only three practices (vocational training, parent involvement, interagency collaboration and service delivery) were cited in over 50 percent of the studies she reviewed as best practices. Three other practices (social skills training, paid employment, and individual transition plans and planning) were identified in at least one-third of the studies examined as best practices. The need to expand research efforts to validate the effectiveness of transition practices, which are promoted in the literature and used in schools, was noted in the early 1990s and continues today.

Professional Commentary

■ "Based on existing research, the field of transition services remains very 'soft.'" (Greene & Albright, 1995, p. 1)

■ "A problematic area in the transition movement has been the lack of research that identifies 'best practices' in curriculums and programs that enhance postsecondary outcomes for students with disabilities." (Neubert, 1997, p. 13)

■ "Only within the past few years, however, have researchers begun to examine the relationship between best practices and student outcomes." (Morningstar et al., 1999, p. 7)

■ "As a field, educators need to determine if transition education really makes a difference in the adult adjustment of individuals with disabilities. . . . Effective procedures must be developed for determining the quantity and quality of transition planning that occur in high school." (Sitlington et al., 2000, p. 336)

■ "In the long term, 'best practices' associated with positive student outcomes must be those supported by evidence of effectiveness." (Kohler, 1993, p. 118)

COMPLIANCE WITH THE TRANSITION MANDATE

One of the more controversial issues that can be raised is whether what occurs in most schools in the name of transition services is in reality only minimal compliance activities. The answer to the implied question is "yes" in a vast majority of settings across the country. Given the complexities of the transition process, the lack of understanding of what practices to implement, and the time demands associated with providing comprehensive transition services, we should not be surprised that the modus operandi is to do what is minimally required by law.

Baer, Simmons, and Flexer (1996) analyzed transition practice in Ohio and found that, while school districts were in compliance on average in nine of fourteen transition policy areas, compliance efforts were generally directed toward paperwork (e.g., transition document developed) aspects of transition rather than on the provision of transition services (e.g., coordination of services).

Some school systems in the country go far beyond what is minimally required by law and provide a vast array of quality transition services. These systems are typically staffed by

TABLE 5 Best and Recommended Practices in Transition Planning and Services

PRACTICE	PATTON & BROWDER (1988)	RUSCH & DESTEFANO (1989)	BATES (1990)	WEHMAN (1990)	HALPERN, LINDSTROM, BENZ, & NELSON (1991)	KOHLER (1993)	MORNINGSTAR (1993)	CLARK & KOLSTOE (1995)	KOHLER, DESTEFANO, WERMUTH, GRAYSON, & MCGINTY (1994)	HUGHES, BOGSEON, KIM, KILLIAN, HARMER, & ALCANTARA (1997)	RUSCH & MILLAR (1998)	KOHLER (1998)	KOHLER & CHAPMAN (1999)
Family network and involvement	•	•	•	•	•	•	•	•	•	•	•	•	•
Individualized and comprehensive transition planning	•	•	•	•	•	•	•	•	•	•	•	•	•
Interagency cooperation and collaboration (including business partnerships)	•	•	•	•	•	•	•	•	•		•	•	•
Focus curriculum on postschool outcomes	•	•	•	•	•	•	•	•	•	•	•	•	•
Student involvement and self-determination			•	•			•			•	•	•	
Social skills training						•		•	•	•			
VR counselors in schools				•									
School-based related services			•						•				•
Follow-up studies and program evaluation		•							•		•		
Personnel preparation		•					•		•		•		
Work experiences/job placement		•		•		•			•		•		
Integrated activities in school and community		•		•		•	•	•	•	•		•	
Flexibility in planning	•											•	
Availability of postschool adult services	•				•		•	•			•		
Administrative support and program structures					•						•	•	•
Comprehensive vocational assessment						•			•	•	•		
Identifying and matching environmental supports										•			
Career pathways and contextual learning													•

Source: From Morningstar, M. E., Kleinhammer-Tramill, J., & Lattin, D. (1999). Using successful models of student-centered transition planning and services for adolescents with disabilities. *Focus on Exceptional Children, 31*(9), 1–19. Reprinted by permission. Complete bibliographic information for the references cited can be found in the original source.

teachers who have received strong training in transition and understand the complexities of delivering effective services.

Professional Commentary

■ "The transition-related mandates of IDEA may have limited accountability, as many educational agencies have developed ways to appear in compliance without changing their educational planning practices in any meaningful way." (Ward & Kohler, 1996a, p. 288)

■ "Currently, the effort under the name of transition planning too often represents perfunctory attempts to comply with federal legislation." (Patton, Polloway, Smith, Edgar, Clark, & Lee, 1996, p. 82)

CURRICULAR IMPLICATIONS OF TRANSITION

An expansive view of transition services, as discussed earlier, has significant implications on curriculum. Curriculum is primarily about the content to which students are exposed during their school careers. In terms of transition, the content, about which we are concerned, involves real-life topics that are needed to function successfully in a variety of adult roles. This content, if it is covered at all, can be addressed in one of two ways. It can be approached proactively, as an ongoing portion of the student's educational program, or dealt with retroactively, after specific needs are identified.

The key issue is that many students who are taking general education classes are not acquiring functional life skills that are necessary for handling the demands of everyday life in the community (Alberto, Taber, Brozovic, & Elliot, 1997). This fact is no more evident than in the data on functional abilities, which were obtained in the National Longitudinal Transition Study (Wagner, Blackorby, Cameto, Hebbeler, & Newman, 1993). These data, as presented in Table 6, clearly show gaps in the functional levels of students across disability categories, as perceived by their parents. A tendency to overlook whether students have mastered the many basic day-to-day skills is common.

Options need to be available for covering important content and developing socially valid skills such as self-determination. Doing so has become more difficult as a result of a number of factors. First, more students with disabilities are receiving a greater part of their education in the general education classroom. Although this setting, and its inherent curricular focus, does not preclude attention to functional topics, few teachers are skilled in infusing real-life content into the existing content of their classes. Second, in an era of standards-based education, while coverage of real-life topics is possible, the reality is that more time will be dedicated to core academic subjects on which students will be tested (Patton & Trainor, 2002). However, the relationship between academics and real-life topics such as occupations provides a natural way to teach applied academics and creates access to the general education curriculum (Eisenman, 2000).

Ways must be developed and refined that introduce education-related activities that correspond to and prepare students for the demands they face as they move from school to community life. In times when it seems like the availability of choices is limited, Edgar and Polloway's (1994) admonition is noteworthy: "We need to offer more options, not fewer" (p. 444).

TABLE 6   Functional Abilities

DISABILITY CATEGORY	PERCENTAGE OF YOUTH WITH PARENTS REPORTING		
	High Self-Care Skills[a]	High Functional Mental Skills[b]	High Community Living Skills[c]
All conditions	86.4	56.9	61.4
Learning disabled	95.5	66.0	74.2
Emotionally disturbed	94.1	65.3	66.9
Speech impaired	91.8	68.9	67.3
Mentally retarded	67.4	32.8	29.4
Visually impaired	51.6	31.8	41.2
Deaf	83.4	44.3	43.4
Hard of hearing	92.3	60.7	45.8
Orthopedically impaired	42.3	50.5	32.5
Other health impaired	65.3	57.3	41.2
Multiply handicapped	34.5	12.8	21.3
Deaf/blind	21.0	6.8	13.2

[a]Skills include dressing oneself, feeding oneself, and getting around outside the home. Scale ranges from 3 to 12. High is 12.

[b]Skills include counting change, reading common signs, telling time on an analog clock, and looking up telephone numbers and using the phone. Scale ranges from 4 to 16. High is 15 or 16.

[c]Skills include using public transportation, buying clothes, arranging a trip out of town, and using community resources, such as a swimming pool and/or library. Scale ranges from 4 to 16. High is 15 or 16.

Source: From Wagner, M., Blackorby, J., Cameto, R., Hebbeler, K., & Newman, L. (1993). *The transition experiences of young people with disabilities: A summary of findings from the national longitudinal transition study of special education students* (pp. 2–13). Menlo Park, CA: SRI International. Copyright 1993 by SRI International. Reprinted with permission.

Professional Commentary

■ "A life skills instruction approach should be part of (i.e., included within existing coursework) or a recognized and approved option (i.e., alternative coursework) to every school curriculum for all students at all grade levels." (Clark et al., 1994, p. 126)

■ "For students whose adult outcomes are other than post-secondary education, the general curriculum, with its academic focus, neglects instruction on the functional life skills necessary for participating within the community." (Alberto et al., 1997, p. 198)

■ "One of the reasons that students with disabilities have not succeeded once they leave school is that the educational process has not prepared students with special learning needs adequately to become self-determined young people." (Wehmeyer & Schalock, 2001, p. 2)

■ "The primary concern of curricular options should be their functionality in terms of the needs of the individual student as related to his or her postschool goals." (Edgar & Polloway, 1994, p. 445)

TRANSITION ASSESSMENT AND PLANS

Two main elements of the transition planning process are the identification of needs and the development of individual plans to address these needs. The federal regulations do not provide guidance on what types of assessment should be conducted or what format individual plans should have to include the required statements.

ASSESSMENT ISSUES

Central to the discussion is the fact that the better the assessment, the better the plans it generates. In general, school-based personnel lack an easy-to-implement system (i.e., framework) for gathering information about the transition needs of students. This should not come as a surprise, since most teachers have not had any training in transition assessment and simply do not know what is available. The result is often a haphazard process of collecting information that is usually narrow in scope (i.e., not comprehensive).

Assessment procedures, which are now available to personnel charged with transition responsibility but which are difficult or time consuming to administer, will not be used. This condition applies to commercially available instruments as well as to informal techniques. The catch here is finding an assessment system that is easy to use and will not take a great amount of teacher or student time yet will provide a comprehensive feel for a student's transition needs.

As is implied by the notion of *comprehensive, transition assessment* is an umbrella term that covers the range of adult domains and encompasses several different types of assessment. Instruments for assessing general transition needs have been developed to cover these areas; however, some areas such as employment and vocational preparation require a more specialized set of procedures and instruments. But, as Leconte (1999) pointed out, most schools do not have a formal vocational evaluation process. As a result, many students with disabilities, who could benefit greatly from a thorough vocational evaluation for helping them plan their lives, do not receive this service.

Roessler, Shearin, and Williams (2000) discuss another assessment issue, that of overlooking data on students during the planning process. They speculate that this occurs for two reasons. First, the assessments that were used do not relate well to the adult domains for which a needs assessment is valuable. Second, they point out that, even when appropriate transition-related data do exist, the transition teams/IEP teams will not use them to develop goals.

Transition assessment can and should be a capacity-building activity (Patton & Dunn, 1998). Although structured around the search to establish "transition needs" (i.e., areas requiring attention), this process provides the opportunity to reaffirm a student's strengths. The features and benefits of a strength-based approach to assessment should be distinctive in all transition assessment procedures.

The time frame for when transition assessment needs to occur has changed as a result of the 1997 IDEA reauthorization. Now that a statement of transition service needs must be in the IEP by the time the student is fourteen years old, school personnel at the middle school level have become key players in the transition planning process. In particular, transition assessment activities have to begin at this level. One of the problems with using more formal instruments with this younger population is that they legitimately respond to most items with

"I don't know." Consequently, more informal techniques such as the development of transition portfolios (see Browning, 1997) need to be used with these students to jump-start their thinking about important issues related to their lives.

Professional Commentary

■ "Transition personnel need to know the features of the different instruments now available for determining transition needs. Furthermore, they must be able to locate and interpret existing assessment data." (Patton & Dunn, 1998, p. 23)

■ "Vocational evaluation has proven to be an effective intervention for improving the vocational and career outcomes of youth and adults with disabilities and special needs." (Leconte, 1999, p. 412)

■ "A portfolio . . . can be used for essentially any student experiences and accomplishments ranging from a given academic subject area, to career development, to job and community preparation." (Browning, 1997, p. 153)

TRANSITION PLANS

Some states require that all students have an individualized transition plan (ITP) that is a separate document from the IEP. Other states include transition goals and statements within the existing IEP document. Many states will use attachments to the IEP to capture transition-related information. Regardless of the type of document used, the critical issue is that both instructional goals and linkage goal statements are listed for all areas of need.

The actual format of ITPs varies greatly. The federal regulations do not provide recommendations on how to structure the transition document; however, most school agencies generally use the postschool activities identified in IDEA as the basis for their transition materials. However, the format of some ITP documents more attractive than others, such as is being guided by the student's preferences and interests and being more comprehensive in nature.

The results of studies of IEPs and ITPs (deFur, Getzel, & Kregel, 1994; Everson, Zhang, & Guillory, 2001; Krom & Prater, 1993; Shearin, Roessler, & Schriner, 1999; Thompson, Fulk, & Piercy, 2000; Wehmeyer, Agran, & Hughes, 2000) are a mixed bag, some pointing to promising features and others to serious problems. Grigal, Test, Beattie, and Wood (1997), in their evaluation of the transition documents that accompany the IEPs of students in North Carolina, found that, while generally in compliance with federal mandate, the goals contained in these documents could be rated as "only adequate to minimal." One of the major problems identified by most of those who have examined ITPs and IEPs closely is the lack of coverage or too little coverage of some important adult-referenced domains (e.g., self-determination, personal care, transportation, family issues). Another issue that arose is the discrepancy between the linkage goals in the ITP generated during the planning process and the actual delivery of these services and supports at a later postschool point in time.

Professional Commentary

■ "Administrators need to work to ensure that teachers have the latitude to infuse learning opportunities in areas such as problem solving, goal setting, and decision making into classroom instruction whether the content is math or functional life skills." (Wehmeyer et al., 2000, p. 67)

■ "The absence of formal linkages is . . . distressing when one considers that self-advocacy was not addressed." (Shearin, Roessler, & Schriner, 1999, p. 14)

■ "Transition planning outcomes and activities must not be disability specific. For example, in the present study, it appears that postschool outcomes may have been decided by disability and not based on student desires." (Grigal et al., 1997, p. 370)

INVOLVEMENT OF STUDENT, FAMILY, AND ADULT SERVICE PROVIDERS

The intent of the transition process is to prepare the student for and to assist the movement to the post–high school world. Accordingly, the key players in this process must share this goal and the array of activities that will accompany it (as emphasized in Figure 1). Thus, it becomes evident that the student, the student's family, and selected adult service providers must actively be involved in this process. The issues discussed in this section focus on the amount and quality of involvement by the key players.

Student

Transition services, as defined in IDEA, should be based on the student's needs, while taking into account the student's preferences and interests. Transition activities, including assessment, planning, and follow-through, necessitate the "active" involvement of the student, whenever this is possible (i.e., some students, due to their pervasive needs, may not be able to participate at the levels suggested in this discussion). Student involvement has benefits for the student and for others who are part of the transition team, as summarized by Wehmeyer (1998) in Table 7.

In reality, students are generally passive recipients of transition services rather than the driving forces that most professionals recommend (Lehmann et al., 1999; Morningstar, Turnbull, & Turnbull, 1995). Most of the time, students do not have the information, experiences, or skills to be active participants in any aspect of the process. They feel no ownership of the transition activities that are taking place around them (Thompson et al., 2000).

To increase student involvement, schools need to prepare students for the transition planning process. This can be done by allowing students to be involved in a variety of meetings and conferences at an early age (Bassett & Lehmann, 2002). Students will also need to be taught the skills needed to be involved in the transition process (see Morningstar et al., 1999). Students also need to be offered as many opportunities as possible to make decisions, set goals, and solve problems.

Family

The reality for most families of students with disabilities is that the parents or guardians will become the service coordinators for their adult children once high school formally ends. As a

TABLE 7   Benefits of Student Involvement

BENEFITS TO STUDENT

- Students may be more motivated to pursue goals they have helped select.
- Students have the opportunity to learn and put in use already learned self-advocacy, leadership, teamwork, effective communication, and other important skills.
- Students who are involved in setting goals have more positive outcomes related to achieving those goals than with goals selected by others.

BENEFITS TO OTHER TEAM MEMBERS AND THE PROCESS

- Students can contribute firsthand information regarding areas that present the greatest and the least amount of difficulty for them and identify strategies that enable them to overcome these difficulties (from Strickland & Turnbull, 1990).
- The student's presence at the IEP meeting can personalize the meeting for team members, particularly if they do not know the student. It also enables other team members to ask the student directly about interests, skills, accommodations, and so forth (from Strickland & Turnbull, 1990).
- By including students in the decision-making process, team members communicate to students that they are expected to behave maturely and responsibly (from Strickland & Turnbull, 1990).

Source: From Wehmeyer, M. L. (1998). Student involvement in transition-planning and transition-program implementation. In F. R. Rusch & J. G. Chadsey (Eds.), *Beyond high school: Transition from school to work* (p. 210). Belmont, CA: Wadsworth Publishing. Reprinted by permission.

result, families become the main, and, in most cases, the only players in the final phase of the transition process.

An interesting dilemma arises in efforts to empower families. Empowering parents can inhibit the development and nurturing of the child's self-determination (Hanley-Maxwell, Whitney-Thomas, & Pogoloff, 1995). Achieving a proper balance between these two competing forces will take time and effort.

Major barriers to family involvement in the transition process also exist. Morningstar and colleagues (1999) identified four major barriers: (1) professional and family misperceptions, (2) limited and conflicting expectations, (3) lack of opportunity, and (4) stress during transition. In addition, families often lack important information about the transition process, postschool outcomes, and community resources (Salembier & Furney, 1997). Too often, transition planning is conducted *for* parents, not *with* them (Patton & Browder, 1988). Lastly, specific barriers can arise for culturally and linguistically diverse (CLD) families. Greene and Nefsky (n.d.) identified six potential barriers to active involvement of CLD families: (1) the CLD family's level of acculturation, (2) cultural group attitudes toward disability, (3) interpersonal communication style differences/language barriers, (4) family knowledge and comfort with the school infrastructure, (5) family perceptions of schools, and (6) special education professional knowledge and sensitivity to cultural diversity. Additional factors, identified by Salembier and Furney (1997), that inhibit parent participation in the transition process are highlighted in Table 8.

For the most part, ways to promote family involvement are straightforward techniques to address the barriers noted above. School-based personnel should strive to create comfortable working relationships with parents, characterized by frequent communication. However, this type of relationship is not achieved immediately and time must be allocated for it to develop.

Interagency Collaboration

The desire to have adult service providers serve as contributing members to the transition process has been emphasized previously (see Figure 1). Interagency collaboration and service delivery was found to be one of the few transition practices that has empirical support to be considered a best practice (Kohler, 1993). The involvement of adult agency and service providers enhances the transition for students because they are able to provide critical information and contribute to the seamless transition to postschool life by ensuring that needed supports and services are in place when the student leaves school.

Federal law requires that interagency linkages be established to increase the effectiveness of the transition services. States address the need to establish interagency planning and cooperation through formal agreements, such as memoranda of understanding (MOU). Typically, interagency agreements are between two state agencies; however, in some states, such as Texas, the agreements involve many governmental agencies.

At the school level, professionals from adult service agencies and other service providers are marginally involved in the transition process of most students. They attend the transition meetings infrequently (deFur et al., 1994), are rarely consulted regarding transition plans

TABLE 8   Factors Inhibiting Parent Involvement

FACTORS CONTRIBUTING TO UNSATISFACTORY PARENT/PROFESSIONAL RELATIONSHIPS

- Teachers and/or adult services representatives fail to attend or leave meetings.
- Team membership changes frequently.
- Professionals do not appear to listen to parents.
- Professionals are not prepared to answer questions and/or seem to lack knowledge about community resources.

FACTORS CONTRIBUTING TO A SENSE THAT IEP/TRANSITION PLANNING MEETINGS ARE PREDETERMINED

- Parent input is not requested prior to meeting.
- IEP/transition goals and objectives appear to have been decided on or written prior to meeting.
- School and/or agency personnel seem to control meeting agenda and discussion.

BARRIERS RELATED TO THE LANGUAGE AND LEGAL ASPECTS OF IEP/TRANSITION PLANNING

- Teachers have not fully explained the purpose of transition planning.
- Language of IEP/transition plan is unclear.
- Legal nature of the IEP makes it difficult to state goals and objectives in language that reflects student needs and interests.

Source: From Salembier, G., & Furney, K. S. (1997). Facilitating participation: Parents' perceptions of their involvement in the IEP/transition planning process. *Career Development for Exceptional Individuals, 20*(1), 29–42. Reprinted by permission.

by school-based personnel (Thompson et al., 2000), and are contacted for use of their services less frequently than one might expect (Colley & Jamison, 1998).

A number of reasons can contribute to this situation. Benz, Johnson, Mikkelsen, and Linstrom (1995) remarked that effective procedures for structuring collaborative efforts are often nonexistent. Another factor is that adult service providers work in different systems that require their time and attention at a higher level of priority, regardless of the agreements that have been made at the state level. Moreover, these providers are under no personal legal obligation to be active participants in the transition process, although federal law suggests that they should. Thus, the result is inevitable—minimal involvement.

Ways to increase better interagency collaboration and involvement focus primarily on ensuring that channels of communication remain open and active. The establishment of state-level and community-level transition teams are also very useful mechanisms (see Blalock & Benz, 1999). Scheduling transition meetings at times that better accommodate service provider's schedules can be helpful. School-based personnel must become as knowledgeable as possible about the array of local adult services so they can "represent" these services at times when they are discussed.

Professional Commentary

■ "Because there seem to be few opportunities for students with disabilities to practice skills related to self-advocacy, empowerment, and leadership activities, it appears that the transition meeting may be an important venue for linking students' involvement to school transition-related activities." (Lehmann et al., 1999, p. 168)

■ "Parents who were most enthusiastic about their participation in transition planning meetings believed that their relationships with professionals had developed over time, were characterized by a sense of trust and shared responsibility, and were based on frequent, interactive communication between parents and professionals." (Salembier & Furney, 1997, p. 39)

■ "In seeking to understand a family's cultural background and experience, professionals should express their interest and respect for the family's customs and traditions by asking them which are important to them rather than assuming which aspects are most important." (Hanley-Maxwell, Pogoloff, & Whitney-Thomas, 1998, p. 254)

■ "IDEA clearly signals that preparing students to move from school to postschool environments is not the *sole* responsibility of public education." (Dunn, 1996, p. 29)

PRESERVICE/IN-SERVICE PREPARATION

The issue of personnel preparation has already been discussed briefly in this chapter. The importance of this issue is supported by the results of the study Bassett et al. (1997) conducted on critical research issues in the field of transition (see Table 4). In this study, researchers identified teacher training as the most important research issue. The DCDT considers this topic to be so critical in the field that it is developing a detailed position paper on it.

The role of secondary special educators is changing, and both preservice preparation programs and in-service professional development efforts must respond to these changes. While transition responsibilities is only one aspect of this change, it is noteworthy because most secondary level teachers do not feel they are competent in areas associated with providing transition services (deFur, 1999; Foley & Mundschenk, 1997).

Wolfe, Boone, Filbert, and Atanasoff (2000) analyzed coverage of transition in the programs of fifty-two universities from across the country. They found that thirty-six of these covered transition in their coursework, with twenty-four of these institutions offering a specific course on transition. Interestingly, Wolfe et al. also found that transition coursework is not required for certification in many states. These results highlight the current state of affairs, in which it is still very unlikely for preservice teachers to acquire the knowledge and skills needed for the new roles at the secondary level.

Professional Commentary

■ "In the area of transition to adult life, there is little formalized preparation of special education personnel." (Sitlington et al., 2000, p. 337)

■ "A common theme . . . was 'lack of knowledge' [of transition team members] . . . including (a) lack of knowledge of adult agency services; (b) lack of professional knowledge; and (c) lack of knowledge of consumer participants and their situations." (Gallivan-Fenlon, 1994, p. 16)

ADDITIONAL RESEARCH NEEDS

The subspecialty area of transition within the larger arena of special education has grown in the last decade. Along with expansion comes the inevitable scrutiny and reevaluation of the field's history and future. This field is at a point where many lines of research need to be encouraged and supported.

One of the major themes covered in this chapter is that we lack certainty about best transition practices. There has been so little research in the area of transition that practitioners are gasping for validation of the many "valued" practices (Everson et al., 2001) that are being used every day. Some of the most pressing areas needing research activity are listed in Table 9.

FINAL THOUGHTS

The future of the field of transition is hard to predict. The bright light has dimmed some on the field. While the mandate still exists, the excitement associated with the transition movement in the 1990s has diminished over time.

Let me share an example of what I mean. I usually can identify a theme or hot topic/issue at every conference sponsored by the DCDT. At the 1999 conference, the dominant theme was "self-determination." The topic that consumed the attention of secondary level practitioners was "standards." One participant commented that there is not time for transition anymore—all of her attention had to be directed to getting her students through the curriculum to prepare them for "high-stakes" tests. Times have changed.

TABLE 9   Areas of Research Activity

CONCEPT OF TRANSITION

- What do educators believe transition planning really is?
- What subtleties exist across disciplines (education, vocational rehabilitation, employment services, housing) regarding what transition is and how it should be implemented?

KEY ELEMENTS OF THE TRANSITION PROCESS

- Which elements of the transition process have the most effect on positive adult outcomes?
- Which elements of the process do school-based practitioners actually do?
- Which elements of the process are school-based practitioners likely to do—i.e., willing to do?

BEST PRACTICES

- For which aspects of the transition planning process is there evidence of effectiveness?
- Which qualitative aspects of transition practices are noteworthy?
- What is the long-term effect (five years or more) of transition practices?
- Can more "recommended" (i.e., nonvalidated) practices be shown to have empirical support for their effectiveness?

COMPLIANCE

- What are schools doing today in the name of transition planning?
- Are the minimum requirements of IDEA being followed?
- What do school-based personnel believe is compliance?
- How wide is the gap between compliance activities and best/recommended practices?
- How have transition planning activities been challenged by families—via hearings or litigation?
- What is the relationship between transition planning and the provisions afforded by Section 504?

CURRICULAR IMPLICATIONS

- To what extent is functional content covered in the curriculum of secondary-level students with disabilities in schools today?
- How can functional topics be addressed in an era of standards-based reform?
- How much attention is actually being given to the development of self-determination?
- How can important functional (i.e., meaningful) content be taught so that it is relevant to students' lives?

TRANSITION ASSESSMENT AND PLANNING

- What types of assessments are most powerful for planning a student's future?
- How early should the assessment process actually begin?
- Are current assessment practices sensitive to cultural and linguistic differences?
- What types of transition-related goals are being included in students' IEPs?
- Is transition planning comprehensive?
- What is the best document for housing information about transition goals?

(continued)

TABLE 9   Continued

INVOLVEMENT (STUDENT, FAMILY, ADULT SERVICES)

- How involved are students, families, and adult service providers in the transition planning process?
- What roles do students, family members, and other participants play at transition planning meetings?
- When should families begin to think about postschool realities?
- How do cultural and linguistic factors impact the transition planning process?
- Do students from different cultural backgrounds still have different outcomes than their European American peers?

PRESERVICE/IN-SERVICE PREPARATION

- How is "transition" typically covered in special education teacher preparation programs?
- Which content about transition should be covered in special education teacher preparation programs?
- How is transition addressed through the professional development activities of schools?
- Are transition specialists/coordinators being adequately prepared for their roles in schools?

Even in the context of a brand-new world in schools, we must remain optimistic that the concept of transition services is sound and should not be abandoned. Promoting the development of self-determined students is the right thing to do. Assisting students and their families to better prepare for the "life after" (school) is justifiable.

REFERENCES

Alberto, P. A., Taber, T. A., Brozovic, S. A., & Elliot, N. E. (1997). Continuing issues of collaborative transition planning in the secondary school. *Journal of Vocational Rehabilitation, 8,* 197–204.

Baer, R., Simmons, T., & Flexer, R. (1996). Transition practice and policy compliance in Ohio: A survey of secondary special educators. *Career Development for Exceptional Individuals, 19,* 61–71.

Bassett, D. S., & Lehmann, J. (2002). *Student-focused conferencing and planning.* Austin, TX: PRO-ED.

Bassett, D. S., Patton, J. R., White, W., Blalock, G., & Smith, T. E. C. (1997). Research issues in career development and transition: An exploratory survey of professionals in the field. *Career Development for Exceptional Individuals, 20,* 81–100.

Benz, M. R., Johnson, D. K., Mikkelsen, K. S., & Linstrom, L. E. (1995). Improving collaboration between schools and vocational rehabilitation: Stakeholder identified barriers and strategies. *Career Development for Exceptional Individuals, 18,* 133–144.

Blalock, G., & Benz, M. R. (1999). *Using community transition teams to improve transition services.* Austin, TX: PRO-ED.

Brolin, D. E. (1995). *Career education: A functional life skills approach* (3rd ed.). Englewood Cliffs, NJ: Prentice-Hall/Merrill.

Brown, L., Nietupski, J., & Hamre-Nietupski, S. (1976). Criterion of ultimate functioning. In M. A. Thomas (Ed.), *Hey, don't forget about me!* (pp. 2–15). Reston, VA: Council for Exceptional Children.

Browning, P. (Ed.). (1997). *Transition in action for youth and young adults with disabilities.* Montgomery, AL: Wells Printing.

Bureau of Education for the Handicapped. (1975, January). *Proceedings of the conference on research needs related to career education for the handicapped.* Washington, DC: U. S. Government Printing Office.

Clark, G. M., Field, S., Patton, J. R., Brolin, D. E., & Sitlington, P. L. (1994). Life skills instruction: A necessary component for all students with disabilities. A position statement of the Division on Career Development and Transition. *Career Development for Exceptional Individuals, 17,* 125–134.

Colley, D. A., & Jamison, D. (1998). Post school results for youth with disabilities: Key indicators and policy implications. *Career Development for Exceptional Individuals, 21,* 145–160.

deFur, S. H. (1999). Special education, transition, and school-based services: Are they meant for each other? In S. H. deFur & J. R. Patton (Eds.), *Transition and school-based services* (pp. 15–50). Austin, TX: PRO-ED.

deFur, S., Getzel, E. E., & Kregel, J. (1994). Individual transition plans: A work in progress. *Journal of Vocational Rehabilitation, 4,* 139–145.

Dunn, C. (1996). A status report on transition planning for individuals with learning disabilities. *Journal of Learning Disabilities, 29,* 17–30.

Edgar, E. (1988). Employment as an outcome for mildly handicapped students: Current status and future directions. *Focus on Exceptional Children, 21*(1), 1–8.

Edgar, E., & Polloway, E. A. (1994). Education for adolescents with disabilities: Curriculum and placement issues. *Journal of Special Education, 27,* 438–452.

Eisenman, L. T. (2000). Characteristics and effects of integrated academic and occupational curricula for students with disabilities: A literature review. *Career Development for Exceptional Individuals, 23,* 105–119.

Everson, J. M., & Guillory, J. D. (1998). Building statewide transition services through collaborative interagency teamwork. In F. R. Rusch & J. G. Chadsey (Eds.), *Beyond high school: Transition from school to work* (pp. 299–318). Baltimore: Paul Brookes.

Everson, J. M., Zhang, D., & Guillory, J. D. (2001). A statewide investigation of individualized transition plans in Louisiana. *Career Development for Exceptional Individuals, 24,* 37–49.

Flexer, R. W., Simmons, T. J., Luft, P., & Baer, R. M. (2001). *Transition planning for secondary students with disabilities.* Upper Saddle River, NJ: Merrill/Prentice Hall.

Foley, R. M., & Mundschenk, N. A. (1997). Collaboration activities and competencies of secondary special educators: A national survey. *Teacher Education and Special Education, 20,* 47–60.

Gallivan-Fenlon, A. (1994). "Their senior year": Family and service provider perspectives on the transition from school to adult life for young adults with disabilities. *JASH, 19,* 11–23.

Greene, G., & Albright, L. (1995). "Best practices" in transition services: Do they exist? *Career Development for Exceptional Individuals, 18,* 1–2.

Greene, G., & Nefsky, P. (n.d.). Transition for culturally and linguistically diverse youth with disabilities: Closing the gaps. *Multiple Voices, 3*(1), 15–24.

Grigal, M., Test, D. W., Beattie, J., & Wood, W. M. (1997). An evaluation of transition components of individualized education programs. *Exceptional Children, 63,* 357–372.

Hanley-Maxwell, C., Pogoloff, S. M., & Whitney-Thomas, J. (1998). Families: The heart of transition. In F. R. Rusch & J. G. Chadsey (Eds.), *Beyond high school: Transition from school to work* (pp. 234–264). Baltimore: Paul Brookes.

Hanley-Maxwell, C., Whitney-Thomas, J., & Pogoloff, S. (1995). The second shock: Parental perspectives of their child's transition from school to adult life. *Journal of the Association for Persons with Severe Handicaps, 201*(1), 3–16.

Halpern, A. S. (1985). Transition: A look at the foundations. *Exceptional Children, 51,* 479–486.

Johnson, J. R., & Rusch, F. R. (1993). Educational reform and special education: Foundations for a national research agenda focused upon secondary education. In P. D. Kohler, J. R. Johnson, J. Chadsey-Rusch, & F. R. Rusch (Eds.), *Transition from school to adult life: Foundations, best practices, and research directions* (pp. 77–104). Champaign-Urbana: University of Illinois, Transition Research Institute.

Kohler, P. D. (1993). Best practices in transition: Substantiated or implied. *Career Development for Exceptional Individuals, 16,* 107–121.

Kohler, P. D. (1996). *A taxonomy for transition programming: Linking research and practice.* Urbana-Champaign, IL: University of Illinois, Transition Research Institute.

Kohler, P. D. (1998). Implementing a transition perspective of education: A comprehensive approach to planning and delivering secondary education and transition services. In F. R. Rusch & J. G. Chadsey (Eds.), *Beyond high school: Transition from school to work* (pp. 179–205). Baltimore: Paul Brookes.

Krom, D. M., & Prater, M. A. (1993). IEP goals for intermediate-aged students with mild mental retardation. *Career Development for Exceptional Individuals, 16,* 87–95.

Lehmann, J. P., Bassett, D. S., & Sands, D. J. (1999). Students' participation in transition-related actions. *Remedial and Special Education, 20,* 160–169.

Leonte, P. J. (1999). Vocational education. In S. H. deFur & J. R. Patton (Eds.), *Transition and school-based services* (pp. 387–417). Austin, TX: PRO-ED.

McMahan, R. (2001). IDEA transition policy compliance and best practice: Perceptions of transition stakeholders. *Career Development for Exceptional Individuals, 24,* 169–184.

Morningstar, M. E., Kleinhammer-Tramill, P. J., & Lattin, D. L. (1999). Using successful models of student-centered transition planning and services for adolescents with disabilities. *Focus on Exceptional Children, 31*(9), 1–19.

Morningstar, M. E., Turnbull, A. P., & Turnbull, H. R. (1995). What do students with disabilities tell us about the importance of family involvement in the transition from school to adult life? *Exceptional Children, 62,* 249–260.

Neubert, D. A. (1997). Time to grow: The history—and future—of preparing youth for adult roles in society. *Teaching Exceptional Children, 29*(5), 5–17.

Patton, J. R., & Browder, P. M. (1988). Transition into the future. In B. L. Ludlow, A. P. Turnbull, & R. Luckasson (Eds.), *Transitions to adult life for people with mental retardation: Principles and practices* (293–311). Baltimore: Paul Brookes.

Patton, J. R., & Dunn, C. (1998). *Transition from school to young adulthood: Basic concepts and recommended practices.* Austin, TX: PRO-ED.

Patton, J. R., Polloway, E. A., Smith, T. E. C., Edgar, E., Clark, G. M., & Lee, S. (1996). Individuals with mild mental retardation: Postsecondary outcomes and implications for educational policy. *Education and Training in Mental Retardation and Developmental Disabilities, 31,* 75–85.

Patton, J. R., & Trainor, A. (2002). Using applied academics to enhance curricular reform in secondary education. In C. Kochhar-Bryant & D. S. Bassett (Eds.), *Aligning transition and standards-based education: Issues and strategies* (pp. 55–75). Arlington, VA: CEC.

Repetto, J. B., White, W. J., & Snauwaert, D. T. (1990). Individualized transition plans (ITP): A national perspective. *Career Development for Exceptional Individuals, 13,* 109–119.

Roessler, R., Shearin, A., & Williams, E. (2000). Three recommendations to improve transition planning in the IEP. *Journal for Vocational Special Needs Education, 22*(2), 31–36.

Rusch, F. R., & Chadsey, J. G. (Eds.). (1998). *Beyond high school: Transition from school to work* (2nd ed.). Belmont, CA: Wadsworth.

Salembier, G., & Furney, K. S. (1997). Facilitating participation: Parents' perceptions of their involvement in the IEP/transition planning process. *Career Development for Exceptional Individuals, 20,* 29–42.

Shearin, A., Roessler, R., & Schriner, K. (1999). *Evaluating the transition component in IEPs of secondary students with disabilities.* Unpublished manuscript, University of Arkansas.

Sitlington, P. L., Clark, G. M., & Kolstoe, O. P. (2000). *Transition education and services for adolescents with disabilities* (3rd ed.). Boston: Allyn & Bacon.

Stodden, R. A. (1998). School-to-work transition: Overview of disability legislation. In F. R. Rusch & J. G. Chadsey (Eds.), *Beyond high school: Transition from school to work* (pp. 60–76). Baltimore: Paul Brookes.

Thompson, J. R., Fulk, B. M., & Piercy, S. W. (2000). Do individualized transition plans match the postschool projections of students with learning disabilities and their parents? *Career Development for Exceptional Individuals, 23,* 3–25.

Wagner, M., Blackorby, J., Cameto, R., Hebbeler, K., & Newman, L. (1993). *The transition experiences of young people with disabilities: A summary of findings from the National Longitudinal Transition Study of special education students.* Menlo Park, CA: SRI International.

Ward, M. J., & Kohler, P. D. (1996a). Promoting self-determination for individuals with disabilities: Content and process. In L. E. Powers, G. H. S. Singer, & J. Sowers (Eds.), *On the road to autonomy: Promoting self-competence in children and youth with disabilities* (pp. 275–290). Baltimore: Paul Brookes.

Ward, M. J., & Kohler, P. D. (1996b). *Teaching self-determination: Content and process.* Baltimore: Paul Brookes.

Wehman, P. (2001). *Life beyond the classroom: Transition strategies for young people with disabilities* (3rd ed.). Baltimore: Paul H. Brookes.

Wehmeyer, M. L. (1998). Student involvement in transition-planning and transition-program implementation. In F. R. Rusch & J. G. Chadsey (Eds.), *Beyond high school: Transition from school to work* (pp. 206–233). Baltimore: Paul Brookes.

Wehmeyer, M. L., Agran, M., & Hughes, C. (2000). A national survey of teachers' promotion of self-determination and student-directed learning. *Journal of Special Education, 34,* 58–68.

Wehmeyer, M. L., & Schalock, R. L. (2001). Self-determination and quality of life: Implications for special education services and supports. *Focus on Exceptional Children, 33* (8), 1–16.

Will, M. (1984). *OSERS programming for the transition of youth with disabilities: Bridges from school to working life.* Washington, DC: Office of Special Education and Rehabilitative Services.

Wimmer, B. D., & Sitlington, P. L. (1981). A survey of research priorities in career education for the handicapped. *Career Development for Exceptional Individuals, 4,* 50–58.

Wolfe, P. S., Boone, R. S., Filbert, M., & Atanasoff, L. M. (2000). Training preservice teachers for inclusion and transition: How well are we doing? *Journal of Vocational Special Needs Education, 22*(2), 20–30.

TRENDS AND ISSUES IN INSTRUCTIONAL AND ASSISTIVE TECHNOLOGY

HERBERT J. RIETH
University of Texas at Austin

LINDA K. COLBURN
Vanderbilt University

DIANE PEDROTTY BRYANT
University of Texas at Austin

INTRODUCTION AND OVERVIEW

This chapter examines trends and issues that have shaped the use of instructional and assistive technology with students with disabilities. The chapter begins with a brief overview of the history of the application of technology to instruct students with disabilities. This is followed by a discussion of issues that have impacted the emergence and refinement of instruction that involves the use of technology. The remainder of the chapter consists of an analysis of four issues that are currently of considerable importance to the field of instructional and assistive technology: hardware and software; training, professional development, and support to enable teachers to use technology; strategies and models to enable teachers to integrate technology into their daily teaching; and the development of new strategies to assess student learning.

HISTORICAL OVERVIEW OF INSTRUCTIONAL TECHNOLOGY

During the 1970s, computer technology was introduced amidst great optimism as the latest and perhaps the most potent innovation designed to transform and enhance the learning of students with disabilities. The optimism was premised on the belief that computer software could (1) simplify the individualization of instruction, (2) provide immediate feedback and consistent error correction procedures, (3) create opportunities for students to emit and practice responses, (4) increase student motivation, (5) provide immediate reinforcement for correct responses, and (6) provide frequent opportunities for students to make responses (Budoff, Thormann, & Gras, 1984). Computer technology, it was reasoned, held potential to enhance the individualization of instruction by accommodating students' needs, interests, current knowledge, and learning styles, thereby improving their performance and producing better outcomes (President's Committee of Advisors on Science and Technology [PCAST], 1997; Rieth, Bryant, & Woodward, 2001).

The professional literature, from the 1970s to the early 1990s, was dominated by studies comparing computer-based instruction (CBI) with traditional instruction. Overall, the results were mixed and supported the conclusion that the effectiveness of CBI for improving education was limited (Okolo, Bahr, & Rieth, 1993; Roschelle, Pea, Hoadley, Gordin, & Means, 2000; Woodward, Gallagher, & Rieth, 2001). These studies suggested that certain computer-based applications enhanced learning for students at various achievement levels. Reviews and meta-analyses conducted by Ellis and Sabornie (1986); Fitzgerald and Koury (1996); Okolo et al. (1993); Schmidt, Weinstein, Niemic, and Walberg (1985), and Shiah, Mastropieri, and Scruggs (1995) provided additional support that CBI can, under certain conditions, enhance the learning of students with mild disabilities. Analyses by Okolo et al. (1993), Woodward and Rieth (1997) and Woodward et al. (2001) provided detailed descriptions of research studies that used technology to teach students with disabilities.

The focus of the research conducted during the late 1980s and early 1990s was inextricably altered by an article written by Clark (1983). Clark portrayed technology as a vehicle capable of delivering instructional procedures demonstrated as effective in enhancing student learning. Subsequent to the publication of this article, the research agenda gradually shifted from comparisons of the efficacy of CBI and traditional instruction to analyses of the effectiveness of software that employed proven learning principles. These included (1) increased opportunities to practice key responses, (2) increased access to immediate and detailed feedback, (3) distribution of practice, (4) development of cognitive strategies, and (5) analyses of motivational strategies (Woodward et al., 2001).

Although early reports of the positive effects of CBI for students with mild disabilities were encouraging, evidence has accumulated over the years to suggest that these students have not uniformly benefited from instructional technology. In fact, more recent literature related to this issue has revealed difficulties involved in translating a promising innovation into a consistently effective educational practice (Woodward & Rieth, 1997).

ISSUES AFFECTING THE IMPLEMENTATION OF TECHNOLOGY

Over the years a series of issues have been identified that interfere with effective implementation of technology and thereby reduce its overall impact. For example, Rieth, Bahr, Okolo, Polsgrove, and Eckert (1988) reported that despite findings demonstrating that the use of microcomputers was related to increased student task engagement and decreased off-task behavior, only 60 percent of the teachers in their sample chose to use them for instruction. Furthermore, the teachers who used computers for instruction were observed to use them for only 25.3 percent of the instructional period. The infrequent use was attributed to a lack of appropriate software, logistical problems in scheduling access to the computer, and a lack of training and support for teachers. The aforementioned issues have frequently been cited as barriers to effectively implementing technology in classroom settings that include students with disabilities (Woodward et al., 2001).

More recently, Means (1994) and Roschelle, Pea, Hoadley, Gordin, and Means (2000) suggested several reasons for the varying results associated with classroom applications of technology. First, the limitations of available hardware and software coupled with the wide variation in the way schools use technology has produced differential effects across schools. Second, often teachers are not instructed to use technology effectively (Means, 1994). Third, successful use of technology requires concurrent reforms in other areas such as curriculum modification and teacher professional development. The process required to attain agreement regarding the content and implementation of curricular change and staff development is time consuming and fraught with complexity, thereby contributing to the variability of the results associated with the use of instructional technology.

The literature on school and classroom change provides insights regarding effective strategies for facilitating the implementation of an instructional innovation for students with disabilities (Evans, 1996; Rosenholtz, 1989). Fullan and Stiegelbauer (1991) reaffirm the difficulty associated with implementing instructional change. They suggest that too often professionals perceive change as a simplified one-dimensional process rather than as a complex, multidimensional process involving people's perceptions of their professional competence and feelings of self-worth. Therefore, professionals must be mindful of this complexity in establishing realistic expectations for the use of and impact of technology on the learning of students with disabilities. For instance, it is unrealistic to assume that teachers trained to implement an instructional innovation will immediately and completely modify their teaching and curriculum in order to incorporate the innovation. Successful implementation requires that teachers must first be active participants in considering the change and then rigorously trained to implement the innovation (Fullan & Stiegelbauer, 1991). Finally, they must be provided support as they endeavor to implement the innovation (Rieth et al., 1988).

CURRENT RESEARCH FOCI

Roschelle et al. (2000) suggest that one of the major scientific accomplishments of the twentieth century has been the advancement of understanding cognitive science and the use of instructional interventions that incorporate this knowledge. For example, it has been shown that learning is most effective when four fundamental characteristics of effective instruction are present: (1) active engagement, (2) participation in groups, (3) frequent interaction and feedback, and (4) connections to real-world contexts. As research has facilitated our understanding about the fundamental characteristics of learning, it has become more apparent that traditional classrooms often do not support learning, whereas instructional technology (when used effectively) can enable ways of teaching that better match how children learn (Roschelle et al., 2000).

Rieth, Bryant, Kinzer, Colburn, Hur, Hartmann, and Choi (2003) and Williams Glaser, Rieth, Kinzer, Colburn, Prestidge, and Peter (1999) incorporated the four fundamental characteristics of effective instruction into a multimedia-based intervention called anchored instruction (Cognition and Technology Group at Vanderbilt [CTGV], 1990). Multimedia anchored instruction is an instructional technique, which begins with a focal event or problem situation presented via a video segment or movie, that provides the opportunity for students to create a mental model or an "anchor" to facilitate learning (Rieth & Kinzer, 2000). The intervention was tested in a series of middle and high school classes that included students with disabilities. The authors reported general and special education students improved their performance on a host of dependent measures including the type and length of interactions and questioning, their general knowledge about important events, research skills, and critical thinking (Rieth et al., 2003). The students flourished in an academic environment that actively involved them in learning and in applying knowledge to solve "real life" problems. This is in direct contrast to traditional instructional environments where they were passive recipients of instruction and their teachers did much of the thinking for them.

Hasselbring (2001) suggests that research over the past several decades has expanded our understanding of human learning. He argues that synergy between technological advances and a deepening understanding of human learning will be an influential force in the future. Basically, there is broad agreement that the next decade will witness substantial work focused on using our increasing understanding of cognition to guide the development of instructional interventions that employ technology. However, if this is to come to fruition, the field needs a better model for helping teachers understand the relationship between technology and learning (Hasselbring, 2001; Hofstetter, 2001). To accomplish this, teachers will need greater access to the latest and best technology, training to effectively use technology, and support systems that include personnel and materials. As a profession, we also will need assessment tools that (1) better match treatment to diagnosis to increase the efficacy of our interventions (Tinker, 2001), (2) more effectively measure higher order thinking, and (3) monitor student performance during group instruction. All of this will occur during a period when technology will become smaller, faster, and cheaper (Hasselbring, 2001).

In the next section we explore four issues that have played and will continue to play an influential role in the research related to effectively using technology to enhance the instructional outcomes attained by students with disabilities. These issues include access to hardware and software; training and support for teachers using technology; strategies and models to enable teachers to integrate technology into their daily teaching; and the development of new strategies to assess student higher order learning.

ISSUES

Access

Over the last twenty years the number of computers in American schools increased steadily, from 250,000 in 1983 to 8.6 million in 1998, while the average number of students per computer fell from approximately forty in 1985 to seven in 1998 (Becker, 2000). As the number of computers in the schools increased, researchers began to examine whether students with disabilities had access to technology and to compare their access with that of their peers without disabilities.

In the mid 1980s, for example, Cosden and a group of researchers at the University of California Santa Barbara (Christensen & Cosden, 1986; Cosden, Gerber, Goldman, Semmel, & Semmel, 1986) conducted a series of studies investigating the amount and type of access that students with disabilities had to technology in special and general education settings. Overall, they reported that students with disabilities appeared to have access to computers that was roughly equivalent to their peers without disabilities (Cosden et al., 1986), although access varied, according to the location of the student's placement. For example, students with disabilities who were placed in special day classes usually worked on computers only in their special education classrooms. This finding is troubling for two reasons. First, students who access computers in special education settings typically only have access to drill and practice software. They do not routinely have access to more sophisticated software that is designed to facilitate higher order thinking and problem solving (Cosden & Abernathy, 1990). If students with disabilities are to have more opportunities to work with complex software applications, teachers will need access to software, training, and time to practice using software successfully. Otherwise, the teachers are likely to continue using computers primarily for drill-and-practice activities (Becker, 2000).

Second, and perhaps more importantly, the students with disabilities are deprived of opportunities to work with their peers on class-related projects. This limitation of access may have multiple side effects that minimize the acquisition of essential academic and social skills (Roschelle et al., 2000). Lou, Abrami, Spence, Poulson, Chambers, and Apollonia (1996) provided evidence indicating that small group learning was an effective instructional strategy for struggling learners. In a subsequent meta-analysis Lou, Abrami, and Apollonia (2001) reported that small group learning (involving computers) produced significantly more positive effects on individual student achievement than individual learning (involving computers). The authors also indicated that the effects of small group learning using computer technology are enhanced when students have prior group learning experience and when the teacher uses cooperative learning strategies (Lou et al., 2001). Research reported by Roschelle et al. (2000) also suggested that students working in small groups involving computers tend to make more rapid and greater progress in learning than students working in large groups.

In a related study that examined the impact of socioeconomic status on computer access, Becker (2000) reported that differences in computer access exist based on a school's socioeconomic status. Although this research did not directly target students with disabilities, the findings are highly relevant to students with disabilities given the overrepresentation of students from low-income groups in special education programs. Interestingly, the differences in access were not reflected in the numbers of computers so much as in type of software and Internet access. Generally, students from low-income families were enrolled in schools that were about one to two years behind schools with students primarily from average-income families and another one to two years behind schools with students mostly from high-income families. The expectation is that this trend will continue well into the future (Becker, 2000).

Overall, the data from these studies suggest students with disabilities are often relegated to working independently on low-level software that will predictably limit student-learning outcomes. The findings create a sense of urgency for conducting research that examines strategies for optimizing access to effective software and to grouping arrangements that enhance the learning outcomes of students with disabilities. There also is a pressing need for research to address the issue of ensuring students equal access to classrooms where teachers have been trained to effectively use computers and to provide instruction using the most sophisticated and creative uses of computers and computer software.

Training and Support

To effectively use educational technology, teachers have to master a variety of powerful hardware and software tools, redesign their lesson plans around technology-enhanced resources, solve logistical problems related to teaching a class of students with a limited number of computers, and take on a complex new role in the technologically transformed classroom (PCAST, 1997). Yet, information reported by PCAST suggests that teachers may receive little technical, pedagogic or administrative support for these fundamental changes, and few colleges of education adequately prepare their graduates to use information technologies in their teaching. Derer, Polsgrove, and Rieth (1996) reported survey data that reaffirmed teacher's perceptions that additional training was required if they were to use computer technology for instruction. The need for training teachers to effectively use technology is further rationalized by broad agreement that the next decades will witness a greater emphasis on instruction focused on higher order thinking skills (Hasselbring, 2001). Teachers will need increased skills to select appropriate software, effectively integrate technology into the curriculum, and devise ways of assessing student work based on potentially complex individual and group projects (PCAST, 1997). The need for additional skills dictates the need for additional training and support systems designed to help teachers effectively employ these new and powerful instructional tools.

Adequately addressing the need for teacher training will require a multifaceted approach encompassing pre- and in-service teacher education. At the preservice level, data suggest that while students in training receive more technology-related instruction than do active teachers, most of the training involves instruction involving the operation of software packages (PCAST, 1997). New teachers typically graduate with little or no experience in using computers to teach and are not prepared to integrate technology into their daily classroom instruction (PCAST, 1997). Langone, Malone, and Clinton (1999) argued for the importance of having technology applications modeled by pre-service teacher trainers but suggest, however, that few students have access to university-based or school-based models of how technology can be used for instruction. Further, if teacher trainees' experiences related to teaching are limited to traditional models of instruction, they are much less likely to be able to employ the more powerful and "higher order thinking" instructional applications of computer technology. Relatedly, Langone et al. (1999) conducted a pilot study to investigate the impact of anchored instruction on the content knowledge test scores of preservice special education teachers. They reported no immediate differences in student performance on posttest measures. However, the anchored instruction group outperformed the traditional instruction group on a follow-up test administered eight weeks after training was provided, suggesting that benefits of training may be more long term (Langone et al., 1999). Overall, the results—although preliminary—provide support for additional research analyzing the impact of technology-based instruction on the ability of teacher trainees to learn about and implement it effectively in the classroom.

Currently employed teachers also will require training and support if they are to effectively implement technology-based instruction. If such training is to succeed, essential conditions for the promotion of instructional change must be accommodated. Berman and McLaughlin (1978) reported the conditions needed to promote change were (1) successful staff training, (2) frequent and regular support systems for teachers and staff, (3) a critical mass of participants committed to adopting the innovation, and (4) administrator awareness of change procedures and support for teachers. Despite the recognized critical importance of these factors, there are few if any studies reported that have employed these principles to train teachers to effectively implement technology.

Technology Integration

Reports from national organizations and government leaders, as well as the scholarly work of prominent educators, have acknowledged that higher order thinking and a capacity for problem solving are critical to the academic and professional success of students in today's classrooms (Bransford, Brown, & Cocking, 2000; OTA, 1995; PCAST, 1997; Sternberg & Spear-Swerling, 1996). Students must be able to collaborate with diverse groups of people, reason and solve new problems, as well as speak and write well in order to meet the expectations of their future employers in business and industry (Dede, 2000; National Education Goals Panel, 1998).

When used effectively as an integral element of instruction, technology can be an instrument for promoting the achievement of these goals and expectations (Bransford et al., 2000; Morgan, 1996; National Education Technology Standards [NETS], 2000). Studies that have examined links between specific uses of technology and higher order thinking have identified positive causal relationships (CTGV, 1992; Wenglinsky, 1998). Additionally, research on the use of video-based anchored instruction involving students with mild disabilities has demonstrated significant improvement in critical thinking skills for these students (Hur, 2001).

Based on research reports, professional standards released in the last decade identify the need to train teachers to offer students, including those with disabilities, meaningful and purposeful uses of technology contextualized within the curriculum (NETS, 2000; OTA, 1995; PCAST, 1997). In contrast, a recent article illustrated that only a few students benefit from access to integrated technology, and unfortunately for a majority of students it is isolated and not integrated into the general curriculum (Peck, Cuban, & Kirkpatrick, 2002). Our schools must provide all students, not just a select few, with the opportunity to develop technological literacy. New technologies are expensive to purchase and require time and intensive effort to implement them effectively; and they will be worth the cost only when used appropriately and equitably (Dede, 2000). According to Dede, to realize the full benefit of learning technologies, we must have "sustained, large-scale innovations" across all facets of schooling (p. 171).

Accomplishing this purpose requires a meaningful integration of technologies across all disciplines through an investment of teacher time for thoughtful planning and careful implementation (Sandholtz, Ringstaff, & Dwyer, 1997; Valovich, 1996). Administrative and technological support is critical, as is the ongoing offering of professional development opportunities (Guhlin, 2002; Willis & Raines, 2001). Successful integration requires the deep curricular expertise of teachers within their discipline. In a recent study of teachers' use of technology, the researcher observed that teachers who fluidly integrated technology also had an identifiable intersection of content knowledge, pedagogical knowledge, and technological knowledge—not just basic competency, but an understanding of how particular uses of technology can support instruction (Pierson, 2001). Beyond knowing how to use technology, classroom teachers must know how to weave it into the curriculum so that it is an integral part of daily instruction. As Colburn (2000) recently observed, those teachers who were the most effective at apparently "seamlessly" integrating technology engaged students in its use nearly every day.

Sometimes unintentionally, teachers' instructional approaches have changed, such as in the previously cited study in which a teacher stated that student-centered instruction was a by-product of technology use (Colburn, 2000). In other cases, teachers have identified a need for instructional change and have employed technology as one means of effecting change. Riel (2000) stated that teachers' roles change when there are "significant shifts in the organization of the learning environments, the orientation of learners, and availability of instructional tools and technology" (p. 1).

For teachers to effectively use technology, they must make the shift from thinking of it as an add-on and outside the curriculum (Stallard & Cocker, 2001). Integrating technology into the classroom curriculum is a more effective way of implementing the use of instructional technologies than is positioning technology as a "stand alone" or supplemental tool. Technology can be an enormously powerful tool that can change the nature of instruction and learning. However, teachers must move from using it simply to expedite the way things have always been done to envisioning how technology can be best used to benefit all students instructionally. Teachers who use multimedia tools to enliven their lectures may be learning personally how to use technology, but they are not providing their students with the opportunity to use technology to research, create, communicate, simulate, or present (NETS, 2000).

In contrast, within an effective educational setting, technology can enable students to become capable information technology users, information seekers, analyzers and evaluators. Students can learn to be problem solvers who are proficient at communicating, collaborating, publishing, and producing multimedia products (NETS, 2000). It is these students who are becoming the citizens of the twenty-first century, a century with new technologies and new literacy and job requirements that we can only begin to imagine today (Dede, 2000).

Developing technological literacy goes far beyond teaching students to word process, create spreadsheets, and create multimedia presentations (Goldberg & Richards, 1995). In this new decade, students must be able to identify accurate information as they search the Internet, they must be taught how to identify and use Gateway sites and on-line school databases, and they must be able to think critically about information obtained through both electronic and non-electronic sources (American Association of School Librarians [AASL] & Association for Educational Communications and Technology [AECT], 1998; Leu & Kinzer, 2000). In addition, students in classrooms today must learn to view and represent information in new ways and for wider audiences.

The push for meaningful technology use in classrooms is only a decade old and there is no question that greater research efforts regarding the added value of the contextualized use of technology are needed. A recent review of the literature acknowledges that it is difficult to separate the impact of instructional uses of technology from other ongoing school reforms and that, additionally, there is a shortage of longitudinal studies examining the effect of these technologies (Roschelle et al., 2000). Researchers have called for a national database to house studies of technology-related interventions that would support the sharing of measures and data from individual projects with the purpose of contributing to a greater shared understanding and to future decision making around public expenditures for educational technologies (Haertel & Means, 2000).

Through the meaningful use of technology in imaginative ways—problem-based learning, simulations, video cases, electronic discussions, virtual worlds, on-line resources, multimedia experiences—we can enhance students' learning opportunities and support their development of deeper understandings. Students can be provided with opportunities to develop technological competencies and engage in the use of strategies for identifying and solving authentic problems, in the classroom and in the real world.

Assessment

Advances in technology and the use of related new instructional methods and strategies are propelling the increased use of alternative assessments. Those include: portfolios, self and group evaluations, rubrics for assessment criteria and developmental benchmarks, as well as performance-based assessments. In particular, educational researchers are focusing on using engaging tasks and authentic classroom projects as a means of looking across a range of student outcomes and linking these to appropriate criteria for assessment (Wiggins, 1993). Gardner and others support the practice of integrating assessment into the daily classroom activity so that teachers and students both are engaged in the process (Gardner, 1993; Resnick & Resnick, 1992; Valencia, McGinley, & Pearson, 1990). This practice provides the potential for using assessment to play a more critical role in both teaching and learning, such that assessment can be used to help students learn (Shepard, 2000).

There is a need for looking more closely at how we can align assessment with current theories of teaching and learning (Shepard, 2000), as our understanding of learning sciences increases and we identify additional opportunities for technological innovation. To better align assessments with "principles of learning," assessment should (1) mirror good instruction; (2) be ongoing and integral to instruction; and (3) provide teachers, parents, and students with information about depth of student understanding (Bransford et al., 2000, p. 244). These authors state that effective teachers routinely identify assessment opportunities, provide students with feedback, and then help them to make connections across tasks, curriculum, and life experiences.

The need for alignment of learning and assessment reflects the reality that today teachers spend considerable time and focus making sure that students do well on state and national standardized tests and on content-specific tests related to the school curriculum. Teachers commonly feel pressured to "teach to the test," which may result in practices that negatively impact the validity of such tests (Miller & Seraphine, 1993). Additionally, it is known that as students advance in school, part of their mastery of the system of schooling is identifying what learning will be evaluated. Thus, students become adept at identifying the elements of learning that will be tested (Bransford et al., 2000). Given the competing needs, research is needed to inform efforts to thoughtfully and accurately balance these needs.

If we consider the potential interplay of technology and assessment, we can identify significant spaces where the two overlap. For the purpose of this discussion we will look at the overlap of using technology to improve on the process of assessment and how the presence or use of technology prompts changes in student learning.

Using Technology to Improve Assessment Process. With the most rapidly developing assessment approaches in special education being devoted to the problem of student instructional performance, we should consider the potential of technology as a medium for the reliable collection, analysis, and reporting of high-quality assessment data. Technology can also reduce the amount of time required to manage the assessment process. For example, curriculum-based measurement (CBM) (Deno, 1985) is a way of systematically measuring student progress in curriculum areas using short tests of no more than 5 minutes in length once or twice a week. CBM has been found to positively impact the achievement of students with mild disabilities (Allinder, Fuchs, & Fuchs, in press). Despite the positive outcomes it produces, CBM was not implemented on a wide-scale basis until computerized programs were developed to administer, score, graph, and consistently apply decision rules. This technology has decreased the amount of time required of teachers to use these tests. Presently, research is ongoing to identify additional ways that technology can be used to expedite the assessment process (for additional information, see the chapter "Issues in Curriculum Based Measurement" in this book, and Greenwood & Rieth, 1994).

Another example of expediting assessment is the use of software to support the collection and analysis of data created from students' use of such tools (McNabb, 2001). Additionally, in classrooms today, there is more work completed in electronic formats. The availability of electronic formats presents opportunities for more readily documenting process over a long term, as these formats allow for the storage of student work on school networks, and the creation of electronic portfolios on video, CDs, and the Web.

Changing Classrooms.   The use of technology has also changed the dynamics of the classroom. The increased use of small-group instruction, electronic work, and problem-solving activities that involve student presentations significantly alters the way students learn and express their understandings. The collaborative nature of multimedia projects makes the task of assessment more complex because students frequently engage in small group work when they conduct research, have discussions, and generate products (Prestidge & Williams Glaser, 2000).

Teachers in these classrooms are increasingly interested in (1) knowing how students' responses have developed over time, (2) providing opportunities for students to think more deeply about their own learning process, (3) identifying the individual's contribution to group learning, as well as learning and participation distributed across the members of a group, (4) providing opportunities for students to give feedback on their own process or product or that of their peers, (5) providing opportunities for students to self-critique by identifying their own strengths and weaknesses, and (6) incorporating thinking and reasoning abilities (Ames & Gahagan, 1995; Colburn, 2002; Prestidge & Williams Glaser, 2000; Resnick & Resnick, 1992), and alternative assessments may provide more ready access to this information and understanding than more traditional forms of assessment. Portfolios, self and group evaluations, and performance-based assessments are some primary examples of alternative assessments used in classrooms today. These are briefly discussed below, followed by a discussion of the importance of using established criteria and the benefits and challenges of the use of alternative assessments.

The portfolio, while not an assessment, provides a basis for evaluating student achievement through the purposeful and systematic collection of student work (Taylor, Phillips, & Joseph, 2002). It typically includes both student and teacher observations of student work. The use of portfolios has grown from the early writing portfolios in literacy classrooms to the use of portfolios in high-stakes accountability programs (see Kentucky Department of Education, 2002; Tindal & Haladyna, 2002; Vermont Department of Education, 2002). The construction of rubrics (discussed below) has made the process of evaluating portfolios more objective and less time consuming (Ediger, 2000). However, there are still issues related to reliability, validity, and the cost of using portfolios on a large scale, and research is ongoing to determine both the level of contribution and the viability of portfolios in high-stakes assessment (Vermont Department of Education, 2002). There is no question, however, that they have become much more commonplace in the classroom and are seen in both K–12 and higher education settings. As discussed earlier, the availability of electronic formats for portfolios has increased both accessibility and usability for students and teachers.

Self-assessment is an important element of alternative assessment, as it enables students to reflect on their learning and to note progress (Pierce & O'Malley, 1992). In elementary and secondary classrooms, and across disciplines, teachers are using both self and group evaluations. Teachers use them for multiple purposes: (1) to provide additional input into the process of assessment, (2) to help students think more critically about their own individual contribution, or the individual contribution of others, to the overall group process and product, and (3) to increase student ownership of learning. Ongoing research has examined the impact of both self and group evaluations on the content that students have learned, the manner in which they learned, and the contexts that support it (Marshall & Weinstein, 1984). This research builds on studies that have identified that students facing learning challenges can learn to be reflective and that this process can lead to improved self-concepts, in addition to improved learning (Ames & Gahagan, 1995; Prestidge & Beaver, 1996).

Performance-based assessments are tasks that require students to demonstrate understanding and expertise through some type of performance (Rothman, 1995). Performance-based assessments need not be lengthy or involved pieces of work. For example, students may demonstrate their knowledge of Spanish vocabulary by creating an audiotape of a dialogue with another student. Or a student might write an essay to demonstrate writing proficiency.

An important element of alternative assessment is the use of established criteria (Wiggins, 1993). Performance standards, rubrics, and scoring guides are all examples of established criteria that may be used in evaluating student performances or products. Rubrics are typically formatted as a matrix and include information about criteria for levels of performance or production matched with a score. Often, the students collaborate with the teacher in establishing the criteria for assessment. In any case, the expectations of the teacher are clearly articulated (Luft, 1997), leading to a "shared understanding of quality" by students and teacher (Penuel, Korbak, & Cole, 2002, p. 52). There are many examples of rubrics and scoring guides on the Web, as well as tools for generating such guides (see Web Resources).

Overall, the use of alternative assessments can provide multiple benefits to students. There is the opportunity for increased student ownership, for example, as students contribute to the development of rubrics used for evaluation of their process and products (Skillings & Ferrell, 2000). Additionally, the opportunity to self-select pieces of work for portfolios that best exemplify their efforts fosters students' sense of ownership and ability to think critically about their process and product. There is also the potential for both students and teachers to reflect and question (in conversation and presentation, in journaling and on-line forms of discourse) as teachers come to an understanding of what students know and as students are challenged to apply their understanding of existing problems to new situations.

One of the benefits of more formative types of assessments is that greater attention can be paid to what students know and can do. Alternative assessments encourage students to capitalize on their strengths and enable teachers to help students improve their learning, rather than focusing solely on what students do not know and cannot do. For example, students of diverse racial or ethnic backgrounds often are penalized under the system of more traditional assessment. Many advocate the use of alternative assessments to provide greater equity for English Language Learners (Abedi, 2001; Darling-Hammond, 1994; Farr & Trumbull, 1997; Garcia & Pearson, 1994).

Implementing more authentic assessments is not without its challenges. Curricular validity, evaluator bias, and the ever-present standardized tests all present themselves as issues to be addressed when considering the use of nontraditional assessments. As in the case of using alternative assessment with English Language Learners, the alternative assessments still have to meet appropriate criteria and ensure assessment validity (Shepard, 1993). Additionally, the limitation of teacher time for exploring new possibilities, examining the possible connections between students' process and products and less traditional assessments, and for constructing new assessments is often an imposing challenge. However, there are considerable on-line supports available to classroom teachers who would like to incorporate the use of these types of assessments. There are a number of Web sites that provide everything from information about linking assessments to standards to templates for designing multimedia rubrics (see Web Resources).

Summary

Traditional assessment methods typically give only a snapshot of a specific point in time. Alternative assessments can provide opportunities for students to demonstrate both a range of abilities, and growth over time. Assessments that are more formative in nature and look at process and products allow for a more comprehensive and balanced view of the student and may result in greater personal and academic gains for both general education and special education students.

ASSISTIVE TECHNOLOGY

Historical Overview of Assistive Technology

A second corpus of literature contributing to the trends and issues associated with the use of technology to instruct persons with disabilities is in the area of assistive technology. Assistive technology is defined in Public Law 100-407 (Technology-Related Assistance Act, United States Congress, 1988) as including any item or piece of equipment that is used to increase, maintain, or improve functional capabilities of individuals with disabilities. Edyburn (2000) defined assistive technology simply as devices and services that enhance the performance of individuals with a disability by enabling them to complete tasks more effectively, efficiently, and independently than otherwise possible. Provenzo (1986) and Brett and Provenzo (1995) argued that the development of inexpensive personal computers in the late 1970s presaged the concept of the computer and adaptive technology as a means of enhancing and extending the capabilities of individuals in the cognitive and physical domains. People with disabilities can use assistive technology to (1) assist them in learning, (2) make the environment more accessible, (3) enable them to compete in the workplace, (4) enhance their independence, and (5) otherwise improve their quality of life (Blackhurst & Lahm, 2000). Assistive technology that employs microcomputers has a 30-year history in the field of special education, with current estimates suggesting that more than 25,000 assistive technology devices have been designed to enhance the life functioning of persons with disabilities (Edyburn, 2000). Given that devices often have to be custom made for individuals, the professional literature has largely reported case studies where the primary concern was: Does the device successfully perform the function for which it was designed, and does it enable the person with disabilities to independently complete a task or tasks that were not otherwise possible? In addition, Edyburn (2000) argued that a limited amount of research informs our knowledge about assistive technology, and he recommends an urgent need for research to help inform the field.

Issues Impacting the Implementation of Assistive Technology

In the next sections of the chapter we explore five issues that play an influential role in the applications and research related to effectively using assistive technology. They include access to hardware and software, training and professional development for teachers, support for teachers using technology, strategies and models to enable teachers to integrate technology into their daily teaching, and the development of new strategies to assess students' higher order learning.

Access

The United States Congress (1988) passed the Technology-Related Assistance for Individuals with Disabilities Act (P.L. 100-407) to provide financial assistance to states to enable them to conduct needs assessments, identify technology resources, provide assistive technology services, and conduct public awareness programs (Blackhurst & Lahm, 2000). An array of services designed for persons with disabilities was included in the act. They include (1) the evaluation of a person's needs for assistive technology devices, (2) purchasing or leasing assistive technology devices for people, (3) designing and fabricating devices, (4) coordinating services offered by those who provide assistive technology services, (5) providing training or technical assistance to a person who uses assistive technology, and (6) training and technical assistance to those who work with people who use assistive technology devices, such as teachers or employers.

The barriers limiting access to technology for individuals with special needs are many, although some are more readily apparent than others. The more obvious barriers are related to hardware access. How do individuals with disabilities overcome the barrier of keyboard and screen? How do they navigate the Internet, function on networked computers, or access augmentative communication devices?

Other significant barriers could be categorized as "people barriers," those in which finances, politics, and attitudes impede the availability of or access to technology. Environment or "barrier-free" access in the home, school, and community constitutes another observable consideration. Research is needed to identify the frequency and magnitude of the barriers to service and equipment.

Training

The Individuals with Disabilities Education Act (IDEA) of 1997 (20 U.S.C. §1400 *et seq.*) supports training in the use of AT devices (Lahm, Bausch, Hasselbring, & Blackhurst, 2001). Training on AT devices is recommended for individuals with disabilities for whom a need for assistive devices has been identified; their families; professionals with whom they interact, such as classroom teachers, job coaches, speech and language pathologists, and occupational therapists (Todis, 1996). Because of the rapidly changing nature of technology innovation and development and changing student needs, training is essential for the successful use and implementation of AT devices (Derer, Polsgrove, & Rieth, 1996; Edyburn & Gardner, 1999; Rieth et al., 2001; Wehmeyer, 1999).

For AT to be implemented properly, educators must possess the knowledge and skills to make decisions about the selection, implementation, and evaluation of AT use (Lahm et al., 2001). Therefore, faculty members will have to explore ways to structure curricula and practica to better prepare teachers to work effectively with students who use AT devices (Bryant, Erin, Lock, Allan, & Resta, 1998). Currently, the professional literature indicates that AT knowledge and skill training can be provided in two ways. First, it can be infused into currently existing courses (Hargrave & Hsu, 2000). Alternatively, it can serve as the foundation for the development of a technology course (Cherup & Linklater, 2000; Ludlow, 2001). Bryant et al. (1998) highly recommend the development of a technology plan to facilitate the infusion and evaluation of technology into higher education personnel preparation programs. Recommended components of the plan include (1) a list of courses that target technology infusion, (2) technology curricula objectives, (3) evaluation procedures, (4) a list of technology tools that are needed for each course, and (5) the necessary support services and personnel to assist faculty with technology infusion efforts.

Infusing technology content into higher education coursework requires professors to make judgments about current curricular content that can be replaced by technology content (Lahm et al., 2001; Bryant et al., 1998). Therefore, higher education faculty must clarify the added value of infusing technology content into their already content-laden courses. Not surprisingly, although professors believe in the importance of technology (OTA, 1995) and the need to include technology in training programs (Task Force on Technology and Teacher Education, 1997), one-half of the teacher education graduates reported insufficient training in technology (Barksdale, 1994).

Ongoing in-service training is the second critical component of a training program. Various in-service training formats have been identified; however, the information needed by professionals varies considerably depending on the disabilities of the students they teach and the devices that may be most appropriate (Rieth et al., 2001). According to Derer et al. (1996), both low- and high-intensity training may be a viable format to prepare professionals to implement AT devices with their students. Additionally, because of the vital role instructional assistants play in the delivery of services to students with more severe disabilities, they too must become competent in the use of AT devices so that they work effectively with students for whom devices have been assigned (Todis, 1996). Finally, Bryant and Bryant (1998) and Carney and Dix (1992) recommend that training include information for professionals to share directly with families and caregivers of students who use AT devices. This is essential when electronic devices are sent home, where complexity of use may exceed family members' capacity to provide assistance. More training for parents may be required for successful implementation to improve outcomes for students with disabilities (Lemons, 2000).

At the in-service level, educators who already have numerous demands placed on their time must view attending AT training as relevant in promoting their ability to address IEP curricular benchmarks and fulfilling the demands of their job (Bryant & Bryant, 2003; McGregor & Pachuski, 1996). As students enter classrooms with upgraded and updated AT devices, teachers will require ongoing professional development to learn about the devices and how best to use them. Thus, educators need time and support to learn the knowledge and skills related to new developments in AT and to make connections between students' use of AT devices and their ability to access the curriculum and instruction.

Support

IDEA (1997) supports measures to promote technology utilization, which must include not only training activities but also technical assistance and support for users and providers. Key support issues such as the maintenance of the technology, technology guidance, and administrative leadership, warrant attention to increase the likelihood of the implementation and continued use of technology and reduce abandonment of technology.

Unfortunately, research suggests that nearly one-third of AT devices are abandoned within the first year of use (Phillips, 1991) because users may lack independence in using devices, training was insufficient, or equipment problems (e.g., maintenance, reliability) interfered with implementation (Phillips, 1992). For instance, Todis (1996) found that students frequently were not using devices adequately because teachers could not solve problems related to the operation and maintenance of the technology. The reliability and durability of AT devices should be evaluated (Bowser & Reed, 1995) because devices that require frequent repairs may not be good solutions for classroom use. Additionally, building level technical assistance is required to ensure that users and providers have timely access to maintenance support and guidance by experts when problems arise.

Technology guidance also is critical at the IEP meeting. Guidance in arriving at decisions regarding the feasibility of AT may be necessary when decision makers lack the knowledge base that is critical for considering a student's need for AT. Decision makers often must decide if (1) the student requires AT to meet his or her needs, (2) the student requires a different type of AT than what is presently being used, (3) the student does not need AT at this time to meet his or her needs, or (4) an AT evaluation is needed (Bryant & Bryant, 2003). Frequently, IEP team members may need support and guidance in this process, as many of them may lack sufficient knowledge about AT devices to promote effective decision making. Therefore, administrators must take an active leadership role in promoting policies that ensure the technology support and guidance for educators with students who use AT devices as a part of their IEP.

Administrators are responsible for identifying, implementing, and enforcing policies and procedures to ensure that AT provisions are instituted. IDEA identifies AT as a special education service, which can be included on an IEP. The intent of this service is to provide the support system that is necessary to properly identify, implement, and evaluate the use of AT devices by individuals with disabilities and to provide the training and technical assistance needed by providers (Lahm et al., 2001; Quality Indicators for AT [QIAT], 2000). Further, IDEA stipulates that educational agencies are responsible for providing or purchasing AT-related services. The use of AT devices in school settings is intended to facilitate the implementation of IEP goals and short-term objectives. Service providers must plan for and implement the integration of the devices into educational settings. Thus, AT administrative policies and procedures that relate to personnel, professional development, the budgetary process, and evaluation are necessary; beyond that, widespread notification and monitoring of these policies and procedures are critical to ensure compliance with the law and equitable institutionalization by IEP decision makers (QIAT, 2000).

Technology Integration

Integrating AT devices into instruction is often quite challenging for general and special education teachers. Challenges may stem from lack of essential training for using the devices, familiarity with *how* to integrate devices into instruction (Lemons, 2000), or perceptions about the feasibility and practicality of integration and implementation. In fact, research has shown that special education teachers who are the recipients of advanced technology preparation are more willing to integrate technology into their instruction (Weber, Schoon, & Forgan, 2001).

Integration of AT devices into instruction can occur as well prepared and reflective teachers design and implement instruction. As teachers design instruction, they think about the curriculum and objectives students will be taught and how instruction will be delivered (e.g., grouping, materials). Teachers must also consider their students with disabilities' abilities and needs, their IEPs, and how AT devices (that may be prescribed as a part of the IEP process) can promote students' active participation in the lesson. It is critical that teachers reflect on the following questions: (1) What is the purpose of the device, and how does the device help the student to access instruction and work assigned to other students? (2) Do I know how to use the device? (3) Does the student know how to use the device? and (4) Is my classroom set up to accommodate the use of the device? (Bryant & Bryant, 2003).

Assessment

AT assessment is often conducted by a multidisciplinary team, using a multidimensional assessment model. The model should consider the dynamic interplay of factors across contexts and over time, including the specific demands of the environment or setting, the strengths and weaknesses of the individual, possible AT solutions, and ongoing evaluation (Bryant & Bryant, 1998; Bryant, Seay, & Bryant, 1999; Raskind & Bryant, 2002). Also, standards and benchmarks are an important component of any assessment model.

Standards for appropriate AT assessment are necessary, and benchmarks to determine student progress with the device must be taken into consideration as multidisciplinary teams make decisions about the benefits of AT. For example, the QIAT, 2000, consortium, which consists of AT specialists that represent various groups (e.g., public schools, higher education, families and users, vendors, staff development leaders, state/federal technology grant recipients), has developed a set of descriptors that serve as guidelines for determining quality AT services. Quality Indicators are specified for six areas including administration, consideration, assessment, IEP development, implementation, and evaluation of effectiveness (QIAT, 2000). Standards and benchmarks can be used to identify best practice in AT assessment procedures and the knowledge and skills necessary to conduct proper assessments. Because AT assessments are continuous in one form or another to ensure that the devices are being used effectively, benchmarks, which are linked to IEP goals and short-term objectives, can provide measures for recognizing the attainment of designated goals.

Finally, AT assessment must be authentic, meaning that it takes place in naturally occurring environments that the individual encounters on a daily basis. Evaluators who are familiar with the student and the setting demands perform the assessment to determine which intervention best meets the needs of the individual at that point in time. The Student, Environments, Tasks, and Tools (SETT) Framework has been proposed as one way to assess an individual's need for AT. The SETT Framework provides a structure for collaborative groups of professionals to work together and think about the AT devices and services that are needed to provide a student with disabilities with access to educational opportunities (Zabala, 2003).

Bryant and Bryant (1993) identified the Adaptations Framework as another example of a process that decision makers can use to conduct an authentic AT assessment of an individual's needs for AT. The Adaptations Framework involves professionals, families, and users in a decision-making process to identify AT devices that would be most beneficial to enable the individual to become more independent and achieve success with the tasks in any environment. The Adaptations Framework involves (1) examining the setting demands and requisite abilities, (2) examining information about the individual's needs and strengths as they relate to the setting demands, (3) determining if AT devices are appropriate and suitably matched to the individual, and (4) evaluating the effectiveness of the device to promote access and success. Based on the Adaptations Framework, AT devices have the potential to enhance an individual's life by promoting access to setting demands, independence, and success. However, the results of research investigating the abandonment of devices (Phillips, 1991) is disappointing, suggesting the importance of investigating the impact of authentic assessment to increase the likelihood that devices are appropriate, help individuals circumvent functional limitations, and are maintained over time as appropriate.

SUMMARY

This chapter has examined trends and issues that have influenced the implementation of instructional and assistive technology with students with disabilities. They have and will continue to impact the emergence and refinement of instruction that involves the use of instructional and assistive technology to improve educational outcomes attained by students with disabilities.

WEB RESOURCES: ASSESSMENT

EXPLORING ISSUES IN ALTERNATIVE ASSESSMENT

http://www.bigchalk.com/cgi-bin/WebObjects/
WOPortal.woa/wa/BCPageDA/sec~ TH~48254~~

http://science.uniserve.edu.au/school/support/
strategy.html

http://www.ncrtec.org/tl/sgsp/index.html

http://www.emtech.net/Alternative_ Assessment.
html

INTEGRATING ASSESSMENT

http://www.ncrel.org/sdrs/areas/issues/methods/
assment/as500.htm

ON-LINE BIBLIOGRAPHY

http://ericae.net/bstore/docs/aalter/htm

PORTFOLIO USE IN THE STATE OF KENTUCKY

http://www.kde.state.ky.us/oapd/curric/Portfolios/
default.asp

USING RUBRICS

http://www.ncsu.edu/midlink/tch.wk.rm.htm

QUESTIONS FOR FURTHER DISCUSSION

1. Identify two strategies for increasing the access that students with disabilities have to computers and to higher-level application software. Justify your choice of strategies and describe how it will be implemented.

2. The ALTOS school district has invited you to design and deliver a staff development program to train the district's teachers to integrate technology in their classroom teaching. Describe, in detail, the steps that you will take and the information that you will collect in order to develop the program, and then describe the program

content and the implementation and support strategies that you will employ.

3. Technology, reportedly, has tremendous potential to enhance student assessment and progress monitoring. Describe two assessment applications of technology and describe the benefits and barriers associated with each application.

4. Select two barriers to the use of assistive technology, and identify and describe at least two strategies to overcome them.

REFERENCES

Abedi, J. (2001). *Assessment and accommodation for English language learners: Issues and recommendations*. Policy Brief 4. Los Angeles: University of California Los Angeles, National Center for Research on Evaluation, Standards, and Student Testing.

Abedi, J., & Baker, E. (1995). A latent-variable modeling approach to assessing inter-rater reliability, topic generalizability, and validity of a content assessment scoring rubric. *Educational and Psychological Measurement, 55,* 701–715.

Allinder, R., Fuchs, L. S., & Fuchs, D. (in press). Issues in curriculum-based assessment. In A. McCray, H. J. Rieth, & P. Sindelar (Eds.), *Critical Issues in Special Education*. Boston: Allyn & Bacon.

American Association of School Librarians and Association for Educational Communications and Technology. (1998). *Information literacy standards for student learning*. Chicago: American Library Association.

Ames, C. K., & Gahagan, H. S. (1995). Self-reflection: Supporting students in taking ownership of evaluation. In C. Dudley-Marling & D. Searle (Eds.), *Who owns learning? Questions of autonomy, choice, and control* (pp. 52–66). Portsmouth, NH: Heinemann.

Barksdale, J. M. (1994). New teachers: Unplugged. *Electronic Learning, 15*(5), 39–45.

Becker, H. J. (2000). Who's wired and who's not: Children's access to and use of computer technology. *The future of children, 10*(2), 44–75

Berman, P., & McLaughlin, M. (1978). Implementation of educational innovation. *Educational Forum, 40*(3), 345–370.

Blackhurst, A. E., & Lahm, E. A. (2000). Foundations of technology and exceptionality. In J. Lindsey (Ed.), *Technology and exceptional individuals* (3rd ed., pp. 3–45). Austin, TX: PRO-ED.

Bowser, G., & Reed, P. (1995). Education TECH points for AT planning. *Journal of Special Education Technology, 12*(4), 325–338.

Bransford, J. D., Brown, A. L., & Cocking, R. R. (2000). How people learn: Brain, mind, experience, and school. Washington, DC: National Academy Press.

Brett, A., & Provenzo, E. F. (1995). *Adaptive technology for special human needs*. Albany, NY: State University of New York Press.

Bryant, B. R., Seay, P. C., & Bryant, D. P. (1999). AT and adaptive behavior. In R. L. Schalock (Ed.), *Adaptive behavior and its measurement* (pp. 81–98). Washington, DC: American Association on Mental Retardation.

Bryant, D. P., & Bryant, B. R. (1998). Using AT adaptations to include students with learning disabilities in cooperative learning activities. *Journal of Learning Disabilities, 31*(1), 41–54.

Bryant, D. P., & Bryant, B. R. (2003). *AT for people with disabilities*. Boston: Allyn & Bacon.

Bryant, D. P., Erin, J., Lock, R., Allan, J., & Resta, P. (1998). Infusing AT into a teacher training program in learning disabilities. *Journal of Learning Disabilities, 31*(1), 55–66.

Budoff, M., Thormann, J., & Gras, A. (1984). *Microcomputers in special education*. Cambridge, MA: Brookline Press.

Carney, J., & Dix, C. (1992). Integrating AT in the classroom and community. In G. Church & S. Glennen (Eds.), *The handbook of AT* (pp. 207–240). San Diego, CA: Singular Publishing Group.

Cherup, S., & Linklater, L. (2000). Integrating technology into preservice education: A model implemented at one small liberal arts college. *Journal of Computing Teacher Education, 16*(3), 18–22.

Christensen, C., & Cosden, M. (1986) The relationship between special education placement and instruction in computer literacy skills. *Journal of Educational Computing Research, 2,* 299–306.

Clark, R. E. (1983). Reconsidering research on learning from media. *Review of Education Research, 53,* 445–459.

Cognition and Technology Group at Vanderbilt. (1990). Anchored instruction and its relationship to situated cognition. *Educational Researcher, 19*(6), 2–10.

Cognition and Technology Group at Vanderbilt. (1992). The Jasper series as an example of anchored instruction: Theory, program description, and assessment data. *Educational Psychologist, 27,* 291–315.

Colburn, L. K. (2000). Integrating technology in your middle school classroom: Some hints from a successful process. *Reading Online, 4*(2). Retrieved November 20, 2002, from http://www. readingonline.org/electronic/elec_index.asp? HREF=/electronic/colburn/index.html.

Colburn, L. K. (2002, April). *The technology infused classroom: Promoting greater teacher and student understanding of student learning across disciplines in the 21st century classroom*. Presentation at the annual meeting of the International Reading Association. San Francisco, CA.

Cosden, M., & Abernathy, T. (1990). Microcomputer use in the schools: Teacher roles and instructional options. *Remedial and Special Education, 11*(5), 31–38.

Cosden, M., Gerber, M., Goldman, S., Semmel, D., & Semmel, M. (1986). Survey of microcomputer access and use by mildly handicapped students in Southern California. *Journal of Special Education Technology, 8*(4),1–13.

Darling-Hammond, L. (1994). Performance-based assessment and educational equity. *Harvard Educational Review, 64* (1), 5–30.

Dede, C. (2000). A new century demands new ways of learning. In D. T. Gordon (Ed.), *The digital classroom* (pp. 171–178). Cambridge, MA: Harvard Education Letter.

Deno, S. L. (1985). Curriculum-based measurement: The emerging alternative. *Exceptional Children, 52,* 219–232.

Derer, K., Polsgrove, L., & Rieth, H. (1996). A survey of AT applications in schools and recommendations for practice. *Journal of Special Education Technology, 13*(2), 62–80.

Ediger, M. (2000). *Assessment with portfolio and rubric use.* (Report No. TM030739). Syracuse, NY: Eric Clearing House on Information & Technology. (ERIC Document Reproduction Service No. Ed 440 127).

Edyburn, D. (2000). Assistive technology and students with mild disabilities. *Focus on Exceptional Children, 32*(9), 1–22.

Edyburn, D., & Gardner, J. (1999). Integrating technology into special education teacher preparation programs: Creating shared visions. *Journal of Special Education Technology, 14*(2), 3–17.

Ellis, E. S., & Sabornie, E. J. (1986). Effective instruction with microcomputer: Promises, practices, and preliminary findings. *Focus on Exceptional Children, 19*(4), 1–16.

Evans, R. (1996). *The human side of school change: Reform, resistance, and the real-life problems of innovation.* San Francisco: Jossey-Bass.

Farr, B., & Trumbull, E. (1997). *Assessment alternatives for diverse classrooms.* Norwood, MA: Christopher Gordon Publishers.

Fitzgerald, G., & Koury, K. (1996). Empirical advances in technology-assisted instruction for students with mild and moderate disabilities. *Journal of Research on Computing in Education, 28,* 526–553.

Fullan, M. G., & Stiegelbauer, S. (1991). *The new meaning of educational change* (2nd edition). New York: Teachers College Press.

Garcia, G. E., & Pearson, P. D. (1994). Assessment and diversity. *Review of Research in Education, 20,* 337–391.

Gardner, H. (1993). *Multiple intelligences: The theory in practice.* New York: Basic Books.

Goldberg, B., & Richards, J. (1995). Leveraging technology in reform: Changing schools and communities into learning organizations. *Educational Technology, 35*(5), 5–16.

Greenwood, C., & Rieth, H. (1994). Current dimensions of technology-based assessment in special education. *Exceptional Children, 61*(2), 105–113.

Guhlin, M. (2002). Teachers must push technology's tidal wave. *Journal of Staff Development, 23*(1), 40–41.

Haertel, G., & Means, B. (2000). Stronger designs for research on educational uses of technology: Conclusions and implications. Menlo Park, CA: SRI International. Retrieved March 14, 2002, from http://www.sri.com/policy/designkt/found.html.

Hargrave, C. P., & Hsu, Y. (2000). Survey of instructional technology courses for preservice teachers. *Journal of Technology and Teacher Education, 8*(4), 303–314.

Hasselbring, T. S. (2001). A possible future of special education technology. *Journal of Special Education Technology, 16*(4), 15–22.

Hofstetter, F. T. (2001). The future's future: Implications of emerging technology for special education program planning. *Journal of Special Education Technology, 16*(4), 7–14.

Hur, S. J. (2001). *Effects of anchored instruction on the critical thinking skills of students with and without mild disabilities.* Unpublished doctoral dissertation, University of Texas, Austin.

Individuals with Disabilities Education Act, 20 U.S.C. §1400 *et seq.* (1997).

Kafai, Y., & Ching, C. (2001). Affordances of collaborative software design planning for elementary students' science talk. *Journal of the Learning Sciences, 10*(3), 323–363.

Kentucky Department of Education. (2002). *Commonwealth Accountabilty Testing System.* Retrieved March 13, 2002, from http://www.lrc.state.ky.us/KRS/158-00/6453.pdf.

Lahm, E. A., Bausch, M. E., Hasselbring, T. S., & Blackhurst, A. E. (2001). National AT Research Institute. *Journal of Special Education Technology, 16*(3), 19–26.

Langone, J. D., Malone, D. M., & Clinton, G. N. (1999). The effects of technology enhance anchored instruction on the knowledge of preservice special educators. *Teacher Education and Special Education, 22*(2), 85–96.

Lemons, C. J. (2000). *Comparison of parent and teacher knowledge and opinions related to augmentative and alternative communication.* Unpublished master's thesis, University of Texas, Austin.

Leu, D. J., & Kinzer, C. K. (2000). The convergence of literacy instruction with networked technologies for information and communication. *Reading Research Quarterly, 35*(1), 108–127.

Lou, Y., Abrami, P. C., & d'Apollonia, S. (2001). Small group and individual learning with technology: A meta-analysis. *Review of Educational Research, 71*(3), 449–521.

Lou, Y., Abrami, C. A., Spence, J. C., Poulsen, C., Chambers, B., & d'Apollonia, S. (1996). Within-class grouping: A meta-analysis. *Review of Educational Research, 66*(3), 423–458.

Ludlow, B. L. (2001). Technology and teacher education in special education: Disaster or deliverance? *Teacher Education and Special Education, 24*(2), 143–153.

Luft, J. A. (1997). Design your own rubric. *Science Scope, 20*, 25–27.

Marshall, H. H., & Weinstein, R. S. (1984). Classroom factors affecting students' self-evaluations: An interactional model. *Review of Educational Research, 54*, 301–325.

McGregor, G., & Pachuski, P. (1996). AT in schools: Are teachers ready, able, and supported? *Journal of Special Education Technology, 13*(1), 4–15.

McNabb, M. (2001). A work in progress. *Learning and Leading with Technology, 28*(3), 45–56.

Means, B. M. (1994). Introduction: Using technology to advance educational goals. In B. M. Means (Ed.), *Technology and education reform* (pp. 1–21). San Francisco: Jossey-Bass.

Miller, M. D., & Seraphine, A. E. (1993). Can test scores remain authentic when teaching to the test? *Educational Assessment, 1*(2), 119–129.

Morgan, T. (1996). Using technology to enhance learning: Changing the chunks. *Learning & Leading with Technology, 23*(5), 49–51.

National Education Goals Panel. (1998). *1998 data volume for the National Education Goals Report.* Washington, DC: U.S. Government Printing Office.

NETS (2000). *National Education Technology Standards For Teachers.* Eugene, OR: International Society for Technology in Education.

Office of Technology Assessment (OTA). (1995). *Teachers and technology: Making the connection* (OTA-CHR-616). Washington, DC: U.S. Government Printing Office.

Okolo, C., Bahr, C., & Rieth, H. (1993). A retrospective of computer-based instruction. *Journal of Special Education Technology, 12*(1), 1–27.

Peck, C., Cuban, L., & Kirkpatrick, H. (2002). Techno-promoter dreams, student realities. *Phi Delta Kappan, 83*(6), 472–480.

Penuel, W. R., Korbak, C., & Cole, K. A. (2002). Designing assessments for student multimedia projects. *Learning & Leading with Technology, 29*(5), 46–52.

Phillips, B. (1991). *Technology abandonment: From the consumer point of view.* Washington, DC: Request Publication.

Phillips, B. (1992). *Perspectives on AT services in vocational rehabilitation: Clients and counselors.* Washington, DC: National Rehabilitation Hospital, AT/ Rehabilitation Engineering Program.

Pierce, L. V., & O'Malley, M. (1992). Performance and portfolio assessment for language minority students (Report No. NCBE-9). Washington, DC: National Clearinghouse for Bilingual Education, Program Guide Series, 9. (ERIC Document Reproduction Service No. ED346747).

Pierson, M. (2001). Technology integration practice as a function of pedagogical expertise. *Journal of Research on Computing in Education, 33*(4) 413–430.

President's Committee of Advisors on Science and Technology (PCAST). (1997). *Report to the president on the use of technology to strengthen K–12 education in the United States.* Washington, DC: Executive Office of the President of the United States.

Prestidge, L., & Beaver, P. (1996, April). *Implications of multimedia anchored instruction for the authentic assessment of the achievement of students with learning disabilities.* Paper presented at the annual meeting of the American Educational Research Association, New York.

Prestidge, L. K., & Williams Glaser, C. (2000). Authentic assessment: Employing appropriate tools for evaluating students' work in 21st century classrooms. *Intervention in School and Clinic, 35*(3), 178–182.

Provenzo, E. F. (1986). *Beyond the Gutenberg galaxy: Microcomputers and the emergence of post-typographic culture.* New York: Teachers College Press.

Quality Indicators for AT Services Consortium. (2000). *Quality Indicators for AT Services.* Retrieved on February 11, 2002, from http://qiat.org/.

Raskind, M., & Bryant, B. R. (2002). *Functional evaluation of AT.* Austin, TX: Psycho-Educational Services.

Resnick, L. B., & Resnick, D. P. (1992). Assessing the thinking curriculum: New tools for educational reform. In B. R. Gifford & M. C. O'Connor (Eds.), *Changing assessments: Alternative views of aptitude, achievement, and instruction* (pp. 37–75). Boston: Kluwer Academic.

Riel, M. (2000). New designs for connected teaching and learning. In *Proceedings of the secretary's conference on educational technology, 2000.* Retrieved on February 14, 2002, from http://www.gse.uci.edu/mriel/whitepaper/learning.html.

Rieth, H. J., Bahr, C., Okolo, C., Polsgrove, L., & Eckert, R. (1988). An analysis of the impact of microcomputers on the secondary special education classroom ecology. *Journal of Educational Computing Research, 4*, 425–441.

Rieth, H. J., Bryant, D. P., Kinzer, C. K., Colburn, L. K., Hur, S. J., Hartmann, P., & Choi, H. S. (2003). An analysis of the impact of anchored instruction on teaching and learning activities in two ninth grade language arts classes. *Remedial and Special Education, 24*(3), 173–184.

Rieth, H. J., Bryant, D. P., & Woodward, J. (2001). Technology applications for persons with disabilities: Benefits, barriers, and solutions (pp. 86–96). In I. Pervova (Ed.), *People, Time, and Society.* St. Petersburg, Russia: St. Petersburg Press.

Rieth, H. J., & Kinzer, C. K. (2000). Multimedia-based anchored instruction. In D. D. Smith (Ed.), *Introduction to special education teaching in an age of challenge* (4th ed.). Boston: Allyn & Bacon.

Roschelle, J. M., Pea, R. D., Hoadley, C. M., Gordin, D. N., and Means, B. M. (2000). Changing how and what children learn in school with computer-based technologies. *The Future of Children, 10*(2) 76–101.

Rosenholtz, S. (1989). *Teachers' workplace: The social organization of schools.* New York: Longman.

Rothman, R. (1995). *Measuring up: Standards, assessment, and school reform.* San Francisco: Jossey-Bass.

Sandholtz, J., Ringstaff, C., & Dwyer, D. (1997). *Teaching with technology: Creating student-centered classrooms.* New York: Teachers College Press.

Schmidt, M., Weinstein, T., Niemic, R., & Walberg, H. J. (1985). Computer-assisted instruction with exceptional children. *Journal of Special Education, 19,* 493–501.

Shepard, L. (1993). Evaluating test validity. *Review of Research in Education, 19,* 405–450.

Shepard, L. (2000, February). *The role of classroom assessment in teaching and learning.* Center for the Study of Evaluation (CSE) Report 517. Boulder, CO: University of Colorado, Center for Research on Evaluation, Standards, and Student Testing.

Shiah, R., Mastropieri, M., & Scruggs, T. (1995). Computer-assisted instruction and students with learning disabilities: Does research support the rhetoric? In M. Mastropieri & T. Scruggs (Eds.), *Advances in learning and behavioral disabilities* (pp. 162–192). Greenwich, CT: JAI.

Skillings, M., & Ferrell, R. (2000). Student-generated rubrics: Bringing students into the assessment process. *The Reading Teacher, 53*(6), 452–455.

Smith, D. D. (Ed.). (2000). *Introduction to special education: Teaching in an age of challenge* (4th ed.). Boston: Allyn & Bacon.

Stallard, C. H., & Cocker, J. S. (2001). The promise of technology in schools: The next 20 years. Lanham, MD: Scarecrow Press.

Sternberg, R. J., & Spear-Swerling, L. (1996). *Teaching for thinking.* Washington, DC: American Psychological Association.

Task Force on Technology and Teacher Education. (1997). *Technology and the new professional teacher: Preparing for the 21st century classroom.* Retrieved on January 16, 2002, from http://www.ncate.org/projects/tech/TECH.htm.

Taylor, G., Phillips, T., & Joseph, D. (2002). *Assessment strategies for individuals with disabilities.* Lewiston, NY: Edwin Mellen Press.

Technology-Related Assistance for Individuals with Disabilities Act of 1988. P.L. 100–407, 29 U.S.C. §2201, 2002 (1988).

Tindal, G., & Haladyna, T. M. (2002). *Large-scale assessment programs for all students: Validity, technical adequacy, and implementation.* Mahwah, NJ: Lawrence Erlbaum.

Tinker, R. (2001). Future technologies for special learners. *Journal of Special Education Technology, 16*(4), 31–38.

Todis, B. (1996). Tools for the task? Perspectives on AT in educational settings. *Journal of Special Education Technology, 13*(2), 49–61.

U.S. Department of Education. (1996, spring). What the research says about student assessment. *Improving America's Schools: A Newsletter on Issues in School Reform.* Retrieved January 18, 2002, from http://www.ed.gov/pubs/IASA/newsletters/assess/pt4.html.

Valencia, S. W., McGinley, W., & Pearson, P. D. (1990). Assessing reading and writing. In G. G. Duffy (Ed.), *Reading in the middle schools.* Newark, DE: International Reading Association.

Valovich, D. (1996). Strategic planning for the successful integration of technology in a private school (Report No. ED400786). (ERIC Document Reproduction Service).

Vermont Department of Education. (2002). Programs and services: Standards and assessment. Retrieved January 18, 2002, from http://www.state.vt.us/educ/new/html/pgm_standards.html.

Weber, R. K., Schoon, P. L., & Forgan, J. (2001). Special educators' technology literacy: Identifying the void. *Proceedings of SITE 2001,* 2641–2646.

Wehmeyer, M. L. (1999). AT and students with mental retardation: Utilization and barriers. *Journal of Special Education Technology, 14*(1), 48–58.

Wenglinsky, H. (1998). *Does it compute? The relationship between educational technology and student achievement in mathematics.* Princeton, NJ: Educational Testing Services, Policy Information Center. Retrieved October 15, 2002, from www.ets.org/research/pic/pir.html.

Wiggins, G. (1993). *Assessing student performance.* San Francisco: Jossey-Bass.

Williams Glaser, C., Rieth, H. J., Kinzer, C. K., Prestige, L. K., & Peter, J. (1999). A description of the impact of multimedia anchored instruction on classroom interactions. *Journal of Special Education Technology, 14*(2), 27–53.

Willis, E. M., & Raines, P. (2001). Technology in secondary education. *T. H. E. Journal, 29*(2), 54–64.

Woodward, J., & Rieth, H. J. (1997). An historical review of technology research in special education. *Review of Educational Research, 67*(4), 503–536.

Woodward, J., Gallagher, D., & Rieth, H. J. (2000). Historical review of technology research in special education. In L. Cuban & J. Woodward (Eds.), *Technology, curriculum and professional development.* (pp. 3–26). San Francisco: Corwin Press.

Zabala, J. (2003). *Personal perspective.* In D. P. Bryant & B. R. Bryant, *AT for people with disabilities* (pp. 27–29). Boston: Allyn & Bacon.

CONTEMPORARY ISSUES IN REHABILITATION COUNSELING

Interface with and Implications for Special Education

JAMES SCHALLER

University of Texas at Austin

NANCY K. YANG

Educational and Research Consultant

SOPHIE CHIEN-HUEY CHANG

National Taiwan Normal University

Just as the field of special education is facing a number of issues, many of which are addressed throughout this book, so too is the field of vocational rehabilitation counseling. Contemporary rehabilitation counseling practice is a multifaceted profession with a rich history and a promising future; however, there are many challenges as well (Hanley-Maxwell, Szymanski, & Owens-Johnson, 1998; Jenkins, Patterson, & Szymanski, 1998). While there are differences between the fields of special education and rehabilitation counseling, there are also many similarities, and contemporary and emerging issues facing the field of rehabilitation counseling have direct implications for special education practitioners. Therefore, the purpose of this chapter is to discuss each of the following issues and provide specific suggestions for special education practitioners. The selected issues are (1) a brief overview of philosophical, historical, and programmatic aspects of vocational rehabilitation counseling; (2) issues of ethnicity and culture; and (3) person-centered planning.

PHILOSOPHICAL, HISTORICAL, AND PROGRAMMATIC ASPECTS

Special education and rehabilitation counseling are two major state/federally funded service-delivery systems for individuals with disabilities and their families. Although there has been much rhetoric about linkages between these two systems (e.g., school-to-community transition issues), finding common ground has been difficult (Hanley-Maxwell et al., 1998; Szymanski, King, Parker, & Jenkins, 1989). The need for coordination between these two systems has been debated in the literature for over twenty years, with both education and vocational rehabilitation perspectives represented (e.g., Dysseguard, 1980; Hanley-Maxwell et al., 1998; McInerney & Karan, 1981; Szymanski, 1984).

Unfortunately, practitioners from each field may be unaware of histories and issues affecting the other profession and the effects of these on current practices within each profession. This is unfortunate, because many students with disabilities who receive special education services will eventually seek services from adult service-delivery systems, of which the state/federal vocational rehabilitation (VR) counseling system is one of the largest, unaware of the similarities and differences between the two systems. This lack of knowledge may have significant consequences both for the student and/or their family.

Although state/federal VR counselors have a responsibility to work with transition-age students with disabilities (Hanley-Maxwell et al., 1998) while they are still in school, special education practitioners also have a responsibility to provide essential information about adult services to assist students with disabilities and their families when the student is moving from one system to the next. Therefore, special education practitioners must have a rudimentary understanding of the state/federal VR system. The following brief overview of philosophical, legislative, and programmatic aspects of vocational rehabilitation counseling highlights similarities and differences between VR counseling and special education with suggestions for special education practitioners.

Philosophical Aspects

Rehabilitation has been defined as "a holistic and integrated program of medical, physical, psychosocial, and vocational interventions that empower a person with a disability to achieve a personally fulfilling, socially meaningful, and functionally effective interaction with the world" (Banja, 1990, p. 615). The process of providing rehabilitation services has been defined as "a comprehensive sequence of services, mutually planned by consumer and rehabilitation counselor to maximize employability, independence, integration, and participation of people with disabilities in the workplace and community" (Jenkins et al., 1998, p. 2). The underlying philosophy for rehabilitation counseling has long included a belief in, and advocacy for, rights of people with disabilities, including the inalienable worth of all people; the importance of membership in society; and the importance of an individual's involvement in the choice of rehabilitation goals, services, and service providers (Talbot, 1961; Wright, 1959).

Legislation

Just as special education is a service-delivery system created through federal legislation, so to is the state/federal VR system (Hanley-Maxwell et al., 1998). Rehabilitation services for people with disabilities began in the United States with private philanthropic and voluntary charitable organizations who encouraged states to establish vocational rehabilitation programs; this occurred prior to passage of the first federal civilian rehabilitation legislation (Jenkins et al., 1998; Obermann, 1965). Eventually, pressure was brought to bear at the federal level and resulted in the first federal legislation, known as the Smith-Hughes Act of 1917 (Public Law [P.L.] 64-347). This act created the Federal Board of Vocational Education for retraining dislocated industrial workers. One year later, the Soldier Rehabilitation Act of 1918 (P.L. 65-178) authorized vocational training and placement for veterans with disabilities (Obermann, 1965; Wright, 1980).

With the passage of the Smith-Fess Act in 1920 (P.L. 66-236), services for civilians with physical disabilities began; services mandated under this act were limited to vocational guidance and job placement (Jenkins et al., 1998). Over the years federal legislation has mandated expansion of state/federal VR services to include people with mental retardation, mental illness, blindness, deafness, migratory agricultural workers with disabilities and family members, individuals with HIV/AIDS, individuals with alcohol and other drug abuse histories and individuals with disabilities (Jones, 1990; President's Committee on Employment of People with Disabilities and U.S. Architectural and Transportation Barriers Compliance Board, 1990). Federal legislation also created the state/federal vocational rehabilitation program and provided funding for colleges and universities for preservice preparation of rehabilitation professionals at the undergraduate and graduate level (Jenkins et al., 1998). The state/federal VR program is funded primarily through federal tax dollars, with each state contributing to its own program as well.

PROGRAMMATIC ASPECTS

The state/federal VR program is implemented in each state through statewide offices. However, the title of the agency may vary from state to state. For example, the state/federal VR program may be called a "division" (e.g., state division of rehabilitation services), a "commission" (e.g., Texas Rehabilitation Commission or Texas Commission for the Blind), or an "office" or "service" (Wright, 1980). Regardless of the title, the state/federal VR agency, through rehabilitation counselors, provides services as well as purchased services from vendors in the community, with the primary goal of assisting an individual with a disability in getting and keeping competitive employment. Services may include assessment for both eligibility determination and vocational needs, vocational counseling, physical and mental restoration (e.g., corrective surgery or therapeutic treatment), prosthetic or orthotic devices, vocational training, postsecondary education, vocational education, assistive technology, job search and/or job placement, or supported employment services (Brabham, Mandeville, & Koch, 1998).

A major difference between special education and state/federal VR agencies is that special education is an entitlement program, whereas the VR agency relies on eligibility determination before providing services, a difference discussed in more depth later. The agency determines eligibility case-by-case, basing its decision on (1) whether an individual has a physical or mental disability, (2) whether the individual's disability constitutes or results in a substantial impediment to employment, and (3) a presumption that the individual can benefit from the provision of vocational rehabilitation services in terms of an employment outcome (Brabham et al., 1998). A determination of eligibility must be made within sixty days after an individual has applied for services.

Once determined eligible, the counselor, individual, and/or family work cooperatively to develop an individualized plan of employment (IPE), which may include a long-term vocational goal, intermediate rehabilitation objectives, vocational rehabilitation services and assessment services, and service providers. Included in the development of the IPE is a process called *informed choice*. Individuals and/or their families receive information about policies and procedures related to informed choice; counselors assist those seeking assistance in acquiring information necessary to make an informed choice about specific services. Counselors also give information about providers of services, cost, accessibility, and duration of services, consumer satisfaction with services, qualifications of potential service providers, and the degree to which services are offered in integrated settings (Brabham et al., 1998). Once the IPE has been developed and agreed on, an individual progresses through the objectives of the plan toward the employment goal based on the individual's abilities, interests, and informed choice.

Once employed, the counselor, individual, and employer must consider the employment satisfactory and agree that the individual is performing well on the job for a minimum of ninety days. If there are no problems, the counselor can close the case at the ninety-day mark after an assessment for postemployment services has been completed. Postemployment services may be provided to assist an individual in keeping the job after the case is closed, and may consist of counselor follow-up visits to the job site or supports from co-workers, for example.

As mentioned previously, special education is an entitlement system, whereas the state/federal VR system is an eligibility system, with counselors having up to sixty days to determine eligibility. If a student and/or the family is unaware that it is necessary to apply for state/federal VR services, or that an eligibility determination could take up to sixty days, the student could be sitting at home for an extended period of time after graduating or aging out of special education. As one professional with a daughter with disabilities puts it, "The little yellow special education school bus may have been coming for approximately twenty-one years, but if the student graduates on a Friday, and there are no services in place, there will be no little yellow state/federal VR school bus on Monday morning" (S. Dumas, personal communication, October 10, 2001).

This situation can have serious consequences for families who have depended on the educational system for as much as two decades, especially if the child has severe disabilities. A family may have come to rely on the educational system as a beneficial, predictable daylong placement for the child. In addition, the child may have also been receiving services such as supported employment in community-based sites while in school, which will end when the student graduates. But without adult services in place on graduation, the student with disabilities could be sitting at home.

This situation can be avoided if the student and the family are aware that, although a counselor in a state/federal VR agency cannot begin providing services while the student is still receiving special education services, the counselor can take the student's application and start a file; the counselor can also discuss potential vocational goals with the student and the family.

Another difference between special education and the state/federal VR system is that students who receive special education services because of a mild disability, such as a learning disability or speech impairment, might not be eligible for state/federal VR services; this could occur because the disability is not defined as a handicap to employment at that time (Jenkins et al., 1998; Szymanski et al., 1989). However, it may also be possible that a student with a physical disability who did not receive special education services could be eligible for state/federal VR services. This possibility is one more reason students with disabilities and/or their families need to contact the local state/federal VR agency before they graduate from high school.

Another difference between special education and the state/federal VR system is location of services. In special education, most professionals, teachers, family members, and the student meet in one location to discuss issues related to individualized education plans (IEPs) or admission, review, and dismissal (ARD), with many of the services being provided within the school or on school grounds. However, with state/federal VR services an individual and the family may need to travel to the state/federal VR office for meetings with the VR counselor, travel to another agency for assessments for eligibility determination or for information related to determination of IPE goals, and travel to one or more agencies for services once the IPE has been initiated.

Finally, it is also important for students with disabilities and their families to know about the client assistance program (CAP). Each state has a CAP, which assists people with disabilities who are receiving or attempting to receive services from the state/federal VR agency or independent-living centers. The CAP assists people with disabilities by providing information on rights, employment, independent living, and VR services. Awareness of the CAP is also important because many families and/or individuals with a disability may come to adult VR services with little understanding of their rights and obligations within that system. The CAP can assist people with disabilities and/or their families by providing legal advice and assistance regarding services and if necessary regarding complaints, grievances, and appeals.

This brief overview of the state/federal VR system provides context for one of the major adult service-delivery systems that many students with disabilities may be eligible for and participate in after leaving special education. Rehabilitation counselors have a responsibility to establish working relationships not only with transition-age students with disabilities but also with schools and school districts (Hanley-Maxwell et al., 1998). However, since special education teachers and professionals also have access to students with disabilities and their families for extended periods, teachers and professionals may provide critically needed information to students with disabilities and their families about the state/federal VR service-delivery system.

ETHNICITY AND CULTURE

Just as issues of ethnicity and culture have received attention for decades in special education literature, so too have these issues been central in VR counseling. For example, the overrepresentation of students from culturally diverse backgrounds in special education has been acknowledged for over thirty years. The field of special education continues to struggle with ways to improve policies and practices in educational services for students with disabilities who are from culturally diverse backgrounds and to provide preservice teacher training in cultural diversity (Artiles & Trent, 1994; Dunn, 1968; Harry, 1992; Ladson-Billings, 1994; Serna, Forness, & Nielsen, 1998).

Similarly, while the field of VR counseling has historically acknowledged importance of issues of culture in service delivery and provided specific suggestions for promoting culturally competent services (Ayers, 1967; Kunce & Cope, 1969), these suggestions have not been effectively incorporated into rehabilitation counseling service-delivery systems (Schaller, Parker, Garcia, 1998; Wilson, Harley, McCormick, Jolivette, & Jackson, 2001). The following sections will provide an overview of research on race and the acceptance for services and discuss issues of ethnicity and culture in service provision.

Overview of Research on Race and Acceptance for Services

One of the issues in special education has been the overrepresentation of students from culturally diverse backgrounds in special education (Artiles & Trent, 1994; Dunn, 1968; Harry, 1992; Ladson-Billings, 1994), whereas an issue in VR services has been the relationship between race and the acceptance for services. Some studies indicate that European Americans receive higher acceptance rates for services than African Americans or individuals from other culturally diverse groups, including Latino, Native American, and Asian American (Dziekan & Okocha, 1993; Feist-Price, 1995; Herbert & Martinez, 1992; Wilson, 2000).

As mentioned previously, the state/federal VR system is an eligibility system with counselors determining eligibility on a case-by-case basis. Research on issues of eligibility for services and race/ethnicity in the field of VR counseling has not yielded consistent findings, and has also raised issues concerning research methodologies across studies (Wheaton, 1995; Wilson et al., 2001). For example, the first study on this topic was in 1980 when Atkins and Wright found that African Americans were accepted proportionately less often than European Americans for VR services; however, the researchers did not determine whether the difference was statistically significant (Atkins & Wright, 1980).

Twelve years later, Herbert and Martinez (1992) found that African Americans and Latinos were statistically significantly more likely to be determined ineligible for VR services than European Americans. Dziekan and Okocha (1993), in reviewing data from 1985 through 1989, found that European Americans were accepted for services at a statistically higher rate than individuals from culturally diverse backgrounds (e.g., African American, Latino, Native American, and Asian American) in each of the five years reviewed (Dziekan & Okocha, 1993). In addition, Feist-Price (1995) also found that African Americans were not accepted for services as often as European Americans.

On the other hand, Wheaton (1995), Peterson (1996), and Wilson (1999) all found no difference between African Americans and European Americans on acceptance rates for services. Because of the divergence in findings across the various studies, it is still not clear if acceptance for services is influenced by race or other variables such as socioeconomic status, geographic location, educational level, or a combination of variables.

More recently, Wilson (2000) used logistic regression and step-wise entry to examine acceptance for services based on race, education, work status at time of application, and source of support (e.g., family, state program). He found that source of support and race were statistically significant, with European Americans more likely than African Americans to be accepted for services.

Acceptance for VR services is a complex issue that may depend on a combination of factors, and research is still critically needed to examine and hopefully clarify some of this complexity. Meanwhile, however, community perceptions may continue to play a critical role in determining the extent of utilization of services from an agency, and it is imperative that services be viewed as a community resource (Harry, 1992). Parents from culturally diverse backgrounds may have little choice over which schools their children attend; however, they do have more choice when it comes to adult services. Just as critical are perceptions of special education services by families from culturally diverse backgrounds with children with disabilities, as perceptions may affect participation in school as well (Harry, Allen, & McLaughlin, 1995). Therefore, the need for addressing issues of ethnicity and culture in the provision of both special education and VR services remains critical.

Issues of Ethnicity and Culture

Researchers have identified a number of issues related to ethnicity and culture that are found in both VR services and special education (Arkansas Research and Training Center in Vocational Rehabilitation [ARTCVR], 1995; Harry & Anderson, 1994; Isaacs & Benjamin, 1991). Isaacs and Benjamin (1991) point to two in particular: how disability is defined and the communication process.

Defining Disability.　Definitions and conceptions of disability are often defined by parameters of normalcy held by a given culture or society (Mercer, 1973). Cultural and societal perceptions of normalcy may influence perceptions of causation of disability, what qualifies as a disability, behavioral expectations regarding people perceived as having disabilities, and expected behaviors of others in response to a person with a disability (Arnold, 1987). Perceptions of disability will vary, not only among individuals and families from European American backgrounds, but also those from culturally diverse backgrounds.

An example directly related to special education is Harry and Anderson's (1994) review of the referral process of children for special education, and how teacher perceptions of behavior and language among children and young adults from culturally diverse groups, specifically African American males, may lead to a designation of disability for children and young adults from culturally diverse backgrounds. In essence, Harry and Anderson (1994) contend that teachers may hold different views from their students about what constitutes "normal" behavior and language for students in school. These cultural differences may result in misunderstandings and conflict when students from culturally diverse backgrounds exhibit language and behaviors outside of teachers' "norms." This may result in teachers' assigning labels of deviance and disability to these students. This process, Harry and Anderson (1994) contend, leads to a distressing outcome of interpreting the strengths and talents of African American males as deficits.

Another example of culture affecting definitions and response to disability is Mardiros's (1989) study with Mexican American parents. The parents she talked with used both biomedical and sociocultural explanations for their child's disability. Biomedical explanations included genetics, cerebral aneurysm, and premature birth. Sociocultural or folk explanations included divine intervention and holding negative attitudes toward people with disabilities. While parents relied on formal medical services, they also used informal community-based supports for material resources, emotional support, and information.

There are traditional Native American languages that do not have words for constructs such as mental retardation, disability, and handicap. Instead, these languages emphasize meaningful roles an individual with a disability may play in the community (Locust, 1988). Trevino (1996) also found that the term *disability* was not used by Mexican and Mexican American migrant and seasonal farm workers who participated in her study, yet all participants had chronic and severe health problems considered as disabilities by the state/federal VR agency.

Again, more closely related to special education, Latino and African American parents' interpretations of their children's difficulties in school may be different from those of special education professionals (Harry, 1992; Harry et al., 1995). Although parents may acknowledge their child is having difficulties in school, they may not accept the label or etiology used by school staff for the problem. As a result, parents may feel the school is labeling the child without considering other factors such as classroom environment, instructional practices, and information parents may have already conveyed about the child's learning style and interactions with school staff. Parents may also disagree with school officials about labels and etiologies because of discriminatory practices, such as the use of intelligence tests and tracking to remove students from culturally diverse backgrounds from regular education classrooms (Dunn, 1968; Harry et al., 1995; Thomas, 1985). In addition, parents may genuinely disagree with educational officials' position that mild deficits in academic skills are a handicap worthy of a disability label, and parents may reject a within-child etiology by questioning the efficacy of instruction.

Finally, societies from different countries may also hold different perceptions of disability. For example, educators and clinicians in the United States have for years recognized attention deficit hyperactive disorder (ADHD). However, ADHD was not recognized as a disability in Taiwan until the Special Education Law of 1997 (Yang & Schaller, 1997), and students in preservice teacher training programs did not receive specific diagnostic criteria related to ADHD until two years later.

These examples are only a few illustrations of how the meaning of disability may be constructed by individuals from different cultures or societies, or not constructed at all. However, the construct of disability is central to both special education and VR counseling services (Harry & Anderson, 1994; Skrtic, 1991; Szymanski & Treuba, 1994). While the field of VR counseling may include a growing recognition of a more comprehensive, environmental conceptualization of disability (Jenkins et al., 1998; Nosek, 1988), both special education and VR counseling continue to use definitions of disability based on pathological and statistical models (Harry & Anderson, 1994; Skrtic, 1991).

For example, Mercer (1973) distinguishes between categories of disability based on pathological and statistical models. Mercer noted that a pathological model of disability was "culture blind" because the model could be "transferred readily from one society to another and still retain its power to predict and to illuminate" (p. 8). On the other hand, a statistical model of disability "defined abnormality according to the extent to which an individual varied from the average of the population on a particular trait" (p. 4). Mercer stated that identification of some disabilities (e.g., mental retardation, emotional disturbance) is based on a statistical model that combines concepts and language from the pathological model such as etiology, symptom, syndrome, diagnosis, and prognosis. As a result, statistical identification of disability provides an air of objectivity to conclusions based on parameters of normalcy defined by a given group. However, by definition, both pathological and statistical models of disability limit perceptions and interpretations of disability.

In addition, professionals from both special education and VR counseling typically receive training in universities that prize an objectivist approach to professional knowledge and use various logical positivist methodologies to generate new knowledge (Skrtic, 1991). According to the positivist tradition, this knowledge is objective and cumulative. It is the result of a process defined as scientific and quantifiable because the observer is separated from the observed and thus the knowledge produced from any value system. Individuals may be educated over a prolonged period of time during which they access knowledge in the form of theories and propositions that contain general principles that are applied to particular cases. In this way preprofessionals are socialized into value systems, norms, and behavioral patterns of a profession and existing service-delivery systems.

Harry (1992) has stated that the language used to describe this system is often high in level of abstraction and low in context. She noted that the term, *service-delivery system* does not convey the ambiguities or complex patterns of interactions that are embedded in professional work (p. 112). Instead, the term conveys an expectation of services provided in a precise manner and delivered in a predictable fashion.

Unfortunately, this process of professional knowledge generation and transmission may also make professionals in special education and VR counseling susceptible to the delusion that their approach to generating new knowledge and associated practices is objective and inherently correct (Skrtic, 1991). Just as unfortunate is the lack of tolerance for experiences and values not held by the majority culture (Harry et al., 1995). A result may be to only deny peoples' experiences and perceptions (e.g., definitions and meanings of disability) but demean and dehumanize people as well (Szymanski & Trueba, 1994). Historically, special education and VR counseling as large service-delivery systems have not included or valued alternative perceptions and definitions of disability, as well as needs and strengths of people from culturally diverse backgrounds (ARTCVR, 1992; Dunn, 1968). Instead, service systems have found people and children from culturally diverse backgrounds to be less intelligent, more pathological, and more deviant than European Americans, resulting in assignment of more severe and less retractable labels of disability and provision of services of questionable efficacy (Akoto, 1994; Baca & Cervantes, 1989; Dana, 1993, 1995; Harry, 1992; Harry et al., 1995; Hoover, Politzer, & Taylor, 1987; Marcus & Stickney, 1981; McShane & Plas, 1984). It is for these reasons that the issue of how disability is defined is critical.

The Communication Process.   The process of communication between parents and students with disabilities from culturally diverse backgrounds and special education and VR counselors is critical, as individuals and families from culturally diverse backgrounds have a need for information (Harry, 1992; Harry et al., 1995; Schaller et al., 1998). However, both special education and VR agencies commonly use "low-context communication," which can quickly create language barriers for people from culturally diverse backgrounds.

For example, Hall's (1977) definition of low-context communication, in which emphasis is placed on information contained in the words used and interpersonal aspects of the communication process, exemplifies communication often used by professionals. The goal of this form of communication is objectivity, assuming that this objectivity will lead to greater precision of meaning. However, this objectivity only happens if all individuals in the communication process share the same meaning in the language used. Low-context communication, with its emphasis on objective information devoid of interpersonal sensitivity, often results in interactions with little meaning for consumers (Harry, 1992; Skrtic, 1991). As a result, this type of communication can effectively silence individuals and family members who may then have little functional understanding of their rights, obligations, and service options within either special education or VR counseling systems (Harry, 1992).

In addition, language is a medium for expression of cultural values (Chaika, 1982). Terms taken for granted by special educators or VR counselors, such as placement options or individualized plan of employment (IPE), may have little meaning and convey values that are at odds with the family's values (Gudykunst & Kim, 1997). Both special education and VR counseling have a history of focusing on the individual and promoting individual independence, which can conflict with traditional family values that stress interdependence, family rights over individual rights, and family cohesion (Isaacs & Benjamin, 1991).

Acknowledgment of the importance of families is also critical (Isaacs & Benjamin, 1991). Because families from culturally diverse backgrounds might not be like the so-called typical European American family, service providers have often viewed these families as deficient (Alston & Turner, 1994; Harry, 1992). This perspective precludes acknowledging and valuing strengths of families, as well as adaptations families have made for survival and advancement in a hostile environment (Hill, 1971). For example, educational achievement and work have traditionally been valued among families from ethnically diverse backgrounds regardless of socioeconomic level (Alston, McCowan, & Turner, 1994; Hill, 1971). Extended families, including in-laws, other relatives, and friends, provide mutually supportive relationships of interdependence that may include emotional, economic, and enculturation support. Therefore, *family* should be defined by an individual and his or her family in a way that makes sense for them, and acknowledging the importance of family may be key for developing appropriate and effective interventions within both special education and VR counseling services.

Interactions that include support for the student with the disability, an atmosphere of respect for parents, and effective parent participation in conferences and meetings have been noted by Harry (1992) and Harry et al. (1995). Some of the commonalties across these interactions also mirror assumptions of what constitutes professional behavior from a family perspective; these assumptions include respect for others during social relationships by expressing interest in others and being willing to listen to them, taking time to establish relationships and trust, and acknowledging the decision-making processes of parents while also providing information and suggestions for consideration and negotiation.

PERSON-CENTERED PLANNING

Person-centered planning began as a purposeful search for new methods of planning for services with people with disabilities, especially severe disabilities, that placed their desires, dreams, and choices at the center of the planning process (O'Brien, O'Brien, & Mount, 1997; Marrone, Hoff, & Helm, 1997). The planning process seeks to improve the understanding of the experiences of people with disabilities and their families and facilitates effective problem solving among consumers, their families and friends, and special education and VR counseling practitioners. A number of planning processes are under the umbrella of person-centered planning, including "lifestyle planning" (O'Brien et al., 1997), "personal futures planning," "McGill action planning," and "essential lifestyle planning" (Kincaid, 1996). While each of these planning processes has distinct characteristics, they also share a common foundation of beliefs, one of which is that the person with a disability and those who know and love the person are the primary authorities on that individual's life direction (O'Brien & Lovett, 1992).

A number of states endorse the use of person-centered planning (PCP) as a means of reforming their service-delivery systems, and several states require it for people considered to be in protected classes (O'Brien et al., 1997). Foundations of PCP are reviewed below, as are implications for special education and VR counseling practitioners and objections to PCP.

Foundations of Person-Centered Planning

PCP grew from dissatisfaction with existing models of service-delivery systems for people with severe disabilities. These models were viewed as offering a limited selection of services to children and people with disabilities and their families, thereby keeping people with disabilities in subservient roles with little real choice over services or how services were offered (O'Brien et al., 1997; Marrone et al., 1997; Racino, 1994). In addition to a limited selection of services, people with disabilities had little real choice over how services were offered. A history of segregation and congregation within both society and the public school system, despite litigation and legislation intended to change such practices, for people with severe disabilities also contributed to the development of PCP (Falvey, 1995).

The PCP process assists individuals with disabilities and their families and friends in defining a desirable future and steps toward that future. Core information that is needed is not a disability label but the preferences and desires of the individual, such as (1) people to associate with, (2) settings to spend time in, and (3) activities to engage in (Smull & Danehey, 1994). The following are essential questions: "Who is this person? What community opportunities will enable this person to pursue his or her interests in a positive way?" (O'Brien & Lovett, 1992, p. 1). This information emerges from multiple meetings with the child or person with a disability, family members, friends, and professionals. The meetings are run using a facilitator with the goal of developing immediate, practical steps to take. The participants work collaboratively to clarify and define the individual's interests and needs, secure services and supports that assist the individual to meet those interests and needs and therefore to work toward the future the individual has defined as desirable, and to build on existing capacities in service-delivery systems. This process creates tension between what is available and what is needed for an individual to pursue a desirable future (O'Brien & Lovett, 1992). The following are some of the key aspects that have emerged from the PCP processes:

1. Being present in and participating in the community.
2. Gaining and maintaining satisfying relationships.
3. Expressing preferences and making choices in everyday life.
4. Having opportunities to fulfill respected roles in everyday life.
5. Continuing to develop personal competencies (Kincaid, 1996, pp. 440–441).

Information gained from professional/technical assessments of the focus person may be helpful, but this information is placed in the larger context of a person's history and desired future, thereby subordinating professional/technical information to personal knowledge of the focus person. As mentioned, short- and long-term goals are formed during meetings; these goals reflect what is important to the focus individual, and steps are spelled out to reach those goals. Follow-up actions and replanning are a part of the process.

This process may not sound all that different from current service delivery in special education and VR counseling, as both of these services use an individualized planning process such as the IEP and IPE. However, PCP has implications for practitioners in both special education and VR counseling.

Implications for Special Education. As mentioned previously, a driving force for development of PCP has been a history of segregation and institutionalization for people with severe disabilities, including segregation in the public school system. As a result, parents and supporters of children and people with severe disabilities may, through PCP, push for increased integrative practices for their sons and daughters in public school. In addition, the use of professional-technical information and the subordination of this information to personal knowledge of the focus person in PCP has implications for parent–professional interactions. As a result, families and/or individuals with disabilities who have participated in PCP may experience tension between what the school offers and what have been defined as steps toward reaching a desirable future for a child or person with a disability. There are several reasons for this.

First, while federal legislation may guarantee a child with a disability a free and appropriate education in the least restrictive environment, placement may vary among school districts or even schools within a district (Choate, 1997). For example, placement decisions, while considering assessment information about a child's unique educational needs, may also be based on the level of training teachers have to provide services in less restrictive settings such as regular education classrooms or resource rooms with students with severe disabilities. The argument that special education is a service, not a place, may fall on the less-than-receptive ears. Parents may have experienced special education services in a particular setting in one school district but be told when they move to another district that their child will not receive an appropriate education in a least restrictive setting, such as a regular education classroom or resource room, because teachers in this district lack the necessary training.

Second, parents may be increasingly aware of criticisms leveled at special education and, therefore, be less accepting of the primacy of professional decision making as it relates to placement decisions for their children. For example, parents may be aware of issues such as overrepresentation of students from culturally diverse backgrounds in special education (Artiles & Trent, 1994; Harry & Anderson, 1994; Ladson-Billings, 1994; Serna et al., 1998); variability in provision of educational services and quality of practitioners from one school system to the next (Choate, 1997; Gable & Hendrickson, 1997); and the effects of teachers' age, gender, and teaching experience on their perceptions and ratings of students with disabilities (e.g., particularly those with mental retardation and attention deficit hyperactivity disorder) (Moberg, 1995; Yang, 1996). These concerns may undermine parents' confidence in teachers' recommendations for services and placement for their children with severe disabilities.

Finally, parents may also wish to alter the power structure of their interactions with educational professionals (Harry & Anderson, 1994; O'Brien & Lovett, 1992). Despite the professed good intentions of professionals during conferences and meetings with parents, many interactions are structured in such a way that professionals report and parents listen, implying that initiative and authority are in the hands of professionals (Harry & Anderson, 1994). An analysis of the dynamics of professionals' power over parents provided by Gliedman and Roth (1980) illustrates four types of power: the power of the group, that is, the accumulated perspectives of several professionals overpowering parent's attempts at offering dissenting viewpoints; the power of kindness, the apparent kindness of professionals deterring parents from expressing dissenting viewpoints; the power of manipulation, professionals purposely using technical language, knowledge, and authority to overpower parents and gain their consent; and finally, the power of need, parents' need for services and assistance works inhibiting their ability to disagree with the very people who control provision of those services.

The intent of PCP is to assist an individual with a disability and their family in defining a desirable future, and to specify and work toward steps to that future. In so doing, PCP may challenge service-delivery systems. Despite many capable professionals who care about what happens to children and people with disabilities they work with, many service-delivery systems, even when using individualized program planning decrease uncertainty in provision of services by reducing the variety of services offered. This may occur through specification of people with disabilities' daily routines in pre-existing service options that are viewed as best matching the person's disabling condition. In so doing, the purpose and effect of individual planning is to make the service-delivery systems more stable by teaching staff, parents, and individuals with disabilities to think about individual needs in ways that match the system's routines (O'Brien & Lovett, 1992). In essence, an intent of PCP is to work and learn collaboratively through a process of mutual adaptation in which services change to create new supports for individuals with disabilities, the individual with a disability responds to new demands and rewards of the new situation, and everyone including parents and professionals learns from the interaction and continues to change.

Implications for Vocational Rehabilitation Counseling.   State/federal VR counseling has a long history of using a goal-oriented, consumer-controlled service planning and delivery process. This process was first legislated in 1973 through the Rehabilitation Act and later extended through the 1992 Rehabilitation Act amendments, which emphasized consumer choice in service delivery (Jenkins et al., 1998; Marrone et al., 1997). Even with such a history, the state/federal VR counseling system has been criticized by people with disabilities, their advocates, and rehabilitation providers for not embodying a truly PCP and service-delivery process.

As a result, the PCP process has been suggested for and used with people with a wide range of disabilities, including youths with emotional disturbance or mental illness and people with psychiatric disabilities (Hagner, Cheney, & Malloy, 1999), people with developmental disabilities (Bradley, Ashbaugh, & Blaney, 1994), and students with learning disabilities (Michaels, 1997). For people with severe disabilities, development of a vocational profile may be useful.

The vocational profile is a planning tool designed to assist people with disabilities, their families and friends, and service providers to collaborate in generating specific employment outcomes (Callahan & Garner, 1997; Hagner & DiLeo, 1993; Wilkes, 1998). This approach uses ecological assessment to gather information that may include an individual's residential history and transportation availability, educational and vocational programming experience, informal and formal work experience, learning and performance characteristics including instructional and environmental strategies, preferences for different types of work, and social connections. This approach may also include community visits by service providers and consumers as a means of gathering more information about the individual's interests and abilities, as well as for occupational exploration. A technology needs assessment may also be completed to identify assistive devices and adaptations in the workplace, for communication, and mobility.

The necessary information is collected by the rehabilitation professional, and meetings with family and friends are held to develop a career vision, identify potential employment locations, and organize the collective efforts of those participating in the process on the part of the person with the disability. The purpose of vocational profiles developed through a PCP process is to increase the choices available to people with disabilities and their families, their control over identifying employment outcomes, and their access to services to achieve those outcomes.

Objections to Person-Centered Planning.   Some people view PCP as a nice concept but impractical for actual use and implementation. A number of objections to PCP have been raised and are discussed briefly.

The line between the interests of the family and the family member with a disability who may not have functional communication or a history of exercising choice may be very fine. Family members may not have the resources or desire to assist in the PCP process or may be viewed as being overly concerned for the safety, security, or happiness for the family member with a disability (Bradley et al., 1994; Marrone et al., 1997). Practitioners of PCP have noted, however, that any problems arising from family members concerns, except in situations that are abusive or extremely dysfunctional, have been occasions for collaborative problem solving, planning, and goal achievement (Marrone et al., 1997).

PCP has been described as too time consuming to be done by special education practitioners or VR counselors and is a case management issue best left to other professionals (Bradley et al., 1994; Marrone et al., 1997; O'Brien & Lovett, 1992). Any planning process that brings together a mix of people with a variety of perspectives, even if that process is meant to gather interested parties on behalf of a person with a disability in a manner that leads to immediate action, may take more time than a generic process of planning under the control of professionals. However, a PCP process may be better suited than other alternatives to bringing resources together and producing opportunities for action that attend to the focus person's desires and needs.

A final objection to PCP is that it may not be an appropriate planning process for all people with disabilities (Marrone et al., 1997). PCP has not been promoted as the only response to issues of service delivery and interactions with service providers for people with disabilities. It may not be appropriate for families or individuals who are not comfortable with open discussion of employment or life issues. And it may not be appropriate for families or individuals with disabilities who are from cultures that do not value open, group problem-solving approaches (Bradley et al., 1994; Marrone et al., 1997; O'Brien & Lovett, 1992).

SUMMARY

Contemporary practice in the fields of special education and vocational rehabilitation counseling is more complex and challenging than ever before. These challenges require that both fields continue to work collaboratively and expand research efforts that address the issues discussed here in order to provide educational and rehabilitation services that consider the strengths and needs of all children and individuals with disabilities as well as their families.

QUESTIONS FOR FURTHER DISCUSSION

1. Please discuss similarities and differences of the special education and rehabilitation counseling service-delivery systems.

2. Describe how issues of culture may impact definitions of disability and communication between special educators and parents/students from culturally diverse backgrounds.

3. What is person-centered planning?

4. Use of person-centered planning by individuals with disabilities may have implications for special educators. What are these implications?

REFERENCES

Akoto, A. (1994). Notes on an Afrikan-centered pedagogy. In M. Shujaa (Ed.), *Too much schooling too little education: A paradox of black life in white societies* (pp. 319–338). Trenton, NJ: Africa World Press.

Alston, R., McCowan, C., & Turner, W. (1994). Family functioning as a correlate of disability adjustment for African Americans. *Rehabilitation Counseling Bulletin, 37*(4), 277–289.

Alston, R., & Turner, W. (1994). A family strengths model of adjustment to disability for African American clients. *Journal of Counseling & Development, 72*(4), 378–383.

Arkansas Research and Training Center in Vocational Rehabilitation. (1995). *American Indian rehabilitation programs: Unmet needs.* Fayetteville: University of Arkansas, Hot Springs Rehabilitation Center.

Arnold, B. (1987). *Disability, rehabilitation, and the Mexican American.* Edinburg, TX: Pan American University.

Artiles, A., & Trent, S. (1994). Overrepresentation of minority students in special education: A continuing debate. *Journal of Special Education, 27*(4), 410–437.

Atkins, B., & Wright, G. (1980). Three views: Vocational rehabilitation of blacks: The statement. *Journal of Rehabilitation, 46,* 40–46.

Ayers, G. (1967). *Rehabilitating the culturally disadvantaged.* Mankato, MN: Mankato State College.

Baca, L., & Cervantes, H. (1989). Assessment procedures for the exceptional child. In L. Baca & H. Cervantes (Eds.), *The Bilingual Special Education Interface* (pp. 153–177). Columbus, OH: Merrill Publishing.

Banja, J. (1990). Rehabilitation and empowerment. *Archives of Physical Medicine and Rehabilitation, 71,* 614–615.

Brabham, R., Mandeville, K., & Koch, L. (1998). The state-federal vocational rehabilitation program. In R. Parker & E. Szymanski (Eds.), *Rehabilitation counseling: Basics and beyond* (3rd ed., pp. 41–70). Austin, TX: PRO-ED.

Bradley, V., Ashbaugh, J., & Blaney, B. (Eds.). (1994). *Creating individual supports for people with developmental disabilities: A mandate for change at many levels.* London: Brookes.

Callahan, M., & Garner, J. (1997). *Keys to the workplace: Skills and supports for people with disabilities.* Baltimore: Brookes.

Chaika, E. (1982). *Language: The social mirror.* Rowley, MA: Newbury House.

Choate, J. (Ed.) (1997). *Successful inclusive teaching: Proven ways to detect and correct special needs* (2nd ed). Needham Heights, MA: Allyn & Bacon.

Dana, R. (1993). *Multicultural assessment perspectives for professional psychology.* Boston: Allyn & Bacon.

Dana, R. (1995). Impact of the use of standard psychological assessment on the diagnosis and treatment of ethnic minorities. In J. Aponte, R. Young Rivers, & J. Wohl (Eds.), *Psychological Interventions and Cultural Diversity* (pp. 57–73). Boston: Allyn & Bacon.

Dunn, L. (1968). Special education for the mildly mentally retarded: Is much of it justifiable? *Exceptional Children, 23,* 5–21.

Dysseguard, B. (1980). *The role of special education in the overall rehabilitation program.* New York: World Rehabilitation Fund.

Dziekan, K., & Okocha, A. (1993). Accessibility of rehabilitation services: Comparison by racial-ethnic status. *Rehabilitation Counseling Bulletin, 36,* 183–189.

Falvey, M. (Ed.). (1995). *Inclusive and heterogeneous schooling: Assessment, curriculum, and instruction.* London: Brookes.

Feist-Price, S. (1995). African Americans with disabilities and equity in vocational rehabilitation services: One state's review. *Rehabilitation Counseling Bulletin, 39,* 119–129.

Gable, R., & Hendrickson, J. (1997). Teaching all the students: A mandate for educators. In J. Choate (Ed.). *Successful inclusive teaching: Proven ways to detect and correct special needs* (2nd ed., pp. 3–17). Needham Heights, MA: Allyn & Bacon.

Gliedman, J., & Roth, W. (1980). *The unexpected minority: Handicapped children in America.* New York: Harcourt Brace Jovanovich.

Gudykunst, W., & Kim, Y. (1997). *Communicating with strangers: An approach to intercultural communication* (3rd ed.). New York: McGraw Hill.

Hagner, D., Cheney, D., & Malloy, J. (1999). Career-related outcomes of a model demonstration for young adults with emotional disturbance. *Rehabilitation Counseling Bulletin, 42*(3), 228–242.

Hagner, D., & DiLeo, D. (1993). *Working together: Workplace culture, supported employment, and persons with disabilities.* Cambridge, MA: Brookline.

Hall, E. (1977). *Beyond culture.* New York: Anchor.

Hanley-Maxwell, C., Szymanski, E., & Owens-Johnson, L. (1998). School-to-adult-life transition and supported employment. In R. Parker & E. Szymanski (Eds.), *Rehabilitation counseling: Basics and beyond* (3rd ed., pp. 143–179). Austin, TX: PRO-ED.

Harry, B. (1992). *Cultural diversity, families, and the special education system: Communication and empowerment.* New York: Teachers College Press.

Harry, B., Allen, N., & McLaughlin, M. (1995). Communication versus compliance: African-American parents' involvement in special education. *Exceptional Children, 61*(4), 364–377.

Harry, B., & Anderson, M. (1994). The disproportionate placement of African American males in special education programs: A critique of the process. *Journal of Negro Education, 63*(4), 602–619.

Herbert, J., & Martinez, M. (1992). Client ethnicity and vocational rehabilitation case service outcome. *Journal of Job Placement, 8,* 10–16.

Hill, R. (1971). *The strengths of black families.* New York: Emerson Hall.

Hoover, M., Politzer, R., & Taylor, O. (1987). Bias in reading tests for black language speakers: A sociolinguistic perspective. *Negro Educational Review, 38,* 81–98.

Isaacs, M., & Benjamin, M. (1991). *Towards a culturally competent system of care: Programs which utilize culturally competent principles* (Vol. II). Washington, DC: Georgetown University Child Development Center, Center for Child Health and Mental Health Policy, Child and Adolescent Service System Program Technical Assistance Center.

Jenkins, W., Patterson, J., & Szymanski, E. (1998). Philosophical, historical, and legislative aspects of the rehabilitation counseling profession. In R. Parker & E. Szymanski (Eds.), *Rehabilitation counseling: Basics and beyond* (3rd ed., pp. 1–40). Austin, TX: PRO-ED.

Jones, E. (1990). ADA: What's next? *Worklife, 3*(2), 26–27.

Kincaid, D. (1996). Person-centered planning. In L. Koegel, R. Koegel, & G. Dunlap (Eds.), *Positive behavioral support: Including people with difficult behavior in the community* (pp. 439–465). London: Brookes.

Kunce, J., & Cope, C. (Eds.). (1969). *Rehabilitation and the culturally disadvantaged.* Columbia: University of Missouri, Regional Rehabilitation Research Institute.

Ladson-Billings, G. (1994). *The dreamkeepers: Successful teachers of African-American children.* San Francisco: Jossey-Bass.

Locust, C. (1988). Wounding the spirit: Discrimination and traditional American Indian belief systems. *Harvard Educational Review, 58*(3), 315–330.

Marcus, L., & Stickney, B. (1981). *Race and education.* Springfield, IL: Charles Thomas.

Mardiros, M. (1989). Conception of childhood disability among Mexican American parents. *Medical Anthropology, 12,* 55–68.

Marrone, J., Hoff, D., & Helm, D. (1997). Person-centered planning for the millennium: We're old enough to remember when PCP was just a drug. *Journal of Vocational Rehabilitation, 8*(1), 285–297.

McInerney, M., & Karan, O. (1981). Federal legislation and the integration of special education and vocational rehabilitation. *Mental Retardation, 2,* 21–23.

McShane, D., & Plas, J. (1984). The cognitive functioning of American Indian children: Moving from the WISC to the WISC-R. *School Psychology Review, 13,* 61–73.

Mercer, J. (1973). *Labeling the mentally retarded.* Berkeley: University of California Press.

Michaels, C. (1997). Preparation for employment: Counseling practices for promoting personal competency. In P. Gerber & D. Brown (Eds.), *Learning disabilities and employment* (pp. 187–212). Austin, TX: PRO-ED.

Moberg, S. (1995). Impact of teachers' dogmatism and pessimistic stereotype on the effect of EMR-class label on teachers' judgments in Finland. *Education & Training in Mental Retardation and Developmental Disabilities, 30*(2), 141–150.

Nosek, M. (1988). Independent living and rehabilitation counseling. In S. Rubin & N. Rubin (Eds.), *Contemporary challenges to the rehabilitation counseling profession* (pp. 45–60). Baltimore: Brookes.

Obermann, C. (1965). *A history of vocational rehabilitation in America.* New York: Arno Press.

O'Brien, C., O'Brien, J., & Mount, B. (1997). Person-centered planning has arrived . . . or has it? *Mental Retardation, 35*(6), 480–484.

O'Brien, J., & Lovett, H. (1992). *Finding a way toward everyday lives: The contribution of person centered planning.* Harrisburg, PA: Pennsylvania Office of Mental Retardation.

Peterson, G. (1996). *An analysis of participation, progress, and outcome of individuals from diverse racial and ethnic backgrounds in the public vocational rehabilitation program in Nevada.* Unpublished doctoral dissertation, University of Northern Colorado.

President's Committee on Employment of People with Disabilities and U.S. Architectural and Transportation Barriers Compliance Board. (1990). *Americans with Disabilities Act (ADA) in Brief.* Washington, DC: Authors.

Racino, J. (1994). Creating change in states, agencies, and communities. In V. Bradley, J. Ashbaugh, & B. Blaney (Eds.). *Creating individual supports for people with developmental disabilities: A mandate for change at many levels* (pp. 171–196). London: Brookes.

Schaller, J., & Parker, R., & Garcia, S. (1998). Moving toward culturally competent rehabilitation counseling services: Issues and practices. *Journal of Applied Rehabilitation Counseling, 29*(2), 40–48.

Serna, L., Forness, S., & Nielsen, M. (1998). Intervention versus affirmation: Proposed solutions to the problem of disproportionate minority representation in special education. *Journal of Special Education, 32*(1), 48–51.

Skrtic, T. (1991). Behind special education: A critical analysis of the professional culture and school organization. Denver, CO: Love.

Smull, M., & Danehey, A. (1994). Increasing quality while reducing costs: The challenge of the 1990s. In V. Bradley, J. Ashbaugh, & B. Blaney (Eds.), *Creating individual supports for people with developmental disabilities: A mandate for change at many levels* (pp. 59–78). London: Brookes.

Szymanski, E. (1984). Rehabilitation counselors in school settings. *Journal of Applied Rehabilitation Counseling, 15*(4), 10–13.

Szymanski, E., King, J., Parker, R., & Jenkins, W. (1989). The state-federal rehabilitation program: Overview and interface with special education. *Exceptional Children, 36,* 70–77.

Szymanski, E., & Trueba, H. (1994). Castification of people with disabilities: Potential disempowering aspects of classification in disability services. *Journal of Rehabilitation, 60*(3), 12–20.

Talbot, H. (1961). A concept of rehabilitation. *Rehabilitation Literature, 22,* 358–364.

Thomas, W. (1985). Schooling as a political instrument of social control: School response to Black migrant youth in Buffalo, New York, 1917–1940. *Teachers College Record, 86*(4), 579–592.

Trevino, B. (1996). *The meaning of disability in the lives of migrant and seasonal farmworkers with chronic and severe health problems: A qualitative study.* Unpublished doctoral dissertation, University of Wisconsin, Madison.

Wheaton, J. (1995). Vocational rehabilitation acceptance for European Americans and African Americans: Another look. *Rehabilitation Counseling Bulletin, 38,* 224–231.

Wilkes, D. (1998). *Person centered planning: Rocketship to the stars.* Richardson, TX: Author.

Wilson, K. (1999). Vocational rehabilitation acceptance: A tale of two races in a large midwestern state. *Journal of Applied Rehabilitation Counseling, 30,* 25–31.

Wilson, K. (2000). Predicting vocational rehabilitation counseling acceptance based on race, education, work status, and source of support at application. *Rehabilitation Counseling Bulletin, 43,* 97–105.

Wilson, K., Harley, D., McCormick, K., Jolivette, K., & Jackson, R. (2001). A literature review of vocational rehabilitation acceptance and explaining bias in the rehabilitation process. *Journal of Applied Rehabilitation Counseling, 32*(1), 24–35.

Wright, B. (Ed.). (1959). *Psychology and rehabilitation.* Washington, DC: American Psychological Association.

Wright, G. (1980). *Total rehabilitation.* Boston: Little, Brown.

Yang, K. (1996). *Teachers' perceptions of attention-deficit/ hyperactivity disorder in Taiwan: Implications for universalistic and cultural relativistic perspectives of disability.* Unpublished doctoral dissertation, University of Texas, Austin.

Yang, K., & Schaller, J. (1997). Teachers' ratings of Attention-Deficit Hyperactivity Disorder and decisions for referral for services in Taiwan. *Journal of Child and Family Studies, 6*(1), 249–261.

■ ■ ■ ■ ■

TEACHER EDUCATION
Toward a Qualified Teacher for Every Classroom

MARY T. BROWNELL
University of Florida

MICHAEL S. ROSENBERG
Johns Hopkins University

PAUL T. SINDELAR
University of Florida

DEBORAH DEUTSCH SMITH
Vanderbilt University

Public interest in teacher education has never been keener, and never before has its warrant been questioned so fundamentally. Recently, the Abell Foundation (2001), on the basis of a critical analysis of the research on teacher quality and student achievement, advocated the *elimination* of coursework requirements for teacher licensure. It characterized licensure as "an inhospitable process" (p. v) that discourages capable people from entering the field. Hess (2001) concurred. He conjectured that "spending time and money on preparation and courses of study that may bear little relation to what it takes to be a good teacher discourages some talented people from entering the profession" (p. 1). He also argued that licensure costs more than it yields in benefits. These reports represent the latest in a series of increasingly hostile and politicized analyses aimed at deregulating the process of teacher preparation (Cochran-Smith & Fries, 2001). Public interest in the issue has been sharpened by the fact that even proponents of teacher education are recommending fundamental reform as well. Cochran-Smith and Fries (2001) characterize this point of view as the professionalization position.

The professionalism position is represented best by the National Commission on Teaching & America's Future (NCTAF) and its spokesperson, Linda Darling-Hammond

(NCTAF, 1996, 1997). Building on the K–12 standards movement, NCTAF and other proponents advocate improving teacher education by linking it and professional development to performance standards such as those promulgated by the National Board of Professional Teaching Standards (NBPTS) for experienced teachers and the Interstate New Teachers Assessment and Support Consortium (INTASC) for novices. According to this perspective, teacher education programs must be accredited through review by the National Council for Accreditation of Teacher Education (NCATE) and its member organizations, whose standards are aligned with NBPTS and INTASC. Advocates of professionalization also support assessing teachers on performance standards. On this point, they differ with deregulationists, who consider student achievement, not teacher performance, the standard with which to evaluate teacher education reform.

Although special education is not identified in this debate, the ability of teachers to instruct all students successfully has become a rhetorical high ground that both sides have claimed (Cochran-Smith & Fries, 2000). Besides, prominent or not, special education teacher education is part of the larger enterprise and, as such, is buffeted by the same ideological storm (e.g., Sindelar & Rosenberg, 2000). Furthermore, special education teacher education has its own problems—chronic and critical teacher shortages, among others, separate from the debate about the merits of teacher education generally. In response to both the larger conceptual issues besetting teacher education generally and the problems particular to our field, the Office of Special Education Programs (OSEP) has funded a personnel preparation policy center. We are affiliated with that center—the Center on Personnel Studies in Special Education, or COPSSE—and in this chapter we lay out what the literature has to say about the three broad issues that OSEP has asked us to consider: supply and demand, professional preparation, and certification and licensure. In the process, we will describe contemporary best practices—to the extent possible—and identify critical questions that remain unanswered by the research.

SUPPLY AND DEMAND

A plethora of evidence points to the fact that U.S. schools are experiencing a continuing, severe shortage of qualified personnel. For example, recent data from the U.S. Department of Education (http://www.ideadata.org/tables25th/ar_ac2.htm) reveal that, during the 2000–2001 school year, 43,799 special education positions were filled by teachers who were less than fully qualified, 11.5 percent of the entire special education workforce. An additional 3,733 teachers were needed to replace teachers who were less than fully qualified and were teaching children with disabilities aged 3 to 5, 11 percent of the preschool workforce. Substantial shortages exist in other special education disciplines, including para-educators (6.7 percent), speech/language therapists (3.5 percent), audiologists (4 percent), and school psychologists (3.7 percent). On the other hand, shortages of occupational therapists and physical therapists were both about 2.4 percent (IDEAdata.org).

It is noteworthy that teacher shortages are not evenly distributed throughout the United States. They vary from state to state, ranging from 1 percent or less in five jurisdictions to 28 percent in Hawaii (IDEAdata.org). Yet, dramatic as it is, state-to-state variability is not as predictable (and therefore as amenable to correction) as variability that results from demographics. Evidence suggests that more severe shortages exist in areas where the most vulnerable students are being taught, that is, in poor urban areas and remote rural areas (Darling-Hammond & Sclan, 1996; NASDSE, 1996). Another critical factor related to the supply of and demand for personnel concerns the limited number of teachers from culturally and linguistically diverse groups (Artiles & Trent, 1997; Smith-Davis, 2000).

To its credit, special education teacher education has prepared and sustained a qualified workforce that now exceeds 350,000 professionals. There is a substantial capacity to prepare teachers; in fact, in 1996–1997, the 850 or so special education programs in this country (National Association of State Directors of Teacher Education and Certification [NASDTEC], 2000) produced 22,158 bachelor's and master's degree graduates. In spite of this seemingly high productivity, new graduates constitute a small percentage of all new hires. In an analysis of sources of 1990–1991 teacher supply, for example, Boe, Cook, Bobbitt, and Terhanian (1998) found that nearly 70 percent of 23,182 new hires were teachers from a reserve pool (of experienced teachers returning to the workforce and first-time teachers who delayed entry into the field). By contrast, the 6,311 teachers with recent degrees in teacher preparation made up little more than one-fourth of all new hires. The number of degrees awarded exceeds the number of teachers with recent degrees for two reasons. Many master's degree recipients are practicing teachers, and many newly graduated teachers decline to enter the workforce immediately.

Furthermore, attrition is a significant factor in the demand for special education teachers. Teachers leave the field for a variety of reasons, though many who do leave later return to the classroom (Ingersoll, 2001; Lauritzen & Friedman, 1993). In fact, in interviews with ninety-three teachers leaving special education jobs in Florida, Brownell, Smith, McNellis, and Miller (1997) reported that less than 20 percent of them were leaving for work in a non-educational field or were not otherwise planning to return to teaching. Nonetheless, beginning teachers are especially vulnerable to attrition, and they remain at risk for up to five years (Singer, 1993). Teachers who lack current certification also are at greater risk to leave teaching (Miller, Brownell, & Smith, 1999). Thus, Boe et al.'s finding that one-third of newly hired beginning teachers were not fully qualified is especially disturbing, given the serious risk of attrition to which beginning teachers teaching out of field are exposed.

It is apparent that under current conditions, the supply of special education teachers is insufficient to meet the demand of the ever-increasing numbers of students with disabilities (Boe, 1998; Boe & Barkanic, 2000). It is likely that this shortage will become more severe simply because of increasing enrollments, a wave of retirements, and attrition (Recruiting New Teachers, 1999). The implications of these teacher shortages are obvious, as over 500,000 students with disabilities are taught each year by teachers who probably are not well prepared to meet their complex learning needs.

Throughout this analysis, we have made the assumption that qualified teachers—teachers with standard licenses who have completed conventional teacher education programs—are more effective in their work with students with disabilities than individuals who are less than fully qualified. Without this assumption, of course, shortages would not be an issue, because 99 percent of special education teaching positions are filled (albeit with many unqualified teachers). Of course, the validity of the assumption that qualified teachers make a difference is an empirical question, a question that research must address: What is the nature of special education teacher preparation and its impact on teachers' knowledge, skills, and dispositions?

PROFESSIONAL PREPARATION

To produce an adequate supply of appropriate and qualified personnel, we must develop a better understanding of two critical issues. First, we need to understand better how to recruit culturally and linguistically diverse individuals into special education personnel preparation programs. Second, we need more knowledge about the impact of teacher education on teachers' knowledge, skills, and dispositions. We discuss these topics in the following sections.

Recruitment into Programs

Available recruitment data suggest that many young people, particularly males and persons of color, do not pursue teaching as a career. In fact, Darling-Hammond (1996) estimated that only 9 percent of entering college freshmen are considering teaching. Although similar statistics are not available for prospective special education teachers, chronic shortages in these areas suggest that most students do not consider special education as a career option, either (Boe, Cook, Bobbitt, & Terhanian, 1998; U.S. Department of Education, 1999). More disturbing is the insufficient supply of minority recruits into special education careers. As the special education student population has grown increasingly diverse in terms of race, culture, and language, the population of special education teachers has not (Olson & Jerald, 1998; Olson, 2000). Teaching is not the only special education workforce that lacks diversity. In fact, critical shortages of culturally and linguistically diverse personnel characterize most related services professions. For example, membership data from the American Speech-Language-Hearing Association and the National Association of School Psychologists reveal that only 7.3 percent and 8 percent of their members are from minority backgrounds (Guillory, 2000; NASP, 1999).

It is critical to study factors that influence the recruitment of personnel into special education. Although the federal government has made a substantial investment in increasing the numbers and diversity of qualified personnel to serve students with disabilities, we do not know how effective these initiatives and other recruitment strategies have been. Some available information suggests that states such as Connecticut, some OSEP-funded institutions, and some alternative route programs have recruited successfully, particularly students who are culturally and linguistically diverse (Center for the Study of Teaching and Policy, 1998; Hurwitz, 2000; Rosenberg & Rock, 1994). Overall, however, this information is not readily available, and we have little knowledge of how state and federal recruitment incentives are influencing the quantity and diversity of students pursuing special education careers.

What Does High-Quality Personnel Preparation Look Like?

Advocates of professionalization contend that because it results in better-prepared teachers, accreditation of teacher education programs is an essential element of standards-based reform. The Council for Exceptional Children (CEC) is special education's NCATE affiliate and, as such, oversees the accreditation of special education programs. As a result, teacher preparation, pre-kindergarten through the twelfth grade, is shaped by competencies developed by CEC and its divisions. Currently, CEC is working to align its standards to those of INTASC and the NBPTS. Historically in special education, competencies were more likely to have been developed through a process of consensus building than by systematic study of classroom practice (Bricker & Slentz, 1988; McCollum, McLean, McCartan, & Kaiser,

1989). Although this competency-based approach to teacher education has resulted in a narrow and technical orientation to teacher education (Blanton, 1992), teacher educators are becoming more aware that "the education profession requires a foundation broader than that of technical knowledge" (Spodek, Saracho, & Peters, 1988, p. 70).

Teacher educators also recognize the limitations of traditional university classroom instruction and are concerned that lecturing does not promote the type of teacher thinking necessary for complex school environments (Tom, 1997). Lectures that primarily involve the dissemination of information combined with limited field-based opportunities to apply knowledge do not produce high-quality graduates (Blanton, 1992; Richardson, 1996). Competent teachers are those who have a well-developed conceptual foundation that cuts across philosophical orientations (Sprinthall & Thies-Sprinthall, 1983), resulting in teachers who are flexible, responsive, adaptable, and empathetic (Blanton, 1992). To develop these kinds of teachers, Howey (1996) has suggested that preparation programs incorporate the following features: (1) a coherent program focus, (2) program content and instructional pedagogy based on the research on children's and adults' learning, and (3) field-based teacher education pedagogy.

Coherent Program Focus.   Teacher education programs tend to have a technical orientation that results in programs "that superficially engage students in a large number of disparate and unconnected ideas and practices" (Howey, 1996, p. 150). By contrast, a coherent program focus improves program quality by providing a framework for faculty as they develop and implement the program and students, as they learn, integrate, and apply information. Such a focus also provides teacher educators with a shared vision about program purposes and goals, and facilitates collaboration among them. Finally, a coherent program focus and shared vision promote the development of collaborative problem solving, professional growth, and clear links between theory and practice (Howey, 1996; Kagan, 1990).

Although basing teacher education on a conceptual framework seems necessary and has intellectual appeal, there are many unanswered questions about its impact. Good general teacher education programs rely on explicit conceptual frameworks (Howey, 1996). Historically, special education programs have been competency driven, although that may be changing: Accreditation now requires explicit conceptual frameworks for all programs. Unified programs—programs in which the preparation of classroom and special education teachers is merged—are prominent in the special education literature (Blanton, Griffin, Winn, & Pugach, 1997) and are based on a coherent vision of teacher education. That vision emphasizes equal access to high-quality teaching and commitment to all students, and stipulates that responsibility for the education of students with disabilities is shared between classroom teachers and special educators. Thus, unified preparation makes sense. That vision also is eclectic. It seems to us that unified programs have a stronger element of constructivism than most special education programs—and a stronger element of direct instruction than most elementary programs.

We need to know whether establishing a coherent vision matters. If so, we need to determine the extent to which teacher educators in our field guide program development on the basis of conceptual frameworks, and whether such frameworks affect how graduates think about their work, what they know and can do, and what their students learn. We also have questions about alternative certification programs. Are they based on a coherent vision or driven by licensure requirements? How does the vision underlying an alternative program compare to those underlying more traditional special education preparation?

Research-Based Program Content.   With a vision in place, teacher educators may specify program content, and that content should be research based. Research examining links between student achievement and teaching suggests that "what teachers know and do is the most important influence on what students learn" (National Commission on Teaching & America's Future, 1996). Yet in spite of research on effective practices, there is reason to believe that preservice students in elementary and special education are graduating with insufficient knowledge of academic content and research-based strategies. Furthermore, many practicing special and general education teachers do not engage in research-based practices (Gersten, Vaughn, Deshler, & Schiller, 1997; Malouf & Schiller, 1995).

Although recommendations about teacher education content abound, we do not know the extent to which conventional and alternative certification programs are embracing this advice. We do not know how shifts in preparation from categorical to noncategorical and unified programs affect program content. More importantly, we are uncertain about the degree to which preparation programs—traditional or alternative, special or general education—change prospective teachers' practices. For example, Richardson (1996) contended that entering teacher beliefs and school context where teachers practice may well overpower the impact of teacher education.

Field-Based Teacher Education Pedagogy.   In far too many college classrooms, teacher educators disseminate information through lecture and demonstration (Blanton, 1992; Howey, 1996; Tom, 1997), and what is taught is disconnected from what happens in classrooms. Research suggests that more effective teacher education must (1) move away from lecture and demonstration to incorporate extensive modeling, (2) provide opportunities for preservice students to reflect collaboratively on what they are learning, (3) invent ways of challenging students' beliefs, particularly about diversity, and (4) provide extensive clinical experience that is linked closely to what students are learning in their program (Sprinthall, Reiman, & Thies-Sprinthall, 1996; Tom, 1997).

Although the arguments for improving teacher education pedagogy are compelling and logical, we do not know the extent to which teacher education institutions have been successful in accomplishing methodological reform. Professional development schools (PDSs)—schools in which improving classroom practice and teacher education occur together—have been proposed as a vehicle for reforming teacher education pedagogy. However, the literature on PDSs suggests that many colleges have been unsuccessful in forging strong partnerships with schools (see Valli, Cooper, & Frankes, 1997). Programs that have succeeded in establishing strong school/university collaboration have failed to evaluate their impact on teacher development. Furthermore, in special education, scale is a problem. PDSs have no more special education programs than schools generally, so opportunities for training special education teachers there are limited. These critical issues must be addressed if we are to gain a better understanding of how to prepare all teachers for their work with challenging students.

Variability of Special Education Teacher Preparation

In the discussion to this point, we have spoken of special education teacher education as if it were a uniform process, belying its remarkable diversity. Special education teachers may be prepared and licensed to work with students with different kinds of disabilities, with different degrees of disability, or at different age levels, depending on the state in which a teacher is trained and the manner in which that state structures licensure. Today, few states are strictly categorical. Many more are eclectic in the sense of offering both categorical and non-categorical licenses. A small but increasing number of states have begun to differentiate licensure on the basis of the severity of the disability. California is a case in point; it offers licenses in mild/moderate disabled and moderate/severe disabled. Massachusetts differentiates between teachers of students with special needs and teachers of students with intensive special needs. A dozen other states draw similar distinctions.

Thus, in the context of special education, the question of the effectiveness of teacher preparation is a complicated one. There is movement afoot to standardize the process by establishing common standards (INTASC and NBPTS) and accreditation (through NCATE and CEC), but it is hard to imagine states relinquishing their prerogative to define special education practice as they see fit. At this point, we see nothing fundamentally wrong with this situation. After all, we know so little about the process of teacher education generally that one licensure/training structure cannot be judged better than another. In the absence of reliable student outcomes data, it is hard to argue that teachers in a given state are better as a group than teachers in another state, in spite of the fact that the requirements for certification in the two states may differ dramatically.

CERTIFICATION AND LICENSURE

Although it is generally agreed that a highly trained workforce is necessary to provide educational services to students with disabilities, issues related to the licensure of personnel remain controversial. What constitutes appropriate professional standards for special educators, who should deliver licensure programs, and the relationship between certification status and student performance continue to fuel dissention among policy makers, teacher educators, and state and district personnel. We begin this section by summarizing why it is believed that we need to license teachers. We then review two critical and controversial certification issues: (1) the role of standards in special education teacher preparation and (2) alternative routes to teacher licensure.

Teacher Licensure

Education professionals regard licensure as an index of qualification and competence. Although the notion of using a "professional model" for licensing teachers has been questioned (e.g., Angus & Mirel, 2001), a standard teaching certificate generally means that an individual has been prepared in a state-approved teacher preparation program that has combined aspects of specific subject matter knowledge and knowledge of teaching and learning (Darling-Hammond, 2000b). States exercise the authority for licensing teachers, often by approving programs of study at colleges and universities (Sykes, 1999). Teacher education programs usually include courses and field experiences, within a required framework established by the state. Although requirements vary greatly across states, there is general recognition among those in the educational community that valid and explicit professional standards are prerequisites for high-quality teacher preparation (Clemson-Ingram & Fessler, 1997; O'Shea, Hammitte, Mainzer, & Crutchfield, 2000).

According to Sykes (1999) states license teachers to protect children from the potentially harmful effects of unqualified personnel. Licensure is a safeguard that ensures that competent individuals are caring for and educating our children. It is also designed to guarantee a common standard of teacher quality across localities within a specific state; "fairness dictates that *where* a child lives in a state should not determine his or her access to qualified teachers" (p. 33). (It is ironic—and unfair—that *where* children live often influences the likelihood that they will be taught by fully qualified teachers.) Finally, the licensure of teachers prevents hiring practices that abuse the public trust; state mandated job-related qualifications serve to counteract nepotism and the use of teaching positions as currency in systems of local patronage.

Standards in Special Education Teacher Preparation

Standards are important in that they provide explicit performance-based guidelines as to what we expect of teachers. Unfortunately, because teacher quality is difficult to measure and guarantee, promulgating standards is and has always been an uphill battle (Sykes, 2000). Still, a number of prominent professional groups (INTASC, NBPTS, NCATE, NCTAF) and scholars (Darling-Hammond, 1999; Galluzzo, 1999) have contributed their views of what successful teachers need to know and to be able to do and have speculated about how standards-based efforts may be reconciled and aligned.

In special education, the Council for Exceptional Children (CEC) remains at the center of efforts to develop, refine, and advocate for standards for the preparation of teachers of students with disabilities. CEC has provided a structure (Council for Exceptional Children, 2001) that delineates the essential knowledge and skills that those entering the profession need to acquire (O'Shea et al., 2000). These standards are used by many states in the process of reviewing and evaluating teacher preparation programs. Moreover, CEC, in conjunction with other organizations (e.g., NCATE), offers technical assistance to states in the development of licensing standards and to teacher education programs in ways to meet the standards (Mainzer & Horvath, 2001). These integrated policy and technical assistance efforts initiated and sustained by CEC have the potential for becoming a formal national certification process, a move that some (e.g., Otis-Wilborn & Winn, 2000; Swan & Sirvis, 1992) believe could strengthen the quality of teachers entering the profession.

Still, the development and use of standards, as well as the movement toward national certification for special educators, are controversial. Sindelar and Kilgore (1995) observed that it is doubtful that agreement can be reached regarding how best to certify teachers. For example, differences in opinion regarding special education's relationship to general education—complete unification of the two systems into an inclusive framework (e.g., Stainback, Stainback, & Ayres, 1996) versus segregated special education for those who need it (Lieberman, 1996)—suggest that we currently lack consensus about best practice, a consensus we need to build national standards for teacher preparation. Also, there is little agreement about whether it is best to prepare and license special educators categorically by disability or through a multicategorical framework (Eichinger & Downing, 2000) or if it is best to prepare teachers in dual licensure programs (general and special education) rather than in special education alone. Although there are clear trends toward generic licensure and licensure structures based on severity, and growth in dual licensure programs, there is no clear empirical basis for the superiority of any one approach over another (Mainzer & Horvath, 2001). Therefore, it is apparent that many critical aspects of special education teacher licensure standards are more likely the result of logic and persuasion than of a strong foundation of rigorous empirical re-search and analysis.

There is little disagreement, however, about the need for teacher preparation programs to adhere to high standards of professional practice (National Commission on Teaching & America's Future, 1996). It is generally recognized (e.g., O'Shea et al., 2000; Otis-Wilborn & Winn, 2000) that the relationship between the accreditation of special education prepara-tion programs (i.e., ensuring that programs do adhere to high standards) and the actual credentialing of special educators must be strong and direct. Factors that influence the devel-opment of individual special education programs include both an articulation of the core val-ues shared by faculty and evidence that national standards are embedded in the program. A recent special issue of *Teacher Education and Special Education* (Johnson & Bauer, 2000) illustrated how a number of training programs are ensuring that their programs reflect national standards and core values. Still, proceeding as if we have a fixed and agreed on licensure structure seems both premature and constraining. More empirical work on the performance outcomes of graduates from specific preparation programs and licensure frameworks may provide guidance in coming to consensus on many of these critical standards-based issues.

Alternative Routes to Licensure

At the same time that rigorous teacher preparation standards are being hailed as the bedrock of teacher quality, shortages necessitate that districts hire less than fully qualified personnel, sometimes in large numbers. Darling-Hammond (2000b) pointed out that well over one-fourth of all newly hired teachers have either no license or a substandard license in areas they are hired to teach. In special education, that figure exceeds 30 percent (Boe et al., 1997). These same data indicate that the problem is most acute in poverty-laden urban and rural schools with high minority enrollments. It is not surprising that the demand for competent teachers in urban schools has been a major impetus for the emergence and dramatic growth of alternative route (AR) programs. Still, identifying the critical features of AR programs is diffi-cult because programs instituted by states, districts, and universities vary greatly, with options ranging from Spartan emergency certification survival training to sophisticated, technology-based programs for individuals with unique life experiences (Feistritzer, 1998; Hillkirk, 2000). Rosenberg and Sindelar (2001) observed that AR programs have become so diverse that treating them as a homogeneous class no longer makes sense.

At the most basic level, however, the defining characteristic of AR preparation lies in what is avoided: AR programs provide access to a teaching credential that circumvents *con-ventional* college and university preparation (Hawley, 1992). AR programs may prepare teachers in nontraditional ways and may allow entry to the education profession for individu-als who lack conventional teacher preparation (Roth & Lutz, 1986). As noted by Feistritzer (1998), AR programs have "opened doors to teaching for persons from other careers, from the military, from liberal arts colleges, former teachers who want to upgrade their credentials and get back into teaching and for people who trained to teach years ago but never did" (p. 1). To the extent that AR programs contribute uniquely to the supply of special education teachers, they may both increase and diversify teacher supply.

According to Rosenberg and Sindelar (2001), the extent to which a program is alterna-tive may be assessed by considering three factors: the length and structure of program, the manner in which the program is delivered, and the population of participants. Length and structure of the program refer to the number of credits or academic units required to attain licensure and the types of activities employed to foster the acquisition of the content. For the most part, AR programs are usually shorter than traditional programs and are structured to allow candidates to enter the teaching force immediately or soon after beginning their studies. Delivery mode refers to how instruction is presented; in general, AR programs tend to rely more heavily on field experiences than traditional teacher preparation and less on formal classroom instruction. Finally, AR candidates typically do not have a substantial background in general or special education; their bachelor's degrees (if they have one) are usually in other fields. In comparison to traditional programs, AR programs tend to attract proportionally more males; persons over twenty-five; minorities; individuals who have had business, industry, or military experience; and math, science, and foreign language majors (Edelen-Smith & Sileo, 1996; Hawley, 1992; Roth & Lutz, 1986).

In a comprehensive review of AR programs in special education, Rosenberg and Sindelar (2001) found very little analysis in the professional literature of specific AR programs. They conjectured that the small number of programs described in the literature represented only a fraction of all AR programs—the tip of the iceberg, if you will—and that a large underground economy for teaching credentials is in place in many areas of the nation. Although few in number, studies of special education AR training allow for several generalizations about what makes such training effective. First, there must be meaningful collaboration between districts and universities, with adequate time and effort allocated to develop and sustain partnerships. Second, AR programs are most effective when content is substantive, rigorous, and programmatic. Although research to support this assertion is limited, existing research is unequivocal: Extensive degree-linked AR programs are superior to those that make extensive use of unanchored courses and activities that lack a thematic approach (Daunic & Sindelar, 1998; Rosenberg & Rock, 1994). Finally, successful AR programs make use of both university supervisors and building-based coaches and mentors. Initial data indicate that beginning teachers believe contact with mentors and supervisors must occur weekly to be effective and, in addition to curriculum and behavior management, assistance in the areas of emotional support and the procedural mechanics of the job must be provided (Lloyd, Wood, & Moreno, 2000; Whitaker, 2000).

Consistent with their iceberg metaphor, Rosenberg and Sindelar (2001) also reported that much of what we need to know about AR in special education lurks below the surface, hidden and potentially dangerous. For example, the authors found only eight empirical studies on AR in special education, not nearly enough research to allay concern about the proliferation of alternatives to conventional teacher education. They advocate for more research in which the teaching competence of program graduates is assessed through valid, reliable, and independent judgments of performance. These authors also expressed concern about the lack of explicit professional standards in AR programs and the professionalism of AR candidates. With few existing standards for AR programs, and the variety of programs being offered, very little is known about how much of the special education knowledge base candidates have mastered or how they were inducted into the field. Most disturbing, however, is how little is known about the professionalism of AR candidates. One must ask: Is it reasonable to expect teachers to respect and remain in a challenging profession that has multiple, nonstandardized paths to training and employment, some that require little formal training? At present, this question remains unanswered.

FUTURE RESEARCH IN TEACHER EDUCATION

In the current political context, all significant research in teacher education must consider the extent to which teacher education makes a difference for students with disabilities. Those of us operating within the professionalization paradigm have accepted the proposition that teacher education matters, perhaps without serious consideration of the evidence that bears on the issue. Now that the evidentiary warrant has been challenged by proponents of deregulation, it is imperative that teacher education research tackle *fundamental* questions of efficacy and import. Do teachers who have completed rigorous teacher education affect what students with disabilities learn and how they behave more so than teachers who have not? If so, how can we recruit and best prepare an adequate supply of diverse special education personnel?

In the paragraphs that follow, we lay out specific questions for special education teacher education researchers to address. We have organized them under the supply and demand, professional preparation, and certification and licensure headings. Ultimately, the work of COPSSE involves developing a research agenda and conducting original studies to guide policy development and personnel preparation practice. Those of us affiliated with the COPSSE must next identify the most pertinent questions and, among them, those most amenable to investigation.

Although teacher shortages are real and substantial, there is much about them—and much about solving the problems they present—that is poorly understood. For example, are shortages a function of geography and socioeconomic status, as they seem to be? If so, what policies have proven effective in encouraging special education teachers to work in disadvantaged urban and rural schools? It is essential to identify factors (such as the conditions of teaching and teacher salaries) that influence the supply of teachers available to schools, and we need to understand the role of attrition on the demand side of the equation. We need to know what is happening to the size of the reserve pool of special education teachers and what factors influence reserve pool members' decisions to return to teaching. We need to know how best to diversify the special education workforce and to identify what factors influence culturally and linguistically diverse candidates to enter teaching. About recruitment more generally, we must ascertain how local, state, and federal recruitment practices influence special education supply and demand.

We have noted that the fundamental question in teacher education research today is an efficacy question: Does what we do matter? Addressing the complexity of teacher education will require us to answer many other questions as well. For one thing, we must identify appropriate and technically adequate outcome measures for teacher education research. This issue is especially important because deregulationists have rejected teacher outcomes in favor of student achievement measures. In our field, student achievement is difficult to parse and a teacher's impact on it is difficult if not impossible to isolate. How can special education teachers be held accountable for achievement when most students with disabilities spend the majority of their school day in general education classes? What teacher outcome measures are sufficiently reliable and valid to be credible to a skeptical public?

With a set of reliable outcome measures in hand, teacher education researchers may turn their attention to identifying essential elements of effective teacher preparation. For example, how do program structure and content affect outcomes? How much field experience is enough, and how much supervision do students require to optimize what they learn from the experience? In turn, we need to ascertain how factors in the institutional, state, and national contexts affect program structure and content. We also need to know more about alternative routes. How do conventional and alternative programs compare on program content and structure, and how do differences affect beginning teacher competence? Fundamental questions about teacher education students also remain unanswered. For example, how do students' age and ethnic background mediate the effects of personnel preparation? Their beliefs about teaching and learning? Their experience and prior training?

In a sense, the diverse policies that govern how states license teachers constitute natural variation, which is amenable to study. What can we learn from the states about how best to organize teacher licensure and teacher preparation? How do differences in certification routes affect the quality and quantity of personnel, particularly in relation to the nature of students' needs (i.e., mild disabilities versus severe cognitive disabilities)? The relative efficacy of alternative versus conventional routes remains an issue, as does ascertaining how certification and licensure at the state level align with national professional standards and research in special education.

Teacher education research is not easy to conduct, which may explain why the existing knowledge base is sparse and incoherent. With deregulation being considered seriously as an alternative to teacher education reform, it is imperative that researchers in our field address fundamental questions related to the warrant of what we do. That concern applies to special education as well as to teacher education writ large, even though we have concerns of another nature to address. Persistent shortages of qualified personnel have thwarted our best effort to provide a free, appropriate public education to all students with disabilities. Can it be argued legitimately that special education has failed when it has never been implemented universally as it was intended: with a qualified teacher in every classroom?

QUESTIONS FOR FURTHER DISCUSSION

1. Concerns over special education teacher shortages and the need to have a qualified teacher for every child with a disability have many policy makers advocating for alternative routes to the classroom as a key policy strategy in increasing teacher supply. In your state, how is the demand for teachers influencing the nature of special education preparation?

2. According to many policy makers, bright individuals with content area preparation have the skills necessary to teach students and should be able to enter the classroom without necessarily completing teacher education programs. While this logic may have some relevance for math

and science teachers, what do you perceive are the issues around applying this logic to special education teaching?

3. From your perspective, what are the implications of increasing alternative routes to the classroom on special education teaching as a profession?

4. In many states, teachers are prepared noncategorically for kindergarten through twelfth grade. As a special educator, what do you believe are the benefits and disadvantages of this type of preparation for teaching students with disabilities? Given that shortages are unlikely to abate

in the near future, what must happen in schools and universities to address the needs of teachers prepared under broad certification structures?

5. How is the policy context in your state (e.g., standards for student learning, demand for special education teachers, proliferation of alternative routes, standards for teacher preparation) affecting the preparation and retention of special education teachers?

REFERENCES

The Abell Foundation. (2001). *Teacher certification reconsidered: Stumbling for quality.* Baltimore: Author. Retrieved on October 23, 2001, from http://www.abell.org/.

Angus, D. L., & Mirel, J. (2001). *Professionalism and the public good: A brief history of teacher certification.* Washington, DC: Thomas B. Fordham Foundation.

Artiles, A. J., & Trent, S. C. (1997). Forging a research program in multicultural preservice teacher education in special education: A proposed analytic scheme. In J. W. Lloyd, E. J. Kameenui, & D. Chard (Eds.), *Issues in educating students with disabilities* (pp. 275–304). Mahwah, NJ: Erlbaum.

Blanton, L. P. (1992). Preservice education: Essential knowledge for the effective special education teacher. *Teacher Education and Special Education, 15,* 87–96.

Blanton, L. P., Griffin, C. C., Winn, J. A., & Pugach, M. C. (1997). *Teacher education in transition: Collaborative programs to prepare general and special educators.* Denver, CO: Love.

Boe, E. (1998). Special education teachers: National trends in demand and shortage. *Twentieth Annual Report to Congress on the Implementation of IDEA* (pp. III-1–III-23). Washington, DC: U.S. Department of Education, OSEP, OSERS.

Boe, E. E., & Barkanic, G. (2000, April). *Critical factors in developing a highly qualified national teaching force.* Paper presented at the meetings of the American Education Research Association, New Orleans, LA.

Boe, E. E., Cook, L. H., Bobbitt, S. A., & Terhanian, G. (1998). The shortage of fully certified teachers in special and general education. *Teacher Education and Special Education, 21,* 1–21.

Bricker, D., & Sentz, K. (1998). Personnel preparation: Handicapped infants. In M. C. Wang, M. C. Reynolds, & H. F. Walberg (Eds.), *Handbook of special education: Research and practice* (Vols. 1–3). Elmsford, NY: Pergamon Books.

Brownell, M. T., Smith, S. W., McNellis, J. R., & Miller, M.

D. (1997). Attrition in special education: Why teachers leave the classroom and where they go. *Exceptionality, 7,* 143–155.

Center for the Study of Teaching and Policy (1998, December). *What states are doing to improve the quality of teaching: A brief review of current patterns and trends.* Seattle: University of Washington.

Clemson-Ingram, R., & Fessler, R. (1997). The Maryland redesign of teacher education: A commitment to system reform. *Action in Teacher Education, 19*(1), 1–15.

Cochran-Smith, M., & Fries, M. A. (2001). Sticks, stones, and ideology: The discourse of reform in teacher education. *Educational Researcher, 30*(8), 3–15.

Council for Exceptional Children. (2001). *The CEC standards for the preparation of special educators.* Arlington, VA: Author.

Darling-Hammond, L. (1999). Solving the dilemmas of teacher supply, demand, and standards. *Quality Teaching, 9*(1), 3–4.

Darling-Hammond, L. (2000a). *Studies of excellence in teacher education.* Washington, DC: AACTE Publications.

Darling-Hammond, L. (2000b, January). Teacher quality and student achievement: A review of state policy evidence. *Education Policy Analysis Archives* [Online serial], 1(8). Retrieved December 10, 2001, from http://olam.ed.asu.edu/epaa/v8n1.

Darling-Hammond, L., & Sclan, E. M. (1996). *Who teaches and why.* In J. Sikula, T. J. Buttery, & E. Guyton (Eds.), *Handbook of research on teacher education* (2nd ed., pp. 67–101). New York: Macmillan.

Daunic, A., & Sindelar, P. T. (1998). *Teaching competence. Project SEART-C Technical Manuscript No. 3* (Technical Report No. 98-1). Gainesville, FL: University of Florida, Center for School Improvement.

Edelen-Smith, P., & Sileo, T. W. (1996). The alternative basic certification program in special education: In search of quantity and quality in special education. *Teacher Education and Special Education, 19,* 313–330.

Eichinger, J., & Downing, J. (2000). Restructuring special education certification: What should be done? *Journal of the Association for Persons with Severe Handicaps, 25*(2), 109–112.

Feistritzer, C. E. (1998, February). Alternative teacher certification—An overview [On-line report]. Retrieved January 25, 2001, from http://www.ncei.com/Alt-Teacher-Cert.htm.

Galluzzo, G. (1999). *Aligning standards to improve teacher preparation and practice.* Washington, DC: National Council for Accreditation of Teacher Education.

Gersten, R., Vaughn, S., Deshler, D., & Schiller, E. (1997). What we know about using research findings: Implications for improving special education practice. *Journal of Learning Disabilities, 30,* 466–476.

Guillory, B. L. (2000). Project access: A program to improve service delivery for culturally and linguistically diverse populations with speech, language, and hearing disorders. *Teacher Education and Special Education, 23,* 271–280.

Hawley, W. D. (1992). The theory and practice of alternative certification: Implications for the improvement of teaching. In W. D. Hawley (Ed.), *The alternative certification of teachers* (pp. 3–34). Washington, DC: Eric Clearinghouse on Teacher Education.

Hess, F. M. (2001). *Tear down this wall: The case for a radical overhaul of teacher certification.* Washington, DC: Progressive Policy Institute. Retrieved December 11, 2001, from http://www.ppionline.org/documents/teacher_certification.pdf.

Hillkirk, R. K. (2000). Effective models for alternative programs in teacher education. In D. J. McIntyre & D. M. Byrd (Eds.), *Research on effective models for teacher education: Association of teacher educators' yearbook VIII* (pp. 195–202). Thousand Oaks, CA: Corwin Press.

Howey, K. (1996). Designing coherent and effective teacher education programs. In J. Sikula, T. J. Buttery, & E. Guyton (Eds.), *Handbook of research on teacher education* (pp. 143–170). New York: Simon & Schuster Macmillan.

Hurwitz, B. D. (2000, May). *Recruiting and retaining diverse groups of students in special education preservice programs.* Paper presented at Florida's 6th annual Comprehensive System of Personnel Development Conference, Clearwater Beach, FL.

IDEAdata.org (n.d.). Data tables for OSEP state reported data: Table AC3. Number and Type of Other Personnel Employed (in Full-Time Equivalency) to Provide Special Education and Related Services for Children and Youth Ages 3–21 with Disabilities by Personnel Category, During the 2000–2001 School Year. Retrieved March 27, 2003, from http://www.ideadata.org/arc_toc3.asp#partbPEN.

Ingersoll, R. M. (2001). Teacher turnover and teacher shortages: An organizational analysis. *American Educational Research Journal, 38,* 499–534.

Johnson, L. J., & Bauer, A. M. (Eds.). (2000). *Teacher Education and Special Education, 23*(2).

Kagan, D. M. (1990). Teacher's workplace meets the professors of teaching: A chance encounter at 30,000 feet. *Journal of Teacher Education, 41*(5), 46–53.

Lauritzen, P., & Friedman, S. J. (1993). Meeting the supply/demand requirements of the individuals with disabilities education act. *Teacher Education and Special Education, 16,* 221–229.

Lieberman, L. (1996). Preserving special education: For those who need it. In W. Stainback & S. Stainback (Eds.), *Controversial issues confronting special education: Divergent perspectives* (pp. 16–28). Boston: Allyn & Bacon.

Lloyd, S. R., Wood, T. A., & Moreno, G. (2000). What's a mentor to do? *Teaching Exceptional Children, 33*(1), 38–42.

Mainzer, R., & Horvath, M. (2001). *Issues in the preparation and licensing of teachers.* Arlington, VA: CEC.

Malouf, D. B., & Schiller, E. P. (1995). Practice and research in special education. *Exceptional Children, 61*(5), 414–424.

Miller, M. D., Brownell, M. T., & Smith, S. W. (1999). Factors that predict teachers staying in, leaving, or transferring from the special education classroom. *Exceptional Children, 65,* 201–218.

National Association of School Psychologists. (1999, November). NASP membership database. Bethesda, MD: Author.

National Association of State Directors of Special Education. (1996, December). Special educator supply and demand in rural areas: Facing the issues. *Liaison Bulletin, 26,* 1–7.

National Association of State Directors of Teacher Education and Certification. (2000). *The NASDTEC manual on the preparation and certification of educational personnel* (5th ed.). Dubuque, IA: Kendall/Hunt.

National Commission on Teaching & America's Future. (1996). *What matters most: Teaching for America's future.* New York: Author.

National Commission on Teaching & America's Future. (1997). *Doing what matters most: Investing in quality teaching.* New York: Author.

Olson, L. (2000). Finding and keeping competent teachers. Quality counts: Who should teach. *Education Week Special Issue, 19*(18), 12–17.

Olson, L., & Jerald, C. (1998). The teaching challenge. Quality counts: The urban challenge. *Education Week Special Issue, 17*(17), 16–17.

O'Shea, D. J., Hammitte, D., Mainzer, R., & Crutchfield,

M. D. (2000). From teacher preparation to continuing professional development. *Teacher Education and Special Education, 23*(2), 71–77.

Otis-Wilborn, A., & Winn, J. (2000). The process and impact of standards-based teacher education reform. *Teacher Education and Special Education, 23,* 78–92.

Recruiting New Teachers. (1999). Teaching at a demographic crossroads. *Future Teacher, 6*(1), 2.

Richardson, V. (1996). The role of attitudes and beliefs in learning to teach. In J. Sikula, T. J. Buttery, & E. Guyton (Eds.), *Handbook of research on teacher education* (pp. 102–119). New York: Simon & Schuster Macmillan.

Rosenberg, M.S., & Rock, E. E. (1994). Alternative certification in special education: Efficacy of a collaborative, field-based teacher preparation program. *Teacher Education and Special Education, 17*(3), 141–153.

Rosenberg, M. S., & Sindelar, P. T. (2001). *The proliferation of alternative routes to certification in special education: A critical review of the literature.* Arlington, VA: National Clearinghouse for Professions in Special Education, CEC.

Roth, R. A., & Lutz, P. R. (1986). *Alternative certification: Issues and perspectives.* Charleston, WV: Appalachia Education Laboratory. (ERIC Document Reproduction Service No. ED 296 980).

Sindelar, P. T., & Kilgore, K. L. (1995). Teacher education. In M. C. Wang, M. C. Reynolds, & H. J. Walberg (Eds.), *Handbook of special and remedial education: Research and practice* (2nd ed., pp. 393–432). New York: Elsevier Science.

Sindelar, P. T., Rennells, M. S., Daunic, A., Austrich, C., & Eisele, M. (1999*). Systematic evaluation of alternative routes to teaching competence: Project SEART-C final report* (Technical Report No. 10). Gainesville, FL: Center for School Improvement.

Sindelar, P. T., & Rosenberg, M. S. (2000). Serving too many masters: The proliferation of ill conceived and contradictory policies and practices in teacher education. *Journal of Teacher Education, 51*(3), 188–193.

Singer, J. D. (1993). Are special educators' career paths special? Results from 1 13-year longitudinal study. *Exceptional Children, 59,* 262–279.

Smith-Davis, J. (2000). *Issues arising from insufficient diversity among education personnel.* Nashville, TN: Peabody College and Vanderbilt University, Alliance Project.

Spodek, B., Saracho, O N., & Peters, D. (1998). *Professionalism and the early childhood practitioner.* New York: Columbia University Press.

Sprinthall, B., & Thies-Sprinthall, L. (1983). *The teacher as an adult learner: A cognitive developmental view.* In G. A. Griffin (Ed.), *Staff development* (Eighty-second yearbook of the National Society for the Study of Education, pp. 13–35). Chicago: University of Chicago Press.

Sprinthall, N. A., Reiman, A. J., & Thies-Sprinthall, L. (1996). Teacher professional development. In J. Sikula, T. J. Buttery, & E. Guyton (Eds.*), Handbook of research on teacher education* (pp. 666–703). New York: Simon & Schuster Macmillan.

Stainback, S., Stainback, W., & Ayres, B. (1996). Schools as inclusive communities. In W. Stainback & S. Stainback (Eds.), *Controversial issues confronting special education: Divergent perspectives* (p. 31–43). Boston: Allyn & Bacon.

Swan, W., & Sirvis, S. (1992). The CEC common core of knowledge and skills essential for all beginning special education teachers. *Teaching Exceptional Children, 25,* 16–20.

Sykes, G. (1999). No standards or new standards? The future of teacher certification. In R. Roth (Ed.), *The role of the university in the preparation of teachers* (pp. 31– 40). Philadelphia: Falmer Press.

Tom, A. R. (1997). *Redesigning teacher education.* Albany: State University of New York Press.

U.S. Department of Education. (1999). *Twenty-first annual report to Congress on developing a highly trained teacher workforce.* Washington, DC: Author.

Valli, L., Cooper, D., & Frankes, L. (1997). Professional development schools and equity: A critical analysis of rhetoric and research. In M. Apple (Ed.), *Review of research in education* (Vol. 22, pp. 251–304). Washington, DC: American Educational Research Association.

Whitaker, S. D. (2000). Mentoring beginning special education teachers and the relationship to attrition. *Exceptional Children, 66*(4), 546–566.

Whitten, T. M., & Westling, D. L. (1985). Competencies for teachers of the severely and profoundly handicapped: A review. *Teacher Education and Special Education, 8,* 104–111.

LEADERSHIP PERSONNEL IN SPECIAL EDUCATION

Can Persistent Shortages Be Resolved?

DEBORAH DEUTSCH SMITH
GEORGINE M. PION
NAOMI CHOWDHURI TYLER
Vanderbilt University

The laws of supply and demand dictate that the value of a product generally increases when its supply is scarce and its demand is high. Several examples come to mind: rising energy prices, the cost of fruit when droughts and floods destroy farmers' crops, and even the price of tickets to sold-out concerts and plays. However, these types of goods are not the only products to which supply and demand principles apply. Today, in our postindustrial society, valued products include specialized services, knowledge, and expertise. Thus, individuals with highly specialized training and skills are valued commodities, and an inadequate supply of such talent attracts both the public's and national policy makers' attention (Kucher, 2001; Rabin & Eisenberg, 2001).

In several fields, there have been organized responses to address this problem. For example, data projecting a dearth of primary care physicians have triggered efforts by states and medical schools to make careers in family practice and primary care specialties more attractive (Weissert & Silberman, 1998), and these efforts are meeting with some initial success. Hospitals and healthcare agencies are similarly experiencing difficulty recruiting and retaining registered nurses (Federation of Nurses and Health Professionals, 2001). This current shortage, coupled with projections of dire future shortages at a time when aging baby boomers will need expert medical attention, has caused hospitals to instate such recruiting incentives as flexible schedules, housing programs, and retention pay bonuses (Sprayberry, 2000). Concerns about the nationwide shortage of information technology (IT) workers have sparked the establishment of congressional commissions and immigration legislation to increase supply. Warnings about college faculty shortages have led to increased graduate student enrollments in some disciplines or, as in the case of business professors, six-figure salaries for new Ph.D.s (Mangan, 2001). Predictions regarding a shortfall of teachers due to increasing school enrollments and teacher retirements have prompted several states, such as Florida, to enact new legislation aimed at addressing the problem.

The field of special education has also experienced serious problems in meeting the demand for the skills and expertise of its professionals. That there is an insufficient supply of special education teachers for the nation's schools is well known. As noted in the *Twenty-Third Annual Report to Congress on the Implementation of the Individuals with Disabilities Education Act* (U.S. Department of Education, 2001), this shortage is substantial and persistent. Projections by the U.S. Department of Labor in 2001, as cited in *Bright Futures for Exceptional Learners* (Kozleski, Mainzer, Deshler, Coleman, & Rodriguez-Walling, 2000), foresee that more than 200,000 new special education teachers will be needed within the next five years. According to data collected for the upcoming *Twenty-Fifth Annual Report to Congress on the Implementation of the Individuals with Disabilities Education Act* (U.S. Department of Education, 2003), the situation is further exacerbated by the fact that approximately 48,000 special education teacher positions are currently occupied by unqualified personnel— a situation that affects over 720,000 children. In fact, the shortage may be considerably greater, given that many states fail to report classrooms where long-term substitute teachers are attempting to provide appropriate educational services to students with disabilities. Thus, it is hardly surprising that meeting the accelerating demand for special education teachers was ranked among their highest priorities by 98 percent of all school districts in 1999 (Kozleski et al., 2000).

At the same time, efforts to address this shortage have met with mixed results. The obvious solution to reducing this shortage is, of course, to train more special education teachers. For nearly thirty years, the federal government, state education agencies (SEAs), and other organizations have designed several different strategies to increase the supply of special education personnel. These strategies have involved recruiting more students into existing undergraduate teacher preparation programs, facilitating the entry of graduates in other disciplines into special certification programs, developing new training programs or expanding the capacity of available training programs to enroll more students, and financing the training of individuals who will become faculty in these programs. Despite these committed and concerted efforts, however, chronic shortages of special education teachers have persisted.

Although there have been several initiatives to train general education teachers and use new technologies to better meet the needs of students with disabilities (e.g., Brown & John, 2000; Gloeckler, 1999), the majority of America's teachers and related service providers are trained by college and university faculty in special education departments. Thus, maintaining an adequate supply of qualified special education faculty, most of whom now must have the doctoral degree, is important.

Unfortunately, faculty shortfalls also have existed for nearly two decades (Sindelar & Taylor, 1988; Smith & Lovett, 1987; Tawney & DeHaas-Warner, 1993). This situation can be traced to at least three sources:

> *Little or no growth in the production of doctorates.* Since 1920, approximately 11,000 doctoral degrees in special education have been awarded by U.S. colleges and universities (Harmon, 1978; Henderson, Clarke, & Reynolds, 1996; Sanderson, Dugoni,

Hoffer, & Selfa, 1999). Approximately 75 percent (or 8,200) of these degrees have been earned since 1970. In contrast to other disciplines that have witnessed growth in doctoral production, however, the annual number of doctoral degrees in special education has not grown. For example, whereas in 1980 nearly 350 doctorates in special education were awarded, only 248 were conferred in 1998—a loss of almost 30 percent (Coyle & Bae, 1987; Sanderson et al., 1999). In contrast, the number of degrees in psychology rose 15 percent (from approximately 3,100 to about 3,600), and doctorates in curriculum and instruction grew by 9 percent (from 815 to 885).

Little increase in the proportion of new doctorates who pursue academic careers. The proportion of new doctorates who become full-time faculty has not increased for more than a decade. As will be discussed later in this chapter, the reasons are several but include expanded career opportunities for leadership personnel and certain characteristics of new doctorates that may affect their ability to pursue academic careers.

Constant demand for new faculty. Between 1982 and 1989, the number of special education faculty positions advertised each year more than doubled (Sindelar, Buck, Carpenter, & Watanabe, 1993). Since 1992, the number of estimated job openings for junior faculty has hovered around 250 each year (Smith, Pion, Tyler, Sindelar, & Rosenberg, 2001)—a number that exceeds the total number of special education doctorates awarded annually.

Unlike other professions in which shortfalls have occurred, efforts to remedy this deficit have suffered from limited resources and lack of systematic examination. Not surprisingly, the magnitude of the problem has not decreased.

Furthermore, there is the distinct possibility that this situation may worsen over the next decade. Faculty vacancies are expected to increase as professors trained in the early 1970s retire from their positions (Magner, 2000). In addition, the expected "career-life" of special education faculty has shortened, even among faculty who were trained more recently. In 1986, the average age of an assistant professor in special education was thirty-six years (Smith & Lovett, 1987). Given that most faculty still retire at the age of 65, this meant that the professor would be teaching, interacting with students, and fulfilling other faculty responsibilities for about thirty years. However, recent research indicates that thirty-six is now the *average age at which individuals first enroll in special education doctoral programs* (Smith et al., 2001). Consequently, the beginning assistant professor is now typically forty-one years old. Assuming no change in the typical retirement age and that newly hired faculty do not leave academe, this means that the typical junior faculty member has an expected career life of about twenty-four years.

The purpose of this chapter is to summarize what is known about the chronic faculty shortage in special education. This is not to say that shortages of leadership personnel in other key employment sectors (e.g., schools and direct service organizations) do not exist. For example, local education agencies (LEAs) have recently expressed concern over the difficulties encountered in filling positions (e.g., special education director) created by retiring special education doctorates (J. Thomason, personal communication, 2001). Unfortunately, however, supply and demand in these sectors has received little empirical attention. Unlike many other disciplines (e.g., psychology, nursing, and engineering), special education has not systematically monitored how its leadership personnel is utilized. This lack of data hinders understanding the nature and magnitude of these shortages, and thus identifying promising strategies to address the shortage must rely too heavily on speculation, opinion, anecdotal evidence, and limited empirical data.

Another reason for focusing on special education's faculty shortage concerns both its short- and long-term negative consequences. First, because university programs bear the chief responsibility for producing special education personnel, faculty shortages hamper the ability to adequately staff courses, supervise students, provide tailored assistance to individual students, and produce high-quality educators. Second, the preparation of fewer special education teachers not only means fewer personnel to address the needs of students with disabilities but also fewer individuals who will pursue advanced degrees in special education. The latter only exacerbates the possibility of even larger shortages of trained faculty in future years. Finally, because faculty are the primary researchers in the field, the generation of new knowledge, particularly with respect to effective practices, is impaired. This in turn affects the eventual welfare of individuals with disabilities.

This chapter identifies several factors that contribute to the faculty shortage in special education and its seeming intractability. First, a brief history of the doctoral training system in special education—the chief supplier of leadership personnel—is provided. Second, the pool of doctoral graduates (i.e., those individuals who are candidates for leadership positions), is described in terms of their employment settings, work activities, and other key characteristics. Following this is an explication of the factors underlying the chronic discrepancy between the demand for college and university faculty and the supply of individuals who can assume these positions. Finally, the capacity of the current training system to redress the supply and demand imbalance is discussed, along with implications for the discipline.

Much of the information in this chapter is based on previous surveys of doctoral departments and new special education doctorates. We also draw heavily on analyses of data from a set of studies that we and our colleagues (Paul Sindelar at the University of Florida and Michael Rosenberg at Johns Hopkins University) have recently completed. These efforts involved interviewing 120 search coordinators for faculty positions that were advertised in 1997–98, obtaining information on all special education doctoral programs in the summer and fall of 1999, and surveying current students and recent graduates of these programs in the fall and winter of 1999. Response rates to these surveys were 69 percent, 100 percent, 81 percent, and 89 percent, respectively. A more detailed description of the methodology and findings of these efforts can be found in Smith et al. (2001).

ORIGINS OF SPECIAL EDUCATION
DOCTORAL TRAINING EFFORTS

Although the history of special education can be traced back to France in the late 1700s and Itard and his work with Victor, *l'enfant sauvage*, education for American students with disabilities was not consistently available until the middle of the twentieth century. It did not become an entitlement until the enactment of the Individuals with Disabilities Education Act (IDEA) in 1975. This legislation created a huge demand for special education teachers and service providers and spawned the development of personnel preparation programs in colleges of education across the nation (e.g., Boe, Bobbitt, Cook, & Barkanic, 1998; Boe, Cook, Bobbitt, & Terhanian, 1998; U.S. Department of Education, 1998). Since that time, institutions of higher education have *never* been able to produce, recruit, and retain sufficient numbers of teachers, administrators, and other service providers to meet the demand. The result is that many students with disabilities have been left with no qualified special educators to provide them with the appropriate education guaranteed by IDEA.

Leadership training, a term for doctoral studies in special education, began after the end of World War II. Programs were developed without a national plan and seemed to emerge in no predictable or orderly fashion. According to the records at the Bureau for the Education of the Handicapped (now the Office of Special Education Programs in the U.S. Department of Education), twenty-seven doctoral programs relating to the needs of special needs students were in operation in 1954 (Schofer, 1964; Smith & Salzberg, 1994). Few of these programs were comprehensive, and the majority were in "speech correction." Only fourteen programs provided doctoral preparation in at least one area typically considered as special education (e.g., "mental retardation," "socially maladjusted," "visually handicapped," "crippled"). In 1958, Public Law (P.L.) 85-926 was passed, which provided federal support to assist with the preparation of special educators. With its implementation, fifteen doctoral programs received support in academic year 1959–60 for preparing teacher educators in the area of mental retardation.

THE DEVELOPMENT AND EXPANSION OF SPECIAL EDUCATION DOCTORAL PROGRAMS

As the national commitment to the education of students with disabilities grew during the 1960s, federal funding in this area continued to increase. This, in turn, stimulated dramatic growth in special education at colleges and universities across the nation. The federal role in special education's development has been twofold: (1) to provide incentives to individuals to influence their career choices; and (2) to create high-quality training programs in higher education institutions that support the special education effort. According to Schofer (1964), two years after the initiation of P.L. 85-926, twenty-one colleges and universities had active special education programs receiving federal support (and four additional programs had received "start-up" funds). Three years later, in 1964, 139 colleges and universities had special education personnel preparation programs—nearly a 700 percent increase. Although there is no national database of doctoral programs that has been consistently updated, it is generally acknowledged that the number of doctoral special education programs has increased significantly. Whereas fourteen programs existed in 1954, there were eighty-five in 1987 (Pierce, Smith, & Clark, 1992; Schofer, 1964; Teacher Education Division of the Council for Exceptional Children, 1987).

Despite the fact that some special education doctoral programs close their doors or are downsized to emphasis areas within another major and that new programs are being established, the number of programs across the nation has remained relatively consistent, hovering in the high eighties. Currently, there are eighty-four programs that offer a formal degree in special education, along with six programs that report having special education as an emphasis within another degree area (e.g., curriculum and instruction).

CAREER CHOICES OF RECENT DOCTORATES

Since 1985, these eighty-four special education doctoral programs as a whole have produced, on average, about 255 doctorates each year. Over time, the demographics of these graduates have changed. For example, the participation of women, already strong, continued to increase; whereas 68.5 percent of 1985 doctorates were women, this grew to 82.3 percent of 1998 doctorate recipients (Coyle, 1986; Sanderson et al., 1999). More members from underrepresented groups earned degrees. In 1985, approximately 6.6 percent of new special education doctorates were African American, 1.6 percent were Hispanic,[1] 1.2 percent were Asian or Pacific Islander, and less than 1 percent were Native American. The corresponding figures for 1998 doctorates were 10.7 percent, 5.8 percent, 4.0 percent, and 1.3 percent. During this time period, the proportion of graduates who were foreign citizens also rose from 4 percent to 7 percent. Given that these individuals typically return to their home countries after receiving their degree and that doctoral production has remained relatively stable, this means that the pool of newly trained leadership personnel may, in fact, have become slightly smaller over recent years.

TRENDS IN THE EMPLOYMENT SETTINGS AND WORK ACTIVITIES OF NEW DOCTORATES

The average numbers of new doctorates and estimated openings for junior faculty have been nearly identical for the past several years. Thus, faculty demand would essentially be met if all new doctoral recipients moved into faculty jobs upon graduation. However, employment opportunities for leadership personnel have broadened, and graduates now have several other career paths from which to choose.

As estimated by Bunsen and Bullock (1988), approximately 85 percent of doctorates who earned their degrees in the 1960s moved into faculty positions upon graduation. Thirty years later, however, enthusiasm for the academic life appears to have waned considerably. Among 1989–91 doctorates, approximately 59 percent reported that their first job was in a college or university; 37 percent were in tenure-line faculty positions, and 22 percent held jobs as non-tenure-track faculty or coordinators on federally funded projects (Pierce & Smith, 1994). Forty-two percent were working in settings outside academe. During this time period, warnings about the increasing difficulties of hiring new faculty also began appearing in the literature (e.g., Sindelar et al., 1993; Sindelar & Taylor, 1988; Smith & Lovett, 1987).

Surveys of more recent cohorts indicate that very little has changed. Among 1994–98 doctorates, approximately 51 percent were employed full-time in institutions of higher education (IHEs) (see Figure 1). Two-fifths held tenure-line faculty positions, and 18 percent were working in other types of roles at colleges and universities. Among this latter group, the majority (62 percent) were serving in non-tenure-track faculty appointments, approximately 9 percent were primarily involved in management of projects or educational programs, and 8 percent held other types of staff positions. Another 21 percent were in research positions, although very few of these involved formal postdoctoral research training. At a time when postdoctoral training is becoming more commonplace in such disciplines as psychology, and as research methodologies and data analytic techniques are becoming increasingly

[1]The authors recognize the fact that terms used to refer to different racial, ethnic, and cultural groups are continuously changing and often reflect regional or political preference. Terminology used in this paper reflects that used in the various reports and studies cited.

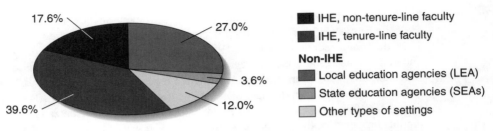

FIGURE 1   Employment Settings of 1994–98 Doctorates in Special Education

Note: Data are from the Survey of Careers of Doctorates in Special Education and include those working full-time in the U.S. (see Smith et al., 2001, for a description of this survey).

sophisticated, this has implications for the ability of new graduates to successfully compete for faculty positions in which research is valued and a key criterion for career advancement (Heward, 1995).

Figure 1 also depicts the nonacademic employment settings of 1994–98 special education doctorates. The most common choice by far were schools and school system district offices (27 percent)—a figure that was slightly larger than the 23 percent reported by Pierce and Smith (1994) for 1989–91 new doctorates. The remaining graduates were distributed across a wide range of work environments. Four percent were working in state education agencies (SEAs) and 12 percent were in a variety of other settings, which included educational settings such as adult vocational centers (2 percent), freestanding research institutes not affiliated with a university (2 percent), hospitals and residential treatment centers (1 percent), and federal government agencies (less than 1 percent). Another 5 percent were in private practice or employed by nonprofit agencies, for-profit companies, or settings not previously mentioned.

Profiling the job responsibilities of recent doctorates also highlights the roles in which leadership personnel are involved and the shared and unique contributions of employment sectors. Not surprisingly, the major responsibility of tenure-line faculty was teaching—78 percent reported it as their primary activity (see Table 1). This was less true for those working in non-tenure-track positions in IHEs; here, the jobs of nearly one-third focused on program and project management, almost the same fraction were essentially hired for undergraduate teaching, and another 20 percent were primarily engaged in research. In LEAs—the most frequent nonacademic employer of special education doctorates—slightly more than two-fifths (44 percent) spent the majority of their time in administration. One-fifth (21 percent) were in positions that primarily involved direct services (e.g., assessment, treatment, and consultation), and 27 percent were classroom teachers. Those working in other types of nonacademic settings held a variety of roles. Approximately 38 percent were primarily administrators, 22 percent focused their energies on providing direct services, and 15 percent were primarily conducting research. Another 22 percent described their chief responsibility as policy analysis, program development, technical assistance, or another type of activity.

As Table 1 indicates, however, recent graduates also were engaged in several activities in addition to their primary role. Regardless of the job, more than half of all individuals reported spending at least 10 percent of their time in management and supervision of personnel or students. It also is apparent that the bulk of research in special education continues to be carried out by those in academic environments—82 percent of tenure-line faculty and 69 per-

TABLE 1   Job Characteristics of 1994–98 Special Education Doctorates by Type of Full-Time Employment

CHARACTERISTIC	TYPE OF FULL-TIME EMPLOYMENT				
	Tenure-line faculty position in IHE (n = 272)	Other position in IHE (n = 117)	Position in LEA (n = 185)	Position in Other Non-IHE Setting (n = 109)	Total (n = 683)
Primary work activity (%)					
Direct services	0.0	6.8	21.4	22.4	10.5
Management and supervision	7.4	32.5	44.0	38.3	26.4
Research	9.9	19.7	1.1	15.0	10.0
Teaching	78.3	31.6	26.9	2.8	44.5
Other	4.4	9.4	6.6	21.5	8.6
Percentage involved in[a]					
Applied research	61.4	48.7	13.0	34.9	41.9
Basic research	20.6	20.5	5.4	10.1	14.8
Direct services	23.5	30.8	61.6	56.0	40.3
Management and supervision	56.3	69.2	66.0	62.4	62.1
Teaching	98.9	70.1	44.3	28.4	68.0
Other	32.7	23.3	14.1	38.0	26.9
Current job satisfaction (%)					
Completely or mostly satisfied	77.4	77.1	73.4	82.4	77.1
Mixed	18.5	18.6	19.0	12.0	17.7
Completely or mostly dissatisfied	4.1	4.2	7.6	5.6	5.3
Median salary in 2000 (9 months)[b]	$42,000	$37,544	$51,000	$45,000	$43,000

[a]This refers to the percentage of individuals who reported spending at least 10 percent of their time in this activity. Percents do not add to 100.0 given that people are involved in multiple activities.

[b]In order to compare salaries across employment sectors, median salaries have been adjusted to reflect a nine- to ten-month period.

Source: Data reported from surveys completed by doctoral graduates on the Survey of Careers of Recent Doctorates.

cent of those in other types of college and university positions devoted a portion of their time to basic or applied research. A notable, although substantially smaller, proportion of doctorates in such nonacademic settings as SEAs, contract research institutes, and the federal government also were engaged in research (45 percent). Given this distribution of the discipline's research effort, it becomes clear that faculty shortfalls not only weaken the profession's ability to train new special education teachers but also can impede the development of knowledge about, and its applications to, students and other individuals with disabilities.

Other data presented in Table 1 provide some insight about the leadership workforce. First, over three-quarters of recent special education doctorates (77 percent) were "completely" or "mostly" satisfied with their jobs. Those in IHEs were somewhat more likely to express satisfaction than those working in LEAs (77 percent versus 73 percent) and somewhat less likely than those working in other nonacademic environments (82 percent). For faculty, dissatisfaction typically centered around salary; whereas 57 percent of graduates working in LEAs and 71 percent of those working in other nonacademic settings were content with their current salary and benefits package, this was true for only 43 percent of tenure-line faculty and 48 percent of those in other IHE positions.

Furthermore, reported salary levels were consistent with these differential satisfaction levels. The median salary for recent graduates in tenure-line faculty positions was $42,000—a figure that was 18 percent lower than that of their counterparts in LEAs and 8 percent lower than that of individuals working in other nonacademic positions. These pay disparities were even sharper for those in non-tenure-line positions in colleges and universities, in which the median salary was $37,544. Thus, academic compensation may function as a strong disincentive for pursuing (and remaining in) a faculty position. In fact, for the academic year 1999–2000, the average special education faculty salary for all ranks was about $53,000 in public universities and $48,000 in private institutions—figures that were 8 percent and 14 percent lower than the average for all faculty in the fifty-four disciplines surveyed (Howe, 2000). Even among fields in education, special education faculty salaries were lower than those earned by faculty in teacher education programs (by about 2 percent).

At the same time, pay is not the only factor that contributes to job satisfaction. For example, those working in LEAs had higher salaries but were considerably more likely to be dissatisfied with their opportunities for scholarly pursuits. Only 29 percent said they were satisfied, 37 percent expressed mixed views, and 34 percent were dissatisfied. These satisfaction levels were significantly lower than those expressed by personnel in other types of nonacademic settings (the corresponding figures were 38 percent, 38 percent, and 23 percent, respectively) and substantially lower than those for individuals working in IHEs (54 percent, 30 percent, and 16 percent). Although this may not be surprising, given that the academic environment is the locus of research efforts and places the most value on scholarship, these data suggest that a substantial portion of individuals working in LEAs may have job responsibilities that differ little from those they had before receiving the doctorate (classroom teaching, assessment, and other types of direct services). In fact, approximately one-third of respondents who were working in LEAs rated their level of responsibility, degree of interesting work, and expected managerial responsibilities as being very little or not at all affected by earning their doctoral degree. Inasmuch as earning a doctoral degree requires a substantial investment of time, energy, and resources, this may signal that a noticeable fraction of special education doctorates are not being used in ways appropriate to their advanced training.

FACTORS AFFECTING CAREER DECISIONS OF RECENT GRADUATES

In addition to understanding the work done by leadership personnel and their views on their work conditions, understanding the similarities and differences among those who pursued faculty versus other types of positions can help identify ways to increase the number of individuals pursuing faculty careers. Table 2 presents information on selected characteristics that have been shown to affect career choices. As can be seen, career choices were not significantly related to such demographic variables as gender, race/ethnicity, and marital status. However, those choosing faculty careers were different than those who pursued other career options in several other ways related to their educational backgrounds, training, and behaviors associated with their first job.

TABLE 2   Demographic and Training Characteristics of 1994–98 Special Education Doctorates by Type of Full-Time Employment

CHARACTERISTIC	TYPE OF FULL-TIME EMPLOYMENT				
	Tenure-line faculty position in IHE (n = 272)	Other position in IHE (n = 117)	Position in LEA (n = 185)	Position in Other Non-IHE Setting (n = 109)	Total (n = 683)
Percentage who were women	77.9	83.9	75.8	81.7	79.0
Percentage who were underrepresented minorities	16.0	12.9	21.8	13.2	16.6
Percentage who were married or living together	70.3	67.0	71.4	67.0	69.5
Average age at entering doctoral program	35.6[a,b]	36.6	37.1	36.9	36.4
Percentage who relocated to enroll in doctoral study	45.0[a,b,c]	30.5[b]	16.2[c]	28.4	32.1
Percentage who planned a faculty career when beginning doctoral program	86.9[a,b,c]	72.2[b,c]	53.9	52.2	70.6
Percentage whose primary source of support for doctoral study was:					
TA, RA, traineeship, or fellowship	61.3[b,c]	58.3[b]	35.6[c]	48.2	51.7
Earnings from outside job	17.7[b,c]	15.7[b,c]	40.6	32.4	25.9
Average years spent in doctoral study	5.1[a,b,c]	5.7	6.3	5.9	5.7
Age at receipt of doctoral degree (years)	40.3[b,c]	41.7	43.3	42.7	41.7
Percentage who relocated for job after graduation	63.2[a,b,c]	28.8[b]	13.0[c]	30.3	38.5

[a]Significantly different from group with other position in IHE ($p < .05$).

[b]Significantly different from group with position in LEA ($p < .05$).

[c]Significantly different from group with position in other non-IHE setting ($p < .05$).

Source: Data reported from surveys completed by doctoral graduates on the Survey of Careers of Recent Doctorates.

The factors affecting career decisions of recent graduates, as indicated in Table 2, can be summarized as follows.

Applying to and Selecting a Doctoral Training Program.   Consistent with prior research on earlier cohorts (Smith & Pierce, 1995; Tyler & Smith, 1999), tenure-track assistant professors were considerably more likely to relocate to enroll in a doctoral program than their counterparts in other types of positions. Whereas 45 percent moved at least one hundred miles to begin doctoral study, this was true for only 31 percent of those with nontenure-track appointments in IHEs, 28 percent of those who were working in other nonacademic settings, and 16 percent of those employed in LEAs. In fact, those working in academic and nonacademic settings were significantly more likely to have relocated than graduates who held positions in schools and school district system offices. Compared to tenure-line faculty, individuals in LEAs also were more likely to indicate that not having to relocate was their primary reason for choosing a doctoral program. In addition, these characteristics do not seem to have changed for students currently enrolled in special education doctoral programs. In Spring 2000, approximately the same percentage as that for 1994–98 graduates (30 percent) moved to enroll as a doctoral student. This group was younger than other doctoral students, and fewer had children living with them. They also were more likely to be enrolled full-time (Smith et al., 2001).

Career Goals in Graduate School.   Whereas 87 percent of those in tenure-line faculty positions and 72 percent of those in nontenure-line positions entered their doctoral program with academic career plans, this was true for significantly smaller proportions of those in nonacademic settings. It is noteworthy that 71 percent overall had faculty intentions when they began their doctoral study—a considerably higher proportion than the proportion of current doctoral students (44 percent) with such career expectations (Smith et al., 2001).

Primary Source of Support for Doctoral Study.   How one's graduate education is financed was clearly connected to career paths. Those in academic settings—whether in tenure-line or other types of appointments—were significantly more likely than their nonacademic counterparts to have primarily relied on teaching assistantships, research assistantships, traineeships, or fellowships for financing their doctoral study; that is, 61 percent of tenure-track faculty and 58 percent of individuals in nontenure-track appointments reported this type of institutional support as the most important as compared to only 36 percent of those working in LEAs and 48 percent of those employed by other organizations. Having to primarily rely on outside jobs was considerably more characteristic of graduates in these latter two types of settings.

Age at Completing the Doctorate.   Those who gravitated toward faculty positions were typically 16–24 months younger when they received their degree than those who did not have such appointments. This was a function of two factors: first, they were younger when they began doctoral study, and second, they completed the degree in less time. In contrast, there were no differences between individuals with other types of positions in academic institutions and those working in nonacademic settings.

Limited Geographic Mobility on Receipt of the Degree.   Junior faculty were twice as likely as those in SEAs and other nonacademic environments and those in IHEs (in nontenure-line position) to relocate to take their job and nearly four more times as likely to move as those who took positions in the schools. Once again, those in LEAs were significantly less likely to move to another geographic area than their counterparts in other types of settings.

These findings have several implications. First, those taking tenure-track faculty jobs are more likely to have relocated for doctoral study, and they also are more likely to be younger than those taking positions outside of academe. These findings are consistent with earlier studies (Smith & Pierce, 1995; Tyler & Smith, 1999). Current doctoral students, however, are much less likely to share these same characteristics (Smith et al., 2001); they were a year older, on average, when they began doctoral study (36.7) than recent graduates who are now in faculty positions (35.6), and a smaller percentage relocated to begin doctoral study (30 percent versus 45 percent of current faculty). Thus, the likelihood of future graduates, at least in the short term, embarking more frequently on academic career paths is questionable.

Second, individuals' early career intentions clearly are strong predictors of later career choices. Increasing the pool of faculty must necessarily involve recruiting more graduate students who want to teach and do research. At present, approximately 44 percent of doctoral students report that they plan faculty careers (Smith et al., 2001). This proportion is noticeably smaller than that for 1995–96 doctorates (61 percent).

Also evident is the fact that a large proportion of those in nonacademic jobs enrolled with academic plans but changed their expectations sometime before taking their first job. Although the exact reasons are unclear, the most likely candidates had experiences while students that reduced the attractiveness of the faculty career and the lower salaries offered by colleges and universities. Thus, doctoral training programs must not only attract students who aspire to be faculty but also must work at nurturing these career goals.

Third, recent research documents the strong role that graduate student support plays in career decisions (Smith et al., 2001). For example, certain types of financial support increase the ability to concentrate on one's studies full-time; this, in turn, decreases the time spent earning the degree. When doctoral study is primarily supported by teaching and research assistantships, fellowships, or traineeships, this greatly increases the probability that graduates will choose an academic career path. This is not only because of full-time attendance but also because of the valuable experiences associated with these mechanisms of support. In contrast, supporting oneself primarily through outside jobs is less likely to result in the decision to take a faculty job after graduation.

Finally, the consistency of these patterns across the last ten years suggests that creative solutions must be developed to facilitate entry into a faculty position. Promising strategies appear to be those that can recruit and support more students who have academic aspirations, are at the stage when accepting a faculty job does not mean a marked decline in earnings, and have the flexibility to consider positions outside their immediate locale. These initiatives are mostly in the province of doctoral programs themselves. However, as discussed in the next section, the degree to which they can be implemented without external assistance is questionable.

DOCTORAL TRAINING PROGRAMS AND THE CURRENT PIPELINE

The eighty-four special education doctoral programs differ in several regards, including the number of full-time faculty, full-time and part-time students, and degrees awarded annually. This variability has implications for future leadership personnel preparation. For example, having fewer full-time faculty often restricts the number of new students who can be admitted, because working with doctoral students involves activities that cannot be easily assumed by adjunct or part-time faculty (e.g., supervising student theses and guiding student research). Having fewer full-time students in turn affects program yield in terms of doctoral production.

This is because pursuing doctoral study on a part-time basis tends to extend the time required to complete the degree.

In Spring 1999, 1,028 faculty worked at the nation's doctoral programs. Of these, 770 (75 percent) were full-time. A noticeable fraction of the programs (27 percent) had five or fewer full-time faculty members. Another 43 percent of the programs had between six and ten faculty, 18 percent had eleven to fifteen full-time faculty, and 12 percent were staffed by more than fifteen faculty. In addition, approximately half (51 percent) of these departments were not fully staffed, as indicated by the fact that they reported searches for one or more faculty were under way.

A total of 1,888 doctoral students were enrolled in these eighty-four doctoral programs. Although this number appears impressive, there also is some suggestion that the typical special education doctoral program has become smaller in terms of student enrollments (see Figure 2). Although the proportion of very small programs (those with less than ten students) has remained at 5 to 7 percent, the proportion of very large programs (forty or more students) has declined noticeably, from 30 percent for the 1992–93 academic year to 16 percent during 1998–99. At the same time, the percentages of programs with ten to nineteen students and twenty to twenty-nine students each rose by 5 percentage points. Given that the total number of programs has been reasonably stable, this means that the larger programs most likely have smaller doctoral student populations.

Another change has occurred with regard to full-time enrollments. For the 1990–91 academic year, Pierce, Smith, and Clarke (1992) found that 44 percent of all doctoral students were enrolled full-time. However, a most recent study indicated that full-time students now make up 38 percent of all doctoral enrollments, with the remainder nearly equally divided between those who were taking classes on a part-time basis (38 percent) and those who were working on their dissertation (32 percent) (Smith et al., 2001). Additional evidence of changes in full-time enrollments is documented by previous studies that examined member schools of

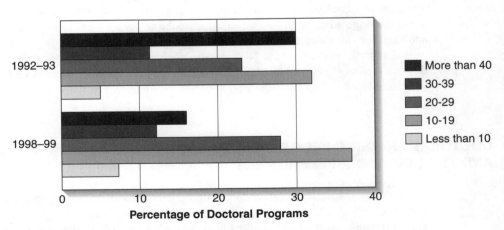

FIGURE 2   Changes in Doctoral Student Enrollments: Academic Years 1992–93 and 1998–99

Note: Data are from the Doctoral Program Survey and only include HECSE schools.

the Higher Education Consortium in Special Education (HECSE), an organization representing institutions with special education doctoral programs. In the early 1990s, 62 percent of HECSE programs surveyed reported that 50 percent or more of their students were attending full-time (Bos, Roberts, Rieth, & Derer, 1995). By 1999, this percentage had dropped by nearly half to 33 percent of the HECSE programs (Smith et al., 2001). Whereas only 14 percent of the departments had 26–49 percent of their students attending full-time in 1992, this was true of 36 percent of doctoral programs in spring 1999.

Looking at it another way, approximately 30 percent (twenty-three programs) had six to ten full-time students, and 15 percent (nineteen programs) had more than eleven students pursuing the doctorate full-time. What is striking is that *half of the programs had five or fewer full-time students*. In fact, twenty-one programs (27 percent) had two or fewer. This is a sobering statistic in terms of the diminished opportunities for students to share ideas outside of class, study and work together on group projects, interact informally with faculty, provide peer support to each other throughout the process of earning the degree, and essentially become familiar figures in the department. Not surprisingly, this also affects doctoral production and departments' ability to nourish and replenish the pool of special leadership personnel. Over a three-year period (1996–98), approximately 38 percent of the programs graduated an average of three new Ph.D.s or Ed.D.s per year. Nearly the same percentage (41 percent) produced an average of one or none at all per year. When HECSE schools are the focus for the purpose of comparison, the percentage of programs that graduated an average of three or more doctorates each year was 41 percent—a figure that was considerably smaller than the 57 percent reported almost ten years earlier (Bos et al., 1992).

These shifts have serious implications for the capacity of special education doctoral programs to provide adequate numbers of leadership personnel. In other words, a noticeable percentage of departments have small faculties, and regardless of their size, doctoral programs may not be operating at full strength, given that approximately half were trying to recruit additional faculty members. Increasing numbers of students are enrolling part-time, which not only affects the culture of graduate education but also slows progress toward the degree. In addition, the pool of applicants to special education doctoral programs is not large, and most are accepted. In the fall of 1998, nearly half of all programs (48 percent) received fewer than five applications—a fact that is not surprising, given that 72 percent of all current doctoral students reported that they had applied to only one doctoral program and only 30 percent relocated to begin doctoral study (Smith et al., 2001).

The result was that acceptance rates are high; approximately half of the programs accepted two-thirds of their applicants, and 19 percent accepted all of their applicants. This situation is unlike many other disciplines: for example, the acceptance role for doctoral programs in psychology was 21 percent (Pate, 2001). In all likelihood, this situation puts constraints on doctoral programs in terms of expanding their doctoral student populations, particularly in terms of attracting applicants who are likely candidates for faculty positions. As previously noted, one characteristic that distinguishes graduates who become assistant professors from their nonacademic counterparts is having relocated to attend graduate school; a larger percentage of this group also apply to more than one program. However, these characteristics do not describe the typical graduate student applicant in special education, most of whom have been working in schools, are older, and may have other responsibilities that make it difficult to attend graduate school outside their local community.

Another factor restricting doctoral programs' ability to enhance recruitment involves the availability of financial support, which is linked to full-time enrollment status and ultimately a shorter time to the degree. As of spring 1999, the largest supporter of full-time students was the U.S. Department of Education, through training and research grants awarded to special education doctoral programs and faculty (Smith et al., 2001). However, congressional appropriations for these types of awards have not increased for some time. In addition, stipends have not kept pace with inflation and are noticeably lower than those available for students in other disciplines. Doctoral programs have neither the resources to provide more assistance to their graduate students nor the means to recruit additional students through financial aid packages. Consequently, students must accumulate considerable debt during their doctoral studies—debt that has become increasingly difficult to repay on assistant professorship salaries. This, along with the inability of many applicants to relocate to begin doctoral study, has negative effects, given that the most important reasons underlying current doctoral students' choice of a doctoral program were the amount of financial aid they received and not having to relocate (Smith et al., 2001).

CONCLUSION

From an individual school's perspective, the magnitude of the supply and demand imbalance may be hard to perceive. The inability to fill a faculty position within a program may seem a minor inconvenience—a microproblem when compared to other challenges facing deans and provosts. Moreover, a readily available supply of individuals who are willing to teach part-time can often be tapped for teaching courses associated with the open faculty slot. However, full-time and part-time faculty are not interchangeable. In other words, although adjunct faculty can be exceptional teachers and enrich course material through their own experiences, their part-time status does not let them fulfill other faculty responsibilities such as advising students, serving on departmental committees, and supervising student theses. When faculty positions remain unfilled for a period of time, the position can eventually be lost by the department, thus permanently reducing faculty resources. When considered from a national perspective, the full significance and magnitude of the problem becomes obvious; that is, unfilled faculty positions result in fewer faculty, which results in fewer graduates. This leads to fewer teachers and related service providers and thus, fewer direct services provided to children with disabilities.

Keep in mind the principles of supply and demand economics presented at the beginning of this chapter. The public's initial reaction to information about a chronic and serious shortage of doctoral-level special educators may well be "So what?" To students with disabilities and their families, the impact of an undersupply of special education doctorates may pale compared to the problems encountered by the current shortages of qualified special education teachers. This shortage has persisted for more than two decades and is well documented in each year's *Annual Report to Congress on the Implementation of IDEA*.

However, this problem is intrinsically linked to the supply of special education leadership personnel for academic positions. The primary reason is that the initial preparation of special educators typically is the responsibility of faculty working at institutions of higher education. A shortage of faculty results in a shortage of teachers and other direct service personnel who provide an appropriate education to students with disabilities.

Although precise predictions are unavailable, some simple, yet conservative, logic models have been generated to describe the magnitude of the situation. For example, representatives from the U.S. Department of Education's Office of Special Education Programs (OSEP), the Council for Exceptional Children, and the Professions in Special Education Clearinghouse conservatively estimate that a typical faculty member can be credited for the preparation of at least twenty-five new teachers each year. Even though the precise ratio of special education teachers serving students with disabilities is not available, reasonable estimates place the ratio somewhere between 16:1 and 20:1. Using the 16:1 ratio, each faculty position left unfilled would result in 400 students with disabilities without a teacher to provide them with an appropriate education. Recent research indicates that the annual shortage of faculty is about 240 per year (Smith et al., 2001). Therefore, the result, at a minimum, is an annual shortage of 6,000 teachers, which leaves 96,000 students with disabilities underserved. (If the 20:1 ratio is applied, the number of students left without qualified teachers is even more staggering.) This annual and projected shortfall compounds the current problem of a high number of unqualified teachers. It is apparent that a shortage of faculty is important, and it does make a difference in the lives of students with disabilities and their families.

Results from previous research detail a serious and persistent shortage of faculty available to prepare the next generation of special educators. For many reasons, the implications of this situation are dire. First, the impact of shortage on the ability to generate new knowledge will hamper the continued development of proven and effective practices that improve services to children and youth with disabilities. Second, the number of service providers available to give an appropriate education to these students will be further reduced. The continued undersupply of special education personnel who work in schools should be a concern to parents, policy makers, professionals, as well as all those who have a stake in this problem.

The situation is complicated by several factors that seem difficult to change. While some strategies are obvious and appear promising in terms of increasing the supply of qualified personnel for faculty positions, most of them are difficult to implement. For example, recruiting applicants for doctoral programs who are committed to academic careers and who have more flexibility in making career decisions is one clear solution; however, targeted recruitment that is effective and produces sufficient yield will require complex and expensive actions. Such actions might include spending substantial time and effort in the recruitment process, allocating funds for moving expenses, supporting these students at reasonable levels throughout the course of their doctoral study, and providing attractive startup packages and salaries to finalists for academic positions.

As the laws of supply and demand have shown, increased demand for a valued product tends to lead to increases in production. What remains to be seen is whether any of the strategies for increasing production listed above will be aggressively used to address the supply/demand imbalance or existing techniques will continue to be used to address teacher shortages. For example, districts desperate for special education teachers have commonly hired individuals with degrees in other concentrations (drama or political science) and placed them in special education classrooms under contingencies such as taking additional special education classes from local universities in the evenings. Will universities follow suit, recruiting faculty from other departments to fill special education faculty vacancies? As business schools across the country face similar faculty shortages, discussions are already taking place regarding hiring from outside the field or hiring individuals without doctorates (Mangan, 2001). Other in-depth studies of teacher shortages indicate that teachers with certification in other areas tend to feel less effective, are less satisfied with their jobs, and burn out at higher rates than their peers whose specialty areas are consistent with their teaching assignments (Zabel & Zabel, 2001). These data are compelling and underscore the point that well-prepared, effective teachers must be trained by those knowledgeable in the field.

Strategies can also be borrowed from other professions to respond to the faculty shortage. In medicine and certain other scientific disciplines, for example, efforts have been made to reduce the time required to earn postgraduate degrees. Given that so many students in special education are enrolling in doctoral study at a late age and attending part-time, serious thought should be given to how these problems can be resolved. For example, many years typically pass between earning a B.A. and earning a Ph.D. Although some of this is attributable to the time required to earn the doctorate (about six years), key contributors are the amount of time taken off between receipt of the bachelor's degree and enrolling in a master's program (the mean is six years) and the elapsed time between receipt of the master's degree and enrolling in a special education doctoral program (the mean is again six years). Part of this time, of course, is targeted at obtaining the teaching experience required by doctoral programs, but part of it is also associated with the lack of financial assistance and the need to pay for one's graduate education itself. Doctoral program coordinators and university administrators, along with state and federal policy makers, must work together to develop and test innovative strategies for reducing the time between earning a B.A. and enrolling in doctoral study. For example, one strategy might be continuing enrollment between degrees and while teaching; this could provide the continuing connections students need to pursue advanced degrees in a timelier fashion.

Also important will be channeling more financial assistance to individuals wishing to become special education leadership personnel, especially those with faculty intentions. This will require the fiscal involvement of local, state, and federal governments. Current fellowship and training grant programs should be expanded. Attention also should be directed to exploring other financial aid strategies that have appeared promising in other professions (e.g., loan repayment programs). This can help not only in fostering full-time doctoral study but also speedier degree completion and less constraints on career choices due to educational debt burden. Partnerships among colleges with and without doctoral degree programs could develop relatively seamless transitions for students to continue graduate study, incentives (e.g., relocation allowances) might be developed to encourage individuals to relocate for doctoral study, and moving expenses could be provided to students who relocate.

The effectiveness of the above suggestions needs to be tested, and such solutions must be implemented strategically. The public also must be educated with regard to how their concerns over too few special education teachers are partly a product of too few faculties to train them. The public can thus bring to the attention of policy makers, higher education administrators, and other key constituencies the need to remedy the faculty shortage.

QUESTIONS FOR FURTHER DISCUSSION

1. How has the production of doctoral graduates changed over the last two decades?

2. Do you think there is a problem with the current doctoral production levels in special education? Justify your answer.

3. The total number of doctoral programs in special education has remained relatively stable for several decades, but the size of the student enrollment is shrinking. Why do you think the numbers in the program have diminished? Is this a problem? Why or why not?

4. As you learned from this chapter, doctoral production is only one piece of this puzzle. Increased career options for doctoral graduates that diminish the appeal of working in a college or university setting also contribute to faculty shortages. What do you think policy makers could do to address these issues?

5. Should federal funding be targeted differently to address the problems discussed in this chapter? What are your suggestions?

REFERENCES

Boe, E. E., Bobbitt, S. A., Cook, L. H., & Barkanic, G. (1998). National trends in teacher supply and turnover for special and general education (1998-DAR1). Philadelphia: University of Pennsylvania, Center for Research and Evaluation in Social Policy.

Boe, E. E., Cook, L. H., Bobbitt, S. A., & Terhanian, G. (1998). The shortage of fully certified teachers in special and general education. *Teacher Education and Special Education, 21,* 1–21.

Bos, C., Roberts, R., Rieth, H., & Derer, K. (1995). Doctoral preparation in special education: Current status and trends. *Teacher Education and Special Education, 18,* 147–155.

Brown, K. S., & John, D. M. (2000, February). *Meeting the twin challenges: Improving teacher quality and supply in State Pilot Project for "Special Education Transition Certification."* Paper presented at the fifty-second annual meeting of the American Association of Colleges for Teacher Education, Chicago, IL.

Bunsen, T., & Bullock, L. M. (1988). Current status of leadership training. In C. A. Kochhar (Ed.), *Excellence in doctoral leadership training: Special education and related service. Report of a national conference* (pp. 8–11). Washington, DC: George Washington University.

Coyle, S. (1986). *Summary report 1985: Doctorate recipients from United States universities.* Washington, DC: National Academy Press.

Coyle, S., & Bae, Y. (1987). *Summary report 1986: Doctorate recipients from United States universities.* Washington, DC: National Academy Press.

Federation of Nurses and Health Professionals. (2001). *The nurse shortage: Perspectives from direct care nurses and former direct care nurses.* Washington, DC: Peter D. Hart Research Associates.

Gloeckler, L. C. (1999). *Special analysis report: Special education personnel.* Albany: New York State Education Department.

Harmon, L. R. (1978). *A century of doctorates: Data analyses of growth and change.* Washington, DC: National Academy of Sciences.

Henderson, P. H., Clarke, J. E., & Reynolds, M. A. (1996). *Summary report 1995: Doctorate recipients from United States universities.* Washington, DC: National Academy Press.

Heward, W. L. (1995). Introduction to the topical issue: Training special education faculty for the 21st century. *Teacher Education and Special Education, 18,* 192–204.

Howe, R. D. (2000). *Salary-trend study of faculty in special education for the years 1996–97 and 1999–2000.* Boone, NC: Appalachian State University.

Kozleski, E., R., & Deshler, D. (2000). *Bright futures for exceptional learners: An action agenda to achieve quality conditions for teaching and learning.* Arlington, VA: Council for Exceptional Children.

Kucher, K. (2001, June 9). Six hospitals to help fund "Nurses Now"; $1.3 million effort aims to boost graduates in field. *San Diego Union-Tribune,* p. B-1.

Magner, D. K. (2000, March 17). The imminent surge in retirements. *Chronicle of Higher Education, 46,* A18–A20.

Mangan, K. S. (2001, May 4). A shortage of business professors leads to six-figure salaries for new Ph.D.s. *Chronicle of Higher Education, 47,* A12–A13.

Pate, W. E., III. (2001). *Analyses of data from Graduate Study in Psychology: 1999–2000.* Washington DC: Research Office, American Psychological Association.

Pierce, T. B., & Smith, D. D. (1994). Career choices of recent special education graduates holding doctoral degrees. *Teacher Education and Special Education, 17,* 129–136.

Pierce, T. B., Smith, D. D., & Clarke, J. (1992). Special education leadership: Supply and demand revisited. *Teacher Education and Special Education, 15,* 175–183.

Rabin, R., & Eisenberg, C. (2001, February 25). Shortage of nurses worsens; "Doorstep of a crisis" reached as demand outpaces supply. *Nassau and Suffolk Edition*, p. A-2.

Sanderson, A. R., Dugoni, B., Hoffer, T., & Selfa, L. (1999). *Doctorate Recipients from United States universities: Summary report 1998*. Chicago, IL: University of Chicago, National Opinion Research Center.

Schofer, R. (1964). *Public Law 85-926*. Unpublished manuscript.

Sindelar, P. T., Buck, G. H., Carpenter, S., & Watanabe, A. K. (1993). Supply and demand of leadership personnel in special education: A follow-up study with analysis of failed searches. *Teacher Education and Special Education, 16*, 240–248.

Sindelar, P. T., & Taylor, C. (1988). The supply of doctoral graduates and the demand for university faculty in special education and communication disorders. In C. A. Kochhar (Ed.), *Excellence in doctoral leadership training: Special education and related service. Report of a national conference* (pp. 23–32). Washington, DC: George Washington University.

Smith, D. D., & Lovett, D. (1987). The supply and demand of special education faculty members: Will the supply meet the demand? *Teacher Education and Special Education, 10*, 88–96.

Smith, D. D., & Pierce, T. (1995). The state of special education leadership training and college and university faculty: What we know and what we don't. *Teacher Education and Special Education, 18*, 150–165.

Smith, D. D., Pion, G. M., Tyler, N. C., Sindelar, P., & Rosenberg, M. (2001). *The study of special education leadership personnel with particular attention to the professoriate*. (H920T97006-100A). Nashville, TN: Vanderbilt University.

Smith, D. D., & Salzberg, C. (1994). The shortage of special education faculty: Toward a better understanding. *Teacher Education and Special Education, 17*, 52–61.

Sprayberry, N. (2000, December 29). Lack of nurses has hospitals feeling blue. *The Tennessean*, p. B-1.

Tawney, J. W., & DeHaas-Warner, S. (1993). Assessing demand for special education faculty in higher education: A pilot study and a prototype for a national registry. *Teacher Education and Special Education, 16*, 283–293.

Teacher Education Division of the Council for Exceptional Children. (1987*). National directory of special education personnel preparation programs*. Reston, VA: National Information Center for Children and Youth with Handicaps.

Tyler, N. C., & Smith, D. D. (1999). Career decisions of doctoral graduates in special education. *Teacher Education and Special Education, 22*, 1–13.

U.S. Department of Education. (1998). *Twentieth annual report to Congress on the implementation of the Individuals with Disabilities Education Act*. Washington, DC: Author.

U.S. Department of Education. (2001). *Twenty-third annual report to Congress on the implementation of the Individuals with Disabilities Education Act*. Washington, DC: Author.

U.S. Department of Education. (2003). *Total Number of Teachers Employed (in Full-Time Equivalency) to Provide Special Education and Related Services for Children and Youth Ages 3–5 with Disabilities, during the 2000–2001 School Year*. [Data file]. Available from the U.S. Office of Special Education Programs web site, http://www.ideadata.org/tables25th\ar_ac1.htm.

Weissert, C. S., & Silberman, S. K. (1998). Sending a policy signal: State legislatures, medical schools, and primary care mandates. *Journal of Health Politics, Policy, and Law, 23*, 743–770.

Zabel, R. H., & Zabel, M. K. (2001). Revisiting burnout among special education teachers: Do age, experience, and preparation still matter? *Teacher Education and Special Education, 24*, 128–139.

PART IV   SPECIAL EDUCATION FUTURES

PUBLIC POLICY

From Access to Accountability in Special Education

MICHAEL L. HARDMAN

University of Utah

KATHERINE NAGLE

University of Maryland

In twenty-first-century America, access to education for every child on an equal basis is national policy. Everyone can learn, and no one should be denied the opportunity for an education because of race, cultural background, socioeconomic status, physical disability, or mental limitation. In today's schools, we teach every student. Such was the not the case, however, a mere three decades ago. In fact, for more than two centuries, education policy in many states was exclusive, rejecting significant numbers of students with learning, physical, and behavioral differences. Historically, the implied purpose of education was to teach only those students who had the greatest potential to learn—the most academically capable. A school's program did not have to be altered in order to fit the unique needs or capabilities of a given child. On the contrary, the child had to fit into the existing program or face exclusion from public education. At the national level, many policy makers held the view that the U.S. Constitution was clear on the federal role: Education is the sole responsibility of the states. As such, federal policy remained silent while many states openly excluded children with disabilities from public schools until well into the twentieth century.

The evolution, or as some would say the revolution, of inclusive education policy is a recent phenomenon rooted in the Fourteenth Amendment to the U.S. Constitution and manifested through the civil rights movement of the 1950s and 1960s. For students with disabilities, the revolution reached its pinnacle in 1975 with the passage of the Education for All Handicapped Children Act (20 U.S.C. §1400 *et seq.*), renamed the Individuals with Disabilities Education Act (IDEA) in 1990. For the past thirty years, the policy debate has evolved from "whether students with disabilities should receive special education" to issues of "what constitutes a free and appropriate public education," and "how should it be implemented."

In this chapter, we examine the evolution of public policy from two perspectives: (1) affirming the right of every student with a disability to access a free and appropriate education, and (2) moving from access to improving results and ensuring accountability for student learning. In the first section, the emerging role of federal policy that eventually led to the passage of IDEA is examined in the context of its revolutionary impact at the state and local levels. IDEA is the only federal education statute in history that mandates from a state agency to the classroom teacher a specific process that must be followed in order to ensure students receive an appropriate educational experience. The evolution of special education practice in the United States has to a large extent been framed by the requirements of IDEA.

The second half of the chapter focuses on the "second policy revolution" in special education: moving beyond access to improving results and establishing accountability for students with disabilities within the general education system. Prior to 1997, the policy debates concerning the efficacy of public education did not involve special education to any great extent. Special education's relationship to and purpose within general education were ill-defined because of its existence as a separate system that only intermittently interacted with its larger counterpart. This changed with the passage of the 1997 amendments to IDEA (referred to as IDEA '97). These amendments represented a considerable overhaul in the dual system of public education, envisioning a merger of the two systems to an extent never before attempted. Among other changes, IDEA '97 requires that every individualized education plan (IEP) must state how the student is to be involved and make progress in the general curriculum as well as meet each of the child's other educational needs that result from the disability. The law mandates that most students with disabilities must participate in state- or districtwide assessments of student achievement and what, if any, modifications in the administration of these assessments are necessary to ensure participation. Furthermore, if it is determined that a student is unable to participate in the state or district's assessment of achievement, there must be a statement of why that assessment is inappropriate and how the student will be assessed (an alternate assessment system). To ensure that the IEP team is knowledgeable from a general education perspective, IDEA '97 requires that a general education teacher participate as a member of the student's team.

PUBLIC POLICY AND ACCESS TO A FREE
AND APPROPRIATE EDUCATION

For most of the twentieth century, public education for students with disabilities was either nonexistent or consisted of programs that placed students in segregated classrooms or separate schools. It was not until the civil rights movement of the 1950s that education was reaffirmed as a right and not a privilege by the U.S. Supreme Court's landmark decision in *Brown v. Board of Education* (1954). The Court ruled that education must be made available to everyone on an equal basis. Although advocates for children with disabilities saw the Court's decision to strike down segregation on the basis of race as a clear precedent for ending the exclusion of students with disabilities from public schools, it would be another twenty-five years before the federal courts would confront the issue head-on. Most states continued to exclude students with disabilities well into the 1960s. For example, North Carolina allowed school districts to define certain children as "uneducable," and parents could be prosecuted if they challenged such a decision. It was not until 1971 that the Pennsylvania Association for Retarded Children filed and won a class action suit charging that the Pennsylvania schools should be required to accommodate children who were intellectually different (*Pennsylvania Association for Retarded Children v. Commonwealth*). *Mills v. Board of Education of the District of Columbia* (1972) expanded the court's decision in Pennsylvania and ordered the District of Columbia schools to provide public education to every school-age child with a disability. By 1975, the right to education for students with disabilities had become a national public policy issue. It was estimated that at least half of the school-age children with disabilities in the United States were not receiving an appropriate education, and 25 percent were being totally excluded from school.

Given the litigation in various states and the fact that students with disabilities were being denied access to education, Congress saw the need to pass the Education for All Handicapped Children Act mandating that public education be made available to students with disabilities between the ages of six and twenty-one. The age level was extended down to three years with the passage of the Education of the Handicapped Amendments of 1986. The basic tenets of IDEA addressed in this chapter are (1) eligibility based on an identified disability, (2) access to a free and appropriate public education, (3) an individualized education program, and (4) access to a continuum of placements consistent with individual need (referred to as the "least restrictive environment").

Eligibility and Labeling

A student is eligible to receive specialized services under IDEA if two conditions are met. First, the child must be identified as having one of the thirteen disability conditions identified in federal law or in a state's special education law. Second, the special education and related services are an essential component of a student's receiving an appropriate education.

Future Issues. Should federal policy continue to support the use of disability labels in determining eligibility for special education and related services? No other process polarizes professionals and parents more than the federal requirement to label students by disability condition before appropriate services can be delivered. While IDEA '97 gave states the option to eliminate disability categories up to age nine, labeling continues to drive eligibility for special education throughout the United States. Proponents of labeling argue that from a policy perspective it is not in the best interests of students with disabilities to end the practice (Fuchs & Fuchs, 1991; Kauffman, 1991; Walker & Bullis, 1991). Parents want political visibility for their own children, fearing that any attempt to eliminate disability categories from the law would result in a loss of services. Continued categorization is necessary to ensure that all eligible students receive special education. The elimination of disability categories under IDEA would allow school districts to take the limited resources available and focus on students perceived to be the easiest and least costly to serve.

Opponents of labeling argue that labeling by disability category is detrimental to the concept of individualization (e.g., Reynolds, 1991; Ysseldyke, Algozzine, & Thurlow, 1992). Disability categories fail to define clearly or to differentiate adequately the needs of students with disabilities. Labeling is considered a demeaning process that causes stigma and leads to discrimination, isolation, and neglect of students with disabilities (Kliewer & Biklen, 1996; Reynolds, 1991).

Looking beyond IDEA, it is evident that public policy at the federal level has been moving away from the use of disability categories. For example, the Americans with Disabilities Act (ADA) uses a generic definition of disability first defined in §504 of the Vocational Rehabilitation Act of 1973 (29 U.S.C. §794 *et seq*.). This definition describes disability as physical or mental impairment that substantially limits one or more life activities. ADA shifts the emphasis away from characteristics by disability condition to the functional needs and abilities of the individual. In contrast, some analysts view IDEA as paradoxical and internally inconsistent with regard to labeling. Research suggests that although labeling is used to establish eligibility for special education services by determining disability classification, no clear relationship may exist between a label and the instructional needs of a given student. Furthermore, some researchers argue that the assessments used to establish eligibility by disability category (1) have little or no relevance to the planning and delivery of instruction and (2) result in the disproportionate representation of children from ethnically and culturally diverse backgrounds in special education programs (Gottlieb, Alter, & Gottlieb, 1991; MacMillan & Hendrick, 1993; National Research Council, 1997; Welch & Sheridan, 1995).

Free and Appropriate Public Education

IDEA is based on the value that every child is entitled to a free and appropriate public education (FAPE) consistent with individual ability and need. The provisions of IDEA related to FAPE are based on the Fourteenth Amendment to the U.S. Constitution, which guarantees equal protection under the law. No student with a disability can be excluded from a public education because of a disability (the zero-reject principle).

Future Issues.   Should federal policy further refine the definition of a free and appropriate education? Over the past two decades, federal courts have repeatedly had to interpret congressional intent regarding the FAPE provision of IDEA. The U.S. Supreme Court in *Hendrick Hudson District Board of Education v. Rowley* (1982) stated that an appropriate education consists of "specially designed instruction" and related services that are "individually designed to provide educational benefit" (458 U.S. 176, at 201), frequently referred to as the "some educational benefit" standard. Unless a state's own laws establish otherwise, a state need not provide an ideal education for all students with disabilities but merely a beneficial one. In adopting a "some educational benefit" standard, the Court examined the legislative history of IDEA and concluded that meaningful access to public education was the basic purpose of the statute. In so doing, it rejected such purposes as self-sufficiency and maximization of potential.

   After the *Rowley* decision, political pundits wondered what would guide the courts in deciding how much "educational benefit" was enough to provide "meaningful" access. A number of lower court decisions over the last decade have probed this issue. Most have adopted a "meaningful progress" standard as the measure of benefit (see Huefner, 1991). In other words, trivial progress toward educational goals is not sufficient. Although the concept of meaningful progress expands on the concept of educational benefit, it too requires some way to measure progress or benefit. It also requires a judgment as to whether the measured progress is substantial enough to be meaningful to the student.

   Although it can be argued that access to a free public education for students with disabilities has been achieved as we begin the twenty-first century, the issue of what defines "an appropriate education" remains at issue. Some would argue that the term *appropriate education* remains extremely broad, difficult to substantiate, and provides little guidance to school districts attempting to assess the efficacy of a special education program for each student. Should appropriate be defined by how well students acquire basic skills within the limited context of the classroom? Or, should it be defined by how well students are prepared to contribute over the long term to the economic and social well-being of the community in which they live? If the latter, then shouldn't states and school districts be required to track the postschool outcomes for students with disabilities in order to determine whether special education has had a meaningful impact on a person's quality of life?

Others disagree with the above premise, arguing that a free and appropriate education is defined by "academic progress." Laski (1997) suggests that "a student with a disability is entitled to an education that yields real benefits. . . . Although no court has established any one standard for all students with disabilities, there are standards that require a measure of 'academic progress'" (p. 79). Florian and Pullin (2000) indicate, however, that academic progress alone does not signify the provision of FAPE. Based on court decisions and federal regulations following the *Rowley* case, these authors suggest that the definition of appropriate education under IDEA has broad meaning and that it includes the services necessary for a student to attain "desired outcomes, as well as any programming needed to address their supplemental individualized needs" (p. 20). To take this argument one step further, IDEA '97 suggests that academic progress is defined within the framework of the general education curriculum:

■ Do the IEP goals enable a student to be involved and make progress in the general curriculum?

■ Will this push for more and more students to access the general education curriculum as a component of FAPE create even more questions for the future?

■ Is the curriculum broad enough to meet the diverse needs and functioning levels of students with disabilities?

■ Will participation of students with disabilities in the general education curriculum result in higher academic achievement?

■ Are the knowledge and skills learned in the general education curriculum the same ones that are necessary for the successful transition out of school and into adult life? (McLaughlin & Tilstone, 2000)

IDEA '97 and its provisions for students with disabilities to access the general education curriculum will be discussed in more detail later.

An Individualized Education Plan

The vehicle for delivering a free and appropriate public education to every eligible student with a disability is the IEP. The IEP provides an opportunity for parents and professionals to join together in developing and delivering specially designed instruction to meet a student's needs. The intended result of the IEP process is to ensure continuity from day to day and year to year in the delivery of educational services. The IEP also promotes effective communication between school personnel and the student's family. IDEA '97 mandates that a student's IEP must include the following elements:

> A statement of the child's present levels of educational performance, including how the child's disability affects involvement and progress in the general curriculum. For preschool children the statement must describe how the disability affects the child's participation in appropriate activities.

■ A statement of measurable annual goals, including benchmarks or short-term objectives related to meeting the child's needs that result from the disability. The annual goals should enable the child to be involved and make progress in the general curriculum and meet each of the child's other educational needs that result from the disability.

■ A statement of the special education and related services and supplementary aids or services to be provided to, or on behalf of, the child.

■ A statement of any individual modifications in the administration of state- or district-wide assessments of student achievement that are needed in order for the child to participate in such assessment. If the IEP team determines that the child will not participate in a particular state- or districtwide assessment of student achievement (or part of such an assessment), the team must state why that assessment is not appropriate for the child and how the child will be assessed.

■ The projected date for the beginning of the services and modifications and the anticipated frequency, location, and duration of those services and modifications.

■ A statement of how the child's progress toward the annual goals will be measured and how the child's parents will be regularly informed (such as by periodic report cards), at least as often as parents are informed of their nondisabled children's progress, of their child's progress toward the annual goals (IDEA 1997, 20 U.S.C. §1400 *et seq.*).

Future Issues.   Should the IEP be altered in federal policy to ensure its effectiveness both as an instructional planning document and accountability tool? The intent of the IEP as defined in IDEA is to facilitate effective instructional planning. However, many professionals and parents seem to agree that the IEP has become mechanistic, concerned more with procedure than results (Laski, 1997; McLaughlin, 1998; National Council on Disability, 1995; Smith, 1990). Some practitioners consider the IEP a detriment to appropriate programming and perceive it as a paperwork monster (Kozleski, Mainzer, & Deshler, 2000). Giangreco, Cloninger, and Iverson (1994) reported that IEPs are generally vague, consisting of broad goal statements that are inconsistent with the instructional demands of classroom settings. Additionally, IEP goals and objectives are discipline-referenced—meaning that they are based on or linked with values or professional agendas associated with the specific discipline of team members (e.g., psychology, social work, speech and language, occupational therapy). Consequently, many of the goals are for staff rather than students. Elliott and Sheridan (1992) identified a number of other problems regarding the overall effectiveness of IEP teams. IEP meetings are characterized by disproportionate participation and input. School psychologists and special educators tend to make the most contributions, while classroom teachers and parents contribute very little.

Although many in the field agree that the IEP has its problems, there is less consensus regarding what should be done about it. One position is to eliminate the IEP altogether because it has failed to meet its original intent as either an effective planning document or accountability tool. Meyer (1997) agrees with the need to eliminate current IEP requirements for students with disabilities but advocates for some broader criteria directed at the needs of all students. She recommends that future education policy require that every child, with and without disabilities, have an IEP "consisting of a statement of student support needs to access valued curricular outcomes" (p. 82).

The above positions are somewhat tempered by the view that while the IEP has its problems, it can be fixed in policy. McLaughlin (1998) suggests linking the IEP directly to the general curriculum in federal policy. She further suggests that while the IEP has become a powerful monitoring device for adherence to specific legal procedures and timelines, it must become much more of an accountability tool focusing on broad plans and student outcomes rather than small, discreet objectives.

Another viewpoint suggests that there is less need for policy changes to fix the IEP and more need for adherence to current provisions in IDEA. Laski (1997) argues that the problems with the IEP do not lie in current policy but in the fact that professionals have "ignored and trivialized important legal requirements [within IDEA]" (p. 77). His view is backed by the National Council on Disability (NCD) in its 1995 study on improving the implementation of IDEA. The NCD suggests that the problems with the IEP lie in the failure of states and the federal government to comply with IDEA provisions. The agency makes several recommendations:

■ Establish a renewed emphasis on the most basic purposes of the IEP to ensure that every student receiving special education is provided with an individualized package of supports and services designed to maximize educational achievement.

■ Monitor state and local school district progress in improving the quality of IEPs. The monitoring should include developing new approaches, such as sampling parent and student satisfaction and eliciting input from teachers and other educators about ways to improve IEPs.

■ Provide greater flexibility on the amount of specificity required in parts of the IEP, such as day-to-day instruction and the delivery of related services. Such flexibility will lead to greater satisfaction by parents and students and will reduce burdensome paper work.

A Continuum of Placements (Education in the Least Restrictive Environment)

All students have the right to learn in an environment consistent with their academic, social, and physical needs. IDEA states that to the maximum extent appropriate, students with disabilities are to be educated with students who are not disabled. Removal of a child from the regular education environment is to occur only when the nature and severity of the child's disability are such that education in regular classes with supplementary aids or services cannot be achieved satisfactorily (34 C.F.R. §300.550(b)). Federal regulations require a "continuum of alternative placements" that school districts must provide if the child cannot be satisfactorily educated in regular classes. However, whenever possible students should be educated in or close to the school they would attend if not disabled (see 34 C.F.R. §300.552(a)(3) and §330.552(c)).

Future Issues.   Should the continuum of placements be eliminated in federal regulation? Placement data from the U.S. Department of Education (2000) suggests that 96 percent of students with disabilities between the ages of six and twenty-one receive their education in a general education school. Of these, 46 percent are removed from general education classes for less than 21 percent of the school day and 20 percent are removed for more than 60 percent of the school day (U.S. Department of Education, 2000). Analyses of U.S. Department of Education placement data over the past thirty years point out the significant variability in the proportion of students with disabilities served in various settings across states. For example,

Lipsky and Gartner (1996) examined data for the 1992–1993 school year and found that the placement rates of students with learning disabilities in general education classes ranged nationally from 2.37 percent in California to 93.59 percent in Vermont. For the 1997–1998 school year, the U.S. Department of Education (2000) reported that more than 9 percent of all students with disabilities between the ages of six and twenty-one in New York were served in separate schools, yet in Florida (another large state) less than 3 percent were served outside of the general education environment.

For some parents and professionals, these data raise serious questions about the validity of the continuum of placements. It is unlikely that such variability can be explained solely by differences in prevalence rates of students with disabilities. A number of analysts have suggested that such differences are more likely attributable to the philosophical orientation of school district administrators and to historical patterns of service delivery (Lipsky & Gartner, 1996; Sailor, Wilson, & Gerry, 1991; Snell, 1991).

While there is a consensus that students with disabilities will require differing types of services to meet their educational needs, there is significant disagreement about whether the range of services can only be delivered through a "continuum of alternative placements" (cf., Lieberman, 1996; Lipsky & Gartner, 1996). Criticism of the continuum concept began almost immediately after the enactment of IDEA in 1975 (Reynolds, 1978; Reynolds & Birch, 1977). Since that time, a number of analysts have criticized the concept for being too oriented to where services were provided rather than the level of services and supports that children need to succeed in the general education class (Lilly, 1986; Reynolds, 1991; Sailor, Gee, & Karasoff, 1993; Snell, 1991; Taylor, 1988; Wang, 1988).

Proponents in favor of maintaining the continuum argue that the research does not support the premise that full-time placement in a general education classroom is superior to special education classes for all students with disabilities (Baker & Zigmond, 1995; Dupre, 1997; Fox & Ysseldyke, 1997; Fuchs & Fuchs, 1991; Hocutt, 1996; Kauffman & Hallahan, 1997; Lieberman, 1996). Additionally, general education teachers have little expertise in assisting students with learning and behavioral difficulties and are already overburdened with large class sizes and inadequate support services. On the other hand, special educators have been specifically trained to individualize instruction, develop instructional strategies, and use proven techniques that facilitate learning for students with disabilities. This results in more specialized academic and social instruction in a pullout setting, where students can more effectively prepare to return to the general education classroom. Specialized pullout settings also allow for centralization of both human and material resources. Supporters of the continuum also contend that if practitioners and consumers don't believe special education is broken, why fix it. In general, both parents and professionals are quite satisfied with the special education continuum of placements (Guterman, 1995). In the study of inclusive education programs in four states, Morra (1994) found that inclusion programs were viewed by the schools as not being for everyone. School districts indicated that they were struggling with the difficult challenges of "(1) severely emotionally disturbed students who disrupt classrooms and (2) students with learning disabilities who may need a more highly focused, less distracting learning environment than that presented by the general education classroom" (p. 1).

The original intent of the continuum was to ensure that the IEP would be delivered in an environment consistent with the needs of each student. The question now is whether the continuum of alternative placements is the only viable means to ensure that student needs are met. While some argue that the continuum is a necessary element of public policy, others believe that placement and service delivery are erroneously perceived as synonymous.

MOVING FROM ACCESS TO IMPROVING RESULTS AND ENSURING ACCOUNTABILITY FOR STUDENT LEARNING

IDEA 1997 represents a considerable overhaul of federal policy with the primary intent of improving results for students with disabilities within the context of general education. In its findings on the history of IDEA, the 105th Congress noted that the implementation of IDEA has been impeded by low expectations and an insufficient focus on applying research on proven methods of teaching and learning for children with disabilities. "Over 20 years of research and experience has demonstrated that the education of children with disabilities can be made more effective by having high expectations for such children and ensuring their access in the general curriculum to the maximum extent possible" (IDEA 1997, 20 U.S.C. §1400 *et seq.*). Implicit in IDEA 1997 was the concern that although students with disabilities now had access to education, mere access proved insufficient to generate the valued outcomes of employment, independence, and community involvement that were the spirit of the law. Among the substantive changes designed to improve results, Congress embedded into law two new tenets: (1) access, involvement, and progress in a challenging general education curriculum and (2) the need to make education accountable for student learning.

Access, Involvement, and Progress in the General Education Curriculum

Implicit in the requirement for access to the general curriculum is the belief that the only way students with disabilities can be as successful as their nondisabled peers is to ensure they have an opportunity to learn the same instructional content. To ensure compliance with this provision, a student's IEP must have a statement of measurable annual goals, including benchmarks or short-term objectives, that enable the child to be involved and progress in the general curriculum. Furthermore, the school district must ensure that the IEP team reviews each child's IEP periodically to address any lack of expected progress in the general curriculum (IDEA 1997, 20 U.S.C. §1400 *et seq.*).

Future Issues. *Will access to the general curriculum improve results for all students with disabilities?* Although federal policy makers appear convinced that the key to success for students with disabilities lies in their access to the general curriculum, the issue has engendered considerable and often heated debate in the field of special education.

Supporters of this provision argue that access to the general curriculum will enable students with disabilities to experience a wider variety of subjects at a deeper level. This would give students with disabilities exposure to high-order thinking skills such as problem solving, enable them to develop collaborative skills, and engender a sense of responsibility and self-esteem (McLaughlin & Tilstone, 2000). The provision also promotes more collaboration among special and general educators, requiring them to develop more challenging learner goals and raise expectations for students with disabilities (McLaughlin, Henderson, & Rhim, 1998). Eyer (1999) suggests that mandating access to the general curriculum will require a redefinition of FAPE. She suggests that the judicial interpretation of FAPE, as enunciated by the U.S. Supreme Court in *Rowley*, is no longer consistent with federal special education law. The relevant changes to IDEA '97 and the legislative history suggest that Congress, mindful of the poor results for students with disabilities and the rising costs of special education, saw an opportunity to endorse higher societal expectations for these students. The silence of IDEA '97 on the validity of *Rowley* suggests that the Court may need to revisit this issue. Failure to do so may jeopardize congressional intent because the lower courts could continue to follow a standard of FAPE that rests on an outdated legislative agenda (Eyer, 1999).

Opponents of the IDEA '97 provisions raise several concerns. Some educators suggest that finding sufficient instructional time to assist those students with disabilities who struggle with the new subject matter would be difficult at best. In addition, some special educators voice the concern that access to the general curriculum may come at the cost of teaching critical functional and independent living skills. In a study by McLaughlin and Tilstone (2000), middle and high school teachers questioned the relevance of some academic subjects to students with disabilities (McLaughlin & Tilstone, 2000). Additionally, opponents point out that special educators have not played a major role at the state level in planning and implementing changes in the general curriculum. This puts them in the difficult position of having to teach a challenging curriculum that they have no control over.

Given the lack of concrete evidence that access to the general curriculum will indeed improve student results, the issue will undoubtedly remain controversial. As McLaughlin and Tilstone (2000) point out, "What is not yet evident, however, is whether such access will lead to sustained higher levels of achievement among students with disabilities and whether the skills gained through this curriculum are the ones that will prove necessary for successful transitions from school" (p. 62).

The debate sparked by IDEA '97 has prompted a renewed call for reform of the current dual system of education that purports to eliminate distinctions among students but in the view of some creates a caste-like system that treats some children differently, and arguably better, than others. At the heart of this argument is the belief that special education policy has served its purpose of obtaining access for students with disabilities and should be dismantled. The new focus for discourse should be on how best to educate all students, not just a few who manifest the required disability characteristics. The goal of the current educational reform movement is to make schools more effective for all students. However, the encroachment of a separate federally mandated special education system into general education schools may make such a goal more difficult to achieve. One possible scenario would be for the federal government to increase its substantive authority by becoming more vigorously involved in the broader context of education. Alternatively, the role of the federal government could be circumscribed, leaving the states to decide the provision and implementation of special education services.

The statutory call for access to the general curriculum has also raised the call for full federal funding of IDEA (Barnes, 2000; Eyer, 1999). It may prove expensive for some students, especially those with more intense instructional needs, to have access to the general curriculum. As such, the cost of special education will continue to increase. When IDEA first became law, federal funding of special education was to reach 40 percent of the national average per pupil expenditure. However, even at its height, federal funding has never reached more than 12 percent of the national average. Some analysts suggest that failing to fully fund IDEA will jeopardize the goal of increasing results for students with disabilities and compromise the needs of other students (Huefner, 2000; Traub, 1999).

The Supreme Court's decision in *Cedar Rapids Community School District v. Garret F.* has intensified this fear. The Court determined that Garret F. could gain access to an appropriate public education only if he received a constellation of related services that had to be provided by the school district at no cost to the parents. Even though the school district argued that the costs of the services were too burdensome and thus were exempt from the IDEA mandate, the Court was not convinced.

Given the IDEA '97 provision regarding access to the general curriculum, is there a need to redesign teacher education programs? Access to the general curriculum increases the expectation that general and special educators will collaborate in the delivery of instruction to a degree never before attempted. This will have important effects on the preservice preparation of every educator and has prompted calls for more integrated teacher preparation programs (Hardman, McDonnell, & Welch, 1998; Trubowitz & Longo, 1997).

Supporters of merged teacher preparation programs argue that neither special educators nor regular educators can respond adequately to the growing diversity in the schools (Pugach, 1996). If students with disabilities are to benefit from access to the general curriculum, then all educators need to have the skills necessary to adapt both curriculum and pedagogy and to deliver challenging subject matter. Evidence suggests that merged programs are successful in preparing teachers to teach all students (Ryan, Callaghan, Krajewski, & Flaherty, 1996). Spinelli (1998) argues that teacher preparation programs for all educators should include alternative instruction and assessment practices, emphasize best practices for all students, and provide training in collaboration skills.

Opponents of merged teacher preparation argue that such programs ignore the needs of some students with disabilities, especially those with low-incidence disabilities. For example, children with autism, visual impairments, hearing impairments, and those who are deaf/blind have needs that only a trained specialist can serve. Kauffman (1999) argues that the only way teachers can be trained appropriately in these skills is in separate programs. The move toward cross- or noncategorical training is prompted primarily by the desire to cut costs and a reluctance to admit that general education cannot educate some children appropriately in the mainstream.

A second issue concerns teachers' being expected to teach the new curriculum within the content areas. The emphasis on constructivist principles that emphasize student-directed learning does not fit comfortably with teachers who have internalized the traditional methods of teaching, such as through lecture, individual assignments, and board work (National Research Council, 1997). Supporters of separate teacher preparation argue that constructivist strategies do not work for all students and that their dominance in merged programs will mean that techniques such as direct instruction and individualization will be neglected (Kauffman, 1999).

Accountability for Student Learning

During the 1980s, education and policy literature began to reflect the view that if education were to be effective for all children there was a need for a systemic approach to reform. Such an effort must involve all levels of the education system rather than being top-down impositions or isolated pockets of local excellence. Florian and Pullin (2000) indicate that for many reformers, curriculum standards are at the core of comprehensive reform and are the only way to overcome a decentralized and fragmented education system. Many pundits view standards-based reform as a way to get into classrooms and marry the vitality of teacher-initiated change with the structure and stability available at the centralized level (National Research Council, 1997).

The rationale behind standards-based education is a belief that all students can learn at a high standard if instructed effectively. In addition, supporters believe that the only way of ensuring student learning is by establishing systemwide accountability. Congress clearly accepted this rationale for students with disabilities. A crucial component of the intent of IDEA '97 to improve results for students with disabilities is the requirement that they be included in state- and districtwide assessments, with required modifications and adaptations as necessary.

In addition, states and districts had to establish alternate assessments for students who are unable to participate in a state or district's testing program to ensure inclusion within the accountability system.

Future Issues.   Is it in the best interests of students with disabilities to be included in district- and statewide assessments of achievement? Supporters argue that the inclusion of students with disabilities in standards-based reform is important for moral and practical reasons (National Research Council, 1997). The explicit link between IDEA '97 and the general curriculum is welcomed, as it demonstrates a willingness to accept that students with disabilities are part of the entire student body. If students with disabilities are placed within the sphere of the accountability mechanism, then schools are forced to be serious about educating them effectively. Thus, from a moral standpoint supporters see this requirement as a direct negation of prior public policy that excluded and devalued students with disabilities.

Another argument for including students with disabilities in systemwide accountability is one of equal opportunity in relation to nondisabled peers. If students with disabilities are to have an equal chance of achieving desired postschool outcomes, they must have access, as appropriate, to the same curriculum as nondisabled students. Expectations for students with disabilities have been low, resulting in lower achievement. Supporters believe that the inclusion of students with disabilities in all aspects of reform could be a potent vehicle for change (National Research Council, 1997).

Others disagree with the above rationale and argue that establishing content standards for students with disabilities at the state level is inconsistent with the concept of individualization and not in the best interests of students with disabilities or their nondisabled peers. Some educators fear that if all students are expected to reach the same standard, then the bar will be lowered to accommodate those with less ability. If the bar isn't lowered, then students with disabilities will routinely fail to meet the standard. However, as suggested by Rouse, Shriner, and Danielson (2000), if states accept differential standards between general parameters, who decides which students are expected to achieve what content?

Clearly, the concept of common standards for all has been met with ambivalence by some educators. McLaughlin et al. (1998) report that some teachers feel powerless because they believe it is not possible for all students to reach the required standards. These teachers suggest that the focus of including all students in system assessments should be on demonstrating progress rather than on absolute criteria. In addition, teachers indicated that there was a lack of clarity regarding which standards would need to be individualized and whether such individualization should apply to what students learned (the content) or just to performance.

Another important issue for students with disabilities who are included within the accountability system is high school graduation. The failure to graduate has serious repercussions in today's society, and students who continually fail to reach required standards will not get the high school diploma in a high-stakes testing system. An ostensible reason for ensuring student access to the general curriculum was the need to improve results. Ironically, it is possible that the requirement of high standards in the general curriculum may further compromise the graduation rate of some students with disabilities (Geenan & Ysseldyke, 1997).

Some special educators voice the concern that inclusion in statewide testing may damage the self-esteem of students with disabilities if they do not perform well. McLaughlin et al. (1998) reported that some teachers admitted that they would help their students to do well at the expense of providing a valid picture of the student's performance. These special educators expressed concern that valuable instruction time would be spent teaching content in academic areas rather than concentrating on the acquisition of critical functional life skills. Others felt that they were being asked to choose between two values: inclusion or standards-based reform. They pointed out that to facilitate a student's mastery of academic skills they were forced to remove them from the general education class, thus compromising the inclusion of students with their same-aged peers.

Kauffman (1999) argues that it is unrealistic and potentially damaging to expect all students to cope with a common standard. While there is no denying the need to improve results in both general and special education, students with disabilities will never catch up with their nondisabled peers. It is also possible that if general education is able to improve student results, then students with disabilities will be even further behind.

How will student learning be assessed? Whether schools hold students with disabilities to the same standard or not, the issue of how to assess learning remains controversial. The most cost-effective method of assessing and comparing performance over many students is by use of standardized multiple-choice tests. However, research suggests that some of the accommodations required by students with disabilities may invalidate the test instrument. In addition, multiple-choice questions do not necessarily allow students to demonstrate the full depth of their knowledge (Rouse et al., 2000).

Although standardized achievement tests are the most common method of measuring performance, some states and districts have developed more authentic methods of assessment. (Madaus & Kellaghan, 1993). Authentic assessments of student learning include individual or group performance of a particular skill, portfolio presentations and projects, exhibitions, and demonstrations (Rouse et al., 2000).

However, evidence from the United Kingdom suggests that the effective use of authentic assessments has a long way to go (Madaus & Kellaghan, 1993). Madaus & Kellaghan pointed out that although the use of authentic testing may be appealing on an emotional level, at a practical and technical level there are many issues to be resolved. Authentic assessments are time consuming to create and monitor. Researchers raise questions as to the technical adequacy of comparing performance-based assessments over many students. Finally, although the careful training of scorers was essential, it was difficult to accomplish at a practical level (Rouse et al., 2000).

What is the purpose of assessing student learning? There are several purposes behind the call for assessment of student learning (Rouse et al., 2000). First, there is the demand that public education be accountable for student performance. Although system accountability has traditionally focused on nondisabled students, recent federal education reforms have adopted increasingly unified approaches. These culminated in the requirements of IDEA '97 that students with disabilities participate where appropriate in districtwide and statewide assessments and that schools publicly report their performance (Sebba, Thurlow, & Goertz, 2000).

Proponents of the inclusion of students in districtwide and statewide tests argue that if students know that their promotion to a higher grade level or their graduation depends on their attaining a particular standard, this will be an incentive to them to perform at a higher level. They point out that special education students have traditionally not been held accountable for the achievement of IEP goals, and this resulted in a lowering of individual expectations and failure to learn essential skills. As a corollary, special educators were not held accountable for the poor performance of their students and largely regarded the IEP as paper compliance rather than an accountability tool (Sebba et al., 2000). Including students in districtwide and statewide testing will force teachers to use the IEP as an accountability blueprint, altering goals and objectives as necessary to ensure student progress in the general curriculum.

Some educators, while accepting the premise that standards-based reform should apply to all students, express unease about the inclusion of test scores from students with disabilities and its impact on teacher accountability. McLaughlin et al. (1998) reported that teachers and principals were anxious about the consequences of publishing low scores. General educators felt particularly strongly about the possibility of teachers being blamed for the negative effects of publicly available scores that include scores for students with disabilities (Geenan & Ysseldyke, 1997; McLaughlin et al., 1998).

SUMMARY

Although few would disagree with the intent of IDEA '97 to improve the educational performance of students with disabilities, the means to achieve this goal remain controversial. There is little research that directly supports the assumption implicit in IDEA '97 that access to the general curriculum and inclusion in districtwide and statewide testing systems will improve student results. Clearly, there is an urgent need for investigations into the efficacy of the IDEA '97 reforms because public policy is outpacing research and practice by several years (Rouse et al., 2000). As the line between general and special education becomes increasingly blurred, there is a need to redefine and renegotiate the roles of all educators. What we do not know is whether special education can retain its individual identity and rights-based rationale and still fully participate in a reformed system that purports to afford all children an education that is both equitable and excellent.

QUESTIONS FOR FURTHER DISCUSSION

1. Should federal policy continue to support the use of disability labels in determining eligibility for special education and related services?

2. Should federal policy further refine the definition of free and appropriate public education?

3. Should the IEP be altered in federal policy to ensure its effectiveness as both an instructional planning document and an accountability tool?

4. Should the continuum of placements be eliminated in federal regulation?

5. Will access to the general curriculum improve results for all students with disabilities?

6. Given the IDEA provision regarding access to the general curriculum, is there a need to redesign teacher education programs?

7. Is it in the best interests of students with disabilities to be included in district- and statewide assessments of achievement?

REFERENCES

Baker, J. M., & Zigmond, N. (1995). The meaning and practice of inclusion for students with learning disabilities: Themes and implications from the five cases. *Journal of Special Education, 29,* 163–180.

Barnes, J. (2000). Casenote: The practice of pediatrics in pedagogy? The costly combination in *Cedar Rapids Community School District v. Garret F. University of Richmond Law Review, 34,* 305–327.

Blake, C. (1999). Deficit ideology and reform in the United States. In H. Daniels & P. Garner (Eds.), *World yearbook of education 1999: Inclusive education.* London: Kogan Page.

Bowers, T., & Parrish, T. (2000). Funding of special education in the United States and England and Wales. In M. L. McLaughlin & M. Rouse (Eds.), *Special education and school reform in the United States and Britain* (pp. 167–193). New York: Routledge.

Corbett, G. F. (1999). Special education, equal protection and education finance: Does the Individuals with

Disabilities Education Act violate a general education student's fundamental right to education? *Boston College Law Review, 40,* 633–672.

Dupre, A. P. (1997). Disability and the public schools: The case against "inclusion." *Washington Law Review, 72,* 775–858.

Elliott, S. N., & Sheridan, S. M. (1992). Consulting and teaming: Problem solving among educators, parents, and support personnel. *Elementary School Journal, 92,* 261–284.

Eyer, T. L. (1999). Greater expectations: How the 1997 IDEA amendments raise the basic floor of opportunity for children with disabilities. *Dickinson Law Journal, 103,* 613–637.

Florian, L., & Pullin, D. (2000). Defining difference: A comparative perspective on legal and policy issues in education reform and special educational needs. In M. J. McLaughlin & M. Rouse (Eds.), *Special education and school reform in the United States and Britain* (pp. 11–37). London: Routledge.

Fox, N., & Ysseldyke, J. E. (1997). Implementing inclusion at the middle school level: Lessons from a negative example. *Exceptional Children, 64,* 81–98.

Fuchs, D., & Fuchs, L. (1991). Framing the REI debate: Abolitionists versus conservationists. In J. W. Lloyd, N. N. Singh, & A. C. Repp (Eds.), *The regular education initiative: Alternative perspectives on concepts, issues, and models* (pp. 241–255). Sycamore, IL: Sycamore.

Geenan, K., & Ysseldyke, J. (1997). Educational standards and students with disabilities. *Educational Forum, 61*(2), 220–229.

Giangreco, M. F., Cloninger, C., & Iverson, V. (1994). *Choosing options and accommodations for children (COACH): A guide to planning inclusive education.* Baltimore: Paul H. Brookes.

Gottlieb, J., Alter, M., & Gottlieb, B. W. (1991). Mainstreaming academically handicapped children in urban schools. In J. W. Lloyd, N. N. Singh, & A. C. Repp (Eds.), *The regular education initiative: Alternative perspectives on concepts, issues, and models* (pp. 95–112). Sycamore, IL: Sycamore.

Guterman, B. R. (1995). The validity of categorical learning disabilities services: The consumers' view. *Exceptional Children, 62,* 111–124.

Hardman, M., McDonnell, J. M., & Welch, M. (1998). *Special education in an era of school reform: Preparing special education teachers.* Washington, DC: Federal Resource Center for Special Education.

Hocutt, A. M. (1996). Effectiveness of special education: Is placement the critical factor? In D. Terman (Ed.), *The future of children: Special education* (pp. 77–102). Los Angeles: David and Lucille Packard Foundation.

Huefner, D.S. (1991). Judicial review of the special education program requirements under the Education for All Handicapped Children Act: Where have we been

and where should we be going? *Harvard Journal of Law and Public Policy, 14,* 483–516.

Huefner, D. S. (2000). *Getting comfortable with special education law: A framework for working with children with disabilities.* Norwood, MA: Christopher Gordon.

Individuals with Disabilities Education Act, 20 U.S.C. §1400 *et seq.* (1997).

Kauffman, J. M. (1991). Restructuring in sociopolitical context: Reservations about the effects of current reform proposals on students with disabilities. In J. W. Lloyd, N. N. Singh, & A. C. Repp (Eds.), *The regular education initiative: Alternative perspectives on concepts, issues, and models* (pp. 57–66). Sycamore, IL: Sycamore.

Kauffman, J. M. (1999). Commentary: Today's special education and its messages for tomorrow. *Journal of Special Education, 32*(4), 244–254.

Kauffman, J. M., & Hallahan, D. P. (1997). A diversity of restrictive environments: Placement as a problem of social ecology. In J. W. Lloyd, E. J. Kameenui, & D. Chard (Eds.), *Issues in educating students with disabilities* (pp. 325–342). Hillsdale, NJ: Erlbaum.

Kliewer, C., & Biklen, D. (1996). Labeling: Who wants to be retarded. In W. Stainback & S. Stainback (Eds.), *Controversial issues confronting special education: Divergent perspectives* (pp. 83–95). Boston: Allyn & Bacon.

Kozleski, E., Mainzer, R., & Deshler, D. (2000). *Bright futures for exceptional learners.* Reston, VA: Council for Exceptional Children.

Laski, F. (1997). IDEA, Amended or not, the past is prologue. *Journal of the Association for Persons with Severe Handicaps, 22*(2), 77–79.

Lieberman, L. M. (1996). Preserving special education . . . for those who need it. In W. Stainback and S. Stainback (Eds.), *Controversial issues confronting special education: Divergent perspectives* (2nd ed., pp. 16–28). Boston: Allyn & Bacon.

Lilly, S. M. (1986, March). The relationship between general and special education: A new face on an old issue. *Counterpoint,* 10.

Lipsky, D. K., & Gartner, A. (1996). Inclusive education and school restructuring. In W. Stainback and S. Stainback (Eds.), *Controversial issues confronting special education: Divergent perspectives* (2nd ed., pp. 3–15). Boston: Allyn & Bacon.

MacMillan, D. L. & Henrick, I. G. (1993). Evolution and legacies. In J. I. Goodlad & T. C. Lovitt (Eds.), *Integrating general and special education* (pp. 23–48). New York: Merrill.

Madaus, G. F., & Kellaghan, T. (1993). The British experience with "authentic" testing. *Phi Delta Kappan, 74*(6), 458–466.

McLaughlin, M. J. (1998). *Special education in an era of school reform: An overview.* Washington, DC:

Federal Resource Center, Academy for Educational Development.

McLaughlin, M. J., & Tilstone, C. (2000). Standards and curriculum. The core of educational reform. In M. Rouse & M. J. McLaughlin (Eds.), *Special education and school reform in the United States and Britain* (pp. 38–65). London: Routledge.

McLaughlin, M. J., Henderson, K., & Rhim, L. (1998). *Snapshots of reform: How five local districts are interpreting standards-based reform for students with disabilities.* Alexandria, VA: Center for Policy Research on the Impact of General and Special Education Reform. (ERIC Document Reproduction Service No. ED 423653)

Meyer, L. H. (1997). Tinkering around the edges. *Journal of the Association for Persons with Severe Handicaps, 22*(2), 80–82.

Morra, L. G. (1994, April 28). *Districts grapple with inclusion programs.* Testimony before the U.S. House of Representatives on special education reform. Washington, DC: U.S. General Accounting Office.

National Council on Disability. (1995). *Improving the implementation of the Individuals with Disabilities Education Act: Making schools work for America's children.* Washington, DC: Author.

National Research Council (1997). *Educating one and all: Students with disabilities and standards-based reform.* Washington, DC: National Academy Press.

Pugach, M. C. (1996). Unifying the preparation of prospective teachers. In W. Stainback & S. Stainback (Eds.), *Controversial issues confronting special education: Divergent perspectives* (pp. 239–252). Boston, MA: Allyn & Bacon.

Reynolds, M. C. (1978). *Futures of education for exceptional students.* Reston, VA: Council for Exceptional Children.

Reynolds, M. C. (1991). Classification and labeling. In J. W. Lloyd, N. N. Singh, & A. C. Repp (Eds.), *The regular education initiative: Alternative perspectives on concepts, issues, and models* (pp. 29–41). Sycamore, IL: Sycamore.

Reynolds, M. C., & Birch, J. W. (1977). *Teaching exceptional children in all America's schools.* Reston, VA: Council for Exceptional Children.

Rouse, M., Shriner, J. G., & Danielson, L. (2000). National assessment and special education in the United States and England and Wales. In M. J. McLaughlin & M. Rouse (Eds.), *Special education and school reform in the United States and Britain* (pp. 66–97). New York: Routledge.

Ryan, L., Callaghan, J., Krajewski, J., & Flaherty, T. (1996). A merged elementary/special education program in a 4-year liberal arts college: Providence College. In L. P. Blanton, C. G. Griffin, J. A. Winn, & M. C. Pugach (Eds.), *Teacher education in transition: Collaborative programs to prepare general and special educators* (pp. 66–83). Denver, CO: Love.

Sailor, W., Gee, K., & Karasoff, P. (1993). Full inclusion and school restructuring. In M. E. Snell (Ed.), *Instruction of Students with Severe Disabilities* (4th ed., pp. 1–30). New York: Merrill.

Sailor, W., Wilson, W. C., & Gerry, M. (1991). Policy implications of emergent full inclusion models for the education of students with severe disabilities. In M. C. Wang, M. C. Reynolds, & H. J. Walberg (Eds.), *Handbook of special education: Research and practice* (pp. 175–196). New York: Pergamon Press.

Sebba, J., Thurlow, M. L., & Goertz, M. (2000). Educational accountability and students with disabilities in the United States and England and Wales. In M. J. McLaughlin & M. Rouse (Eds.), *Special education and school reform in the United States and Britain* (pp. 98–125). New York: Routledge.

Skrtic, T. M. (1991). Behind special education. A critical analysis of professional culture and school organization. Denver, CO: Love.

Smith, S. W. (1990). Individual education programs in special education: From intent to acquiescence. *Exceptional Children, 57,* 6–14.

Snell, M. E. (1991). Schools are for all kids: The importance of integration for students with severe disabilities and their peers. In J. W. Lloyd, N. N. Singh, & A. C. Repp (Eds.), *The regular education initiative: Alternate perspectives on concepts, issues, and models* (pp. 133–148). Sycamore, IL: Sycamore.

Taylor, S. (1988). Caught in the continuum: A critical analysis of the principle of the least restrictive environment. *Journal of the Association for Persons with Severe Handicaps, 13*(1), 41–53.

Traub, L. M. (1999). Comment: The Individuals with Disabilities Education Act: A free appropriate education—at what cost? *Hamline Law Review, 22,* 663–687.

U.S. Department of Education. (2000). To assure the free appropriate public education of all children with disabilities. *Twenty-second annual report to Congress on the implementation of the Individuals with Disabilities Education Act.* Washington, DC: U.S. Government Printing Office.

Walker, H. M., & Bullis, M. (1991) Behavior disorders and the social context of regular class integration: A conceptual dilemma. In J. W. Lloyd, N. N. Singh, & A. C. Repp (Eds.), *The regular education initiative: Alternative perspectives on concepts, issues, and models* (pp. 75–93). Sycamore, IL: Sycamore.

Wang, M. C. (1988, May 4). A promising approach for reforming special education. *Education Week, 7*(32), 36, 28.

Welch, M., & Sheridan, S. M. (1995). *Educational partnerships: Serving students at risk.* Fort Worth, TX: Harcourt Brace.

Ysseldyke, J. E., Algozzine, B., & Thurlow, M. (1992). *Critical issues in special and remedial education* (2nd ed.). Boston: Houghton Mifflin.

INDEX